THE LIFE AND TIMES OF JACK L. RHEA

Former Director of Camping,
Philmont Scout Ranch

*Jack Rhea in 1966 as Director of Professional Training
at the BSA National Office.*

THE LIFE AND TIMES
OF JACK L. RHEA

Former Director of Camping,
Philmont Scout Ranch

Philmont Staff Association

Dedication

This book is dedicated to the memory of Jack L. Rhea:
loyal Scouter, Philmont visionary, and inspirational leader.

THE LIFE AND TIMES OF JACK L. RHEA

ISBN: 978-0-9830497-2-2

Library of Congress Control Number: 9780983049722

Published by the Philmont Staff Association.

Editing, writing, and project management by William F. Cass.

Cover art: *Cathedral Rock – Autumn Afternoon*, by former Philmont staffer, Dawn Chandler.
 Oil on canvas, 18 x 12 inches.
 Dawn Chandler copyright 2012.
 Reproduced with permission of the artist.
 Prints are available.
 To view more of Dawn Chandler's landscapes of northern
 New Mexico, please visit www.taosdawn.com

Book design and typesetting by Pam Dooley Graphics, Gulph Mills, Pennsylvania.

This book is set in Times New Roman.

Printed and bound in the United States of America by McNaughton & Gunn, Inc., Saline, Michigan.

TABLE OF CONTENTS

Introduction

It would be entirely appropriate to describe Jack L. Rhea's years as Philmont's director of camping as "Philmont's Golden Age." The attendance and staff grew rapidly, awareness of Philmont Scout Ranch as a national treasure increased by leaps and bounds, and fundamental changes in program, services, and facilities were made – changes which have withstood the test of time.

Many of Philmont's most iconic leaders served in the Rhea era, including Mister Clarence Dunn, Boss Sanchez, and Doc Loomis. Waite Phillips himself was well-acquainted with Jack Rhea. The seasonal staff's composition evolved from essentially southwestern to truly national. From their swelling ranks in the mid-50s through the early 60s emerged a small company of idea men who in a few short years would make outsized, lasting contributions to Philmont's programs and even its infrastructure. Jack hired them all and would have been the first to say that his success depended on the key contributions of his seasonal and permanent staff subordinates.

It would be hard to imagine a leader more suited for the role of camping chief than Jack Rhea. He was a westerner who had first-hand experience with farming and ranching. His most formative years had been spent high in the Colorado Rockies, and he had even visited Philmont before it became Philturn Rockymountain Scoutcamp.

During the most cataclysmic event of his generation, Jack commanded young men in battle. Like many members of "The Greatest Generation," Jack remained silent about his experiences in World War II. Fortunately, in-depth records from Jack's wartime service still exist which is why that heretofore concealed period in his life is explored at length in this book.

In the early 1950s, the "Volunteer" Training Center was a responsibility of the director of camping. When he arrived at Philmont, Jack brought a wealth of training experience; he had just completed two years of expanding Wood Badge and, indeed, his experience in training dated back to 1942 when he was an Army battalion training and operations officer. He was on the Wood Badge staff at Philmont in the early 1950s and was also involved in training Philmont Guides, the forerunners to today's Philmont Rangers.

How appropriate it is that Jack Rhea began climbing Scouting's trail as a Lone Scout, one who was later able to join a regular troop in Kansas and later become an Eagle Scout. And climb that trail he did – right to the inner circle of the National Executive Staff. The second point of the Scout Law, loyalty, is certainly one that characterizes Jack's life: a tireless council volunteer while he was a busy, young school teacher, an early Scouting organizer for German boys during the Occupation in 1945, and a ready participant for all kinds of Scouting events well into his retirement which followed a very productive career with the Boy Scouts of America.

This book actually began with a manuscript created by Jack himself. It was meant to be strictly a memoir of his youth and concluded in the autumn of 1938, just before Jack went into professional Scouting. Following Jack's death in May of 2010, the manuscript was generously made available to the Philmont Staff Association (PSA) Publications Committee by the Rhea family. With their approval, the manuscript became a book project and a member of the PSA board of directors, Bill Cass, was assigned as editor/project manager. Jack's original manuscript was augmented where necessary and edited to transform it from an autobiography to a biography for consistency with the rest of the book. There followed considerable primary and secondary research into Jack's military experiences and many interviews with both seasonal and permanent staff from the 1940s through the 1960s.

In keeping with the easy-reading nature of PSA books, the use of footnotes has not been employed in the text. However, considerable research was required to bring this book to fruition and for that reason the many sources are listed in the bibliography. The "interviews" portion of the bibliography also serves as an appendix to the "Acknowledgements" section because many people contributed their recollections, essays, documents, and photographs to this project. This book also serves as an in-depth history of Philmont Scout Ranch in the Rhea era (late 1954 through late 1962), and for that reason the two major introductions made by Jack Rhea, the twelve-day expedition and the Philmont Rangers, are examined in great depth. To better understand the magnitude of Jack Rhea's innovations, a picture of Philmont in the early 1950s is presented along with a profile of Jack's predecessor, George Bullock, the man who has truly never received enough credit for Philmont's gathering momentum in the immediate post-World War II period.

Over the years, Philmont place names have changed; this book will utilize the current place names. So, to eliminate potential confusion in the pages that follow; Carson-Maxwell became Rayado, Clear Creek Mountain became Waite Phillips Mountain, or more casually, Mount Phillips, and Rayado, located at the confluence of the Rayado and Agua Fria Creeks, became Fish Camp.

This book, and others in the Philmont Staff Association's growing list of titles, is dedicated to exploring and maintaining Philmont's heritage. With the passage of years and then the decades, it is so easy to lose sight of those who changed the Philmont landscape. Living for the day, we take so much for granted at present – including many of the remarkable, leading-edge benefits brought to the Ranch during the Rhea years. In their day, they were substantial changes.

Jack was a bold and decisive man who was committed to American youth, a man who started his adult life as a school teacher and later turned professional Scouter. If you think of Philmont as the keystone in the arch-way of BSA's High Adventure programs, the following pages will show you that Jack Rhea was one of the most important architects and stonemasons in the creation of that structure.

Publications Committee
Philmont Staff Association

Acknowledgements

First and foremost, we have Jack Rhea himself to thank because the 1985 memoir he wrote about his youth forms the basis for Part I of this book. Jack's grown children, Julie, Carol, Ron, and Bart, turned over that manuscript to the Philmont Staff Association's Publication Committee, gave their blessing to the book project, and followed up with hours of interviews. They also graciously provided photographs, documents, and many mementos from Jack's years in Scouting as a youth, professional, and volunteer. Other members of the Rhea family helped too; nephew Peter Rhea's extensive Rhea family genealogy and stories of his father, Jack's brother Ralph, were of great value. John Eilert's recollections of his Uncle Jack at Philmont were very important in portraying what Jack Rhea considered the apex of his Scouting career: his eight years as director of camping at Philmont.

Several periods in Jack's early life were expanded upon in Part I. Sally Altick Keller was the source of significant insights and documents relating to Jack's service as a teacher and later the principal at Wichita Country Day School. For three years as a youngster and later as a wrangler, Jack Rhea lived on a ranch high in the Colorado Rockies. What was the VC Bar Ranch near Lake City, Colorado, is now the Lake Fork Club. Its manager, Lonnie Reel, shared period photographs and information on the club's colorful history.

While most historians believe that all of the millions of military service records from World War II were destroyed in a horrendous fire at the National Personnel Records Center in St. Louis in 1973, the fact is that thousands out of the millions did survive. Fortunately, Jack Rhea's file was among the very few to come through that tragedy, and like most its singed edges show evidence of that fire. Its complete legibility, however, was a rosetta stone which was essentially a diary of Jack's perilous and remarkable journey through the war. Jack's division, the 100th Infantry Division (the "Century" Division), created the post-war 100th Infantry Division Association which was among the most "historian-friendly" of all World War II unit associations. Ms. Patti Bonn, the group's executive director, was a constant source of research support as was Jeffrey Kozak of the Marshall Foundation at the Virginia Military Institute which is the repository of 100th Division records and memorabilia. Sadly, with its membership now decimated by the passing of all but a handful of its stalwarts, the association has just been dissolved as of this writing.

Mr. Robert Fair, a professor emeritus at the University of Virginia, the association's last president, and an infantryman in Jack's regiment, provided an excellent critique of the book's Part II, the "War Years." Another man with a 100th Division connection, Edward Longacre, the noted military historian and son of a 100th Division artilleryman, read the Part II manuscript and made constructive suggestions for its improvement. The Philmont Staff Association's Ken Davis is a published author, historian, and like Jack Rhea, an infantry graduate from Fort Benning's Officer Candidate School. As a retired colonel with thirty-one years of Army active/reserve service, Ken critiqued Part II of the manuscript with an expert's touch.

Critiquing a manuscript is an essential part of the publishing process and in that regard, Parts III and IV, got a good working over from a team very experienced in Scouting and Philmont, starting with Ed Pease, chairman of the PSA Publications Committee. Former Philmont Rangers Allan Rouse, Gayle Reams, Ned Gold, Greg Hobbs, and Dave Caffey all pointed out shortcomings and made helpful suggestions, additions, and corrections. Allan Rouse also provided the invaluable research assistance which led to contacting all but one of the Philmont Rangers of 1957 known to be alive at this writing. Ranger historian, Marty Tschetter, was the source of important background information, including monographs on key figures of the early Ranger years. Those who knew Jack best, his daughters and sons, made sure the manuscript was on the right track as well.

At Philmont Scout Ranch, Director of Program Mark Anderson supported the project with manpower, transportation, and access to the Philmont Museum where Librarian Robin Taylor had relevant files and the copy machine ready and waiting. She also scanned many of the photos in Parts III and IV. Philmont Staff Association Executive Director Randy Saunders saved countless hours by digging out old staff rosters and following through on a multitude of other research requests.

Those people named above are really the tip of an iceberg. Many people helped on this project – ranging from a small town newspaper editor in rural Colorado to a Scouting historian in Fort Dodge, Iowa. Members of the Philmont Staff Association (especially those whose staff days date back to the 1940s through the early 1960s) were delighted to respond to a call requesting information relating to Jack Rhea. Fortunately, everybody who contributed information, anecdotes, and photos is listed in the bibliography under the "interviews" section. That list is a long one, including many people who were perfect strangers at the outset of this project, but it is a list well worth reading.

William F. Cass
Publications Committee, Philmont Staff Association.
Autumn 2012

Part I
THE COWBOY

Rhea Family Collection

*Jack Rhea at The Philmont Ranch in
1936 when he was guiding tours for
the Wichita Country Day School.*

CHAPTER 1

From Kintail To The Rockies

Jack Lloyd Rhea was born on the family farm near the village of Springfield, in southwestern Missouri, on a July Fourth. That is fact, but the year of his birth is less certain since his parents never recorded the birth at the state capital, Jefferson City. Later, when Jack needed a birth certificate, the family concluded that it must have been 1915. Jack was the youngest of seven children born to Charles W. and Goldie Bebee Rhea whose other children were named Louisa, Evelena, Clara, Charles, Ralph, and Joy (Josephine). Due to the tremendous range in ages and the near-constant moves, Jack never became well-acquainted with his oldest siblings. Jack's oldest sister, Louisa, was already eighteen years old when he was born, so Jack was very much the baby of the family.

The name Rhea is one of many derived from the ancient Scotch name "Macrath" or more commonly "Macrae." The list of related names is long and includes Rea, Ray, Wray, Cree, Cray, MacKree, MacCreath, and MacCrea among many more. The name itself means "Son of Grace." In medieval Scotland, the Clan Macrae was aligned with the powerful Clan Mackenzie whose lands in the Scottish Highlands included Kintail, a ruggedly wild and beautiful mountainous area in northwest Scotland on the mainland opposite the Isle of Skye. It was in and around Kintail that the Clan Macrae was originally located late in the fourteenth century. In exchange for providing military services to the Clan Mackenzie, the Macraes were given lands in Kintail. The most prominent feature in the region is the Five Sisters of Kintail, a series of mountain peaks.

In the Jacobite Rebellion of 1745, a few of the Macraes fought beside Bonnie Prince Charlie (Stuart) to the displeasure of the Clan Mackenzie which had come up short in the first Jacobite Rebellion of 1715. At the Battle of Culloden in 1746, the English triumphed again; the resulting oppression that followed convinced many Macraes to cross the seas for America. Many more Macraes and MacRheas left for religious reasons and came to America in the mid-1700s after living in Northern Ireland.

Several Rheas found their niche in politics. John Rhea was a Revolutionary

War soldier who settled in Tennessee and became a lawyer, although most of his career was spent in politics. Following service in the Tennessee House of Representatives, he served as a U.S. Congressman nine times, although not in consecutive terms. John Stockdale Rhea was a lawyer and active in Kentucky and presidential politics, serving several terms as a U.S. Congressman in the late 1800s. He chose not to run for another term and returned to private law practice in 1904. Jack's ancestry in America begins with the arrival of three MacRhea brothers in Virginia. Then a family disagreement caused them to part ways. One stayed in Virginia, one moved to Kentucky, and one, named John, changed his name to Rhea and moved to Greene County, Tennessee, a state in which there are several Rhea place names. William Francis Rhea, a grandson of the original John Rhea was born in Greene County, Tennessee, and later moved to Springfield, Missouri. There he was both a grocery store owner and Methodist minister, serving a circuit of several churches in the area. He married Collie Collett and the couple had three children. A brother, Charles William Rhea was also born in Greene County, Tennessee, and grew up to become a farmer in Springfield, Missouri. In addition to the farm, Charles Rhea raised Missouri mules which typically commanded a good price. It was that farm which forms Jack's first memories, particularly of his brother Ralph, six years older, and sister Joy, four years older. The only clear memories Jack ever had of his older siblings were when the older Rhea children returned home for holidays, especially the Fourth of July when the younger kids got firecrackers. Jack was much more interested in soda and on one birthday he was given a whole case of twenty-four bottles (which he had to share with his brothers and sisters). It was a special occasion when Jack got his favorite flavor – cream soda.

Jack's father had dropped out of high school to take up farming full time, but later became a wheelwright at the Springfield Wagon Works. Before the demand for wheels declined Charles Rhea had advanced to become a foreman, engineer, and later a salesman. The wagon company transitioned into a new line which was building ice plants because many homes now had an "ice box" in the kitchen. Those ice plants turned out 300-pound blocks of ice which were hauled by horse and wagon or trucks to customer locations where smaller blocks were sawed off. The smaller blocks would keep perishables cold in an icebox for two or three days. There was a drawback; the drip pans under the icebox had to be emptied several times a day and frequently at night.

The job was demanding, requiring the elder Rhea to work twelve hours a day: gone at six and home at six. Very frequently, Charles Rhea was gone for long periods when the company built an ice plant at some distance from Springfield because he had to coordinate the construction and start-up. Jack's young life became nomadic because his father eventually concluded that the only way to keep the family together was to simply pick up and move to communities where the work was. Before Jack finished the third grade, he had lived in Missouri, Kansas, and Oklahoma.

The Rheas were a religious family, and Goldie Rhea said grace before the evening meal after which Charles Rhea frequently fell asleep on a couch for several hours, typically waking up just in time to go to bed. After church on Sundays, the Rheas and other families would go to another church member's home for Sunday dinner. Years later Jack would recall how careful he and the other children had to be in the games they played after dinner because they were still wearing their Sunday best clothes. While Jack's family was far from financially well off, they ate well at those Sunday dinners where the food was good and plentiful. Nothing, however, was wasted and Jack was expected to eat every morsel that was put on his plate.

Jack's favorite games included hide and seek or tag which could be played without too much danger of getting his clothes dirty. As a little boy, he was jealous of older boys who owned pocket knives and played "mumblety-peg," a game of skill in which a pocket knife is flipped into the air with the object of sticking it into a peg driven into the ground. In the summer when fireflies were out, Jack and his friends caught them in glass jars, capped the jars to see how much light they could make, and then released them.

The Rhea kids rarely had a "store-bought" toy. They rolled barrel hoops with a stick or made guns from wood, used old tires hung from a tree as swings, and made slingshots from a forked branch and rubber bands. Jack became quite proficient with the slingshot and used small stones or acorns as projectiles. The slingshots were rarely taken to school since punishment in those days was sudden, swift, and painful.

Games of accuracy appealed to Jack and as might be expected, he was an expert marble player. When he knocked his opponent's marbles out of the ring, he got to keep them and vice versa. Jack rarely put a prized shooter marble in the ring. It was a serious game in which the winner was the one who still had marbles in the ring. Even at that early age, Jack had developed a hunter's eye – one that proved useful during more trying times ahead.

Being talented in the popular games of the day served Jack well, considering the itinerant lifestyle the family followed and the need to make friends in new communities. While he was in second grade, the Rheas were living on a farm near Baxter Springs, in southeast Kansas, where an ice plant was under construction. Charles Rhea was practically an absentee father and was gone for many days at a time, although he might be home for an occasional Sunday afternoon. Goldie operated a beauty shop in town. The farm had a storm cellar which was essentially a small, underground room with a gently, sloping roof barely above ground level. The cellar's principal purpose was storing corn, potatoes, apples, pears, and canned fruits and vegetables. One evening, an ominous storm was descending upon them with a darkening sky and howling winds. Goldie tried to gather up seven-year old Jack, his older brother Ralph, and the remaining sisters to make a run for the storm cellar. The tornado was upon them before they could get out of the house. Jack was terrified and had visions of the already shaking house being torn to smithereens. By this point, the wind was absolutely shrieking. Then, in as strong and as sure a voice as Jack had ever heard, Goldie said, "Let's not be afraid. He is here." Then one of the sisters started playing the piano. The Rheas started singing their favorite hymns and nearly drowned out the sound of the wind. The tornado passed with very little damage to the Rhea farm, although some of the neighboring farms suffered severe damage.

For work on the farm or when he was playing, Jack wore overalls. Like all of his clothes, they were hand-me-downs. He took very good care of his church clothes and changed out of them immediately upon arriving home. In between, he had separate clothes for school, but the overalls were his favorites, even when they had holes in the knees and the bottoms were frayed. They had been washed so many times that their color was faded beyond recognition, and they started looking rather peculiar as Jack grew taller. Ralph got to the point where he was ashamed of his brother and then forcibly took the old overalls off and made young Jack accept a new pair. Many years later, Jack marveled at how antique clothes could command a high price and how brand new designer jeans were being sold with patches and holes.

Jack always had to work, and that meant chores on the farm and part-time jobs in town. His first and most memorable job was taking tickets at the movie theater in town. He had to use a step ladder to sit on in order to be as tall as the adult movie-goers. Each ticket cost ten cents which was exactly Jack's pay for the night. Making fifty cents each week convinced him that he was the richest kid in town and, on top of that, he got to see all of the movies. His favorites were the cowboys, including his idols Tom Mix, William S. Hart, Buck Jones, and Hoot Gibson. In that era, there was plenty of violence and shooting, but no sex and profanity. Seeing the hero kiss the young lady he had just saved from some terrible fate would bring a chorus of "Oooohhs" from the audience. The final outcomes were always certain. The Indians and bad guys always lost or rode hard out of Dodge just as the hero galloped into town on a white stallion. Jack loved the cartoons which also were silent in that pre-talkie era when many of the movies had captions at the bottom of the screen.

Taking tickets provided Jack with some income which he learned to save. One of his fondest childhood memories was having enough money to buy every member of his family a Christmas present. They all got a handkerchief. Jack also worked in a grocery store, starting as a delivery boy for those customers who called in their orders. At first, he hand-carried the grocery bags to customers' homes, but then decided he had to have a bicycle. He did not have the money to buy a brand new bike, but figured he could build one out of spare parts and pay for those parts he could not scrounge. When the bike was completed, Jack's total out-of-pocket cost came to one dollar, sixty cents.

The bike solved a lot of problems, except for one: the little old lady with a small, vicious black dog. Jack had to be very cautious when making a delivery at that house because the terrier always picked a new spot to lie in waiting for the ambush. Fido invariably attacked when Jack was trying to ring the doorbell and holding onto the bags at the same time. Jack was bitten several times, but the little woman just laughed it off saying, "Oh, all he wants to do is play." With holes in his pants and blood dripping down his leg, Jack did not see it that way.

On one occasion the lady came into the grocery store with her dog while Jack was up a ladder, stocking canned goods on the top shelf. The pooch immediately ran over to the ladder and barked. Startled, Jack turned and a couple of cans fell out of the carton he was cradling in his right arm. One of the falling cans hit the mutt right on the nose. The dog's owner was aghast, but said nothing. On Jack's next trip to deliver her groceries, the dog launched an attack, but suddenly stopped short, turned tail, and retreated beneath the porch. It was Jack's last encounter with the terrier.

Jack enjoyed certain fringe benefits from working at the store which, like most stores of that era, had a high, pressed tin ceiling, shelves reaching to the ceiling and stocked with much more than just groceries, and a waxed, wooden planked floor. In the summer, there was a large tub packed with ice and watermelons. One of Jack's jobs was to take a knife and cut out a small cylindrical section from each melon. A plug was placed in the hole so a customer could just pull out the plug and look inside to see that the melon was indeed perfectly ripe. Naturally, somebody had to consume the little melon cylinder, and that was usually Jack.

Lunch was one of the benefits too, and Jack was allowed to slice bread, meat, and cheese for sandwiches. Unlike today's modern in-store delis, Jack's choices were limited to about two or three choices of meat and cheese. Jack dipped out flour, lard, peanut butter, sugar, rice and other items from cans, sacks, and barrels. The store sold no fresh vegetables or dairy products to speak of; the customers grew their own, kept their own cows, and frequently bartered with neighbors. Because customers were so self-sufficient in those days, Jack never sold bread, pies, cakes, or rolls. Butchers traveled the streets, selling meat from their wagons. Children, for five cents, could fill a bag with candy that they had picked out themselves.

Jack was not allowed to handle money, but was trusted with ringing up customer purchases on the adding machine, a great contrivance with a keyboard and big handle to perform the addition and punch out the transaction tape. The machine could only add; multiplication, division, and subtraction were not part of the machine's capability. One of the adults collected the customer's money. If asked, Jack would show the tape to the customer, but he was never questioned about the accuracy of his work, not even when he and the owner added all of the tapes at the end of the day and compared the sum with the cash in the register.

Saturday nights were important because the Rhea family came to the grocery store to do their weekly shopping and to pay for anything that had been picked up during the week. The store owner always threw in a free bag of candy to be divided among the Rhea kids.

The Rheas grew their own vegetables and butchered their own meat. If it was a hog, the Rheas had plenty of pork roast, pork chops, ground pork, pork stews, and pork pot pie. The hams were sugar cured and kept in a spring house where it was cool. Bacon was cured, sausage ground, and head cheese made from scraps. The fat was rendered in a big copper kettle and put away for later use. Jack's favorite meals were always beef for which the Rheas kept several steers. There were chickens, geese, and ducks, all of which wound up on the table as did the chickens' eggs. Jack learned hunting early and the results were meals of wild turkey, pheasants, rabbits, and squirrels. The family always had two or three milk cows which kept them in milk, cream, butter, buttermilk, and cheese.

As expected, the Rhea family garden was a large one and planted in potatoes, peas, carrots, lettuce, squash, turnips, and other vegetables. When autumn came, those Rhea kids still at home helped in picking fruits and vegetables for the canning with which they also helped. Goldie Rhea was an excellent cook and knew how to make left-overs appetizing. Jack loved to watch and frequently helped her in the kitchen.

Ralph and Jack also took extra vegetables into town to sell door-to-door. Ralph always had Jack knock on the doors, knowing that a little boy would sell more than a teenager. Ralph was the money manager in the enterprise, but Jack always got his share which was invariably spent on Saturday night movies and chewing gum. Frequently, the movie house would have what was known as a bank night in which there was a drawing for a prize based on ticket numbers. Jack had never won anything in his life, but got lucky on one of those bank nights when he won a fifty-foot garden hose. He never won anything else again in a raffle or drawing, but that hose had special meaning for him considering the hours and hours he had spent pumping water from a well and hand-carrying it to water the garden.

Religion ran deep in the Rhea family, and Jack attended both Sunday school and the main church service, but he was having an increasingly difficult time with Sunday school because he felt that the teacher was not spending enough time on Bible study. Rather the teacher was concentrating on why the students were so bad and what to do about it. Jack thought all of that was a complete waste of time. Like most towns of that day, there were "blue laws" which prohibited certain establishments such as theaters, taverns, stores, and cafes from being open on Sundays.

The Sunday school teacher launched into a tirade about the evils of such businesses being open on the Lord's day. The rant continued for several Sundays in a row which was provoked by a movement in the community to allow the theater to operate on Sunday afternoons and evenings.

The debate in Sunday school culminated with the teacher's asking those students in favor of banning Sunday movies to raise their hands. Slowly a few hands went up, followed by more and more, even from those who secretly were in favor of Sunday movies. Only one hand was not raised – Jack Rhea's. The teacher was nearly apoplectic.

"Jack Rhea, are you in favor of having movies in our town on Sundays?"

"I don't know. But I do think that those who want to go should have the right to."

The teacher promptly threw Jack out of the class and ordered him never to return. Jack never did return to that Sunday school or any other. Jack's mother was behind him 100 percent, saying that if Jack really believed in something, he should back it up with action, not just words. The expulsion did not shake Jack's belief in God one bit; it just added to the strong self-confidence that would become a Jack Rhea hallmark.

A New Future in Colorado

By that point, all of the moves required by the ice plant business and the longing to return to farming were becoming too much for the Rhea family. The elder Rhea truly missed raising horses and mules. The one good aspect of the ice plant work was that it allowed the family to save some money. Charles Rhea had been attracted by information on a ranch that might be available near Lake City, a small, out-of-the-way town southwest of Gunnison, Colorado. The ranch was on the western side of the Continental Divide and on the banks of the Lake Fork of the Gunnison River, just a few miles north of the remote village of Lake City. With some borrowed money from his older children, Charles had enough money to start his venture. It was not large in terms of total acreage, but that was immaterial anyway since the ranch had grazing rights on the Uncompaghre National Forest on the one side and the Gunnison National Forest (now part of the Rio Grande National Forest) on the other. It was, indeed, an immediate post-frontier wilderness. There were no other immediately neighboring ranchers in the area and loggers had not yet discovered it. In a word, it was unspoiled. The area was beautiful with alpine meadows, snow-capped peaks, streams loaded with trout, and all kinds of game including deer, elk, and bear.

Jack could sense his father's enthusiasm and knew what the ranch would mean: at long last he would have a real father, not an absentee dad who never had any time for his family. Jack had prayed that this day would come and now it had.

When Jack was nine years old, Charles Rhea moved his family to the VC Bar Ranch. The time came to start the journey west. Jack always had the impression that Charles Rhea bought the place, but a review of records in Lake City strongly suggests that he leased either the entire ranch or a portion of it. The older Rhea siblings had flown from the nest, leaving just Ralph, Joy, and Jack to make the trip with their parents. Jack, although he had been praying for this opportunity, was quite aware that he had never been very far from home. And here he was about to undertake a journey of several hundred miles. Charles bought a Ford truck and a Model T touring car for the journey in which he drove the truck and Ralph drove the car. Everybody else took turns riding in the two vehicles which never stopped at a restaurant. To conserve money, the Rheas bought groceries on the way and had a lot of soup along with prepared, canned meals. For water, they stopped at roadside springs and even clean-looking streams.

The vehicles were hard-pressed to top seventy or eighty miles a day, so the 300-mile trip was not completed with interstate efficiency. On their third day, they approached Pueblo, Colorado, and wondered if they would ever get to the other side of the mountains which were so tantalizing on the western horizon. Driving on mid-1920s mountain roads in Colorado proved to be slow and occasionally hazardous, especially considering the daily afternoon rains and unpaved mountain roads. Getting stuck happened more than once, and that meant all but the driver had to get out and push. Another problem was complicated by the incline and altitude which caused vapor lock; with carburetors starved, the Rheas had to sit and wait for the engines to cool. That was fine with Jack who stretched his legs and luxuriated in the scenery, especially considering his flat land Missouri upbringing. Once in a while, the convoy would get above the timberline where the vistas were breathtaking, but most of the time in the mountains was spent among tall conifers where the view was blocked.

Jack was fascinated by the new trees, flowers, vines, and like any new Philmont camper, also with the ground squirrels. He would toss them crumbs and was amazed at how close they would come to his hands. Taking all of this natural beauty in, Jack again thought to himself that God was indeed nearby. They spent one night in Creede, about 100 road miles south of Gunnison. Creede was then still a mining town, but its heyday as a wide open frontier town filled with gamblers, saloons, and gunfighters was in the past. In the mid-1920s, the bars had been reduced to just one along with several stores where the Rheas bought supplies.

Late the next day, the family crossed the Continental Divide and arrived in Lake City, a town that Jack would come to know well in the years ahead. Although more of a village by then, Lake City owed its existence to the late nineteenth century silver boom. While there was an occasional confrontation between sheriff and desperado, Lake City never developed a reputation as wide-open and lawless as did many other Colorado mining towns of that era. Charles Rhea was not the first Rhea to arrive in Lake City. That distinction belonged to a distant relative from Chillicothe, Missouri. That man, Luther Rhea, a silver miner, proved to be an exception to the comparative peace and order in Lake City and had been killed by one Jack Wells following a dispute on Election Day, 13 November 1877. Wells, a stonemason, came out second in an altercation in which he was thoroughly thrashed by Rhea. Following the fisticuffs, Wells, truly bloodied at that point, got up from the ground, armed himself, stalked Rhea, and shot him stone dead. Wells was nearly lynched by an outraged mob of witnesses after the shooting, but was quickly locked up by the sheriff. He was eventually tried and convicted of first degree murder.

In the morning, the Rheas drove the few remaining miles to their new home, the VC Bar Ranch, and found that it was truly a beautiful place. At its center was a solidly built, very roomy log home where most of the furnishings had been left by the previous occupants. For the first time in days, Jack slept in a real bed after watching a colorful sunset. He was up very early in the morning and explored the immediate area, beginning with the Lake Fork. The VC Bar Ranch traced its origins back to 1877 when Lake Fork pioneer Daniel C. Baker started ranching on what he initially named the Villa Grove Ranch. The "VC Bar" was actually a cattle brand at first, but as Baker bought surrounding ranches, the VC Bar became the name of the entire property which eventually encompassed over 1,500 acres.

Lake Fork Club Collection via Lonnie Reel

*At center, the bridge over the Lake Fork of the Gunnison River
leads to the VC Bar Ranch. The dirt road at right is today's
Colorado Rte. 149.*

Jack found the Lake Fork clear, cold, and fast with the promise of great fishing where the ripples smoothed out into pools around some of the big rocks. Jack had been a good fisherman back home in Missouri where his quarry was usually sunfish or catfish. Jack ran back to the house, got his fishing pole, and dug some worms to use as bait. He cast the worm into one of the pools and in no time felt a sharp tug; moments later he had caught his first trout. In a short while, he had a nice string of them to take back to the house where his father showed him how to clean the fish which were enjoyed at breakfast – the first of many such breakfasts to come.

Soon, Charles taught the youngest Rhea how to hunt with emphasis on safe gun handling which was carefully explained and demonstrated. Jack carried his .22 caliber rifle with him almost constantly. Very soon, he was hunting for the table and bringing home rabbits, squirrels, and wildfowl. He put a serious dent in the resident rodent population which Charles encouraged since he did not want such pests around the ranch. The prairie dogs and their holes were also a problem since a horse could easily break bones when stepping into them.

Horses were the reason why Charles Rhea bought the ranch: he was going into the horse breeding business. He had bought horses elsewhere in Colorado, including auctions in Montrose and Gunnison. The United States Army Quartermaster Corps was the main customer, and it wanted horses for cavalry and artillery units. The Army set up a program called the "Remount Service" which bought colts and mules at pre-determined prices from qualified breeders; buying horses in auctions had failed since too many sub-standard horses were offered by sellers. The Rheas' colts were destined for cavalry units which were interested only in bay or chestnut-colored horses. Charles Rhea had selected brood mares and stallions most likely to produce colts in those colors. After trucks hauling horses arrived, the VC Bar had over fifty horses with the prospect of many more the following spring.

The lodge and another house were built on a hillside overlooking the stream, and from its porch Red Mountain could be seen in the distance. Like Philmont's Big Red, Jack's Red Mountain in Colorado was a tall one, rising over 11,000 feet. Below the lodge was a relatively flat area covering several acres. Shortly after their arrival, Jack found his father on the porch, gazing out on those acres. Jack had no idea what his dad was thinking, but soon got his answer: corrals, stables, and fences for grazing pastures. As a farm boy, Jack had always been around horses, so helping out on the VC Bar came quite naturally. In the autumn, Ralph and Jack helped their dad sort the horses into two strings. Charles Rhea then hired two horsemen to help move the herd to winter pasture. Charles and one of the wranglers took the first bunch up into the Uncompaghre National Forest's high mountain meadows and left them there for winter grazing in several, separate bands which were located far enough apart so that the stallions did not have to fight each other.

The other wrangler, assisted by Ralph and Jack, took the other half of the herd up to the Gunnison National Forest which, although not as high, offered beautiful mountain meadow country, dotted with little lakes. One lake, on Blue Mesa, became Jack's favorite fishing spot. Young Jack became a superb fly fisherman, frequently using a "dropper" (two flies tied on one leader) to catch two trout on the same line. The horses seemed to be very content with their new surroundings for the next four to five months. So was Jack, although he definitely noticed the change from Missouri and Kansas, especially the cold which occasionally could result in frostbite. The lodge was down in a valley where it was not always as sunny as previous Rhea homes, but the location also shielded the Rheas from winter winds.

On a late October morning, this is the view that greeted Jack as he came out onto the front porch of the Rhea home on the VC Bar Ranch. At top center, Red Mountain stands at 12,815 feet.

Jack's father started building an icehouse, a small, low building well chinked with concrete to keep the sun and weather out. Jack was confused because this little affair had no resemblance to the plants his father had built back in Missouri and Kansas. Jack suddenly understood during the depths of winter when they carved blocks of ice out of nearby ponds. That activity was preceded by hauling in lots of sawdust from a mill in Lake City. The sawdust was dumped by the icehouse, and the Rheas would haul ice up to the icehouse and layer them with sawdust. The process provided ice throughout the summer, and the icehouse was an ideal place to age meat.

The horses would naturally graze in the high country until the weather turned worse later in the autumn at which point the horses would naturally move down the slopes. Snow was not a major problem because the horses had enough intelligence to dig with their hooves until they found grass, unlike cattle which are more likely to simply stand still and starve. In the spring, a roundup would bring all of the horses and new foals back down to the ranch. By the following year, Charles Rhea had acquired nearly 200 brood mares along with ten stallions. Nearly all of the mares would give birth in the spring before the Remount Service buyers came to select colts.

Jack was now old enough to ride with Ralph on one of the roundup teams. Driving the horses down to the waiting corrals was not especially difficult; sometimes finding the horses was challenging. The boys quickly found the horses which were grazing in the lushest meadows, but there were many others scattered over a wide area. To locate those Jack and Ralph rode high up in the mountains to a good vantage point and looked down to detect any movement. Occasionally they were fooled and rode downhill only to find that they had been watching elk or deer instead of horses. The process usually took several days, and the stallions were the most difficult to locate and drive down to the ranch.

There was also a lot of tack that had to be repaired because when the foals were brought down in the spring they had to be halter broken before the Army buyers decided which ones they wanted. With the Army buyers watching, Jack or Ralph had to go into one of the holding corrals (typically containing about twenty-five colts each), halter a colt, and show that it could easily be hand led around the training corral. The colt was brought over to the buyer who conducted a quick physical inspection and then promptly indicated if he wanted the horse or not by sending a hand signal to Charles Rhea. The price was always higher than what the colt could be sold for locally. The fillies were broken in during their second year and sold at auctions. If a colt could not be haltered and walked around the corral, the Army would not buy it. Seldom did a VC Bar Ranch colt fail the test which was critically important because the big money was with the Cavalry. The Rheas treated their horses gently which is why the animals came to trust humans. The few colts that failed were kept by the Rhea family or sent to auctions elsewhere. In later life, Jack admitted that occasionally a favorite colt got "lost" and that he was sure his father was aware of it. But the elder Rhea did not object so long as there were not too many lost colts.

Selling the colts was the easy part; there were difficulties with the stallions because nearly all of them would fight each other unless they were kept in separate stalls over the summer. Only a handful were friendly toward each other and would not fight. For those kept in stalls, Jack had to turn them loose individually in a pasture every day for exercise. While the stallions could be vicious toward each other, most were friendly toward Jack.

After they were taken away, the Cavalry moved the colts to another ranch where they were trained. The Rheas subsequently sold the fillies, remaining colts, and any of the unproductive mares. The VC Bar was becoming known for quality horses which fetched a good price.

CHAPTER 2

The Boy Scout

Jack did not especially enjoy going to school in Lake City. One reason for that was getting up long before daylight, doing chores, saddling his horse, then changing clothes, and riding for nearly an hour to get to school in Lake City. The school was a traditional one-room school house with about thirty students. The teacher administered discipline by telling parents about any infractions. For many students in those days, that meant a painful encounter with a belt, razor strop, or switch at home. Charles and Goldie never spanked or whipped their kids; they had other ways of enforcing proper behavior.

When they moved to Lake City, the Rhea kids, Ralph, Joy, and Jack, were all in elementary school. Jack always remembered the look on Ralph's face when he finished his last day in elementary school in Lake City. Ralph was elated because he now had to be sent to Gunnison for high school, and that was almost sixty miles away. He would have to find a place to live and work for his room and board. Ralph was very busy during his last school year in Lake City because there was much to do; corrals and fences required repairs, hay had to be cut and brought in for storage, and ice had to be cut and stored in the icehouse.

Many of the daily chores Jack had to do were the same as those he had done back in Missouri: raising chickens, collecting eggs, tending the pigs and steers which provided meat, and milking the cow. Ralph and his dad hunted the big game such as elk and deer, while Jack hunted smaller game. Mrs. Rhea and Joy canned the fruits and vegetables for storage.

Most of the Rhea family's shopping was done at the small store in Lake City. Several times a year, the family traveled to Gunnison to buy items not available locally. In Gunnison, they stayed with friends who had a large home, and on one occasion in 1927, the Rheas decided to be in Gunnison for Jack's twelfth birthday on the Fourth of July. Although the Fourth was a big day in Gunnison, it paled in comparison to the community's mid-July "Cattlemen's Days," then in its twenty-sixth year of sponsoring three days of rodeos, races, boxing and wrestling matches, exhibits, and band concerts (it is still going strong). That Fourth of July in 1927 was relatively quiet for Gunnison because many residents left town – to go to Crested Butte to watch the baseball game between the two towns' ball teams. Many families took picnic baskets prepared by Gunnison food stores (excluding Gunnison Fuel and Food which was closed for the holiday). Other townspeople were attracted to the annual fish fry sponsored by Western State College at Irwin Lake which is located twenty-five miles north of Gunnison.

Shopping, however, was the main reason for traveling to Gunnison, and the Rheas were not disappointed with sales at local retailers. Gunnison Fruit and Produce had good bargains on Swift's picnic and premium hams. Fogg's Cash Store slashed prices on some items that appealed more to townspeople; Goldie Rhea would not have been attracted to their hosiery for women "in beautiful light shades of silk" ranging in price from forty-five cents to a dollar and a half, but would have had Jack in mind for another sale item: boy's sturdy shoes for just under three bucks. Goldy was more interested in Miller's Store which was having a July clearance sale on ladies dresses at fifty percent off. There was not much clothing for sale in Lake City which is why the other merchandise on sale at Miller's was appealing: trousers or knickers for two dollars, twenty-five cents. Fancy, all wool knickers were pricey at four dollars, eighty-five cents. Martin's Book Store was offering something that appealed to all little boys – a package of firecrackers for just fifteen cents.

Folks in town from the more isolated communities such as Lake City could stop by the Rose Marie Tearoom Restaurant for a regular dinner, including salad and dessert, for just fifty cents. The tearoom was located next to the Unique Theater which had live performances of the "The Fire Brigade" on the fourth and fifth – with a portion of each ticket's price going to the local fire company. Jack, being more interested in movies, noticed the coming attractions signs which promoted Rudolph Schildkraut in *The Country Doctor*, Norma Shearer in *The Demi Bride*, and Gloria Swanson in *The Love of Senya*. All feature films were shown with news and short subjects.

Other than preparing for Cattlemen's Days, talk on the street that Fourth of July was about the six and one-quarter pound trout caught by a local man. The angler, John McCabe, disqualified himself from winning a cash prize from the local newspaper by admitting that he used a live minnow for bait instead of a more sporting dry fly. Only the week before, a summer visitor from Ohio, Harry Pratt, had taken a three and one-quarter pound trout from the Gunnison using a number ten "California Hackle" fly which was more in keeping with local fishing traditions. There was also news of a Chautauqua (a road show consisting of oratory, music, comedy routines, dramatic readings, etc.) coming to town. Gunnisonians were looking forward to the Redpath-Horner Chautauqua which was featuring Irish singers, stand-up comedian Charles Plattenburg, *Saturday Evening Post* feature writer A.B. McDonald speaking on prohibition and the possibility of beer coming back soon, and the Hawaiian music of George Vierra among other featured performers.

One of the children of the family the Rheas were visiting was a boy who also was twelve years old; he and his father were going to a rally in downtown Gunnison. The big meeting was all about the Boy Scouts of America and how to sign up. At the meeting, there was even a representative from the BSA National Office in New York City. The man's name was E. Urner Goodman, a name known to every Boy Scout as the principal founder of the Order of the Arrow. At the time, Goodman was in his mid-thirties and on his way to becoming the BSA's national program director.

Jack was impressed and wanted to become a Boy Scout. There was a major problem, and that was the lack of a troop in Lake City. Scouting was fine for youth who lived in communities large enough to support one or more active troops, but what was there for a boy like Jack who, for all practical purposes, was living in a wilderness? Jack was crushed, but also saw his dad talking to Goodman who came over to Jack and said, "You can be a Boy Scout!"

"But I can't go to meetings back in Lake City. There's no troop."

"You can be a Lone Scout."

The Lone Scout program had been initiated by the man who brought Scouting to America, the Chicago publisher W.D. Boyce. His Lone Scout program was launched in 1915 quite independent of the BSA, but by the mid-1920s it was absorbed by the BSA. Goodman went on to explain that Jack's father could be his counselor and sign him off on the various requirements as Jack climbed Scouting's advancement ladder – all without having to travel to Gunnison. Jack and his father filled out the application and paid the dues for one year: fifty cents. Jack brought up one concern and that was his lack of a BSA *Handbook for Boys*. Goodman promptly gave Jack a copy and refused Charles Rhea's offer to pay for it. For some reason which always remained a mystery, Jack impulsively asked Goodman to autograph the book. It remained a treasured possession.

That meeting was a life-altering event, but Jack did not realize it at the time. There is a wonderful sequel to that story. Many years later, long after he became an Eagle Scout, Jack became a professional Scouter and was a member of the staff at the National Office working for none other than E. Urner Goodman. Jack attended Goodman's retirement in 1951 and gave him a special gift: the autographed and well-worn *Handbook for Boys* that Goodman had given Jack twenty-four years earlier. As the two men hugged each other, both had tears in their eyes. Had Jack arrived in Lake City just a few years earlier, he could have joined a Boy Scout troop there, but the troop folded before the Rheas arrived. In the intervening years, Scouting has had an occasional presence in Lake City with some sporadic activity in the 1970s through the 1990s, but at this writing the community is without a troop due to a lack of Scout age youth.

Photo Courtesy of Mitch Reis

Lone Scout Division patch from the 1920s.

Then in the beginning of their fourth year at the VC Bar Ranch, the Rhea family's prospects were suddenly bleakened by a letter which arrived from the Remount Service indicating that it was dramatically scaling back its purchases since the Army was rapidly mechanizing its cavalry and artillery units. The Rheas had suddenly lost their only customer. It was a devastating blow to the family and especially to Jack since he could see the handwriting on the wall; he would have to go back to his nomadic, essentially fatherless lifestyle somewhere in Kansas or Missouri. There were more immediate problems: what do with the stallions and over 200 brood mares (none of which had ever been broken for riding) along with a number of colts not sold to the Army. There were also many foals expected the following spring. There was no local market for the colts and mares, but Charles was able to sell the stallions to nearby ranchers, although he certainly could not afford to keep any of the remaining horses for very long.

The solution was to sell the horses elsewhere. Charles announced to his two sons that he had hired two wranglers. They, Ralph, and Jack were going to drive the remaining horses down the Lake Fork Valley to Gunnison – a horse drive that would require three days. At Gunnison, the horses would be put on a train, taken to Denver, and sold. Also on the train were several cattle cars of steers headed for the Denver stockyards. Charles, the two wranglers, and Ralph had to find a place to sleep in the cattle cars as best they could, which was a problem not shared by Jack since the conductor took the him under his wing and put him up in the caboose. It was an exciting ride at the back of a train as it sped downhill and around sharp turns. Gazing out of the window, Jack thought it was like being at the end of a string while boys played "crack the whip."

When they got back to the ranch, the new occupants were there to meet the Rheas. Alvah "Tony" Baker was the son of Daniel Baker; he had recently been married to Kay Arrington. The couple bought the Rheas' personal horses, saddles, and other equipment. While operated by the Rheas, the VC Bar had been a great success which allowed the family to buy a new truck and car. Now they were about to put all of their worldly belongings into those two vehicles and retrace the journey back to their previous lives.

Goldie's prayer was longer than usual when they last gathered around the supper table. She thanked the Lord for the wonderful three years that they had enjoyed at the VC Bar Ranch. Jack watched another glorious sunset that evening, was up early on his last day at the ranch, and caught a string of trout for breakfast just as he had done on his first day at the VC Bar. After breakfast, he went down to the corral to say goodbye to his favorite horses. It would be years before he got back into riding horses regularly. As the family drove away in their little convoy, Jack looked back and just knew that someday he would come back to the VC Bar Ranch. He was right and would someday indeed return to the ranch for more experiences that would further shape the rest of his life.

Scouting in Kansas

While they were driving east, Charles Rhea told the boys that he had bought into an ice plant in Wichita and that he would not have to travel as he had done before. Unfortunately, once they got back to Kansas, Charles worked twelve hours a day, seven days a week. He was never home, and Jack was functionally without a father once again. The situation never changed; in fact, the family was coming apart. After a year of living in Wichita, it was agreed that Charles would take a small apartment near the ice plant and

Goldie would take the kids to live in Kansas City, Missouri, where some of Jack's brothers and sisters had settled. Jack's oldest sister, Louisa, was by then a secretary in Washington, D.C. Clara lived in Mission, Kansas, not far from Kansas City. Her husband was a sheet metal worker in Kansas City. Evelena lived with her husband in Springfield, Missouri, near where Jack had been born. The latter marriage was on the rocks since Evelena's husband was both alcoholic and abusive.

Jack's oldest brother, Charles, had dropped out of high school and was working for an optical company in Kansas City. He became interested in making reading glasses and was a pioneer in bifocal technology. Working in his basement, he developed a technique for fusing a higher magnification section onto the bottom of regular glasses. He called this technique "Cryptox," and he signed a contract to supply lenses to the giant American Optical Company. Unfortunately, he did not patent his process but did make enough money to start his own optical company in Cape Girardeau, Missouri. He helped aspiring young opticians and they in return sent him their business. The business was very profitable and is still going strong, although Charles Rhea sold out in 1963. Ralph and Joy found work with the Unity School of Christianity in Lee's Summit, a suburb of Kansas City. Joy was a corresponding secretary, replying to people all over the world who wrote asking to be remembered in prayer by the Silent Unity. The church met each morning in a time of prayer and meditation for those who had written. Jack knew that the letters, in the thousands, came from all over the world because he was an avid stamp collector. Once the letters were answered, Joy gave Jack the envelopes with the interesting stamps. As might be expected, Stamp Collecting was one of the merit badges Jack earned in Scouts.

Ralph eventually went through the Unity Church's training program and became an ordained minister. One of his assignments was as the minister at the Unity church in Lee's Summit where he proved to be very popular; people came from a wide area and filled the chapel on Sundays.

Jack's life was very busy in Kansas City; he lived in three different homes and attended three different schools. While in Kansas City, Jack enrolled in the Junior Reserve Officers Training Corps (JROTC) not knowing, at the time, what an impact it would have in later life.

Influenced by the movie, *Wings*, Jack and his friends enjoyed going to the Kansas City Airport and pretending they were World War I pilots among the old fighter planes in storage there. Jack and his buddies had joined "Captain Eddie" Rickenbacker and were going to clear the skies over France of that aerial scourge, the bloody Red Baron and his Flying Circus. Jack's comings and goings at home were strictly up to him, so frequently he and his buddies would stay at the airport and watch the big commercial planes land after dark. A large searchlight was located at one end of the airport and it illuminated the runway. When the pilot turned the plane around to taxi to the ramp, a man would spread out his overcoat and stand in front of the searchlight so the pilot would not be blinded. Jack was definitely in awe of the pilots.

Unfortunately, things were not working out for the family, so they moved back to Springfield, taking their model T Ford with them. In one sense, it is a shame that Jack could not have stayed in Kansas City because it was a town in which Scouting was especially strong, a phenomenon related to the dynamic, legendary "Chief" Roe Bartle who was the council executive.

Women in those days seldom drove a car, and Goldie Rhea was no exception. Jack, however, at age fourteen started driving. On one occasion, the Rheas in two cars were driving to Kansas City to see relatives. After a stop in Nevada, Missouri, to see other relatives, the two Rhea cars started again for Kansas City, with Ralph following Jack. Within a few miles, Jack sensed that his brakes were beginning to fail, but fortunately the road was essentially level. He said nothing about it because he did not want to upset his mother. Ralph, however, could sense that something was not quite right, but wrote it off to Jack's inexperience. When they reached the sister's home in Kansas City, Ralph was first to park at the bottom of the driveway which was inclined down. By this point, Jack's brakes were almost completely shot, but Ralph motioned him on, so Jack got the car onto the upper portion of the driveway, shoved the brake pedal to the floor, closed his eyes, and prayed as the car rolled forward. Jack's car softly touched Ralph's at the bottom of the driveway, but there was no damage. Jack thought his guardian angel was certainly on the job that day. Ralph asked what was wrong and how that could have happened with no brakes. "I had help," Jack said. Ralph said nothing but understood completely.

It was at about this time that Jack started showing more interest in family history, which he recalled from his grandfather William Rhea, the circuit riding preacher. Reverend Rhea as Jack remembered him was a tall man with a flowing, full beard. Jack recalled strangers asking the pastor of what denomination he was and hearing the reply, "God's denomination." It was from William Rhea that Jack learned of the family's coming to America via Ireland and settling first in Tennessee.

Jack learned only a little of his mother's side of the family. He did hear of one of Goldie's cousins, William Bebee, a famous explorer and naturalist who is considered one of the founders of what is now known as ecology. Jack got to know one of his uncles quite well. That Bebee, a very likable fellow, was a watchmaker, and a very good one too. Jack was fascinated as the watchmaker would disassemble clocks and even the smallest of watches to identify the problems, correct them, and then reassemble them. There were some problems, however, as the man would disappear after making a little money. The disappearances were caused by alcoholism. Jack's mother, tiring of her brother's sponging on the Rheas finally had enough and banished her brother from the Rhea home. Jack was ordered to drive the man out on the main road for miles and let him off. Bebee got out and said goodbye to Jack whose eyes were filled with tears. The watchmaker was never seen again.

The family problems started again, so the Rheas moved back to Wichita. Charles Rhea, who was Chief Engineer and Superintendent at Independent Ice Company, was still an absentee father. The family rented a farm on the edge of town and had chickens, hogs, and steers. What Jack really wanted was a horse, but that was an unnecessary luxury at that point. Young Jack drove his father to work every morning at 6 A.M. and picked him up every evening at 6 P.M. After dinner, he would take a nap, wake up, and head off for bed.

Rhea Family Collection

*Jack Rhea was a very busy young man in high school and
was a basketball player and member of the Junior ROTC.
The pin in his lapel is that of an Eagle Scout.*

This move was the last for the family; Jack would complete high school
in Wichita, get back into Scouting, and complete college there too. Although
Jack did not continue with Junior ROTC in Springfield or Wichita, he did
enroll in ROTC in college. He was also turning into a good basketball
player, and played the sport for all four years of high school and all four
years of college. In later years, Jack declared that he was not a star player,
just a good regular guard who played in every game. Like the good soldier
that he would become in just a few years, Jack did his best in his assigned
role: keeping the other guy from scoring while trying to get the ball away
from his opponents and get it to one of the forwards who would take the
shot. When the individual scores were posted after the game, it was usually
a zero that appeared after the name "Rhea."

Jack's leadership abilities were recognized early. Shortly before becoming an Eagle Scout, Jack was senior patrol leader in his Troop 37.

During one season, Jack was playing in the state championship game and was assigned to closely guard the other team's star player. Jack was doing his best to prevent the other team's hero from getting a shot from anywhere except the sideline. The other player, completely frustrated at this point, leaned back and threw the ball into Jack's face at point blank range. Jack went down, bleeding profusely from a broken nose. Later, in the locker room where a doctor was working on Jack, the other player came in with tears streaming down his face. He apologized profusely. Good sportsman that Jack was, the two parted as friends. Jack minded the poor sportsmanship even less when he learned that his team had just won the game and the state championship.

Jack's team could not possibly have won a victory against its next opponent: the Harlem Globetrotters. That was in the days of Goose Tatum and others who were real players and sportsmen. The Globetrotters made it a point to stay only two points ahead of the Wichita stars. What the Globetrotters said at the end of the game counted a lot – that they had to play much harder basketball against the boys from Wichita than they usually did against local teams.

Jack Rhea, front row, second from right, served on the Camp Talahi staff.

Jack got back into Scouting in a big way and started climbing the Eagle Trail in the Greater Wichita Council which was a Scouting powerhouse, serving a twelve-county area. Interestingly, the council's first executive was B.B. Dawson who would go onto become Philmont's first director of camping. Jack served on the staff at camp Talahi for several seasons.

He was the senior patrol leader of Troop 37 when he attained Eagle Scout Rank on 13 December 1932. He eventually qualified for a bronze and gold palm to his Eagle award. His Eagle award, certificate, and merit badge sash have all survived through the years. The Eagle requirements have changed over the years, but probably not become any easier. The service project was not required then, and such merit badges as Environmental Science, Personal Business, and Communications were well into the future. An Eagle candidate in the 1930s still had to satisfy tenure and leadership requirements. Many of the same badges were required, i.e., Camping, Lifesaving, First Aid, Pioneering, and Cooking. There were a few that were expanded; "Civics"

*Jack's Eagle Award
survives to this day.*

evolved into the four Citizenship merit badges. Physical Development became Personal Fitness. At least one required badge became optional: Bird Study.

Rhea Family Collection

*Jack Rhea at age 17 –
shortly to become an Eagle Scout.*

As with many Scouts, a quick look at the line-up of merit badges on a sash tells the viewer where the Scout has come from. In Jack's case it was clearly from the farm. Among his badges were Animal Husbandry, Poultry Raising, First Aid to Animals, Farm Mechanics, Farm Records and Management, Farm Home and Its Planning, and Farm Layout and Building Arrangement. He was disappointed in no longer having the contacts to earn what would have been an easy one: Horsemanship. Of personal interests, Jack earned Stamp Collecting, Botany, Marksmanship, and one that has been replaced by Orienteering – Pathfinding. As might be expected, he earned Scholarship which, in one sense could be a harbinger of a future career since Jack did go into education. Had he not gone into education and Scouting, he might have steered a path to journalism because he did earn that merit badge.

While Jack's focus in 1932 was on his reaching the top of the Eagle Trail, the BSA National Office had launched an aggressive, ten-year crusade for dramatic increases in membership. In 1942, the program had long since fallen short, but by then the overwhelming emphasis was on supporting the war effort in which Scouts acted as messengers, helped in war bond rallies, and supported scrap metal drives among other activities. Jack could not have known it in 1932, but someday he would be involved in another massive Scouting membership campaign – one in which he would be a major player and one that would also fall short of its lofty goals.

Jack served as the Scout editor of the Wichita Area Council newspaper and had a weekly show on one of the Wichita radio stations. The 1930s were the Golden Age of Radio, and Jack once interviewed the Lone Ranger, the cowboy hero of millions of boys. His interview with General John "Black Jack" Pershing was memorable. Jack was disappointed to learn that the World War I hero's language was more than salty. Jack just had to accept it as part of the man's normal vocabulary, although it was hardly what Jack had been used to hearing. The great General told Jack to give him a call whenever he wanted to join the Army. Unfortunately, General Pershing's influence had waned by the time Jack was ready to enlist. Attending some out-of-town college was not in the financial reach of the Rheas, so Jack enrolled at the University of Wichita (later to become Wichita State University) where he majored in education and psychology. To say that Jack was a busy young man is an understatement. He was still very much involved in Scouting while at the university and served as an assistant Scoutmaster with his old Troop 37.

Jack Rhea earned enough merit badges to qualify for bronze and gold palms to his Eagle Award.

CHAPTER 3

Teaching

Although the Great Depression darkened many Americans' outlook, there were some people in Wichita who were making big money, very big in fact. It was the opening of the nearby Hull-Silk oil fields that made fortunes for a few people in Wichita. They in turn built great homes and wanted the best private schools for their children. For that reason, a man named Ernest E. Altick founded the Wichita Country Day School (WCDS) in 1929. Altick had a strong record of service to youth and been appointed the executive director of the North Wichita Branch of the Wichita YMCA in 1922, but resigned in 1929 to start WCDS. The new school, for kindergarten through the sixth grade, was located in what had been the suburban home of Mr. and Mrs. George Hyde on 49th Street near the Little Arkansas River. The house, leased by the school, could more accurately be described as a mansion; it was a rambling, two-story structure with many rooms and several smaller buildings. The property at one time had been a working farm. Jack was entering his third year of college when he met Altick. In those days, with two years of college and a certification, one was permitted to become a teacher. In those pre-"middle school" days, kindergarten through sixth grade was considered as elementary school with junior high school starting in the seventh grade

Jack got his teaching credentials before college graduation and was hired by Altick to teach the first grade and drive the school bus for the 1934-35 school year. The school also included extra-curricular activities under the name "Akita Club." Those activities, typically scheduled for Saturdays, included crafts, Indian lore, camping, rifle marksmanship, archery, and many other activities typically associated with Scout camps. Jack's resume was loaded with that type of experience which was one reason why Altick hired Jack in the first place. Similarly, several of the female teachers had previous experience with Girl Scouts and Campfire Girls. Jack continued working for his degree in education, playing basketball, devoting several hours a week to R.O.T.C., and giving what little spare time was left to Scouting. It was a nearly frenzied existence: drive the bus to pick up some of the kids in the morning, teach for one hour, quickly head to the university for classes, back to Wichita Country Day School to drive some of the kindergarten kids home, teach for another hour, and then return to the university. When he had time for lunch, it was usually on the school bus. He still had another class in the afternoon and also drove the school bus yet again later in the afternoon. Many years later, Jack summarized those days as "Busy, but lots of fun."

Altick resigned in late 1935 as the CEO of WCDS to become headmaster of lower and middle schools of the Pembroke Country Day School in Kansas City; it was a move that brought him financial security because WCDS had always struggled financially. Although living in Kansas City and no longer the principal, Altick remained as the chairman of the board of directors of the Wichita Country Day School, Inc. Nevertheless, Altick's move created a crisis at WCDS which was faced with closing its doors until some of the influential parents got together, subsidized the operation, and asked Jack to run the school. The school's management structure changed to the extent that parents shared some of the burden of management; there were committees on membership, endowment, building/grounds, educational policies, etc. In some ways, WCDS was a Montessori school before the Montessori method caught on inasmuch as classes were small and instruction was individualized. WCDS rarely enrolled more than seventy-five students. Although always on shaky financial ground, the school's accreditation was maintained because it was on a very good standing with the local school system. While teaching at WCDS, Jack completed his academic work with a major in education and a minor in child psychology which allowed him to be certified as the school's principal.

Jack loved it – he had found his life's calling: working with kids. He was offered a commission in the Army through R.O.T.C., but turned it down. Several years later, he regretted turning the commission down, but as it would work out, the regret was short-lived. Jack was more interested in pursuing his career in education at that point, and although there were shooting wars in China and Spain, America was not yet as concerned about being drawn into the conflict as it would be several years later.

Jack employed several other qualified teachers who would teach grades one through six. Before the autumn term opened, Jack and his staff spent over a month in preparation, especially studying what the city schools were emphasizing in grades four through six. He was determined to prepare Wichita Country Day School students as well as possible for entry into the seventh grade. Subsequent testing of those students graduating from Country Day confirmed that Jack and his staff were exceeding their expectations.

It was far from an easy job. Some of the very privileged kids were discipline problems, especially since they had been pampered at home and had servants to take care of their every need. With little or no discipline at home, some of the students were demanding and difficult. One young lady in the second grade became an enfante terrible for Jack at first. However, she did straighten out and eventually became a model student. The parents were thunderstruck, and the father asked Jack at a parent-teacher meeting one evening how he had been able to prompt such a transformation. Jack related that he administered a firm but not bodily threatening spanking when the girl misbehaved. The father turned to the mother and out loud said, "See, that's what I have been telling you to do all along."

Western Tours with Students

Through its Akita Club, Wichita Country Day School operated a subsidiary called Camp As-We-Go in which participating students were able to go on long-term tours across much of America during the summer. The school had its Ford bus, a large touring car, and everything else it needed including a truck, kitchen trailer, sleeping bags, folding cots, and plenty of related equipment. Although living in Kansas City, Altick was still on the school's board of directors and continued direct involvement with the summer touring program. Jack's first tours were in the summer of 1935 when he took forty boys on the first tour and then took thirty girls on the second tour. The school offered several tours: one to the Pacific Northwest, a short southwestern tour that focused primarily on Colorado, and a long western tour to California that also saw many of the sights in Arizona, Nevada, and Utah going out and coming back. There was also a northeastern United States tour that was rich in American Revolutionary War history. In 1933 a tour to the Chicago World's Fair was offered. These tours had some built-in flexibility because each year several new stops were added while others were dropped. The short southwestern tour frequently passed close to Philmont and included nearby Capulin Volcano along with Santa Fe. In the years that Jack participated, his involvement was limited to the southwestern and Pacific coast tours, but the experience provided him with a wealth of memories.

The trips were very carefully planned, and the routes and overnight stops were arranged well in advance. The bus, truck, and trailer were very carefully maintained and inspected prior to the departures. The parents were given a copy of the itinerary. Jack telephoned back each evening to one of the parents so any important messages could be relayed. The parents agreed that Jack could control and discipline the children as he saw fit. Parents deposited money with Jack for the kids to buy souvenirs on the trip or presents for those back home. Jack was thunderstruck at amounts some parents were planning to deposit, so he quickly put a cap on how much spending money could be taken on the trip. These were the children of Wichita's most affluent people, so the maximum amount was always deposited.

One of the children, the son of a prosperous banker, went into business for himself by loaning money to other kids and charging exorbitant interest rates. If another youngster ran out of soap, the budding banker charged a penny for each use of his own soap. The young entrepreneur bought expensive presents for his parents and still had more money in his pockets than the amount of the original deposit. Many years later, Jack was hardly surprised to learn that the young man had become a bank president.

One of the cars always preceded the main body; its driver was responsible for scouting out the night's accommodations. The stopping points were usually state or national parks where the group pitched tents after dinner which was cooked by two of the other teachers, Bennie and Sarah Smith, who drove and slept in the kitchen trailer. While the group was on the road in the morning, Bennie or Sarah would be in back of the trailer, making lunch. Then one of them would start readying supper in the trailer during the afternoon ride. After arrival, dinner was cooked and the kids were responsible for the cleanup.

Just before driving the bus down the Big Thompson Canyon (between Loveland and Estes Park, Colorado), Jack sent the other drivers ahead to wait, knowing from past experience there that it was not a good road for convoying. Once all vehicles were together, they would resume their convoy. It was a beautiful area with the road winding around the mountain from which it seemed the view extended for a thousand miles. The unpaved roads, hugging the mountainside, crossed streams and passed through forests where the pines were absolutely majestic.

Approaching one of the turns, Jack applied brake pressure, but his foot suddenly went to the floor: no brakes! Jack quickly downshifted into the lowest gear, praying that the gears would hold and not strip. Fortunately, the bus slowed. Jack quickly whispered to one of the other adults what had happened and asked him to keep the kids engaged by pointing out prominent points in the distance. One of the students asked Jack why they couldn't stop once in a while since the scenery was so stunning, but Jack just told him that they were behind schedule and could not afford the time. Jack was acquainted with this stretch of road and knew that some dangerous, descending curves were up ahead and that in their present condition there was no way to maintain control. In fact, the steepest descents on the entire route were not too far ahead.

Jack was looking and praying for somewhere to ease the bus off the road, but, unfortunately, he was quite literally between a rock and a hard space, or more accurately, a rock and space since beyond the other side of the road was a sheer drop off. The road had been cut out of the mountainside and the right side was loaded with huge boulders. To hit one would result in the bus being bounced off to the left side and over the edge. The drop was hundreds of feet. Jack never prayed so hard. His prayers were answered when he saw a stretch ahead on the right that was loaded with tall grass and weeds. Knowing that there was soft earth beneath the grass, Jack steered for it and as the wheels started sinking into the soft earth, Jack gently turned right, scraping the bus against the bank on the right side. Jack looked skyward and said a prayer of thanks, not knowing that in little more than two decades he would have another terrifying downhill experience.

They were still in a predicament and had no place to go. Jack refused to let the kids off the bus due to the risk of losing some of them over the sheer cliff. Walking the youngsters out, one by one, was not a real way out either even with the other adult on the bus. Backing the bus up was no solution since they would eventually face another downhill stretch anyway. At this point, good fortune intervened when Jack heard a loud honking sound from out in front of the bus. On such roads, it was customary for a driver to blow his horn prior to going around a turn to warn other drivers of oncoming traffic. If the oncoming driver heard nothing, he would proceed, but if the uphill driver replied with honking, the approaching driver would stop, and back up until he found a place to get off the road enough to let the descending driver, who had the right of way, continue his descent. The other adult rushed to the bus to toot the horn in reply, but Jack cut him off just in the nick of time. Jack wanted the other driver to quickly know what a problem the bus was having.

Very shortly, a small truck with two men inside drove up. Jack explained the situation, and the other drivers quickly realized what a predicament the school group was in. The little truck was not an answer to the problem; even if they could have pulled the bus out of the loose dirt, their brakes would never have held up if they had tried to back down the mountain with the bus positioned against its front bumper. The only solution appeared to be for the truck to back up to some location where it could be turned around and driven to the nearest town for help. There was no way help could arrive before dark anyway. At this point, the kids realized the gravity of the situation and several became quite frightened and upset.

Then there was more honking – this time from in back of the bus. It turned out to be another truck whose drivers joined with Jack and the other truck driver in a discussion of the best strategy to get the bus safely down the mountain. Fortunately, both trucks carried heavy tow chains. The group decided to have the truck in back pull the bus back onto the road. The truck in front would attach a chain to the bus and back down the mountain with both trucks using their brakes.

The kids were kept busy by singing and storytelling. Jack claimed that, although he was unafraid because he had confidence in the other drivers, he had never felt so useless, just sitting there steering the bus to keep it on the road. It seemed like hours and hours before they were down to the bottom of the canyon and in level driving distance of a facility that could fix their brakes. The good Samaritans steadfastly refused any money for their help, but Jack did get their names and addresses. The bus finally reached the main body, and after a late dinner the kids promptly went to bed. In the morning, Jack called a meeting and explained fully what had happened. Then the group said prayers of thanks for being brought down safely. Jack then passed out paper and pencils; the group wrote letters to the men who had been responsible for their safe descent. Each of the men replied to Jack with letters addressed to the entire group. That is when Jack learned that when it came to the precious cargo the bus was carrying, he had not been the only one praying fervently.

On one of its stops, the group spent several days at the AZ Ranch near Tres Piedras, New Mexico (about thirty miles northwest of Taos). The ranch was owned by a family whose son had graduated from Wichita Country Day School. The ranch included a lodge, guest cabins, and a string of about twenty-five saddle horses. The ranch employed one wrangler whose job was to take guests out for rides on mountain trails. Learning of Jack's experience with horses, the wrangler suddenly had a new assistant. Jack took the school kids out for rides and even took some other guests out during their short visit to the ranch.

There was one very spirited horse named Tistinata. She was half Arabian, spotted gray in color, and very beautiful. Jack asked if he could ride her.

"Ride her? You can't even get near her!"

With that, the wrangler went up to the corral gate and Tistinata promptly reared up, kicked, snorted, and shook her head menacingly. Jack, for the moment forgot about riding the beauty as the wrangler told more about the mare. Tistinata had been one of the wrangler's favorite horses. Not that long ago she had given birth to a foal and was about to wean it. The wrangler would allow unweaned foals to tag along on trail rides, knowing that the foals would never stray far from their mothers. The wrangler would even pause on the ride if a foal decided it was feeding time – and it was interesting for the guests to watch. Eventually, the foals would be left behind, and when Tistinata's colt had to remain in a corral, Tistinata did not seem to mind at all.

The wrangler had asked one of the boys who worked at the lodge to tie the colt to a hitching post in the corral while he took some guests out for a ride. Instead of putting a halter on the colt and tying that to the post, the boy put a rope around the colt's neck. Then the lad went back to his other chores. The colt got wound up in the rope and suffocated. When the riders returned, they unsaddled the horses and turned them loose in the corral. Tistinata ran over to her now dead colt and kept trying to make it stand. When she realized that it was hopeless, she went absolutely berserk, running and kicking all around the corral. From that day, she was calm around the other horses, but if a human being got near her, she would kick and buck, trying to chase the person away.

As usual, Jack was up early the next morning, and saw the boy who worked at the lodge. He was down at the corral, in tears and sobbing. He was trying to get Tistinata to eat the hay he was pushing through the corral bars.

He looked at Jack and said, "It's all my fault. We were such good friends."

"Keep trying. Just keep talking to her."

Soon, Tistinata calmed down and started eating the hay. Jack and the boy stayed there for a while, feeding the horse, and talking to it in soothing tones. Finally, Jack went to the corral gate, opened it, and walked into the corral. The horse just stood there looking at Jack but not making a move. Several men started walking down to the corral and one of them yelled at Jack to get out of there. The wrangler, who had also shown up, said, "Be quiet. Let's see what happens."

Jack walked to another spot in the corral with a handful of hay and offered it to Tistinata. She spent another minute or so watching Jack, but soon walked over and started eating the hay. Jack reached out and stroked her head. Soon he was rubbing her neck and back. Then he turned, and slowly left the corral, heading for the tack room. He returned with a comb and brush. Tistinata seemed to enjoy the grooming that followed. In a few minutes the horse was calm enough to allow Jack to pick up her feet and clean them off. With a couple more pats on her neck, Jack slowly walked toward the gate – and Tistinata followed him. Jack repeated the process several times during that day in order to get better acquainted with the horse. Then Jack asked permission to ride the horse the next day. The wrangler agreed.

In the morning, Jack saddled her, climbed aboard, and rode her around the corral for a while. Then he opened the gate and went for a ride in the pasture, concluding that she was a perfect horse, almost seeming to sense what Jack wanted to do and then doing it without any directions. Before going to lunch, Jack and several other riders tied their horses to hitching racks in a grove of trees about 100 yards from the lodge. Among the guests was a family with a little boy about eight years of age. Suddenly, from the lodge porch, the boy's father yelled, "Oh, no!" Jack rushed to the porch to see the youngster running across the clearing toward the horses and paying no attention to his father's yells to come back. Along with Tistinata there were about fifteen older, trail-wise trotting horses. They would not be upset by Tistinata or by the approaching boy. Naturally the boy gravitated toward the beautiful mare; the father was nearly frantic by this time, and Jack had to tell him and the other bystanders to keep their voices down, remain calm, and stay on the porch. Although his heart was pounding, Jack walked out to the hitching post as calmly as possible. He watched the little boy walk down the line of horses until he came to Tistinata. The lad crawled under her belly and tried to pull himself up into the saddle from the right side, not knowing that the horses had been trained to let riders mount from the left.

Jack started talking very soothingly to Tistinata, but the boy had actually gotten into the saddle and was digging his heels into her sides the way the he had probably seen it done in western movies. Jack was praying that the horse would not erupt as she always did prior to the previous day. Jack finally approached the horse, still talking to her, and eased the boy out of the saddle with firm instructions to walk back to his father who was already running toward his son. Jack then untied Tistinata's reins; she remained calm and had not moved an inch, even when the boy was crawling beneath her. Jack looked into her eyes and saw no fear or excitement. Although Jack could sense that she was somewhat nervous, he untied the reins from the post, mounted up, and rode her out into the clearing. Sensing that the horse wanted a good run, Jack held the reins loosely and let Tistinata run. For several minutes the horse ran freely all over the meadow, but then slowed to a trot, and returned to the hitching post – all without any guidance from Jack. Both rider and horse were soaked with sweat. Jack dismounted, got some rags, and dried her off. Returning to the lodge, the much-relieved father grabbed Jack in a bear hug and exclaimed that Jack had saved his son's life. Jack corrected the man saying that he had nothing to do with it; Tistinata did.

Fishing was always an important part of these summer road trips, and one year Jack took some of the older boys on a very memorable fishing side trip that started from Eagle Nest, New Mexico. After unloading their horses from a trailer, the group made its way south of Eagle Nest Lake, turned southeast, and rode up to some very broad meadows between the peaks where they came upon a lake where the fishing was really excellent. The kids were catching so many fish that Jack showed them how to remove hooks from those fish not too deeply hooked and return them to the lake. Eventually, the group decided a little exploring was in order and a group of three, including Jack, headed down the little stream that flowed out of the eastern end of the lake. The fishing was good as the stream got larger and entered a canyon. After a while, they encountered some activity where the creek met another larger stream. There was a large lodge near the junction of the two creeks, and there was a lot of lumber and building material lying about where men were working on some other buildings. Jack was told that the lodge was owned by a man who owned a million or more acres of prime cattle, hunting, and fishing country in New Mexico. At the time, Jack did not know that he would return to this location many times in the future. The land owner was Waite Phillips and the lodge was none other than Rayado Lodge at Fish Camp.

CHAPTER 4

Gaucho

Several days later, there was another contact with "The Philmont Ranch" (or just "The Philmont") as it was known by Colfax County residents in its pre-Boy Scouts of America days. After getting back to Tres Piedras, the entire group headed east through the Cimarron Canyon to go to Philmont Ranch where they had been invited to camp for the night. The father of one of the boys on the trip had made arrangements with a Tulsa-based oilman friend, Mr. Waite Phillips, for the group to camp at the ranch. After camping overnight, the group went down to the corrals to see the horses. Phillips was in the forefront of breeding palomino horses, made quite striking by their blond-yellow color. The night before, one of the mares had given birth to a colt, but had died during the delivery. Jack asked the ranch manager, Mr. Roy Cartwright, what was to become of the colt.

"Not much. We don't have another mare that will take him and feed him, and we just don't have enough time to spare for hand-feeding and raising him."

Jack asked, "Could I have him?"

"Sure."

Thus began a truly remarkable partnership. Jack took the colt and put him in the bus which absolutely delighted the kids. All the way home, they took turns feeding him milk, keeping him clean, and taking him out for exercise whenever the bus stopped. By the time Jack got home, he had a healthy, active, and decidedly spoiled colt. Jack found a place to keep the colt and bottle feed him with milk. Soon, the colt was eating regular feed. Jack had lots of help because the kids who had been on the tour that summer adopted the colt as the school mascot. Since the colt was from a state with a strong Spanish heritage, New Mexico, the students named him "Gaucho" after the Argentinian cowboys of the same name. By the time he reached two years of age, Gaucho had developed into a really wonderful palomino stallion.

Gaucho liked people, especially the kids who had been such an important part of his life. Jack started to train him for riding by putting a hackamorc (a bridle with no mouth bit) on him. Jack used this to start riding him around a corral. Gaucho was taught to neck rein in the manner of most cowboy's horses, i.e., laying the rein on one side of the horse's neck resulted in a turn in the opposite direction. Jack also started to ride Gaucho bareback in the corral. The mouth bit was only used to slow down or stop. Later Jack started putting his saddle on the corral fence so Gaucho could see it, smell it, and get used to it. Jack was well-acquainted with the way most cowboy horses were broken: just saddling up and riding a bucking horse until he got too tired to jump and buck any longer. Usually, the bucking stopped almost at once – when the rider had been thrown within a few seconds of mounting. It was usually a slow process involving a lot of thrown riders and waiting for the horse to be" topped off" with some bucking before they would settle down. Jack wanted to avoid that with Gaucho even if it took longer to train him.

When Jack was finished, Gaucho was "gentle broke," to use Jack's own words. The horse never bucked, not even when a blanket and saddle were first placed on him. Getting him used to a bridle with a bit was more challenging since Gaucho would grit his teeth, trying to eject the bit. With patience Jack stayed with it until he could lead the horse around the corral with the bit in place without any resistance. Finally, the day came when Jack fully saddled Gaucho for the first real ride. First came the bridle, on went the blanket and saddle, and finally, he fastened the girth under Gaucho's belly. Gaucho turned his head and eyed Jack who could see that the horse was nervous; still, Gaucho did not cause any trouble. Jack put his foot in the stirrup, grabbed the horn and quickly was aboard, hoping that some wild bucking would not follow. He did nothing for a few moments, but then started walking Gaucho around the corral. Jack savored what followed for the rest of his life.

> One of the nearby men opened the gate and we went out into the pasture. Walking at first, then into a trot, then into a gallop. His gaits were wonderful. No hard bouncing up and down. It was almost like sitting in a rocking chair. We stayed out a long time and both of us enjoyed it. After that when I came into the corral, he eagerly trotted over to me ready for another ride.

Jack later wrote back to Roy Cartwright at Philmont asking if there were any papers on Gaucho's background. By return mail, Jack got some exciting news. It turned out that Gaucho's father was "Old Plaudit," one of the greatest palomino stallions that the breed ever had. Gaucho lived up to every bit of his heritage. One of Jack's friends suggested charging stud fees considering Gaucho's sterling ancestry, and Jack followed through by getting fifteen dollars for service: five dollars down and ten dollars upon arrival of the colt. Jack completed his college education by paying tuition largely derived from those stud fees.

Garden City, Kansas, was a frequent overnight stop on those summer tours. On one occasion, the sky had become very threatening. Having lived in Tornado Alley for years, Jack had a pretty good idea of what was going to happen, especially since he could see some small twisters starting to form as they approached Garden City. The wind went from blowing hard to howling and the rain started coming down in sheets. The bus was rocking back and forth which was scaring the kids. Jack got them started singing – as loud as they could. The rocking chorus went on for over an hour, but eventually the storm passed. Jack was the first out of the bus and found that the twister had passed within a few hundred feet of the bus.

The truck and kitchen trailer were mired down in mud about a mile behind the bus. Jack was forced to turn the bus around and pull the other vehicles out of the mire. The trailer's insides were a shambles with pots, pans, equipment, and food scattered all over. Fortunately, Bennie and Sarah were both riding in the truck's cab and were unhurt, although it was obvious that there would be no hot meal that night. It was also very clear that there would be no camping in the park in Garden City.

The advance party had made arrangements to sleep in the basement of a church where the ladies of the church would fix a hot meal of spaghetti and meat sauce. There also was plenty of bread and butter along with homemade cookies for dessert which the kids absolutely loved. The tornado had roared through on a Saturday, so Jack had the group up and dressed in their best clothes to attend church on Sunday morning. The youth were perfectly behaved and the congregation enjoyed hosting them; on subsequent tours, the church became a regular stop.

First sight of the Rockies was exciting as the group approached Colorado Springs where Jack took the group up Pikes Peak on the cog railway. As so often happens on top of Philmont's Tooth of Time or Baldy Mountain, the kids were overwhelmed by the broad vistas extending before them in all directions – majestic mountains on one side and the broad, sweeping plains on the other. One youngster shouted, "Boy, this is a great country!"

The journey continued to the Grand Canyon's South rim where Jack was anxious for the students to see the colorful, beautiful spectacle the Colorado River was still creating. A park ranger joined the group and explained how the process had begun over a million years before; he also issued a stern warning about staying away from the sheer drop off at the canyon's edge. The young people took the warning to heart, but still appreciated the grand vistas sweeping out from and below the rim.

Jack noticed the remains of an old pine tree just hanging onto an outcropping at the canyon's edge. It appeared to have been hit by lightning more than once in the same place since its gnarled trunk showed several scars running down its sides. Looking at the burns which ran deep into the tree, Jack marveled at how the tree could remain standing for so long. The tree did have one branch that reached out parallel to the rim of the canyon. The guide took the kids one by one and had each grip that branch with one hand, leaning out so they could see all the way down to the bottom of the canyon. Jack was apprehensive at first, but relaxed when he saw the guide made sure each youngster had a firm grip on that branch and that the guide also had a firm grip on the kids' other hands. The branch was almost worn smooth in one section from the grip of so many trusting hands.

Then it was Jack's turn to lean out. Jack described it as "breathtaking," as he gazed at the canyon walls, the vivid colors of many different rocks, and the dancing of sunlight and shadows. Just as Jack was musing about the stunning scenery, his eyes caught another, different color. At the end of the branch was a sprig of green. The branch was alive and so was the tree. Jack always thought that the tree stayed alive because it was serving a worthwhile purpose: helping people safely see the wonders of nature and God's handiwork.

The caravan continued west out to northern California's Big Sur National Forest where the group set up camp. As usual, Jack was up first in the morning since issuing the wake-up call was one of his duties. Typically, Jack would find a secluded spot to sit, think, and say a morning prayer, thanking God for all of the natural beauty the group was enjoying. One morning, Jack was on the edge of a little clearing, sitting on a log when he heard a rustling sound in the branches of a small tree just a few feet away. Soon, a bushy-tailed squirrel scampered down the tree and bounded to the very center of the little clearing. The sun was climbing higher and suddenly a shaft of light poked through the tall redwoods and lit up the clearing almost as if a spotlight had been aimed right there, and the squirrel was at the epicenter of the spotlight. The squirrel must have been a performer since it sat on its hind legs and switched its tail back and forth and then suddenly looked right up at Jack. As the sun continued to climb, the spotlight disappeared and the little clearing returned to the shadows. The squirrel quickly scampered back to its tree and started to climb, but paused and gazed back. Jack always maintained that the squirrel absolutely smiled at him. So Jack smiled back at the squirrel which, after a few moments and a tail-waving, disappeared into the boughs after providing Jack with another special moment in nature.

When the bus stopped, Jack advised the group at what time they had to be back at the bus. That was in a time when there was not much need to worry about kidnapping or molestation by others. Within set boundaries, the kids were free to go and see what was there, although the adults circulated around the boundaries to make sure none of the youth got lost or into any kind of trouble. When everybody got back to the bus, Jack used a numbered call system to make sure all were present, with Jack as number "one." The numbers would be called out in perfect sequence with each kid knowing never to shout his number until the previous number had been called. Jack never forgot number seventeen. Time after time the count would stop at sixteen. Then there was nothing but silence. Jack's irritation mounted every time he had to get off the bus and start looking for the errant boy. Discipline, firm words, and a few scoldings had no effect.

The group stopped at Stanford University whose beautiful campus had been endowed in honor of the son that Leland Stanford, a California railroad magnate had lost. Because his patience was wearing thin at this stop, Jack took the lad aside and firmly told him that if he was absent again, his parents would be contacted and he would promptly be removed from the tour and sent home. Tears welled up, and the boy promised Jack there would never be another problem. The campus tour ended and the kids started counting off after Jack commenced with "One." The silence after sixteen was deafening. Jack, angry at this point, stormed off the bus with plans to make good on his threat. He quickly located a phone where he could make the long distance call, and then set off on a hurried search of the campus.

Jack covered the entire campus from stadium to library and each of the stops the tour had made. The search concluded in the magnificent chapel. Beyond the altar's big cross was a stunning stained glass window. The altar and cross were so strategically placed that they were bathed in multi-colored light from the windows. In that setting, Jack found the boy kneeling in prayer. Jack stood silently as the boy finished, stood up, and turned to leave with a face that was positively radiant. Jack was also praying – that the boy would not be afraid. As it turned out, the youngster was not at all afraid. Jack put his arm around the boy and they walked in perfect silence. The count was resumed and completed with all kids accounted for. Jack sensed a great change at the count after the next stop. Sure enough, the counting ended at sixteen. The kid had not changed, but Jack had. Jack was no longer angry. As Jack told it, he went looking again for a kid that was worth the trouble of the search.

Swinging back east, the caravan reached Salt Lake City after several days of camping and hiking in the Big Sur National Forest. As the group was spending a lot of time outdoors, Jack had tried to make sure the kids knew how to recognize poison ivy with its "leaves of three" and shiny green color. Unfortunately, the lectures did not include a troublesome vine that frequently grows up trees and hangs down from branches: poison oak. Back in California, some of the kids had come into contact with poison oak, and the symptoms were appearing on arms and faces. Rolling into Salt Lake City, Jack stopped at a small clinic, had the scratching kids examined, and loaded up on what he thought must have been a gallon of calamine lotion.

The relief was temporary, and the miserable, itchy kids were scratching vigorously which just made matters worse. One of the major attractions in Salt Lake City, other than the Mormon Tabernacle, was the Great Salt Lake and its promise of the unique swimming experience which bordered on levitation due to the buoyancy effect of its very salty water compared to ocean water. A young lifeguard took interest in the group and showed them how to deal with getting salt water in their eyes: wet their fingers in their mouths and wipe their eyes. Then the young man noticed the poison oak problem. Most kids were interested only in a quick float, especially when the salt water reached their sores. He told Jack that the best cure for poison oak was a thorough, soaking swim. Some of the older kids took the cure without question. Others advanced into the water inch by inch. Others had to be thrown in. Not all went quietly and their protests attracted unwanted attention from other bathers, but the lifeguard explained the problem and solution.

The longer they stayed in, the less painful it was. Soon they were having a wonderful time – the first enjoyable moments in several days of scratching all the way from California. After a while, several of the kids headed for the shower house, but they were intercepted by the lifeguard who told Jack to prohibit any showers. Jack objected thinking what a stinking mess the sleeping bags would become, but the lifeguard insisted that the mess would be worth it. Jack reluctantly accepted the advice, and, to be sure, the sleeping bags were a sight the next morning. The group stretched ropes between trees and beat the bags with sticks, knocking off the patches of caked salt. The group's poison oak sores were still a bit crusty, but the maddening itching had stopped. When the caravan left Salt Lake City the next day, Jack swung by the swimming area to thank the young man, but in spite of his inquiries, the lifeguard who had saved the day could not be found.

Back to the VC Bar Ranch

The 1937-1938 school year commenced several weeks after the group returned from the road tour and with it a very busy life for Jack. There was the teaching, driving during the day, and administrative duties as the school principal. By late 1937, the Wichita Country Day School had outgrown its original suburban location and had made two moves. The second location was in a mansion at 10th and Jefferson and its final facility was in the R.J. Paul property at 1030 South Hillside. Jack was still very busy with Scouting; for all practical purposes it was a second job for him. Since his Troop 37 days, he had progressively served as Scoutmaster for Troops 55 and 6. He had also moved up to the district level and had been an assistant commissioner in two of the council's districts.

Over the years, Tony and Kay Baker at the VC Bar Ranch had stayed in touch with the Rheas. Even ten years after buying the ranch from Charles Rhea, the Bakers had questions about exact boundary lines, grazing and water rights, hunting and fishing agreements, and other issues. The VC Bar Ranch years were an era that Jack longed for in later life – a time when a bill of sale was recorded in the abstract office, money changed hands, and a handshake completed the deal without lawyers, title searches, tax settlements, etc.

The Bakers had turned the VC Bar Ranch into a "dude ranch" with a clientele composed primarily of wealthy Texans. Jack always preferred the term "guest ranch" since he thought calling somebody a dude in those days was a demeaning title. However, years later with four teenagers in his family and then grandchildren, he was always amused how the meaning of the word changed and that being called a "cool dude" was actually a compliment. Jack convinced Ernest Altick to include a week-long layover at the VC Bar Ranch on the 1937 Southwestern Tour. For Jack, it was a wonderful return to the ranch that had meant so much to him as a boy.

In the early spring of 1938, the Bakers had a proposal for Jack who took it as "the offer of a lifetime." The ranch needed horse wranglers who could also serve as trail guides and fishing guides. The Bakers knew that Jack was intimately familiar with not only the VC Bar's 1,500 acres but the Gunnison and Uncompaghre National Forests as well. The pay was thirty dollars a month, room and board included. And Jack could count on generous tips from the well-to-do guests. He could plan on returning to Wichita in late August with several hundred dollars in his pocket, and that was a lot of money in those days. The offer was especially attractive because Jack's salary as a summer guide for Camp As-We-Go was significantly lower than his pay during the regular school year. Jack offered a quick prayer of thanks for the promise of returning to the happiest days of his life. He actually started packing for the trip out to Colorado two months before the spring term ended.

There was a lot to pack into his old Dodge coupe: boots, chaps, spurs, gloves, ropes, flashlight, a Winchester .30-30 rifle, fishing tackle, and more. Then there were two saddles. One was a form fit with a wing-shaped pommel which helped keep Jack securely on the saddle. Jack had actually participated in the construction of it with the saddle maker. The other saddle was for roping; its pommel was narrow with a strong horn to which another horse or animal could be tied. Jack had only one remaining problem; he needed a trailer to haul Gaucho. The solution came in the form of the father of two of Jack's students. The father, who kept a string of polo ponies, had hired Jack to tutor his young son and daughter. Jack was allowed to keep Gaucho in the man's stable. Gaucho was a quarter-horse for whom all of the polo pony maneuvers (fast starts, sudden stops, quick turns, high speed) came quite naturally. Soon enough, Jack and Gaucho were training polo ponies, although Gaucho was excused from one aspect of polo pony training: teaching aggressiveness. Polo ponies have to be ready and able to push another horse out of the way, and that simply was not in Gaucho's nature.

When the polo ponies had reached the age where they were not good at the game, they were used simply as riding horses. At that point they were

gentle, well-trained, and easy-gaited. Once in a while, the old instincts surfaced which meant that the rider had to be alert and very much in control.
One Sunday, the two children and their parents were out for a ride along
with Gaucho and Jack. The boy had become a good rider, and his father
gave him one of the older polo ponies to ride that day. Suddenly, something
spooked the pony which took off at a full gallop. The father galloped after
the boy in spite of Jack's yelling to him to stop. Jack knew that the boy's
pony would only pour on the speed if he heard another horse approaching
from the rear. That is the way they were trained. Jack spurred Gaucho and
rode at a full gallop in an arc swinging around the bolting pony. Jack knew
that the pony would head for him and Gaucho. It worked, as Jack completed the circle with the polo pony following him.

The mother and sister were in tears from fright, but the boy was thrilled.
It had been the best ride of his life. The lad handled it well; the father smiled
at his son with pride, knowing there was going to be another polo player in
the family in just a few years. The boy's father gladly loaned Jack a single
horse trailer for the upcoming journey to Lake City and even had a couple
of his employees fasten a sturdy hitch onto the car. Although the trip would
not start for several more weeks, Jack put a lot of effort into the planning,
especially since he did not remember the details of the family's move to
Lake City years before.

Road maps were not that easily obtained in those days. As it turned
out, his plans were constantly upset by delays associated with dust storms
and rain which also meant muddy roads. He had to allow for time to water,
feed, and exercise Gaucho. The dust storms across western Kansas turned
out to be a real problem even when he could see the big, rolling black clouds
headed toward him in the distance. Before starting in the morning, Jack ran
through a quick checklist: car filled with gasoline, extra gasoline on board
in cans, and plenty of water in wet canvas bags. When he saw a dust storm
approaching, Jack would wet a rag and place it over Gaucho's head. The
horse objected at first but eventually accepted it as Jack talked soothingly
to him.

Some of the journey's sights stayed with Jack forever: the arid land,
dust piled high against a house or barn, and farm wagons almost buried in
dust. He drove for miles seeing no crops or people. Considering the many
times he had moved as a child, Jack identified with the farmers who were
driven off their land in order to survive elsewhere. The roads back then

were hardly up to Interstate 70 standards. There were plenty of rough roads and detours, and the most miserable type of road Jack described as "washboard." Jack drove very slowly over those. He had a cushioned seat and shock absorbers. Poor Gaucho was standing on his feet all the time. Jack never got lost but admitted to being confused more than once, particularly because the roads were very poorly marked. Frequently, he would just follow any traffic heading west. When he was really confused, he would stop and ask somebody. Jack knew the names of the major towns he wanted to reach, but frequently the people he inquired with had never been more than twenty-five miles from their homes. Some of those encounters were priceless.

"How do I get from here to Pueblo?" Jack asked of one grizzled farmer.

"Well, let's see. You take the road to Springdale and then the road to Hickory."

" OK, well what road do I take out of Springdale."

"The one for Hickory."

"But just which road is it from Springdale out to Hickory."

"Oh, shoot, boy everybody knows that one."

Jack just thanked the farmer and drove on. When he got to Springdale he found only one road leading out of town. It led to Hickory. Later Jack pulled up at a crossroads garage named "Tornado Garage." Jack inquired if there might be a better name, at which one of the mechanics indicated that the garage had been flattened by three tornados in recent years.

"Did you ever think about moving away?"

"Why would we do that? Folks rely on us to fix their cars, tractors, and farm equipment. Move away? Who would help them? Our customers come help us rebuild after each tornado hits. We figure that if the good Lord needed us somewhere else, He would tell us."

During the journey west, Jack wrote home to his mother and never had a problem finding the post office in towns through which he passed. The American flag was always flying from the post office. Although Goldie Rhea could not send Jack letters while he was in transit, she did send letters to him at the VC Bar Ranch. Upon arrival, Jack found a small stack of letters waiting for him with all of the news about what was going on at home. Jack's mother always wrote about the good news. Even when things might not be so rosy, she always found something for which to be thankful.

Jack was always on the road early and would stop in the mid-afternoon to take Gaucho on a ride so neither horse nor rider would get too stiff from the long hours on the road. In an age when there was not a Holiday Inn at nearly every highway exit, Jack still had no problems in finding overnight accommodations. It was, indeed, a very different time in America. Staying at a hotel cost about a dollar and a half – make it two dollars if staying on a floor with a bathroom. Gaucho was put up at the local livery stable for fifty cents per night. Sometimes Jack would find himself in villages where there were no hotels, but that posed no problem. He simply pulled up at a farmer's place, explained who he was and where he was going, and asked if he could sleep in the barn with his horse. There was always plenty of clean straw and Jack had a good bedroll. The farmers, knowing a good horse when they saw one, always admired Gaucho. Frequently, children on the farms tagged along behind Gaucho when he was turned out in a pasture. On numerous occasions, Jack was offered good money for Gaucho, but he never was tempted. In the morning, Jack was up early and had breakfast with the family. More often than not, the lady of the house had packed a big lunch for him. None of them ever accepted Jack's offer to pay for lodging and food.

When Jack arrived at the VC Bar Ranch, he noticed some changes. A grand new lodge had been built on the mountainside. Down below on the meadow, close to the flowing Lake Fork, a number of new cabins had been built for the guests. The corrals, stable, and wranglers' bunkhouse were the same as Jack remembered them. Jack saw that many things had not changed as he looked back ten years in time. God's handiwork was still there. The Uncompaghre and Gunnison National Forests were still there and Red Mountain still stood on the horizon, reaching for the sky. In his mind's eye, Jack remembered the trails, the trout pools in the Lake Fork, pristine mountain lakes, and alpine meadows. Jack suddenly felt very much at home.

Lake Fork Club Collection via Lonnie Reel

Tony and Kay Baker, owners of the VC Bar Ranch.

Tony and Kay Baker were expecting Jack. They looked the same to him, but Jack had changed from a twelve-year old boy into a twenty-three year old man with the confidence of being an Eagle Scout, athlete, educator, and superb horseman. Soon Jack met the other wranglers, including the oldest, Frank, who had lived in Lake City all of his life and remembered Jack's father very well. Frank was in his early thirties and was the natural leader of the wranglers. Jack immensely enjoyed working for the Bakers, especially because Tony never bluntly ordered anybody to do anything. It came across as more of a suggestion. If something went wrong, Tony's approach was to say, "Well, let's see if we can do it better next time." It was understood that Tony would not ask somebody to do something unless he knew that person was capable of it if he really tried.

Slender and tall, Kay was quiet, but she seemed to be everywhere all of the time. She was as good with horses as any man on the VC Bar and could shoe a horse with the best of them. Kay took care of the garden, was the bookkeeper, and also the cook. Kay checked the guests in and out, and served as the nurse, doctor, and friend to all. She never tired of listening to the wranglers. When she talked, they all listened closely.

Tony quickly learned each wrangler's strengths and weaknesses. Because he was the youngest, Jack felt he had to work hard to earn the Bakers' respect. Jack brought a lot to the job because he could ride, rope, and saddle and shoe a horse as well as any of the other wranglers. Jack's father had also taught him how to repair tack and other equipment. Jack put in his share of cleaning up in the corral and stable – not always a pleasant task. The others knew that there had been some sort of personal ties between the Rheas and Bakers, but that never translated into any special privileges for Jack; in fact Jack occasionally thought that more was expected of him. He did, however, feel a special kinship with the Bakers.

Tony Baker's sense of humor was that of a good ole boy who liked a classic play on words, especially with the dudes who had little or no experience riding horses.

Tony would say, "For ten cents, I'll take you down to the stable and show you something special."

"What's that?"

"It's a horse that's got his head where his tail should have been."

Then Tony would take the dude down to the stable and show him a horse that had been turned around in its stall. After the laughing died down, Tony collected his dime. That kind of humor was Tony's domain and none of the wranglers ever tried to muscle in on his turf. Another favorite was betting a dude that Tony could run afoot faster than a horse could. Tony would saddle the dude's horse and challenge him to a race from one end of the corral to the other and back. Loser had to pay the other a quarter. And it was agreed that Tony would run afoot while the dude could get the best out of his horse. One of the wranglers would yell, "Go," whereupon Tony would take a ruler out of his vest pocket, measure off a foot on the ground, and jump to it and back. When the laughter subsided, Tony was richer by twenty-five cents.

Typical daily duty for Jack was taking the guests on a half or full day trail ride. If there were not enough guests to need all of the wranglers, one or more of them would remain behind shoeing horses, repairing equipment, pitching hay, or cleaning out the stables. One day, Jack was shoeing a horse and as he was standing behind the horse he sensed that the horse was about to kick him. Charles Rhea had taught his son how to deal with that hazard. Moving away from the horse was a mistake – that just gives the horse a greater arc with which to kick through and means that the victim suffers from the full impact. Jack knew in the split second he had available, the best thing to do was get as close as possible so the horse's foot. That way the foot does not hit – it merely pushes. Even so, a push can be a mighty shove, and Jack was thrown up against a wall. He was uninjured with the exception of having broken off a front tooth.

Jack wasn't smilin' when Kay got him into the truck and drove over fifty miles to Gunnison where a dentist quickly fashioned a gold crown. Interestingly, during Jack's lifetime, the crown fell out several times, but Jack always found it, and had it reattached. The gold tooth was also a source of great amusement for the Rhea children in their earliest years.

Taking the guests on trail rides was a source of great pleasure for Jack, especially because there was so much breathtaking scenery. Several of Colorado's 14,000 foot peaks are nearby, Slumgullion Pass (over 11,000 feet) was just to the south, there were other rushing streams in addition to the Lake Fork, and there were beautiful lakes in the high, alpine meadows. There were very few children among the guests. Jack sometimes got the impression that some of the guests were taking a vacation from their kids. For Texans wanting to escape the heat of late summer, the VC Bar Ranch, at nearly 9,000 above sea level, brought wonderfully cool relief. Jack kept a close eye on what few kids did come to the VC Bar and made sure they got a chance to pet Gaucho, especially during rest stops on the longer trail rides. In addition to enjoying his work, Jack was building up his savings because the tips from guests were adding up.

With an academic background in psychology, sociology, and education, Jack always found the guests to be interesting people. Some of them quickly admitted to knowing practically nothing about horses and there were others who had never ridden on a western saddle. Of those who had ridden before, many had experience only on an English saddle which Jack likened to a leather handkerchief. Here and there were a few experienced riders. Jack had a test to quickly separate the rookies from the real riders. He would take a saddled horse, lead it to the guest, and turn over the reins. If the guest promptly checked the cinch for tightness and the stirrups for length, then Jack figured the riders had enough experience which allowed Jack to spend more time with the inexperienced. The former group got the best horses while the latter group got the more docile animals. The horses had their own personalities. Some preferred only men as riders; others preferred the ladies. Some horses had their own particular horse friends and preferred to be placed next to them on the trail rides.

Once in a while, one of the guests was a self-styled expert rider who would brag and tell the other guests what to do. The wranglers had special techniques for dealing with such "know-it-alls." One scheme was to fix the horse's bridle so that when the rider pulled on the reins the entire bridle would slip off the horse's head and down its neck. The smart aleck would frantically try to shove the bridle back up the horse's neck and over its ears which is nearly impossible. Another deflating approach was to make sure the cinch looked tight but really wasn't. The result of trying to mount up was an ungraceful, slow motion meeting with the ground, usually under the horse. Then there was the old "right-handed" horse trick in which the "experienced" rider was told that his particular horse should be mounted only from the right side. The inevitable result was that the rider never did swing into the saddle because the horse swung away, frequently leaving the rider sitting on the ground. There were only a few horses used in these ploys, and Jack always thought that they enjoyed the antics as much as the wranglers.

If the dude survived all of those corrective measures, Jack had only one other resource, and it was a very trail-wise and gentle horse which had only one bad habit. The horse was remarkably fond of stopping in the middle of a stream crossing and lying down in the gurgling waters. Horses seem to have a sense of just who is in charge when a new rider climbs aboard. If the rider is hesitant and does not show some real authority right away, the horse becomes the leader. If the rider has a firm voice, solid eye contact, a forceful pat, and a firm hand on the reins, the horse knows who is in charge. With such a person, the bathing horse never tried for a cool down in the creek. When the group came to the first stream, Jack always dropped back, got hold of the accomplice horse's reins, and led the expert rider across the creek. The rider usually protested vehemently. Jack would relent and the smart rider was allowed to solo the next stream which invariably resulted in a swim much to the amusement of the other riders.

A violent afternoon storm was the rule rather than the exception – so much so that Jack could almost set his watch by them. A heavy duty rain slicker was tied onto every saddle, and at the first sign of an approaching storm, the raingear was immediately donned. The horses were even used to the break in the routine. Jack and the other wranglers occasionally did not put on their slickers, preferring instead to enjoy the refreshing showers. Jack thought the wranglers' taking care of such details always helped in generating more tips. There was no question about what the horses thought;

they absolutely loved the rain because it helped check the horse flies.

Jack never took a thunderstorm lightly and always had a plan. Guests got off their horses and spread out, preferably not under tall trees. The horses were tied into a string and secured. Guests were told to lie down flat on the ground if they felt any sort of a tingling; that way they would be less of a target. Many guests did not realize that if they heard thunder, the lightning had already struck somewhere else. Jack made no attempt to straighten them out. It just made one more good story about riding across a high, mountain meadow and just barely escaping from being hit by lightning for the guests to tell when they got back to Dallas or Houston.

Gaucho was having every bit the good time as Jack. Gaucho was the only stallion in the string of horses; the rest were geldings. As such, Gaucho became the leader which worked very well for Jack. In the morning, Jack did not have to ride out to the pasture to bring the horses in. He just walked out of the bunkhouse, beat on a tin pan, and heard Gaucho's answer. Very soon, Gaucho would be on his way, with all of the other horses following him. Jack was usually the first in line on the trail rides and often sensed that Gaucho was just as intoxicated with the scenery and pure mountain air as he was.

Frequently, the guests wanted to go fishing, and in Jack they had a talented guide. For Jack, it was a lot of fun and a source of good tips; his guests almost always brought home a nice string of trout. On one occasion, a storm had turned the stream murky and the trout simply were not biting. Jack decided to cross the stream and head for a little cabin where the group could have lunch. His group welcomed the suggestion since the storm seemed to be doubling back toward them. Jack tied the horses to trees and the group stepped over rocks and logs to reach the other side of the creek and the little cabin just beyond. When lunch was completed, Jack gathered up the leftovers and trash and looked out a window toward the waiting horses. Then he saw the bear.

Jack suddenly dropped down to the floor and said, "Get down, there's a bear out there!" The guests all dropped to the floor, most on all fours but some flat on their stomachs. Jack allowed those who wanted to creep to the window for a peek at a large black bear. For most, it was the first time they had seen a bear anyplace except a zoo or circus. Jack admitted years later to staging what followed. But it did seem like such good theater.

So, he whispered to the group, "See that row of trees out there. That's our best escape route. We'll just go from tree to tree and hope the bear doesn't see us. If he chases you, climb a tree." Jack did not mention what good tree climbers black bears really are. Jack then said he would go first and that the guests should watch how he did it and then try it one at a time, making sure the bear could not see them. Jack took off and made sure the bear saw him, knowing that the bear would bolt the minute he saw Jack which is exactly what happened. Knowing that the danger was now gone, Jack readied himself for some fun. Breathlessly, the guests made the run for their lives. Some did not even try to stay dry on the stream crossing and just splashed their way across. The last two to reach the other side of the stream swore that the bear had been chasing them. The group hastily mounted up and headed back for the VC Bar. The stories they were telling got better with each passing mile.

Jack was not sure if Tony, Kay, and the other wranglers approved of Jack's handling of the situation, but his tips certainly made him feel good about it. The guests were convinced that Jack had saved their lives. Jack frequently took other groups to the same cabin for lunch, but the bear proved wildly uncooperative. The bear ploy was one Jack never forgot; he would re-invent it many years later and play it with other groups of "dudes."

Every group of guests got a one-night fishing expedition to a lake on Big Blue Mesa which is north of Lake City and west of Gunnison. The lake is home to some trophy-sized trout. Jack had to pack tents, sleeping bags, fishing tackle, cooking gear, food, and other supplies. It took hours of riding to get up there, and upon arrival many of the guests were saddle sore and ready for a nap. Jack had his hands full on these trips since he had to supervise setting up tents, getting a fire going, and cooking supper. The guests were expected to pitch in and help, but it was obvious that camping was a very new experience for most of them. Jack always maintained that it was on those trips that he most valued his experience as an Eagle Scout because the potential for chaos was always present.

When it came to fishing, some of the guests, who certainly were not rookies, brought their own fishing tackle. That allowed Jack to spend more time with the neophytes. On one occasion, Jack's work was simplified by a trio of guests who declared that they were not interested in fishing. They stayed behind and when Jack returned with the anglers, lo and behold the trio had cooked a tasty stew complete with biscuits. Jack was anxious to get back to the lake since the big trout were most active near dark. Fortunately, only the hard core fishermen were going which meant that Jack did not have to worry about tangled fishing tackle, tying on lures, or removing hooks from caught fish. Instead, he would have time to kick back on a hillside and enjoy watching the guests having a wonderful time catching fish.

There was one man in the group of guests who never really seemed to fit in. He spoke very little, kept to himself, was not fishing, and joined few of the organized activities back at the VC Bar. Jack wondered why the man had paid money to come to the VC Bar and why the loner never really responded to Jack's going out of his way to get the man involved. For some reason, Jack liked the man though. He seemed like a nice enough fellow even though he did not seem to want any friends. That evening, while Jack was perched on a rock looking down at the guests catching fish, he sensed somebody approaching. It was the loner.

"Mind if I join you?"

"Not at all."

"You're not fishing?"

"No, sometimes I enjoy watching our guests catch some really big ones just as much as I enjoy catching them."

After a brief silence, the man indicated that he too liked to see others having fun.

"Jack, you seem to know a lot about people and horses."

"Well, I like them both. That's for sure."

At this point, Jack was thunderstruck. It was the most Jack had heard out of the quiet man since he arrived at the ranch.

"Have you ever been lonely, Jack?"

"No. Seems like no matter where I go, I have somebody with me."

The outsider got up to leave and said, "I'm sorry to have intruded on your privacy."

"No, wait," Jack said.

The man sat down as Jack explained, "Look at that lake. The moon and the way the clouds creep past the moon. The lake. The trees. That owl we're hearing. The coyotes out there somewhere. We're not alone."

"Do you really believe that?"

"Sure I do. Prove me wrong," Jack said.

The man opened up and explained how his wife had died just a few years before and that his children and grandchildren lived so far away that he practically never got to see them. He also admitted that he was truly alone – and that he had nobody to call a friend. Jack told him that nobody is ever truly alone. All they needed to do is live with those around them. Then the man got up to leave, took a few steps, turned and simply said, "Thanks." Over the next few days, Jack was pleased to see that the man opened up and seemed to enjoy himself more.

When Jack got back to the campsite, he found that one of the guests had tripped over a log and had quite a bad bruise on his hip. The hip certainly was going to be in for some abuse on the dirt road (today's Route 149) back to the VC Bar Ranch. The injured man was in real agony, although Jack was sure that there were no broken bones. Jack always carried a well-stocked first aid kit, but it was designed for use with cuts, scratches, burns, blisters, and snake bites. Jack knew that there was really nothing he could do, but it was important to appear that he was doing something positive. He knew that the situation called for desperate measures – and that there was a man in the group who always carried a bottle of whiskey in his pack.

Jack quietly retrieved the bottle, gently rubbed in a copious amount to the injured man's hip, and just as quietly returned the bottle to the pack. The bottle was not missed that evening. The next morning was another story; the drinking man went from person to person demanding to know who had stolen his booze. He finally threatened bodily injury, but nobody spoke up. The injured man still reeked of the whiskey but the man who owned the bottle never detected it because he smelled that way himself nearly all of the time.

Jack had time for fun. Since it was only a little more than three miles down to Lake City, Jack would occasionally saddle some horses and take a few guests down to the town. It was a route he knew well, having made it every day when he went to elementary school in Lake City. Today, Lake City comes alive in the summer when tourists flock to Colorado's High Country. There are art galleries, a theater, restaurants, a lovely town park, and a few saloons. Some of the VC Bar's guests enjoyed stopping at the local watering hole for a drink. The bar was clean, orderly, and well-managed. Jack and the other wranglers were not drinkers and neither were Tony and Kay Baker. The wranglers thought it best to follow Tony and Kay's example in that regard. None of that applied to the guests, however, and on some occasions, Kay had to be summoned with the truck to retrieve some equilibrium-challenged guest whom the wranglers could not trust to remain upright on the trip back to the ranch.

For a wrangler, there was not much opportunity for social life in Lake City. Usually, there was simply not enough time for it and there were not that many young ladies in Lake City to begin with. Jack did, however, find one young lady, they became friends, and went dancing when Jack was able to get some free time in Lake City. Romance was starting to blossom and Jack really looked forward to seeing her. All went well until she came out to see the VC Bar Ranch. She and Jack walked up to one of the rock formations just in back of the main lodge, i.e., the VC Bar's equivalent of Philmont's Lovers Leap. The scene could not have been more romantic. The scent of pine was carried on a mild breeze, there was the soft, rhythmic hooting of an owl, the moonlight-silvered waters of the Lake Fork splashed below, and the mountains were majestic in the twilight. The stars were so big and bright that it seemed as though the young couple could just reach out and touch them.

Jack looked at the girl, gazed at the sky, and then started talking about how wonderful life was, that he was so lucky to have a job at the VC Bar Ranch, how perfect everything was, and best of all, he owned the finest horse in the world. Jack turned to the young lady. But she was not there and was already half way back to the VC Bar lodge. Jack never saw her again.

Just as Jack's father had done, Tony Baker wintered his horses up in the Uncompaghre National Forest. The horses always prospered up there and were in fine shape when they were herded down in the spring. Tony only brought down just enough horses to cover his requirements for guest trail rides. However, the VC Bar's business was picking up and Tony decided to send Jack up into the mountains to bring back more horses to finish the season. Even though it had been a number of years, Tony knew that Jack was familiar with the area. Jack was asked to take a pack horse, camping gear, and provisions for a three to four-day trip up to the high country to drive down enough horses to meet the ranch's growing business.

Early the next morning, Jack saddled up Gaucho and one pack horse for the trip to one particular meadow which would be his starting camp. From there, he knew how to reach other meadows where he was sure to find the horses grazing. After about four hours, Jack reached the meadow where he planned to camp. He located the closest spring for water, pitched his tent, gathered up firewood, and found a suitable tree limb from which to hang his bear bag. Then he covered everything that needed protection from the late afternoon rain.

By early afternoon, Jack and Gaucho were on their way to a command-ing vantage point where they could look out to see the most likely spots where the horses would be grazing. Spotting any movement, Jack would ride out to that spot. Occasionally, he was fooled by elk or deer which would be confirmed when he saw their tracks. Gaucho seemed to enjoy the hunt and needed little guidance. When they did find horses, Jack would start them downhill toward the VC Bar, but would stop when the horses wanted to graze. Late in the afternoon, Jack rode out into a clearing where he saw a large coyote lazily trotting across the other side. Coyotes were not welcome on the ranch because when they were in packs they could kill a colt and were dangerous even for a mare. Jack reached down to the scabbard attached to the side of his saddle and started to pull out his rifle. Suddenly, the coyote stopped, turned, and glared at Jack.

At the same time, something frightened Gaucho and he jumped sideways – something he had never done before and certainly something Jack was not expecting. Jack, being in an awkward position while drawing the rifle from its scabbard, fell from Gaucho with one leg between the saddle and scabbard with the rifle only half out. Jack hit the ground with a broken leg.

CHAPTER 5

Jack and the Shepherd

Gaucho stopped about twenty feet away with both reins dragging on the ground. He was ground hitched and would not move. Jack tried to get Gaucho to come over, but the horse would not move and Jack knew it. Jack had spent hour after hour training Gaucho not to move when he was ground hitched. Somehow, Jack managed to pull himself over that twenty feet which seemed more like twenty miles. He managed to tie Gaucho's reins so they would not touch the ground. Then Jack pointed down the trail and yelled, "Go home Gaucho!" The horse moved out but only went about thirty feet and then stopped and looked at Jack. It was the first time Jack had ever told the horse to leave him. Jack then picked up a stone and threw it at Gaucho, again yelling, "Go home Gaucho." After hesitating just a few seconds, Gaucho threw back his head, and then started down the trail at a gallop. Jack sighed, knowing that it would not be long before Tony came looking for him with Gaucho leading.

By then it was very late afternoon. Jack was not looking forward to the night and its near-freezing temperature. Jack said some prayers and then either fell asleep or passed out. When he woke up, he heard a dog barking and soon saw a sheep dog bounding into the meadow. Jack had worked with sheep dogs before and knew that he had nothing to fear from this dog. In just a few moments, several sheep and then many more came into the meadow. That is when Jack heard some singing in a language he could not understand. Then a Basque shepherd appeared behind the sheep along with a pack mule. The men could not communicate because neither understood the other's language. So, Jack pointed to his leg and gestured with his hands to show a stick being broken. The shepherd kneeled down and tried to straighten Jack's leg which felt much better.

The Basque walked away but returned very shortly with two sturdy sticks with which he expertly splinted Jack's leg, using some rags for rope. The shepherd disappeared yet again and returned, this time with an armful of long, soft grass which quickly became a pad on which Jack's rested his broken leg. Next, the man unpacked a tent from his mule and pitched it over Jack. After clearing the grass and digging a shallow hole, the shepherd started a fire. Taking a leather bucket, he disappeared but did not return as quickly as before. When he did return, it was with fresh, cold water. Jack always said that water was the best drink he ever had. Next, an iron pot was placed over the fire and soon meat and vegetables were boiling away along with a pot of coffee. The shepherd then left to take care of his flock.

Within a few minutes the aroma from the gurgling stew reached Jack – and nearly sickened him! The odor was vile, and Jack was certain the meat had come from the oldest, sickest sheep in the flock. The mutton had probably been aged a bit too long as well. The shepherd returned and tossed in some seasoning including a couple cloves of garlic; the fumes from that alone added insult to injury. Through hand signals, Jack signaled that he was not hungry. The shepherd settled back and enjoyed his dinner which consisted of the entire pot of stew. Then the men started drinking coffee. Up to that point, Jack preferred coffee with plenty of cream and sugar, but he had to go without that night. He actually liked the coffee black, and the more he drank the better he liked it. From that night forward, Jack Rhea was strictly a black coffee drinker.

Then the shepherd opened a little canvas bag containing cookies that were shaped like little biscuits. The shepherd pointed at the cookies and said something that sounded like "piff-news." Jack could not speak Basque, but the word did not sound like French or Spanish to him. Anyway, he took one, bit into it, and almost lost his recently installed gold crown. The cookie was as hard as a stone. The shepherd howled with laughter; then he took several cookies and dropped them into his coffee. So did Jack. After a little soaking, the now-softened cookies tasted wonderful. Jack never went near the stew, but enjoyed more of the hard, little cookies. Jack could not have known it high in that alpine meadow on a summer night in 1938, but the next time he would encounter the little cookies was almost seven years later in the country of their origin. The cookies were actually *pfeffernusse* (German for pepper nuts).

Jack fell asleep that night listening to his new friend singing and playing a small Basque folk guitar. Jack could not understand the lyrics, but he found the music very reassuring and thought that the dog and sheep were similarly pleased by the music. Jack drifted off into slumber. When he woke up, he had his daily, devotional talk with God. His new friend probably thought Jack was still asleep since Jack's eyes were closed during the meditation. Soon the shepherd was breaking camp, packing up, and getting ready to move on. The sheep were well-fed, seemed to have had a lawn mower effect on the meadow grass, and were ready for some greener pastures elsewhere. The shepherd sat down beside Jack and gave him another cup of coffee. The Basque and the cowboy of Scottish descent could not speak to each other, but they were communicating just the same. In a few more minutes, the shepherd took Jack's coffee cup, put it in the pack on his mule, and then turned around. It was a stunning morning with a beautiful sunrise in a sky ablaze with fiery red and yellow clouds. The shepherd smiled, raised his arms, and in perfect English said, "He is here. He is here." Then the shepherd was gone. The sounds of his dog and flock faded in the distance.

Jack later learned that Gaucho had been discovered standing alone at the corral gate by Frank, one of the other wranglers, late in the afternoon following his return from a trail ride. Frank immediately told Tony, but they decided that with darkness rapidly approaching the best approach was to start searching at first light in the morning when the chances of success were better and tracks could be seen best. Four men made up the search party and each was assigned a certain area. When one of the searchers found Jack, three rifle shots would be fired to signal the others. After nearly a full day of searching, Jack's campsite was found and a rifle was fired. It was obvious that Jack had not used the campsite; food was still hanging in the tree, there were no fresh ashes in the fire ring, and Jack's bedroll had not been used. Darkness was approaching, so the dejected riders turned back for the VC Bar.

They returned the next morning and brought Gaucho with them. When they reached the campsite, Tony tied Gaucho's reins to the saddle and turned him loose. Gaucho wasted no time and was quickly headed for Jack. Tony knew they were on the right trail because he could see Gaucho's tracks from two days before. As the riders followed Gaucho, Tony would frequently yell Jack's name. After a while, there was a faint reply to one of Tony's yells. Then the replying yells slowly got louder, and soon Jack could hear riders approaching on the trail. Gaucho was the first to see Jack. He tossed his head back, whinnied, and dashed straight for Jack. Gaucho lowered his head, almost as if talking to Jack who stroked the horse's forehead. Within a few seconds, Tony, Frank, and the other wranglers arrived.

Cabin Duty

Frank said, "Well he's busted his leg all right. Guess we'll have to shoot him." That of course was the usual fate of a horse with a broken leg. The black humor continued with another wrangler who said, "Oh, he's no good to us anymore, so let's just leave him here for the buzzards." The jesting had a wonderful effect on Jack who broke into laughter for the first time in days. Tony disappeared for a while but soon returned with tree branches which were stripped into several sturdy sticks which, along with some soft cotton rope, were used to re-splint Jack's leg. Then the group set about building a travois with which to carry Jack back to the VC Bar since it was obvious that riding was out of the question. The travois, a sled-like carrier, would be towed behind a horse in order to return Jack to the VC Bar. To Gaucho went the honor of towing his master. Jack was riding backwards, and as he was being towed out of the meadow, he look back to where he had last seen the Heaven-sent shepherd and silently said, "Thanks."

When Jack arrived back at the VC Bar, Kay was waiting at the gate with her truck, and with Jack and Frank aboard, she set out for Gunnison. Tony then phoned the doctor with news that a broken leg case was on the way. At this point, Jack was in real pain; the trip down the mountain on the travois had made it worse and the gravel road to Gunnison was not helping matters. Jack never remembered much about the trip, and Frank said Jack was out of it most of the way. The doctor was ready, set the leg quickly, and applied a heavy plaster cast. Jack was given a pair of crutches and told to come back in several weeks. Fortunately, the drive back to the VC Bar was comparatively pain-free, although Jack had developed a ravenous appetite, especially since he had not had a decent meal in three days. On the rare occasions when Kay was gone, Tony did the cooking. Whatever Tony prepared that night came out of cans. Years later, Jack had forgotten exactly what it was he ate that night, but was sure that it tasted a lot better than the shepherd's stew did.

Tony and the other wranglers were trying to figure out what to do with Jack who knew that nobody was going to spend much time taking care of him. Because he had crutches, Jack was mobile enough for "cabin duty," i.e., cooking and general clean-up in the bunkhouse and lodge. As soon as it was obvious that he could get around pretty well, shoveling out the stables was added to his duty roster. Gaucho was waiting for Jack when he hobbled down to the corral and really looked puzzled. Frank said that when the other wranglers started saddling horses, Gaucho always stared directly at the bunkhouse, waiting for Jack to come down to get the day started. To Jack's amazement, Gaucho did not react well to the man who came down to the corral with one big, white leg and a long, heavy stick in his hand. Gaucho would have nothing to do with Jack and acted like he had never seen Jack before. A little soothing talk and petting Gaucho's forehead soon changed things.

Still, there were some heartbreaking moments for Jack when he went down to the corral. As he came down the path to the corral, Gaucho would greet Jack, but then promptly turn and trot over to the door of the tack room where his bridle and saddle were kept, turn around, and look back at Jack. Poor Gaucho could not understand what had happened to Jack. If Jack had asked any of the other wranglers to take Gaucho for a ride, they would have jumped at the chance because they all admired Gaucho immensely. But they never asked and Jack never offered to share his horse with the others. In fact, Jack was not entirely sure how Gaucho would have reacted to another rider. Gaucho could have been a "one-owner" horse who might throw an unfamiliar rider, and Jack was not about to take a chance.

Of all of his temporary duties, Jack enjoyed cooking most of all. It came naturally, since he had been his mother's kitchen helper when he was younger. Goldie Rhea never kept any recipes; she just winged it and cooked according to taste, aroma, and those unique instincts that great cooks have. Kay and a hired lady did the cooking for all VC Bar guests while Jack cooked for Tony and the wranglers. Among Kay's many roles at the ranch was that of gardener. She had a very large garden and grew corn, tomatoes, radishes, turnips, potatoes, and carrots among other vegetables. At nearly 9,000 feet above mean sea level, the corn and tomatoes were not prizewinners, but they were tasty. Kay bought potatoes in forty-pound bags on her infrequent trips to Gunnison along with beans which came in big bags. Peeling potatoes was on the long list of Jack's chores; being a spud peeler was time well-invested, but Jack did not recognize it at the time. It was a very useful skill when he was in Army basic training three years later. Potatoes were on the menu three times a day: fried with breakfast, in a salad for dinner, and baked for supper. Jack frequently varied the menu based on what he had learned from his mother. Several varieties of greens for salads could be picked right in front of the lodge and both water cress and wild onions grew along the Lake Fork.

Lake Fork Club Collection via Lonnie Reel

The VC Bar Ranch with guest cabins and Kay's garden in the foreground.

Jack had an area behind the lodge where he could dig a trench and hang as many as five Dutch ovens over the coals. The ovens were Jack's favorite cooking pots, and the other wranglers kept Jack supplied in firewood, realizing that he could not chop the wood himself and that Jack was a true maestro with Dutch oven recipes. Most of what Jack cooked in the ovens took several hours, and all Jack had to do was periodically keep a hardwood fire going for more coals. Guests would occasionally watch and always ask for a taste of whatever Jack was cooking when he removed the ovens from above the trench. What came out of the ovens was strictly for the wranglers; Kay and an assistant cooked for the guests on a large kerosene stove in the kitchen. Jack always preferred the aroma of wood smoke in contrast to the kerosene fumes emanating from Kay's kitchen.

Other than the canned goods and bulk items bought in Gunnison, the VC Bar Ranch was practically self-sufficient for food. There were chickens and a milk cow. Fresh meat was there just for the taking since Colorado game laws in those days did not prohibit a landowner from shooting an elk or deer for the table. Fresh elk or deer would keep the VC Bar in meat for days. Refrigeration was not a problem since the icehouse Charles Rhea had built years before was still in great shape, and Tony filled it with ice each winter. Jack never served the same elk meal two days in a row. The elk menu was varied: steak, roast, stew, sandwiches, meat loaf, chili, and spaghetti were favorites. Jack always preferred elk which he considered much tastier than venison.

Grouse and wild turkey frequently wound up on the table. One day, a wrangler brought in some rabbits which Jack turned into a delicious stew. One of the other wranglers asked what it was and Jack said, "Prairie dog stew." Jack never heard the end of that one and was always asked what was in the stew before it was served.

Although Jack could not ride Gaucho, he did have time for his second favorite activity: fishing. He knew the Lake Fork like the back of his hand and nearly always returned with enough trout for a big fish fry. There was a reason for Jack's occasionally striking out; when silver mines above Lake City dumped their tailings into Lake San Cristobale, the silt would eventually work its way into the Lake Fork upstream of the VC Bar Ranch. When that happened, the stream became cloudy and the fishing was very difficult. Fortunately, there were nearby lakes in the mountains where guests could fish when the Lake Fork was cloudy. There was a silver lining in the Lake Fork having been cloudy for a couple days; the trout were ravenous when the water cleared and would take nearly any fly.

On Sundays, Jack frequently hobbled down to the Lake Fork to catch some trout for breakfast. The other wranglers went fishing too, but everything they caught went to Kay's kitchen for the guests' meals. The other wranglers were allowed to sleep in on Sunday mornings since no trail rides or other activities were scheduled until the afternoon. Jack tied his own trout flies and rarely had trouble catching enough fish for all wranglers to enjoy for breakfast. Jack's favorite pattern was what he called the "Patriotic Fly" because its hackle was tied from tiny red, white, and blue feathers. Although it may not have resembled any of the local aquatic insects, it worked beautifully – so much so that guests wanted to buy them. Jack couldn't collect any tips from the riding guests, so selling trout flies for twenty-five cents each was his main source of income for several weeks.

Before each meal, a prayer was always said. Kay frequently ate with the wranglers whose meals were usually served later than guests' meals. Kay liked Jack's cooking and there was the added bonus that she did not have to cook it. Kay usually said the prayer, but occasionally asked one of the wranglers to do it. She seemed to know which wranglers were uncomfortable in offering a prayer, so Jack was asked most of all. Jack felt that his prayers were always answered.

In the evening, the wranglers would frequently join Tony, Kay, and the guests by the fireplace in the lodge. The guests were talking about their experiences, how many fish they had caught, how the big ones got away or did not, and what wild animals they had seen. Jack occasionally wondered what those wild animals were thinking and telling each other about all of those strange people they had seen that day.

Lake Fork Club Collection via Lonnie Reel

The VC Bar Ranch, looking northwest.
Kay's kitchen and the main lodge are at right.

When the cast was removed from his leg, Jack was very busy. He had his trail ride duties, tried to catch some trout for breakfast when he could, and was still in demand as a cook. His Dutch ovens were filled with biscuits, cobblers, roasts, stews, beans, and occasionally spaghetti sauce. The vegetables from Kay's garden added more variety and tasty salads. One night Jack and another wrangler decided to go frog hunting along the Lake Fork's banks. Armed with flashlights and ice picks, they had a very successful time of it and had the makings of a fried frogs' legs breakfast. Another wrangler, seeing the legs jumping around in the pan, as frogs' legs do, suddenly lost his appetite. The remaining wranglers ate the meal with great gusto and only when they got up to leave inquired exactly what the meal was. When they were told, Jack suffered a bit of grief, but he reminded the wranglers that they had not inquired before they sat down to the table. After that, Jack always made sure that the men knew what they were eating in advance.

Jack Learns the Truth

The summer was drawing to a close, and in just another week Jack and Gaucho would be headed back to Wichita. Although Jack would always associate a little pain with that summer due to the broken leg, Jack always remembered the fun and excitement of working at the VC Bar Ranch. In the Bakers and the other wranglers, Jack had made some new friends. He stayed in touch with all of them until he was caught up in World War II.

With just a couple days left, Jack went down to the corral to pack Gaucho's bridle, saddle, blanket and other tack into the trailer. He put his gloves, chaps, spurs, slicker, rifle, and other items into his car, but he had a nagging question in his mind. Frank and another wrangler had told Jack that they had been up to the meadow where Jack had been rescued, but had seen nothing to suggest that sheep had been grazing there. Nor did they see any evidence of any cooking fire or anything else that suggested Jack had been there overnight. This was very troubling to Jack who started thinking that what the wranglers were implying might be correct. Had Jack been delirious and just imagined the shepherd, the dog, sheep, being splinted, and sheltered in a tent? Could it all have been nothing more than dreams?

Jack was looking up the mountain trail when he heard Kay approaching. She quietly said, "Go. I've been expecting this. Go find out for yourself." Long before dawn the next morning, Jack got the bridle and walked out into the corral where Gaucho was waiting. Jack quickly put the bridle on and went back for the saddle and blanket. With the saddled cinched, Jack headed for the gate. When the gate was closed, Gaucho needed no direction; in the darkness he was headed straight for the meadow where Jack was rescued. When they arrived there at first light, it was almost déjà vu: a coyote loped across the other side. Jack did not reach for his rifle since it was already packed in his coupe's trunk; he probably would not have reached for it even if it had been in its saddle scabbard. When the coyote reached the far corner of the meadow, he turned and stared at Jack who sensed that it was the same coyote. The coyote then moved to the tree line and looked back again, almost as if saying goodbye.

Jack rode all around the meadow, looking for evidence that sheep had been grazing there recently. There was no evidence, none at all. Jack then started looking for evidence of a tent having been pitched and for the ashes from a cooking fire. Again, there was nothing. Jack was forced to conclude that Frank had been right and that Jack had just imagined it all – perhaps in a pain-induced delirium made worse by exposure and dehydration.

Just as Jack and Gaucho turned to leave, the sun came up. Jack turned to look at the glorious sunrise and on the ridge just above the meadow he saw his shepherd friend. Then just as the shepherd raised his arms, Gaucho suddenly whinnied, momentarily distracting Jack. When he looked back at the ridge, the shepherd was gone. After lingering for a few more minutes, Jack turned Gaucho for their return to the VC Bar. As Gaucho turned, Jack saw something else. There on the ground, almost under Gaucho's hooves, were two sturdy sticks and some strips of cloth – the remains of Jack's splint as fashioned by the shepherd. That was the last full day Jack and Gaucho spent at the VC Bar. An important period in Jack's life had come to a close.

Over the years after Jack left, ownership of the VC Bar passed through a number of hands. Tony and Kay sold out in 1946 to Orville Dowzer, and after a few more changes in ownership, Dallas businessman Bob Goddard bought the ranch and converted it into what it is today, a private sportsmen's residential association called the Lake Fork Club. Among its subsequent owners was Jock Mahoney, a former World War II Marine pilot who starred in a number of television westerns in the 1950s and 1960s (*The Range Rider, Yancy Derringer*). Today, the Lake Fork Club's owner/ members are limited to ninety people and the number of residences on the club's 1,500 acres is restricted to just thirty. What were oxbows in the Lake Fork of the 1930s, have become fishing ponds where some truly monstrous trout cruise the cold waters. Club members can hunt on the property itself or in the adjacent national forests and fish the ponds or well over a mile of the Lake Fork's rushing waters.

Troubles in Wichita and Europe

The tempo of Jack's life went back into overdrive when he returned to Wichita. Although college, basketball, and ROTC were all behind him, his duties at WCDS kept him very busy. He was the school principal, classroom teacher, and a bus driver. Those students who graduated from WCDS were doing very well academically when they entered seventh grade at other schools where they also scored well on standardized tests. Jack might just as well have been a professional Scouter instead of a volunteer since he was spending many hours a week as a scoutmaster and district commissioner. Wichita, then as now, is a city with a great Scouting heritage and a couple of interesting Phillips/Philmont connections. Frank Phillips, one of Waite Phillips' brothers, was a major donor to several councils in Oklahoma and Kansas in the 1930s. The Wichita Area Council, later to become the Quivira Council, was one of those fortunate councils to receive some very welcome Phillips funds during the middle of the Great Depression. Most likely, that connection fueled what grew into the strong relationship between the council and Philmont that exists to this day. In 1940, only two years after Waite Phillips' first gift of land to the Boy Scouts, Wichita Area Council sent 93 Scouts and leaders to what was then Philturn Rockymountain Scoutcamp. It was the largest contingent as of that date. Today, Quivira Council still sends large contingents to Philmont and is the home of many seasonal staffers.

A major change, however, was in the wind in that autumn of 1938 because at the end of the year, the Wichita Country Day School passed out of existence. A review of corporate records in Wichita does not reveal any bankruptcy filing or any other indication of major debt; the records only show that the Wichita Country Day School, a Kansas corporation, was dissolved. The school had always been on the edge of going out of business in spite of the fact that the children who attended came from wealthy homes. The school's chronically precarious financial situation was cited by Altick as his reason for accepting an offer in Kansas City to be the headmaster of a financially more secure school. In its last several years, Country Day School was able to stay open only on the basis of donations and its summer touring business. The leased properties where the school was located over the years had become progressively larger, but each building was vacant for three months of the year which contributed to the importance of Camp As-We-Go as an important revenue center.

The situation came to a head at a mid-September hearing of the Interstate Commerce Commission (ICC) to whom the school had been forced to apply for a contract carrier license. The school made application, but did so anticipating that it would be exempt from certain rules and regulations based on its being an educational tour company. The school, as a not-for-profit organization, had operated relatively unencumbered with most regulations, a situation noted by several railroads and bus companies which saw the school's Camp As-We-Go tour operations as an irritant to their business. With the likes of Southwest Greyhound, Union Pacific Stages, Union Pacific Railroad, Santa Fe Trails Transportation Company, Atchison, Topeka, & Santa Fe Railroad, Missouri Pacific Railroad, Chicago, Rock Island & Pacific Railroad Company, and others lined up to protest Country Day School's request for exemption, it was a matter of giants picking on the little guy.

Although he lived in Kansas City, Ernie Altick was still on the board of directors of Wichita Country Day School, Inc., and he presented the case before the ICC along with the school's lawyer (whose children were Country Day School students). The summer camping operation was growing and included students from the Pembroke Country Day School in Kansas City where Altick was the headmaster. There were ambitious plans for the summer of 1939, including taking students to the 1939 World's Fair in New York. The crux of the matter was whether Country Day School was exempt from certain requirements of the Motor Carrier Act of 1935. If found to qualify for the educational exemption under the Act, Country Day School could avoid the high costs associated with coming into full compliance. Altick pointed out the facts that students were required to take notes on the tours and that they wrote essays and gave speeches on what they learned during the school year. Altick defended the school's 1933 tour to the World's Fair in Chicago, saying that the tour encompassed history along the route, including Abraham Lincoln's home in Illinois. In spite of Altick's presentation, the ICC board saw many of the stops on the Camp As-We-Go itineraries as being more typical of recreational tours. The ICC ruled in favor of the protesting railroad and bus companies. Unable to continue with the reality of significant new costs, Country Day School and its summer tour business shut their doors, forcing Jack Rhea to look for new opportunities. Altick returned to Kansas City where he remained with the Pembroke Country Day School before being recruited to be the assistant director of what is now the highly-regarded Cheley Colorado High Adventure Camps which had been founded in 1921. To this day Pembroke, after several mergers, operates in Kansas City as Pembroke-Hill School. Altick eventually became co-director of Cheley Camps before retiring in 1967. While retired and living in Estes Park, Colorado, he was active in civic and service organizations. A mentor and major influence on Jack Rhea, Altick passed away in 1998 at age ninety-six.

Professional Scouter

Considering his credentials and considerable volunteer work, it can be safely assumed that Jack was strongly encouraged by the new Wichita Area Scout Council Executive, Harold Baker, to join the professional ranks. At a videotaped interview at Philmont nearly forty years later, Jack further explained why he left education to join Scouting as a professional. He said that although he enjoyed teaching and was committed to working with youth, the idea of influencing thousands, if not tens of thousands, of young lives through Scouting, instead of hundreds at a private or public school, was another key factor influencing his decision to change careers.

Jack left in his Dodge coupe for the sixty-second session of the National Training School for Scout Executives at Mortimer L. Schiff Scout Reservation in Mendham, New Jersey, on 20 January 1939. Occasionally, there have been two misconceptions about the training school in those days. The first is that it was free. Indeed it was not, and the cost to Jack was around five hundred dollars, excluding travel expenses to and from Mendham. The second is that there was a guaranteed job waiting for a new graduate. The only assurance was that Jack would be eligible for a position when and if he graduated on 8 March 1939.

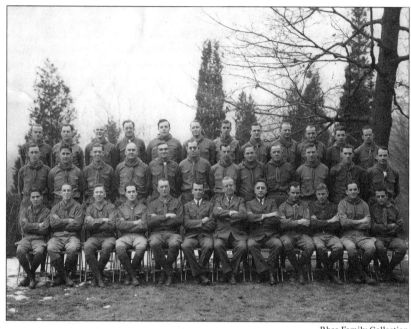

*Jack Rhea graduated from training at Schiff in March 1939 as top man
in his class. Jack is in the front row, second from right,
and Gunnar Berg is fifth from left, front row.*

A major player in Jack's training was the redoubtable Gunnar Berg,
an immigrant from Norway who had been an educator in Seattle. He was
a Scouting volunteer who decided to switch careers and become a professional Scouter. Berg very quickly found himself working for the National
Council in a series of progressively more responsible training roles which
would eventually result in his appointment as director of training. Jack
could not have guessed it at the time, but he would one day have the same
job himself.

The majority of Jack's training amounted to long days in the classroom
and several weekend sessions lasting until noon on Saturday. There were
several permanent instructors assigned to Jack's class. They conducted most
of the instruction, but from time to time were assisted by others, including
officials from the National Office then in New York City which is just under
forty miles to the east. The students studied the history, objectives, and
organization of the Boy Scouts of America and everything a young field

executive needed to know about council operations, including recruiting, camping administration, volunteer training, finance, meeting programs, fund raising, and more. In contrast to today's professional training for new district executives, Jack's training involved considerable Scoutcraft in a patrol setting.

Schiff was an amazingly beautiful piece of real estate; it had been given as a gift to the BSA in 1931 by Mrs. Frieda Schiff in memory of her son, Mortimer Schiff, a president of the BSA who died in 1931. The lake in front of the Schiff mansion was breathtaking. Schiff was also steeped in Revolutionary War history. When Jack's class arrived, the staff encouraged them to explore the property. It had several hiking trials that were distinguished by colors: white trail, yellow trail, blue trail, and green trail, but the most important trail was the Jockey Hollow Trail, site of two winter encampments by General George Washington and his Continental Army.

Jack was housed in a dormitory a few hundred yards from the Schiff mansion and took classes in another building. The dining hall was a huge room on the mansion's second floor that looked out over the lake and the countryside. The mansion was also a museum with huge fireplaces in several of the large rooms. One of the staff pointed out to Jack that there were medallions on the mantles of these fireplaces which had been purchased from mansions in Europe and shipped to this country when the mansion was built. The legend has it that the medallions were awards given to Roman generals when they returned from their conquests. Another striking feature of the mansion was the original Norman Rockwell paintings that hung on many walls. What a treat for Jack to be there and absorb all that Scouting lore.

The candidates were graded on a wide range of criteria of which much was based on the Boy Scout Oath and Law. Like many large organizations of that era, the Boy Scouts of America administered intelligence tests to its job applicants. One of the most widely used tests was the U. S. Army Alpha Intelligence Test, a test that was heavy on verbal skills and one that the Army used to evaluate new personnel. The test score ranged from a zero to 212. "Average" intelligence required a score between forty-five and seventy-four. Anything above 105 was classified as superior. Jack's score was 191 – practically at the top of the scale. Surprisingly, that did not place him at the top of his class because he was in fast company, very fast company, at the sixty-second national training class.

His score placed him fourteenth out of thirty-two on the Army Alpha Intelligence Test. Although his scores on written tests averaged ninety, that effort just placed him in the middle of the class. His test scores on the Constitution and Amendments did place him in the upper third. There were thirty other criteria, including, as might be expected, trustworthiness, loyalty, helpfulness, friendliness, courtesy, spirit of unselfish service, and others such as balanced ego, sense of humor, perseverance, refinement, sense of humor, etc. Jack ranked number one in several categories such as Scouting spirit and placed second, third, or fourth in enough categories for the instructors to rank him as top man – number one in the class on personal qualities.

As a result of the Boy Scouts of America moving its National Office to Texas from New Jersey in 1979, most of Schiff Scout Reservation became a nature preserve, but in its heyday, more than one national BSA leader described Schiff as the spiritual heart of American Scouting. Jack left Schiff during the second week of March 1939 to embark on a new career. The Boy Scouts of America had actually grown, slowly but surely, all throughout the economically troubled 1930s. As Jack left Schiff, the Great Depression was waning, but American concern about international developments was not. The mood on Main Street America might be described as "wait and see" because there was much about which to be concerned. Japan was fighting China on the Asian mainland and the situation in Europe could only be described as "fluid." The Nationalist forces in Spain, aided by Fascist dictatorships in Germany and Italy, were about to walk into Madrid, unopposed, in what was seen as the conclusion of the Spanish Civil War. Germany had occupied Austria and annexed the German-speaking section of Czechoslovakia in 1938. By the end of March 1939, Hitler had annexed the rest of Czechoslovakia. During this period, Italian Dictator Benito Mussolini was saber rattling with his threats to reacquire those portions of the eastern French Riviera which had at one time been under Italian control. Six months after the complete annexation of Czechoslovakia, the European situation would spiral into a war in which Jack Rhea would face the most harrowing experiences of his life.

Jack Rhea in 1939 at the time of his appointment as a field executive with the Boy Scout council in Wichita Falls, Texas.

Jack drove west from Schiff, stopping in Kansas City and Wichita, but his final destination was Wichita Falls, Texas, where he had an interview scheduled with C.E. Peden, the council executive in what is today the Northwest Texas Council. Jack was subsequently employed as a field executive in that council which had four districts: Wichita, Red River, Chisolm Trail, and Greenbelt. The council had a real problem into which Jack was immediately thrust; it was losing its camping facility, Camp Bolder. The land where Bolder was located had just been acquired by the United States Army which would soon be using the area as an artillery range. Fortunately, the Perkins Family Trust provided new land for the council near the Oklahoma border, and building and launching the resulting Camp Perkins was part of Jack Rhea's first job as a professional Scouter.

North Texas Council was always near and dear to Jack. Although Peden retired shortly after World War II, Jack developed a strong friendship with the new council executive, Marvin Smith. The council is still strong and has a number of distinctions. In the post-Wold War II period, it led the nation in the rate at which young men attained Eagle Scout rank. At this writing, the National President of the Boy Scouts of America is a Wichita Falls native, Rex Tillerson. His father was a professional Scouter and council executive in Wichita Falls in the 1950s.

In the late spring of 1941, an opportunity surfaced with the Boy Scout Council in Des Moines, Iowa. Jack went for it and was employed as a field executive with the Des Moines Council on 1 June 1941. The council could trace Scouting activities back to 1910; two years later it applied for a charter as a council in 1912. Over the following few years, the council was listed in the BSA annual report as one of the four strongest in Iowa. In the two years before Jack arrived to be a field executive, the council had average growth of almost eighteen percent per year. It was also a council in transition. The new council executive appointed in 1940, James Hiner, Jr., had remained for only one year, turning the reins over to N. Harold West who would remain in charge until after World War II. The top volunteer leadership, Reverend Clarence Bigelow and Dr. Charles H. Henshaw (president and commissioner, respectively), had been in their positions for several years. In 1921, the council had purchased its first camping facility, the 123-acre Camp Mitigwa which is located on the Des Moines River about twenty miles north of council headquarters. Over the years, Mitigwa expanded to 700 plus acres and is now the oldest of what is now Mid-Iowa Council's three Boy Scout camps.

Jack was doing well as a field executive and was very much involved with the camping operation. The council thought so too; in 1941, the camping honor organization, the Old Guard Honor Society, inducted Jack as a member. Although the Order of the Arrow dates back to 1915 when it was founded by the Philadelphia Council at its Treasure Island Scout Camp, many other councils did not form OA lodges until decades later. The Old Guard's program made it similar to the OA, but its separate membership categories for youth and adult aligned it much more closely with another camping honor society, the Tribe of Mic-O-Say in today's Heart of America

Council (Kansas City, Missouri). The Old Guard was founded in 1931, but it was phased out in 1951 by Mid-Iowa Council (then known as Tall Corn Council) which became affiliated with the Order of the Arrow with the establishment of its Mitigwa Lodge Number 450.

However, in late 1941 Jack received some "greetings" from Uncle Sam. Jack was about to leave his job as a BSA field executive in Des Moines for new employment as Rhea, Jack L., Private, United States Army. It is not known where he did his basic training or where he received advanced training for his first duty assignment which, ironically, was at Fort Des Moines in the same city where he had been employed by the Boy Scouts. In the late 1930s, Fort Des Moines would have held some attraction for Jack since it was home to the 14th Cavalry Regiment which was still riding horses. However, by 1942, the 14th had mechanized and moved out, and other units were starting to move in. While the Fort would very shortly become a major base for a WAAC (Womens Auxilliary Army Corps) Officer Candidate School (OCS) and enlisted training, in early 1942 its resident units included a Signal Corps Photographic Sub-Laboratory, the 7th Ordnance Service Company, 19th Signal Service Company, and a couple of other units assigned to the Seventh Service Command.

The latter command was headquartered in Omaha, Nebraska, and provided a wide range of services to Army installations in the central and northern plains states. Those services ranged from transportation, accounting, purchasing, and training to operation of recruiting and induction centers. Jack was assigned to the 1727th Induction Station as an interviewer in the Classification Section. That was not Jack's idea of actively contributing to the war effort. The time spent as an interviewer was not wasted; Jack could not have known then how useful that experience would prove when he was at a place he could not have dreamed of in 1942: the BSA National Office.

Infantry Officer Candidate School

Accordingly, on 20 May 1942, he applied for admittance to OCS with the goal of gaining a commission as a second lieutenant. In mid-1942, there were twenty-five officer candidate schools in operation, serving many branches of the Army. Among the options available to Jack were the Administrative School, Field Artillery School, Quartermaster School, Armored Force School, Engineer School, and other branches, including Finance, Tank Destroyer, and Ordnance. Although Jack's head may have been turned by the possibility of Cavalry, the Army was not riding horses to battle in 1942, so Jack applied for life in the fast and very high risk lane: Infantry. Jack faced rather daunting odds in selecting the Infantry; nearly fifty percent of Infantry OCS graduates of that era would be killed in action. On top of that, for each infantryman killed, at least another three would be wounded. Any infantry officer coming home from the war without a scratch after commanding a rifle company or platoon was an escapee from the law of averages.

The application was approved; Jack put in another six weeks at the induction center interviewing new arrivals as the first step in determining to which branch of the Army they would be sent. Then he was off to Columbus, Georgia, home of Fort Benning, for thirteen weeks of Infantry OCS. He entered Officer Candidate Course 79-A on 14 July 1942 as a member of the Eighth Company, First Student Training Regiment. The war news on that July fourteenth was not good; the Germans had broken through Russian lines and were again threatening Moscow. Elsewhere the Germans were on a major push toward the Caucasus and its major prize: Russian oil fields. The Royal Air Force was expanding its night bombing of German industrial targets, although accuracy left a lot to be desired. The night before Jack arrived at Fort Benning, the RAF left German war plants in the Ruhr Valley's city of Duisburg in flames. Closer to home, the local selective service board in nearby Columbus announced that the draft of married men would proceed as planned. Baseball provided some diversion to the bleak war news, and the New York Yankees were favorites for the American League pennant with a five-game lead after beating the Detroit Tigers four to three in their latest confrontation. The Yankees had few fans in South Carolina but did go on to win the pennant, although the St. Louis Cardinals triumphed in the five-game 1942 World Series. The war was, however, everybody's concern – from homemakers who were encouraged to save waste household cooking fats to motorists who pleaded with their congressmen to provide relief from high gas prices (for what rationed gas was available).

The day after Jack arrived, another class arrived, and so it went each and every day early in the war; every day one class graduated and another started. Jack's first two days at Fort Benning were spent in orientations and drawing clothing and equipment. Unlike the Army's aviation cadet training, there was no hazing by upperclassmen. There was not time for that type of activity so desperate was the Army to rush more junior officers into the field. Jack was promptly assigned to a fifty-man platoon as part of a 200-man company of new arrivals on an alphabetical basis, thus his closest friends all had last names starting with P, Q, R, S, and T. The platoons occupied newly completed two-story barracks. Had Jack arrived exactly one year earlier, in the month when the Infantry OCS was established at Fort Benning, his accommodations would have been very different: a small tar paper shack housing eight candidates. Each platoon was presided over by a tactical officer, typically a recent, outstanding graduate of OCS himself, who was responsible for training the platoon. He was also responsible for deciding who would and who would not graduate from the course, thus his power was second only to God.

Although there were classes and written exams, there was no grade posted at the end of the course. Jack would either pass or fail, and it was the tactical officer alone who decided who would get gold bars at the end of the ninety-day program. The classroom courses covered tactics, military maps, leadership, traditions and customs of the military, and aircraft recognition among other subjects. Marching and physical training ("PT") became daily aspects of Jack's life; the PT and cross country running and hiking with full packs were by far the most rigorous so far in Jack's life. Many of the lectures were held outside with the candidates seated in bleachers – all in the late summer, Georgia sun. Below the bleachers, on massive tables, the instructors had sand models simulating various types of terrain over which they conducted simulated battles from which the candidates were expected to learn what tactics worked and which did not in a variety of situations.

Jack also learned how to operate all weapons in the infantry inventory from the 37 mm anti-tank cannon right down to the .45 caliber automatic Colt pistol. Candidates also cycled through all positions in a company. Jack could have been its commander one day and a rifleman or top sergeant the next. An extremely important aspect of OCS was what amounted to small scale war games in which each candidate had to function as the platoon commander in different circumstances, i.e., infiltrating, flanking, attacking, and leading night patrols. Unknown to the officer candidate was the "where and when" of how his little force would be opposed and just what the opposition's strength would be. How Jack responded and led his platoon in a rapidly changing situation (enhanced with simulated machine gun fire and realistic shell explosions), were carefully observed by the tactical officer who was essentially functioning as a referee in a micro-war game. Thus, it was only candidates like Jack, with real leadership skills, plenty of situational awareness, and good judgment, who completed the school.

Several times as the course progressed, Jack along with all others had to fill out a card which was turned into the tactical officer. The card had two very simple questions which ran along the following lines. "What candidates in your platoon would you prefer to have lead you in battle? Which candidates in your platoon are the weakest leaders?" Candidates inspiring little or no confidence were doomed. Where Jack came out on that exercise is not known, but based on his performance during his training at Schiff and that he had leadership experience (in ROTC, Wichita Country Day School, and BSA council offices), it can be assumed that he was well-situated among those gathering the most votes of confidence. There was another advantage to those exercises – the day was shortly coming when Lieutenant Rhea would have to quickly size up each man in his company and give orders which could make the difference between life or death.

One of the first announcements made by the tactical officer at the beginning of the course was that the platoon would be decimated and that the washout rate could go as high as fifty percent. It did not take long for the winnowing process to start. At the conclusion of the morning formation's announcements after breakfast, especially early in the course, several candidates would be called out and told to report to the orderly room immediately. The rest of the class was marched off to its regularly scheduled activity. When Jack returned to the barracks in late afternoon, there was no sign of those who had been called out that morning. They were already gone – on their way to an Infantry Replacement Training Center. Thus the pressure to succeed was relentless. Typically, those who washed out were the ones who botched their field exercises and led their men into traps or who had failed to show any leadership ability in the minds of their peers and the tactical officers. There were other ways to wash out. Getting "gigged" (assigned demerits for various offenses or shortcomings) too frequently was grounds for dismissal as was consistent deficiency on written exams. Candidates who washed out plunged into the depths of despair – the shame of failure was without bottom.

Jack completed the three-month Infantry OCS on 14 October 1942, a mild, sunny day in Columbus. The name of Jack's tactical officer has been obscured by the swirling, clouding mists of passing decades, but his prediction of how many of Jack's fellow candidates would fall by the wayside was rather accurate. Only 110 graduated; forty-five percent washed out and became enlisted infantry replacements. On that October day, Jack got his commission and lieutenant's shiny bars. Before the graduation ceremony, he made sure he had a dollar bill in his pocket. In a long-standing Fort Benning tradition, he handed over that dollar to the first enlisted man to salute him following the graduation ceremony. Short of combat in France and Germany two years later, OCS was the most intense period in Jack's life.

On the Columbus home front that mid-October day, citizens were doing their best for the war effort and another Boy Scout-assisted scrap metal drive was under way. One motorist was so moved by the news of a local Marine, Cpl. Edward Raht, being declared missing on Guadalcanal that he drove his smooth-running 1938 Buick into Columbus Salvage Yard, removed the tires, and left the car there to be turned into bullets, bombs, and bombers. As Secretary of War Stimson argued the case for drafting eighteen and nineteen year olds before the House Military Committee, three Army Air Force light bombers flew low over Columbus dropping leaflets urging young men between the ages of eighteen and twenty to enlist. The Columbus Elks also sponsored a gala parade for the same purpose; many of Fort Benning's units were part of the parade which passed the Springer Theater which was showing one of 1942's most popular movies, *Wake Island* with Brian Donlevy, Robert Preston, and William Bendix. When Jack had arrived at Fort Benning, ninety days before, Glen Miller was at the top of the popular music charts with "I've Got A Gal in Kalamazoo." The song was still heard, but not as popular as two others with closer ties to the war: "When the Lights Go On Again All Over the World" and "Praise the Lord and Pass the Ammunition." All three songs could not hold up a candle to what was just around the corner: Bing Crosby with "I'm Dreaming of a White Christmas."

Jack missed watching *Wake Island* in downtown Columbus because he had been granted a brief leave and was already on his way back to Missouri. His new orders were to report to the 100th Infantry Division, "The Century Division," then forming at Fort Jackson, near Columbia, South Carolina.

Part II
THE WAR YEARS

Riflemen from Jack Rhea's 100th Infantry Division under German fire during the taking of Heilbronn, the last major, urban battle in Europe for American armies during World War II.

CHAPTER 6

The "Century" Division

Understanding the role Jack Rhea played in the 100th Infantry Division requires a basic comprehension of the division's organization and history. The division had actually come into existence during World War I and was preparing to ship out to Europe when the war ended on 11 November 1918. The division was demobilized shortly thereafter, but was reactivated on a limited scale in early 1920. However, it languished for years in the peacetime Army until it was fully reactivated on 15 November 1942 at Fort Jackson, which is located about six miles from Columbia, South Carolina. Second Lieutenant Jack Rhea arrived for duty with the 398th Infantry Regiment two days earlier and was just one of about 400 junior officers arriving in mid-November.

The men in Jack's OCS graduating class had been scattered across the Army, joining many of the infantry divisions then in training. Just over five percent of that class was assigned to the 100th Division. Not every enlisted man or non-commissioned officer was thrilled to be placed under the command of a brand new second lieutenant. Although OCS graduates were referred to as "ninety-day wonders," many of them, through a combination of brains, instinct, and courage, earned the undying respect of their men. Captain Robert M. Martz, the 398th Infantry regimental S-1 (personnel officer) was a very busy man, considering all of the many quick assignments he had to make. Nearly all of the newly arrived second lieutenants were assigned to rifle companies as platoon leaders. Jack Rhea was assigned to the 398th Infantry Regiment as the 3rd Battalion S-3 (operations officer), although on an acting or temporary basis because the S-3 function was normally a captain's job. Those were not normal times and there were certainly not enough captains to go around.

There was little to gladden the hearts of those at Fort Jackson, the brass in the Pentagon, or any American in mid-November 1942, although there was definitely cause for some hope. The Japanese navy had suffered a strategic defeat at Midway just five months previously. British General Bernard Law Montgomery had just triumphed at El Alamein and was already pursuing a retreating German General Erwin Rommel out of Egypt. Mercenary American pilots in China, so well known as the Flying Tigers, had been absorbed into the United States Army Air Force as the 23rd Fighter Group and were continuing to shoot down Japanese planes with only minimal losses. Another three squadrons of Americans flying for a foreign government, better known as the Royal Air Force's Eagle Squadrons, had just weeks before been absorbed into the United States Eighth Army Air Force as the 4th Fighter Group. The Fourth would emerge as the top-scoring fighter group in the European war. The First Marine Division on Guadalcanal continued to hold the island and its valuable airfield; the Japanese would abandon Guadalcanal in another three months. Hitler's advance into Russia had been halted, and he was again facing Russia's strongest ally: another brutal winter. The invasion of North Africa had started only a week before and seemed to be progressing according to plan (at that point) when Lt. Rhea arrived at Fort Jackson.

While the Royal Air Force Fighter Command had decisively defeated the German Luftwaffe in the Battle of Britain in 1940, the British had been disastrously routed at the Dieppe Raid on the French coast in mid-August 1942 in what was billed as a dress rehearsal for the eventual invasion of France. The Army's top man in China, General Joseph Stillwell, had been chased out of Burma several months before, personally leading his remnant army on a 150-mile march out of the jungles to safety in India. The swastika still flew over most of Europe, and the rising sun flag covered most of Asia and key islands in the western Pacific. It would be well into 1943 before German submarines became the hunted instead of the hunters. America, in late 1942, was still in the early stage of converting its wealth, manpower, and industrial resources into the might that would topple the Axis powers nearly three years into the future.

Any man or lady on Main Street in Columbia was already thinking about Christmas which was only six weeks away, a fact very much on local retailers' minds. Efrid's Bargain Basement was advertising "Advance Winter Fashions" featuring spun rayon dresses ranging in price from one dollar, ninety-eight cents to two dollars, ninety-five cents. If Jack had needed a two-sided shaving mirror, Walgreen's had just what he was after and at only forty-nine cents. Lifebuoy soap was on sale there too – three bars for eighteen cents (a better deal than the three bars of Lux hand soap the A&P was selling for nineteen cents). Local motorists were discouraged to hear that Harold Ickes, the petroleum coordinator in Washington, was about to announce a further cut of petroleum consumption in all eastern seaboard states.

It was not just petroleum that was rationed. Jack, even though he was living on a military base, was in a land of plenty compared to his family back in Missouri who were issued ration cards limiting a wide variety of consumer essentials, including meat, butter, sugar, shoes, coffee, and many other basics of everyday life. The rationing brought out the best in most people and the worst in a few. Federal Judge George Timmerman sentenced a Columbia youth, seventeen year-old D.F. Jackson to eighteen months in a reformatory for stealing gas ration books from cars parked near the First Baptist Church on Hampton Street. With so many young men away in the service, older homeowners were doing more of their own work around the house, a trend noticed by the Sears store at 1704 Main Street where a gallon of one-coat, master-mixed flat paint was on sale for two dollars, sixty-nine cents. As the war progressed, many items would become harder to find, but Sears in late 1942 was advertising an item that would appeal to any Philmont Ranger of the late 1950s – a drop-forged axe with a thirty-six inch hickory handle for only two dollars, forty-nine cents.

General Burress

Accepting command of the 100th Infantry Division was Major General Withers A. Burress, a Virginian and career soldier who had served as a regimental operations officer with the 2nd Infantry Division in France where he saw action at Chateau-Thierry, the Marne, and St. Mihiel during World War I. It was during the Great War and having seen so much carnage that he acquired an aversion to frontal attacks; his preference for outmaneuvering his enemy would become apparent when the division went into combat in late 1944. The activation ceremony was held at Fort Jackson's outdoor stage area on Sunday, 15 November. The activation was notable for several reasons of which not the least was the fact that the United States Army had by then created 100 infantry divisions. It was also the first division to be activated at Fort Jackson. The ceremony attracted many high-level dignitaries including various state and local officials. General Burress accepted the division's flag from Major General Emil Reinhardt, commanding general of the 100th Division's parent organization, the 76th Infantry Division.

100th Infantry Division Archives, Marshall Foundation

Major General Withers Burress was among a very small minority of
generals who finished the war commanding the same divisions they started
with. Burress was a master of flanking maneuvers and river crossings which
accomplished objectives at minimal cost in his soldiers' lives.

Burress was a 1914 graduate of Virginia Military Institute which also
counted General George Marshall, Army Chief of Staff, among its alumni.
Burress was a star in the classroom as well as on the athletic field. The
school was near and dear to Burress' heart and he had returned in 1922
to teach military science; in the late 1930s, he served a five-year tour as
VMI's commandant of cadets. On Army documents, Burress listed VMI's
location as his residence: Lexington, Virginia. During the inter-war years
he had attended the Infantry School at Fort Benning in Georgia and was a
graduate of the Army's principal schools for promising career officers. By
1940 Burress was on the War Department General Staff and soon thereafter was Assistant Commandant of the Infantry School at Fort Benning.

Jack Rhea had much in common with his commanding general. Both were very enthusiastic hunters and fishermen who had a journalistic streak. Burress had been the editor of VMI's yearbook in his senior year. Although Burress had been known as a tough disciplinarian while at VMI, he stressed the importance of winning respect of soldiers as the best way to have them follow orders. Having been a professional Scouter and worked with many volunteers, Jack Rhea understood that perfectly.

Informally, General Burress was known as "Pinky," in light of his complexion and red hair. It certainly was not a derisive term because he was very well liked and widely respected. In him, the "Centurymen" saw a fine southern gentlemen who was committed to the in-depth training and welfare of every man in the division. His immediate subordinates, the brigadier generals and colonels who were in charge of the infantry, artillery, and staff were career men whose service dated back to World War I. The infantry regimental commanders had all been junior officers during World War I.

The non-commissioned officer cadre, about 1,500 men came from the 76th Infantry Division, then based at Fort Meade, Maryland. Although the largest single group within the division came from the Middle-Atlantic states, the Century Division was eventually composed of men from every state in the union. There was a lot of work to do, and Jack Rhea was at the center of it.

Men of the Third Battalion

Jack, as the operations and training officer, worked very closely with the battalion commander, Lt. Col. Floyd Stayton, a soft-spoken, 40-ish Missourian, and the battalion executive officer, Major Marshall Gilman who was from Newport, New Hampshire. Jack had a lot in common with Stayton who had been a prizewinning basketball coach, president of the Missouri High School Athletic Association, and superintendent of the school system in Appleton City, Missouri. Stayton was a reservist called up immediately after Pearl Harbor. Also on the battalion staff were two men from North Jersey: 2nd Lts. Bernard Boston who was the intelligence officer or S-2 and Sidney Kleinwaks, the supply officer or S-4. Kleinwaks and Stayton had similar educations. Both had graduated from the University of Missouri: Kleinwaks in business administration in 1935 and Stayton with a master's degree in 1934 preceded by a B.A. and an ROTC commission. All of these men would stay together as a team and learn each other's jobs over the next two years until shortly after the division got into combat when the fluid situation created the need for shuffling assignments. As the S-3, Jack was the third highest ranking officer among the nine officers in the headquarters company.

Commanding the 3rd Battalion when Jack joined it was Lt. Col. Floyd Stayton who also came from Missouri where he had been a school system superintendent before he was called up from the Army reserves in early 1942.

At the pointy end of the 100th Division spear were the three infantry regiments: the 397th, 398th, and 399th. Each regiment consisted of 154 officers and 3,100 enlisted men. At the heart of each regiment were three infantry battalions which were supported by a headquarters company, an anti-tank company, a cannon company, a services company, and a medical detachment. Jack's organization, the 3rd battalion of the 398th Regiment, numbered thirty-five officers and 836 enlisted men. As an S-3 Jack was not issued a personal weapon, other than a Colt .45 caliber semi-automatic pistol, but other weapons were available, primarily the .30 caliber M-1 carbine or Thompson .45 caliber submachine gun. The battalion headquarters was, however, armed for defense and included two .50 caliber heavy machine guns, three 57 mm anti-tank guns, and eight bazookas. The battalion also included a heavy weapons company consisting of eight officers and 158 enlisted men who were equipped with six 81 mm mortars and eight .30 caliber machine guns.

Providing each battalion's firepower were four companies each led by a captain. A company included three rifle platoons each led by a lieutenant whose headquarters section was composed of two senior non-coms, two scouts for reconnaissance, two runners (messengers), and a first-aid man attached from the regimental medical detachment. Each platoon, typically numbering forty-two men, was broken down into three squads, each led by two non-commissioned officers heading up a team of two scouts, a two-man Browning automatic rifle team, an ammunition bearer, and five riflemen. Just as one of the battalion's four companies was a heavy weapons company, each company had a weapons platoon; both were equipped with machine guns and mortars (heavier for the battalion, lighter for the platoon). A typical rifleman was nineteen or twenty years of age – some were even younger. Each rifle company was also supported by a headquarters section responsible for food, supplies, and communications. At least, that was the plan – in combat, even with replacements, the manpower levels described above were rarely attained.

The heart of a rifle company was, of course, the rifleman armed with a .30 caliber M-1 Garand semi-automatic rifle or a lighter M-1 .30 caliber semi-automatic carbine. To provide suppressive fire while advancing or covering fire on withdrawal, there was the .30 caliber Browning automatic rifle (BAR), a holdover from World War I as was the Colt .45 pistol.

The rifle companies were supported by 100th Division Artillery, usually referred to simply as "DivArty." That organization consisted of fifty-seven officers and 2,080 enlisted men assigned to the 373rd, 374th, 375th, and 925th Field Artillery Regiments. These regiments operated 105 and 155 mm howitzers, but were also armed with heavy machine guns and bazookas for defense. The artillery regiments had their own support, including supply, truck drivers, mechanics, communications, cooks, etc.

Like most infantry divisions of WWII, the 100th could be described as "self-contained" in that it had a combat engineer battalion, a medical battalion, a mechanized reconnaissance troop, a quartermaster company, a maintenance company which kept the division's trucks and jeeps in operating order, a signals company (responsible for radios and telephones), and military police. All of those units, except the medical battalion, had weapons available for defense, typically bazookas or heavy machine guns. There were also many specialist organizations: Postal Section, Judge Advocate General's Office, Inspector General's Office, 100th Division Band, Surgeon's Office, the Chaplain's Office, Signals, and Engineering Office among others.

At full strength, when it shipped out in late 1944, the Century Division numbered just over 15,000 men. Once in the European Theater of Operations (ETO), the division's capabilities were supported by other Army and Corps assets, including very heavy artillery, tank battalions, tank destroyer battalions, anti-aircraft artillery, and chemical mortar battalions that fired special, very high-explosive rounds or smoke screen projectiles.

Jack's function, operations and training, had varied responsibilities during peace and war. While stateside, he was more heavily involved in training, except during maneuvers of which more later. Once the division went into combat in late 1944, Jack was dominated by operations. As the S-3, Jack's primary duty was to serve as the battalion commander's principal advisor. Lt. Col. Stayton had to be pleased to have Jack Rhea on his staff. Jack had a degree in education, had come from an organization where training was developed to a fine if not overly fine level, had previously been a teacher and star basketball player, and was used to working with adults and older adolescents (a category that included the many of the youngest soldiers in the division). More importantly Jack had been a hunting guide and was a crack shot. He had the professional hunter's feel for terrain and weather, key attributes for an operations officer. And he had turned in an outstanding record at OCS which had contributed to his becoming an acting operations officer immediately without having put in some time leading a rifle platoon.

Jack Trains Infantrymen

While at Fort Jackson, Lieutenant Rhea was occupied with assessing training needs for the battalion and its subordinate units, companies and platoons, conducting the training, and evaluating the results. Once overseas, Jack was a fixture in the battalion command post, planning and coordinating the battalion's operations along with the very critical function of monitoring what were typically very fluid situations when the four companies were engaged in combat. How he reacted to opportunities and threats was of paramount importance. The training element was not ignored while overseas, as it would turn out when the battalion was in reserve. Then Jack conducted specialized training, particularly for the new men arriving from replacement depots and for experienced soldiers going on special operations. Interestingly, his role with the 3rd/398th would perfectly presage his post-war career with the National Office of the BSA: operations and training.

Jack's more immediate focus after arriving at Fort Jackson was the basic training of new men arriving in early December from Army reception centers in the Atlantic seaboard states. The first couple of weeks were spent in military indoctrination, including military discipline, structure of Army units, and other basic orientation. Most surviving Centurymen now remember that period as wet – classes were held out in the open and that December 1942 was very rainy. Basic training followed once a sufficient number of recruits arrived and typically lasted three months, emphasizing physical training, marching and drilling, running obstacle courses (a precursor to the popular BSA cope courses?), and hiking with full packs. The hikes ranged from a few miles to ten or more, and the graduation hike was a 25-miler. Kelty packs and BSA Cruisers with their magic hipbelts were still about fifteen years into the future. Those struggling most on the long hikes were the soldiers carrying a BAR (nearly twenty pounds, not counting ammunition), a .30 caliber machine gun, or a machine gun tripod.

Firearms instruction started late in the basic training phase. At that stage of the war, the M-1 Garand semi-automatic rifle was the standard issue firearm; new recruits became intimately familiar with it and its occasional tendency to mangle an ill-coordinated thumb during inspection of the rifle. The only .30 caliber, bolt-action Springfield rifles from World War I in regular service were those with telescopic sights issued to the few really talented marksmen who became snipers. Nearly ninety percent of the division's men qualified on the M-1. Oddly enough, none of the infantry regiments came out as the top qualifier on the M-1; that honor was taken by the 325th Combat Engineer Battalion with a score of ninety-six percent. Basic training also included work with bayonets, hand grenades, knives, and personal defense without a weapon.

While Lt. Jack Rhea was involved with infantry training, other elements of the Century Division were arriving at Fort Jackson, most notably the division and regimental support units along with the four artillery regiments. Once a soldier was brought up to personal military standards, he might go onto more specialized training if he had been selected for a heavy weapons company, a reconnaissance troop, or other combat specialty.

After a soldier was toughened up and proficient with his weapon, his training moved to a new phase when he had to crawl through an infiltration course complete with trenches, shell holes, barbed wire, and live machine gun rounds zipping by, hardly a yardstick above his head. To make it more realistic, small charges of dynamite were set off nearby. The S-3 officer was, perhaps more importantly, also responsible for training groups of men as they would eventually go into battle in companies, platoons, and squads. To teach basic tactics such as attacking, flanking, defending, and withdrawing, instructors used natural features to the fullest extent possible and even utilized a "Nazi village" which had been built by the combat engineers.

On 2 March 1943, Jack was promoted to First Lieutenant based on the "outstanding performance of his duties as the Operations Officer of the 3rd Battalion, 398th Infantry." By the end of March, the Century Division had completed basic training for its first influx of fresh recruits. Brief furloughs were issued to the lucky, but more field exercises awaited them upon their return. Suddenly, on Saturday 10 April, all passes for the weekend were cancelled. The camp immediately buzzed with all kinds of rumors, including one that the division had just received its overseas movement orders. Actually, General Burress had just been informed that the division would guard the entire South Carolina rail route President Roosevelt would follow on an inspection tour of southern military bases in the middle of the following week. It was a challenging assignment considering the logistical demands. However, the general's staff rapidly completed plans, and had the infantry regiments and artillery regiments (the latter without their howitzers) in place as FDR's train rumbled through South Carolina on 14 April.

Jack temporarily gave up the S-3 post on 26 April to become the acting K Company commander, a slot normally occupied by a captain. This proved to be an interim assignment, and he would return to the S-3 post several months later. While a company commander Jack was responsible for the training and direction of the 192 officers and men in his company.

*The Headquarters Company, 3rd Battalion,
398th Infantry setting up a command post while on
bivouac in the South Carolina woods.*

By June 1943, the infantry regiments were spending much more time on bivouac, up to one week per month. A Philmont ranger would have been very much at home during this phase when the troops learned how to live in the great out-of-doors. The ranger would not have been comfortable with some of the other things accompanying a South Carolina summer: sand fleas, millions of chiggers, and humidity to match the temperature. Having had some Boy Scouting experience was a definite advantage for new recruits. It was not at all uncommon for a platoon leader or senior NCO to ask of new men assigned to his command, "Any of you guys Eagle Scouts?" Many years later, the 100th Infantry Division Association ran a small, informal survey on the value of Scouting to its members during the war. To a man, the respondents cited the ability to work in a team, setting goals, developing self-reliance, and the ability to get by in the woods as how Scouting helped them during what were terribly trying times.

At the beginning of early summer 1943, the Century Division suffered the first round of a series of major setbacks: massive transfers out of the division for a variety of reasons including the needs of the Army Air Forces, demand for paratroopers, opportunities in the Army Specialized Training Program (ASTP), and the intake needs for overseas replacement depots. In other cases, soldiers who were overage or simply physically unfit were discharged or placed in the reserves. The manpower losses came at a critical time since the division was about to embark upon its "D" exercises, i.e., Division level training. Heretofore, training had emphasized offensive and defensive tactics for battalions, companies, and platoons; the third level of training ("RCT" or Regimental Combat Team Training) focused on division-wide activities in which foes were other army units or large groups of the 100th which were designated as foes.

The 100th Division ranged over much of northern South Carolina during these "war games." Some of the exercises, those held back at Fort Jackson, involved using live ammunition and real bombs dropped by B-25 Mitchell medium bombers based at nearby Columbia Army Air Base which is today's Columbia Metropolitan Airport. The division was still not at full arms, but was getting close when the War Department boosted its firepower with the addition of three cannon companies equipped with 105 mm howitzers. Offsetting those gains were the loss of another 1,000 men who were transferred to other divisions whose overseas departures were imminent.

Rhea, Capt. Jack L. O1296148. Infantry, Ranger.

In mid-summer 1943, Jack Rhea was selected for Army Ranger training. Earlier, in the first days of January 1943, General Burress had an opportunity to observe an infantry skills demonstration put on by the men of the 2nd Ranger Battalion which was then in training at Camp Forrest in Tennessee. Burress was convinced that he needed rangers for the 100th Division. During World War II, the Army created six Ranger Battalions. Most were authorized, trained, and activated overseas, although the 2nd and 5th Ranger Battalions originated at Camp Forrest, near Tullahoma, Tennessee. The American Ranger Battalions were based on British Commandos with whom they shared a reputation for daring feats. Among the American rangers' exploits were scaling the cliffs at Pointe du Hoc on D-Day at Normandy, dashing inland to disable the big guns threatening the D-Day invasion fleet, taking out key objectives deep in enemy territory in North Africa and Italy, and rescuing American POWS from behind the Japanese lines in the Philippines. Marine Raiders in the Pacific and the Army's Merrill's Marauders in Burma, although not officially classified as rangers, also fell under the classification of what would later be known as "Special Forces."

With a little lobbying on the part of General Burress, General George Marshall quickly approved a plan for several of the infantry divisions in the Second Army, all based in the southeastern United States, to send small groups of men to the Ranger School at Camp Forrest for training. Men completing that training would return to their original positions, i.e., they would be sprinkled throughout the division and not concentrated all in one dedicated unit as was the case of the original six Ranger Battalions. Since it was impractical to send every Centuryman to ranger training, it was anticipated that those returning from that training would spread what they learned far and wide throughout their squads and platoons.

Accordingly, the regimental commanders of the 100th Division reviewed the files of likely-looking men and "volunteered" them for ranger training. Men selected for this training had to be physically very fit, highly intelligent, and, in the beginning, somewhat older than the average recruit. Each training contingent was composed of about thirty-six men with officers and enlisted men mixed together. That first group was comprised of captains, first lieutenants, and senior non-commissioned officers primarily from rifle companies, although there was token representation from the reconnaissance troop, division artillery, military police, and signals. The first several classes did not include any personnel from regiment or battalion headquarters.

Physical conditioning was an integral part of that first ranger training, and a forced march with an M-1 rifle and seventy-pound field pack occurred almost daily. These forced marches started with a three-mile march which had to be completed in thirty-seven minutes; the 100th Division contingent made it in thirty-three minutes. Then it was five miles in fifty minutes. The marches became progressively more demanding and culminated in a nine-mile final test which had to be covered in two hours. The Centurymen contingent got through the final march with two minutes to spare, but it came at a cost. Although selected by their regimental commanders for their toughness, something had to give and it was usually what little excess body weight the men were carrying. One of the Century's toughest, a twenty-eight year old sergeant and former semi-pro boxer went from 160 to 143 pounds during the training. He said that he was thrilled to have taken ranger training, but if given the chance to take it a second time he would decline. According to the sergeant, the hardest test of all was running 300 yards in 45 seconds, which he and only one other man among the several hundred candidates were able to do.

The ranger course was far more grueling than the advanced training a new recruit could expect, but then Jack Rhea was more than up to it considering his post-frontier upbringing, his record in OCS, his athletic stamina, and the fact that many of his Scouting skills were very useful. In the latter category, he was taught how to improvise bridges, use toggle ropes, and how to stalk enemy soldiers and tanks. There was advanced instruction in activities typically associated with Special Forces: infiltration, patrols and ambushes (particularly at night), individual camouflage, hand-to-hand combat which included judo, crossing streams, construction of and passage through entanglements, use of demolition, and setting up/dismantling booby traps.

When the Ranger School at Camp Forrest was first opened to candidates from infantry divisions in the Second Army, the entire group from the 100th Division completed the training, something that could not be said for every other division's candidates. And the 100th's former boxer emerged as the top-scoring candidate, earning a record 984 points out of a perfect grade of 1,000.

By autumn 1943, both the 2nd and 5th Ranger Battalions had left Camp Forrest for other stations. Well before they left, cadres from the Century and several of the divisions in the Second Army spent several weeks in training to be ranger instructors because General Marshall had decided that infantry divisions would have to take responsibility for training their own rangers. Accordingly, the Second Army Ranger School was closed on 15 February 1943.

Ranger training, when it came to Fort Jackson, was conducted in locations apart from the usual training sites. Compared to regular advanced infantry training, the bar was set much higher for ranger candidates. Fort Jackson included a few enhancements that Camp Forrest could not offer, including running through swamps with rifle and full field pack.

The training Jack and other 100th Division Rangers received, however, was not as extensive as that of the original six Ranger Battalions. There was no in-depth training in large scale amphibious landings, climbing seaside cliffs, and hands-on firing of captured German weapons for Century Rangers. The 2nd and 5th Ranger Battalions got preliminary amphibious training in Florida and were further trained after their arrival in the United Kingdom. General Burress trained as many swimmers (including lifesaving and artificial resuscitation) as he could and used Fort Jackson's Twin Lakes as the site for assault training with GPAs (amphibious jeeps).

Once in combat, the toughest jobs usually involved Century Rangers. That hazardous duty included hit and run raids on German barracks and facilities well behind the lines, night ambush patrols, capturing large groups of Germans for interrogation, and scouting ahead in advance of river crossings. General Burress got his money's worth when he authorized ranger training, particularly in Jack Rhea's case. As an operations and training officer, Jack was able to pass along much of what he learned and could better match men with the missions once in combat.

Jack completed ranger training and was awarded his Century Division Ranger Certificate of Proficiency on 17 August 1943. Fourteen years later, "rangers" was a word that Jack would use in a different context at Philmont Scout Ranch for another group of specially trained, gung-ho, physically-fit, pack-laden, "can-do" young men charged with important tasks at the leading edge of Philmont's camping program. Below his division insignia, Jack was entitled to wear a small red strip with white lettering bearing the word, "RANGER."

Editor's Collection

Jack completed Army Ranger training in the summer of 1943 and put that experience to good use when the 100th Division went into combat in November 1944.

World War II infantry division shoulder sleeve insignia varied considerably although most were done in two colors. Here and there were a few four-color creations of which the most notable were the 101st Airborne, "Screaming Eagles," and the 2nd "Indianhead." Most division graphics were very straightforward: either numerals or a very basic symbol of origin or strength. The Century Division insignia was simple but striking: a blue shield emblazoned with the number "100" in which the upper half of the number was white and the bottom was gold.

While the division insignia was worn on the left shoulder below the shoulder strap, the metal regimental insignia was worn on both shoulder straps between the rank insignia and the strap button. The 398th Infantry Regiment insignia was a blue shield with a wavy bend in silver above a rattlesnake. The regiment's motto was "On the Alert."

The Tennessee Maneuvers

Then, in mid-November 1943, the division packed up and headed north to winter maneuvers in north-central Tennessee. The Centurymen did not know it, but the rotten cold weather, rain, mud, rivers, and mountains of their 15,000 square mile training area perfectly foreshadowed the natural surroundings they would face in exactly twelve months minus, of course, genuine German troops. Jack's role here shifted from training to operations. The 100th Division teamed with the 14th Armored Division as the Blue Forces against the Red Forces consisting of the 35th Infantry Division and the 3rd Cavalry Group. The Century Division was in good company with its ally and foes: they would all go on to distinguish themselves in the fight with Germany. Nobody was killed in the Tennessee maneuvers unless a green-flagged umpire declared that they were quite deceased. Prisoners, sometimes entire companies at a time, were taken. And for Jack Rhea, the 3/398 S-3, it was a valuable experience in that he had a chance to employ the tactics he had been taught at Fort Benning's Infantry OCS on a very large scale.

The exercises were a series of eight assignments spread over two months of quasi-wilderness camping involving a variety of offensive and defensive maneuvers. The judges occasionally shifted assets between forces to put one side at a numerical disadvantage. Bridges had to be taken or defended, night assaults were launched, scouts probed enemy lines, mortar men fired special projectiles to set up smoke screens, the medical staff "treated" the wounded, runners carried messages, pioneer platoons carried ammunition, a retreating enemy was pursued, bridges were "blown up," engineers assembled and took down pontoon bridges, and communications wire was put in place all the way from division to regiment to company command posts.

During the maneuvers, and in its challenging weather, General Burress was not ensconced in some cozy mountain cabin overlooking the Cumberland River. Rather he was with the troops, sharing what they were going through. He was known for being as close to the action as prudence would allow. Tragically, one of his regimental commanders lacked that fine judgment and would pay for it with his life in little more than a year's time.

At the time the combat teams were attacking or retreating across the Cumberland River, few Centurymen could name any river in Germany other than the Rhine. Time would certainly change that shortcoming in geographic awareness and make many a 100th soldier glad that General Burress' expertise in river crossings had been part of the war games.

During the Tennessee maneuvers, Centurymen occasionally heard a throaty snarl in the sky, looked aloft, and saw a P-40 Warhawk fighter roaring by. The maneuvers were not just for infantrymen. The Curtiss P-40s along with some Bell P-39D Airacobras were flown by pilots from the 15th Tactical Reconnaissance Squadron which was developing its skills too. In the near future, the 15th TRS would join the 10th Photographic Reconnaissance Group, ship out to England, and after the invasion, move across France with other tactical recon squadrons and serve as the eyes and ears of the Allied armies as they drove the Germans eastward.

The Century Division was becoming a well-oiled machine. The machine did suffer from a bit of adversity – it rained almost constantly during the division's two months in the Tennessee woods. But there was light at the end of tunnel. Jack Rhea's star was rising at the same time. On 20 September, 1943, Jack got his "railroad ties" (promoted to captain) – a meteoric advance even by wartime standards. Under normal circumstances, a promising young, stateside officer could expect to make captain two years after having been commissioned. Jack Rhea did it in eleven months. Prior to the promotion, he had already relinquished command of Company K and returned to the battalion staff. For Jack Rhea, it may have been a providential move – one in which he quite literally may have dodged a bullet.

His replacement as K Company commander was Captain Randolph Jones, from the little town of Hephzibah, just south of Augusta, Georgia. Jones survived the war, but was severely wounded during combat in France.

Training at Fort Bragg

In mid-January the Centurymen left Tennessee, not for Fort Jackson, but for a new home: Fort Bragg, North Carolina. When Jack arrived at the base, which is located a few miles northwest of Fayetteville, the local draft board had just released the names of nineteen delinquent men who had moved and not notified the board of their new addresses. The public was asked to provide information leading to the draft dodgers' whereabouts. Members of the local Kiwanis Club announced plans for a major variety show to promote the sale of war bonds during the great Fourth Loan Drive. On January fifteenth, marriage licenses were taken out by five couples; four of the men were from Fort Bragg and the fifth was an airman from nearby Pope Army Airfield. Although the B.F. Goodrich store at 223 May Street was advertising Goodrich Silvertown synthetic tires, Todd's Recapping Service urged readers of the *Fayetteville Observer* to come in and have their rubber tires recapped.

The town's basketball team, the Fayetteville Bulldogs, appeared to rally in their latest contest with Durham, but finally went down fighting, 31 to 36, for their fifth straight loss. The Associated Press announced that the sport of golf had suffered a twenty-eight percent decline in 1943 compared to its pre-Pearl Harbor level. Nonetheless, Byron Nelson held a second round lead in the San Francisco Open on January fifteenth. Two days later, he won the tournament, just edging out chief rival Lloyd Mangrum who was about to turn in his golf bag for an M-1 rifle and Army basic training just a few days after the tournament.

Although the Allies' fortunes had improved since Jack's first joining the Century Division, Hollywood turned out many westerns and musicals as a diversion to war news. It also produced many war films, and several were playing in Fayetteville theaters as Jack arrived at Fort Bragg. Errol Flynn was staring in *Northern Pursuit*, an espionage thriller about tracking down Nazi saboteurs in Canada, which was soon to open at the Colony Theater. The Colony was in its last few days of *The North Star*, a film in which Anne Baxter and Dana Andrews played Ukrainian peasants resisting the Nazi juggernaut. Jack's off-duty time was limited, but there was usually time to listen to the radio; the Mills Brothers had the number one song in January 1944 – "Paper Doll" which gave up the top spot late in the month to Glen Gray and "My Heart Tells Me."

The training continued. Some of it was repetitious: requalifying on the rifle ranges for example. There was more training on the coordination of infantry attacks with supporting artillery. Ranger training was also reinstated. Although the vast majority of new rangers came from rifle companies, there were a few representatives from field artillery, the military police, and the 100th Reconnaissance Troop. Some of the training was new: laying, detecting, and disarming land mines. The enlisted manpower drain of mid-1943 continued into early 1944 when the 100th Division lost 3,500 more enlisted men to the upcoming invasion of Europe. There was a trickle of combat-experienced, non-commissioned officers into the division with most having recovered from wounds suffered in the Pacific, North Africa, or Italy, but it was only a trickle. As a rule, it took one full year to create an infantry division. The wholesale transfer of trained men from the 100th to other divisions shipping overseas had the effect of moving the division back to square one to start all over again. The perception of the 100th as strictly a "training division" would create some resentment among the men who had been with the division since its activation in late 1942.

In early March 1944, Jack Rhea was sent on detached duty to Fort Benning to attend the Officers Advanced Infantry Course. He remained at Fort Benning until returning to Fort Bragg on 4 June 1944, thus missing what amounted to a supplemental training period for the regiment. The Advanced Infantry Course was designed for men moving into the S-3 position or assuming command of a company. Grades were issued for the Advanced Course, and Jack emerged with a "superior" rating. When he returned to the 3rd Battalion, it was as the S-3 and no longer in an "acting" capacity.

Almost as soon as he returned to Fort Bragg, he was granted twelve days leave which allowed him the pleasure of returning to Kansas City to see his family and friends. In the following month, the 100th Division lost 120 junior officers to replacement depots. An appalling number of these men were killed during the Allied breakout from the Normandy beachhead. Jack was well-acquainted with two of those dead; Lts. Ladislaus Horvath and Ivan Miklich, both mid-westerners, had been platoon leaders reporting to Jack while he was commander of K Company.

To make good these losses, the Century Division became the recipient of transfers from a variety of Army units including aviation cadets, anti-aircraft artillery, barrage balloons, military police, etc. The largest influx came from the Army Specialized Training Program which was being radically scaled back. Through the ASTP, young enlisted men who had achieved a high score on the Army General Classification Test (AGCT) could attend college preparatory to being commissioned. The AGCT had replaced the old Alpha Test and evaluated much more than verbal skills. There was a rather droll touch to the ASTP acceptance test in that while a score of 110 on the AGCT was required for Officer Candidate School, 120 was the minimum for ASTP which emphasized study on the more useful disciplines such as engineering, languages, psychology, and intelligence, etc.

The ASTP was somewhat similar to the Army Air Force College Detachment Program which was supposed to take bright young men and quickly bring them up to an educational standard required for training as a pilot, navigator, or bombardier. That program was heavy in math and physics, but the early part of its existence was based on holding those men somewhere (away from their draft boards) until enough flight training facilities could be constructed to absorb them. ASTP men had no such protecting authority and comprised a major portion of the Century's intake in 1944, easily making it one of America's smartest infantry divisions. By mid-to late 1944, the Army Air Force was no longer building up its aviation cadet program; large numbers of those highly qualified men who were awaiting assignment to pilot, navigator, or bombardier training were simply reassigned out of cadets and shipped to infantry divisions along with the ASTP transfers, thus also contributing to the division's reputation as a very high I.Q. organization. Many of the college-oriented ASTP men and former aviation cadets took advantage of the GI bill after the war and subsequently went into very productive careers.

There was something going on at Fort Bragg, and it was of a paradoxically unfavorable nature. Like most infantry divisions, the 100th had hosted a few VIPs during regimental or division reviews. And had not General Burress once said that he wanted every man in the 100th to be publicly recognized for his service? The spring of 1944 saw more VIPs coming to see what a sharp outfit the 100th was. Ink started running in the newspapers about these visits. More favorable articles appeared when a sergeant in the 399th Infantry Regiment became the very first soldier to earn the Army's new Expert Infantryman's Badge. Increasingly, the 100th was becoming known simply as just a "show" division, an image enhanced by the rapid pace of visiting congressmen, other politicians, Army top brass, and civilian VIPs. And when a battalion of the division was chosen to march in New York City on the first celebration of Infantry Day along with participating in a very visible position in the great Fifth War Loan Drive, the reputation as a show division was mightily enhanced. The next high point was the division's hosting the North Carolina textile industry's top executives for three days of "soldiering."

Once back at Fort Bragg, the only people who really needed advanced infantry training were the former ASTP troops who brought the division basically up to strength. It was during this period the 398th Combat Team put on a stirring artillery demonstration for military writers from allied nations which certainly added even more laurels to the division's reputation as a show division. Most infantrymen at that time were firing M-1 rifles or carbines on Fort Bragg's rifle ranges. For those not qualifying, the weapons course had to be repeated. Jack Rhea's skill with a rifle did not rub off on his battalion; Company G of the 397th Infantry emerged as the top marksmen, although the anti-tank gunners of the 398th scored higher than all companies from the 397th or 399th. Jack had previously qualified for the Army's Marksmanship Award with the 1903 Springfield rifle while he was in ROTC and later qualified with the M-1 rifle and M-1 carbine while with the 100th Division. The Marksmanship Award actually had three levels: marksman, sharpshooter, and, the highest, expert. Jack, a skilled hunter to begin with, easily qualified as an expert on all three weapons, but never wore the award since most officers rarely wore them in that era.

At Fort Bragg, there were combined exercises involving tanks, artillery, and infantry, more training for snipers, learning about booby-traps, and more night and combined operations. Assuming that the 100th might be involved in an amphibious landing, more men were taught to swim. Finally, assuming that the Germans might not play fair, there was universal training with gas masks.

As with all military units, there were diversions: open post on weekends for some soldiers, four movie theaters on base, a division newspaper (the *Century Sentinel*), dances with local ladies at the service club, visits by entertainers such as Danny Kaye or actors like John Garfield, and even a yearbook, *Century Division 1944*. The movies were first run titles and frequently included such war-oriented films as *In Which We Serve*, with Noel Coward.

General Burress, a trim and compact man, had been a star on the VMI football team in spite of the fact that his physique was not that usually associated with burly football players. There were leagues for nearly every sport at Fort Bragg, including football, baseball, basketball, volleyball, and boxing. At age fifty, Burress was no longer a football player, but it was not at all unusual to find the general in pick-up games of volleyball which added to his growing reputation as a soldier's general.

The interest in sports league standings, dances, and visiting Hollywood stars suddenly took a back seat on 10 August 1944. The Century Division had just been alerted for overseas movement.

CHAPTER 7

The Vosges Campaign

After having received its overseas movement alert, Centurymen started packing, an advance group left for New York Harbor, and by 30 September the division was in its staging area at Camp Kilmer. That base is just north of a town that Jack would come to know very well in later years: North Brunswick, New Jersey, where the Boy Scouts of America was headquartered prior to moving to Texas in 1979. Four days previous to that, an advance group from the division staff left by air for the Century's ultimate destination: Marseille, France. Many of the men had a shorter destination afforded by twelve-hour passes: New York City. To his parents, Jack posted a change of address card. The street/city portion was cryptic: APO #447, c/o Postmaster, N.Y., N.Y.

By the afternoon of 5 October, final physical exams had been passed, inoculations were administered, and 100-pound duffel bags had been collected and shipped to the port of embarkation. After cold weather clothing was distributed, all sorts of rumors started. Were they headed for an invasion of Norway? After short train and Hudson River ferry rides, the Centurymen were at a pier gazing up at the ships that would take them to war. After carrying seventy-pound packs aboard, the men found their way to their decidedly cramped quarters. As an officer, Jack Rhea was assigned to a crowded stateroom with bunks, but he was nowhere near as tightly packed as the enlisted men who were stacked five-high in hammocks with only inches of clearance between one's chest and somebody else's back.

The 100th Division was in good company. Also assigned to convoy UFG-15B were the 103rd Infantry Division and lead elements of the 14th Armored Division. The three divisions were activated at different stations on the same day in November, 1942, and were destined to fight in the same sector after arriving in France. The 100th Division was loaded onto four ships: the USS *George Washington*, the USS *General W.H. George Gordon*, the USS *McAndrews*, and the USS *Mooremac Moon*. The *George Washington* had carried troops to France before – in World War I. The ship had actually been built in Germany as a superbly luxurious cruise liner. It happened to be in an American port when war between the United States and Germany was declared and was promptly seized and put into service. Four other, smaller transport vessels also sailed with the convoy as did the USS *Merak*, a Navy refrigerator ship carrying food to France. Jack Rhea, however, was aboard the *Gordon* with the rest of the 398th Regiment. The *Gordon* was a youngster compared to the *George Washington*, having only been commissioned in June 1944. On mid-morning 6 October, Capt. Jack Rhea's ship sailed past Lady Liberty, headed out to the open sea, and was joined by a destroyer, a small escort carrier, and several destroyer escorts.

After landing in Marseille, the Century Division moved by rail and truck to the Vosges Mountains east of Nancy, fought its way through to Germany, and captured Stuttgart in late April 1945. The dotted line traces the route of a special task force led by Captain Jack Rhea in the closing days of the war.

In less than a month, another Rhea in uniform would sail from New York. It was Ralph Rhea, Jack's brother who was with the 289th Infantry Regiment of the 75th Infantry Division. Compared to the extensive training received by the 100th Division, the 75th was a very green unit and would be headed not for France, but for Wales where it would receive more training before arriving at Le Havre, France, in early December.

Three days after Jack sailed from New York and about 3,400 air miles to the northeast, a Lockheed Lightning roared down a runway at Mount

Farm, an Eighth Army Air Force base just outside of Oxford or about 40 miles west-northwest of London. This particular Lightning, Army Air Force serial number 42-68235, was not a P-38 Lightning; rather, it was an unarmed F-5G Lightning, the photo-reconnaissance version of the familiar twin-engined fighter. The pilot, Flight Officer Edgar L. Vassar, was flying the 7th Photographic Reconnaissance Group's sortie number 7/3505. He took up a southeasterly heading to fly the nearly 400 miles to his objective. His target, the fortress town of Bitche in Alsace, France, is about eighty miles west-northwest of Stuttgart, Germany. In French, Bitche is pronounced as "Beeshe." In German, it comes across as "Bee-che." In English it is pronounced exactly as it looks and would prove to be one too. Vassar's mission was not a success because the objective was only partially visible through breaks in the clouds. On the other hand, Vassar considered it personally successful because after about four hours of flying he returned safely. The last 7th Group pilot to fly to Bitche, Lt. Paul Ballough, was killed on 19 August flying an unarmed Spitfire P.R. Mark XI (the long range, photo recon version of the famous Royal Air Force fighter which equipped one of the group's four squadrons). Bitche would later become the keystone of the 100th's reputation.

October was, of course, still within the Atlantic hurricane season, and Jack's convoy was not spared when it was hit by a hurricane on 10 October. For many Centurymen, ordinary seas were enough to produce classic symptoms of seasickness. Those waiting far back in the interminably long lines to get to the heads to relieve their *mal de mer* found another emergency use for their helmets. Life on the *Gordon* could not possibly be confused with a Holland America or Cunard cruise. Sanitary conditions were nasty and Jack did not get three squares a day as he had gotten stateside. Rather it was two meals a day, although for a few dollars, a G.I. could usually get a bologna sandwich on the "QT" from a Navy messman in the late evening.

There were few diversions aboard the ships. Gambling had been forbidden, but that hardly put an end to the shuffle of cards or the roll of dice. Just getting a breath of fresh air on deck was a wonderful experience. For those lucky enough to be topside for a few moments in calmer waters, there was the amusement of watching dolphins jump the waves just head of the destroyer escorts' bows and seeing that flying fish actually fly. There was a small movie theater aboard the *Gordon*; but there was only one movie available, one in which Deanna Durbin sings "Songs My Mother Taught

Me." For those troops whose quarters were near the theater, the constant repetition of the movie cost Miss Durbin many of her fans in the 100th.

As the battalion S-3, Jack Rhea had training responsibilities on the way to France. The troops still had daily physical training, gas mask drills, and instruction in simple French and German. Centurymen became familiar with such phrases as *"Ou est les Allemands?* (Where are the Germans?), *Hände hoch!* (Hands up!), *Nicht schiessen!* (Don't shoot!), and *Kamerad!* (Surrender!)." With the hurricane spent after several days, there was a stretch of smooth sailing which reached a climax when land was sighted. Although the threat from German submarines on the crossing had been dramatically reduced with the Allies getting the upper hand in the Battle of the Atlantic in mid-1943, there were still a few Nazi submarines at large, and they had left their calling cards at the mouth of the Strait of Gibraltar: two sinking, burning American transport vessels. With the passing view of Gibraltar on the port side, many Centurymen entertained visions of smooth sailing on a sun-drenched Mediterranean. It was not to be; stormy weather was the division's unwelcome companion all the way to Marseille.

In 1939 Marseille had been a beautiful city with its port, ancient fortress, Mediterranean charm, and hilltop cathedral. In October 1944, the harbor was just barely functional, but after successive bombings by German, Italian, and Allied air forces, the city was in ruins and the harbor crowded with half-sunk, derelict ships scuttled by retreating Germans. Troops from Jack's convoy were assigned to the Seventh Army and were among the units to start relieving combat teams of the 3rd , 36th, and 45th Infantry Divisions on the line up in the Vosges Mountains to the northeast. The Vosges (pronounced "Voe-jshh") Mountains are a prominent feature of the Alsace Lorraine region of France which usually conjures up visions of the beautiful city of Strasbourg, crisp white wine in tall, fluted bottles, and quiche Lorraine. The area had been fought over by France and Germany before. In the nineteenth century, Germany took Alsace Lorraine in the Franco-Prussian War which partially explains why there are so many German-sounding place names there. France took it back at the conclusion of World War I and tried with only partial success to eliminate any German influence. The Century Division leaders saw Alsace Lorraine in a different way: mountains, deep forests, an approaching winter (rain-sleet-snow-mud), and a still dangerous German foe.

The 3rd, 36th, and 45th Divisions were badly in need of a rest after fighting in North Africa, Sicily, Italy, and having landed in France during Operation Dragoon, the Invasion of Southern France in August. One alumnus of the 3rd Infantry Division did much to enhance its laurels as a hard-fighting outfit: Lt. Audie Murphy, the most decorated American soldier of World War II. Sergeant Bill Mauldin, the Pulitzer Prize-winning soldier/cartoonist and creator of Joe and Willie, the bone-tired soldiers who came to epitomize the American infantrymen of World War II, was a sergeant in the 45th Division.

Joining the 7th Army at the same time with the Century Division were the 103rd Infantry Division and the 14th Armored Division. The Century was assigned to VI Corps initially, although it would later be temporarily assigned to the XV and XXI Corps and back to VI Corps as conditions changed during the remaining six months of the war. The Seventh Army was commanded by Lt. Gen. Alexander M. Patch, a West Point graduate who had seen action in World War I as an infantry officer and more recently on Guadalcanal in the Pacific war.

At about the same time Jack was landing in Marseille, major decisions were being made about the Seventh Army's supporting Army Air Force units. For the invasion of Southern France, the Twelfth Army Air Force diverted many of its assets from Italy to the island of Corsica and then to France itself. By mid-autumn the Twelfth Tactical Command needed to return many of its units back to Italy. Accordingly, the leaders of the Ninth (based in northern France) and Twelfth Army Air Forces drew up a plan to determine which units would remain, which Army Groups they would support, and how they would be supplied and serviced. The result was the creation of the First Tactical Air Force (Provisional) which, in effect, became the Seventh Army's private Air Force flying, for the most part, P-47 Thunderbolt fighter-bombers, B-26 Marauder medium bombers, and F-6 Mustangs and F-5 Lightnings for tactical reconnaissance.

Upon landing on 16 October, General Burress was ordered to have a combat team, consisting of an infantry regiment, one field artillery regiment, and supporting units along with a skeleton divisional headquarters, on the line in two weeks to relieve the 45th's 179th Infantry Regiment. It was a challenge, considering how much equipment had to be unloaded and how long it would take to get the Centurymen out of Marseille and marched to a staging area. Prior to departure anything that could rust on the salty ocean passage had been liberally coated in Cosmoline, a protective coating whose consistency was somewhere between grease and wax. Cleaning that goop from arms and vehicles was especially time-consuming. By nightfall, the regiment started marching inland. In spite of the secrecy attending the departure from the United States, "Axis Sally," the turncoat Nazi radio propagandist, broadcast a cynical greeting to the Centurymen upon their arrival in Marseille.

Blooding at Raon L'Étape

After a full night of slogging uphill with those heavy packs, Jack's regiment reached the staging area at Septeme, but learned that the 399th Regiment was a jump ahead and would go into the line first. Then the rain started. At Septeme, the regiment set up a temporary camp since it had to return to Marseille to unpack equipment which would subsequently be trucked to the front. Over the next two weeks, the regiment moved by a combination of truck and rail through Dijon and onto its final assembly area at Saint Grogan. Here were the first signs of the shooting war: the rumble of not so distant artillery and the sight of recently vacated foxholes.

If it had not been full of Germans, General Burress would have felt at home in the High Vosges – it was very reminiscent of the Blue Ridge Mountains that surround VMI in Lexington, Virginia. In the upcoming six months of combat, Burress would emerge as a very crafty tactician, one who could walk the tightrope of accomplishing objectives set down for him by his superiors but doing so at a minimum cost of Centurymen lives. He would also prove to be a very mobile general in that he created a traveling divisional command post (CP) consisting of his jeep and a special caravan containing maps and communications equipment. Occasionally, he would take to the air in an artillery spotter plane in order to see the big picture.

Jack's regiment would not be the first into the line, however; the 399th Regiment had won the race and would relieve the 179th Regiment before the 398th could take over from the 45th's 180th Regiment. On 6 November the regiment replaced the 180th and was in the vicinity of St. Barbe, already sending out reconnaissance patrols. The division's first objective was to start breaking the German winter defensive line with the goal of taking Raon L'Étape, a small city in use by the Germans as a supply and communications center. Today Raon L'Étape has a reputation as the scenic gateway to the Vosges Mountains which rise from what is essentially a flat plain to the east. The town is at the confluence of the La Plaine and the

Muerthe Rivers; for centuries both traders and armies have passed through Raon L'Étape.

On 8 November the regiment came under fire for the first time as its position was hit by artillery all day. The advantage was with the Germans because the weather was cold and rainy, the Muerthe River was a natural barrier, and the Germans held the heights that ringed the town. On 9 November, recon patrols sent by the battalion and an inconclusive firefight on one of the hills between the defending Germans and C Company of the 1st Battalion promptly convinced Burress to outflank Raon L'Étape instead of taking it by a costly frontal assault – provided a weaker point elsewhere on the La Plaine could be found after crossing the Muerthe River. C Company's blooding that day involved one soldier killed in action, eleven wounded, and one missing.

During the following week, the battalion crossed the Muerthe in the vicinity of Baccarat along with the 1st Battalion. The artillery battalions subjected the Germans to heavy fire from the original position directly facing Raon L'Étape. While the 1st Battalion was in defensive positions near Baccarat, the *Luftwaffe* (German Air Force) put in an appearance and strafed the battalion command post. Jack Rhea's opposite number in the 1st battalion, the S-3, was seriously wounded in the attack. On 18 November, the battalion was in its staging area northeast of Baccarat, the home of the very fine French crystal of the same name. On that cold day, Jack participated in a briefing of officers from the four companies on the battalion's objectives for the following day: crossing the La Plaine at the village of La Trouche, taking Hill 578 (named for its height in meters) which rose up beyond the fields and woods on the other side of the river, and occupying the village of Moyenmoutier.

The 1st Battalion's Company A had succeeded in crossing the La Plaine River the day before but only at the cost of substantial casualties. The 3rd Battalion crossed the La Plaine at 7:05 A.M. on the nineteenth and met stiff resistance in the fields on the other side of the river. German machine gun nests were silenced by flanking, permitting the battalion's companies to move toward the rising terrain surrounding its primary objective – Hill 578. By early evening on the 20th, Hill 578 belonged to the battalion, but it came at a high price considering the artillery that fell on the battalion and the numerous German counterattacks during the day. The terrain on the way to the top of Hill 578 was rocky, steep, and laden with underbrush – somewhat similar to an ascent from just above Old Abreu to the Notch on the Rayado Canyon ridge trail at Philmont before there was a trail there. While clearing out the woods below the hill, I and L Companies came across something of great interest to Jack Rhea, the former wrangler: artillery pieces still attached to several teams of harnessed horses. The defending Germans, by this time facing fuel shortages thanks to Allied Air Forces, had quickly abandoned their equipment. Some Germans did not flee; the regiment took seventy-five prisoners that day.

Centurymen pursuing retreating German forces northeast of Raon L'Étape. Mountainous, heavily wooded terrain, rainy weather, and German roadblocks complicated the pursuit.

As darkness set in, temperatures dropped even more and a squad-sized contingent from the battalion headquarters staff, including Jack, set out on a task that would endear them forever to the men holding Hill 578. It was a relief mission of sorts led by Major Ernest Janes who had replaced Major Marshall Gilman as the battalion executive officer before the division arrived in France. Janes was a tall Kentuckian whose distinctive appearance was frequently capped off with a large cigar. The plan was to bring hot food in mermite cans (insulated containers) and more ammunition to the nearly frozen Centurymen on top of the hill. It was a trying mission made more difficult by the lack of a moon, fallen trees, and muddy roads. Not long after starting, their jeeps became mired in the mud. Several Centurymen escorting German prisoners to the rear were encountered, but instructions to the POWs in English to start pushing the jeeps had no effect – until Janes gestured with his hands and unholstered and cocked his Colt .45. That the Germans understood. The little convoy got underway again, but eventually encountered a downed tree which completely blocked the road. The balance of the arduous journey was made on foot, to the great relief of the shivering and hungry GIs on the hilltop.

The 3rd Battalion's opponent was the 708th Volks Grenadier Division and it, like the 100th Infantry Division, was untested in combat. Its predecessor division was originally a coastal defense unit that had been badly mauled while it was on the western front from June until September 1944. Although the leadership was very experienced, the average German soldier was as young as eighteen or as old as forty-four. Many of the division's members had previously been members of the *Kriegsmarine* (Navy) or the *Luftwaffe* whose declining fortunes released many men for service elsewhere. What the 708th lacked in experience was partially compensated for by its arms: new MP44 assault rifles and for each squad one MG42, a 7.92 mm light machine gun with a devastatingly high rate of fire.

As the operations officer, Jack Rhea was located at the battalion command post during this action. The "CP" was typically located 600 to 800 yards in back of the actual line of demarcation between the opposing forces; the division command post could be a mile or more behind the front. At the CP during the La Plaine crossing, Jack was not in significant danger of being targeted by an individual German infantryman. That would come later. However, when the battalion command post was located close to the line of demarcation, great care had to be taken. The visible smoke from an ill-advised, impromptu cooking fire could result in a response from German mortars and heavier automatic weapons such as 20 mm cannons. A poorly aimed shot by a German infantryman using a Mauser rifle, while missing its intended, closer target could still occasionally reach the battalion command post area.

Operations in the Vosges Mountains

The typical German soldier in late 1944 was armed with a 7.92 mm Model 98 bolt action Mauser rifle. That was a fine weapon in its day and was comparable to the American Springfield rifle which was first issued in 1903, but it could not begin to compare with a Centuryman's M-1. Increasingly, German infantrymen were armed with a "burp gun," the MP40, which was roughly equivalent to the American Thompson subma-chine gun. The burp gun was ideally suited for fighting in close quarters, such as the dense Vosges forests, and was so named because firing it on full automatic sounded like a hearty, beer-fueled belch. Other firearms included the MP44, considered by many to be the world's first operational assault rifle. Additional weapons included the *panzerfaust* (the German bazooka) and the "potato masher" hand grenade. The former was used primarily against armor or building structures and the latter was strictly a short range anti-personnel weapon. And the Germans had planted anti-personnel mines where Americans were most likely to advance.

The greatest danger to Jack and others at the battalion command post came from German artillery, particularly heavy mortars and the notori-ous 88 mm cannon. Snipers were a constant menace, and when the pace of American advance was swift, there was considerable danger from the occa-sional German patrol or snipers who had been bypassed. Jack, working in conjunction with the battalion intelligence officer, had to be very analytical when the location of battalion command posts were evaluated. They had to provide a clear view of the four infantry companies because both models of mobile radios in use, particularly the handheld "walky-talkies," could be operated only in line-of-sight conditions. Both types of radios frequently malfunctioned, and for that reason telephone lines were laid on the ground from a company's location back to the battalion command post and from there to regiment and division CPs whenever possible. The communications platoon could lay mile-long phone wire from heavy, wooden reels, but those wires were frequently severed by shrapnel. Finally, as a last resort, every squad had runners whose job was to dash between command and observa-tion posts with important messages. Command posts could not be located in funnel points, such as near a village entrance in case the front line collapsed. They had to be close to the rifle companies during an advance but to the rear while in defensive postures. CPs required some sort of shelter offering pro-tection from weather and, most importantly, enemy artillery and mortars.

Another very important tool for a battalion operations officer was his field map. While in France, Jack used topographic maps that are remarkably similar to Philmont's full-Ranch topo maps – the scales are identical: 1 to 50,000. The Army Map Service turned out millions upon millions of maps for the military during World War II and based those maps on nearly any useful scrap of information available – ranging from the work done by Army Air Force photo reconnaissance squadrons to simple pre-war road maps. The Army was fortunate in gaining access to pre-war French military topo maps which had most recently been printed in 1939. The Army Map Service had to do little more than update them with new information gleaned from photos taken by the Army Air Force photo reconnaissance squadrons and then start the printing presses. Those maps with their deeper colors, however, are not as easy to read as Philmont's because there is much more detail in terms of cities, villages, roads, etc. Once in Germany, Jack used all new maps prepared by the Army Map Service. Those maps were very similar to their French counterparts in terms of color and graphic symbols, but the scale was significantly different: 1 to 100,000. Jack's situation map was essentially a topo map overlaid with the locations of the opposing forces – thus the situation map was essentially a very important, real-time map constantly modified based on the reports Jack continually received from company commanders. How accurately Jack assessed the changing situation and how correct his resulting tactics were quite literally determined success or failure – and with it how many 3rd Battalion lives were saved or lost.

A frightening example of what could happen when a regimental or battalion officer failed to remain on station at the command post occurred on 16 November while the 398th Regiment gathered at a staging area near Bertrichamps preparing to cross the La Plaine. On that day, the 397th Regiment, to the northeast, was in support of the 399th on the latter's right flank. Both regiments were making exceptional progress and were poised to move south on the Raon L'Étape-Neaufmaisons road. German resistance was crumbling and the 397th's 1st Battalion was so far out in front that Regiment lost contact with it. The disposition of troops was conveyed to General Burress at Division quite literally in real time thanks to telephone and radio communications. Burress was at once aware that one full battalion was out of touch somewhere in hostile country, unaccounted for. He quickly radioed his old friend, the 397th commander Colonel William Ellis, and told him to promptly locate the missing battalion. Ellis was a World War I combat veteran and had been an instructor at Virginia Military Institute in the late 1930s.

The colonel took the order much too personally and promptly rounded up his driver and quickly drove off in his jeep, *leaving his situation map behind*. Unable to find the battalion, he pressed on and rounded a sharp curve only to run directly into a German patrol which reacted instantly. The battalion independently re-established contact with its regimental CP later that day. Ellis could have ordered a team from the 100th Reconnaissance Troop to find the missing unit, but it was too late. The bullet-riddled bodies of the colonel and his driver were found the next day.

The Germans, knowing that they could not defend Raon L'Étape, withdrew to the southeast with the Centurymen at their heels in a pursue and destroy mission. General Burress had planned on a fast pursuit built around supporting his infantry with the 100th Reconnaissance Troop, and outside assets including the 753rd Tank Battalion, the 69th Armored Field Artillery Battalion, and the 636th Tank Destroyer Battalion. The objective was to prevent the Germans from escaping south to Strasbourg by encircling and confining them between the La Plaine and Brouche Rivers.

The Germans, although in retreat, were still a dangerous enemy and prevented the task force from making rapid progress. In many ways, the trees of the Vosges forests were German allies. The thick forest made it difficult for infantry companies to stay in touch and protect each other's flanks. The terrain was difficult for armor, and the few available roads were so muddy and slippery that tanks had problems. The Germans shelled the advancing Americans with 88 mm cannons whose fused shells exploded in the treetops, creating tree bursts which spread shrapnel and deadly wood splinters in a much wider pattern compared to a shell hitting the earth. The massive trees, once felled, became effective roadblocks. Many roadblocks were mined and some were defended by both machine guns and snipers. Anti-personnel mines faced by Centurymen were of two varieties. The first was the *schu* mine which contained a nearly a half-pound of TNT in a small wooden box. Detonating one almost guaranteed losing a foot at the very least. A more diabolical weapon was the "Bouncing Betty" which popped up about one yard above the ground before exploding.

Making the pursuit even more dangerous was the fact that the Germans had roadblocks already zeroed in with artillery and heavy mortars. Jack's battalion joined with the 2nd Battalion and cleared Germans out of villages and defensive positions from Moyenmoutier up through Senones, Vieux Moulin, Le Vermont, and St. Blaise before completing its mission at Salm.

During the Century's service in Europe, non-secret communications into and out of the regimental headquarters were recorded on dictation equipment and later transcribed into typewritten form where they became part of the monthly operations report. The transcribed reports, officially known as "Infantry Journal: Messages, Incidents, and Orders" are comprised of division-regiment-battalion communications. Jack Rhea's name appears very frequently in these exchanges which read almost like a movie script in which the speaker's name is capitalized and the spoken sentences follow in what is quite literally a conversational tone, albeit usually very cryptic. The dialogue is difficult for the non-military oriented reader because it is abrupt, utilizes code names, frequently contains map reference numbers, and is full of military abbreviations. Nonetheless, through those reports, Jack Rhea's voice, frequently in the midst of battle, still speaks to us nearly seventy years after the division's six months of European combat. Occasionally Jack responds to the regimental commander's questions on what progress is being made, but more frequently the voice on the other end of the line was that of Major Robert Whitus or Captain Joseph Sowul of the regimental operations staff.

After reaching Moyenmoutier, Regiment called to ask Jack what progress had been made. Jack replied:

> RHEA: We kicked off this morning and took the town after we came down hill 578 and met no opposition going up the next hill. Occupied that hill and then into the town at 1130, but we still have a patrol up on that hill tonight. The people in this town were very glad to see American soldiers.

With Salm taken, the Vosges campaign was successfully winding down for the Century Division, although the Germans created problems during their retreat as another radio exchange illustrates; this conversation was between Jack and Captain Sowul of the regimental operations staff.

> RHEA: We're consolidating and organizing our positions right now for the big push tomorrow morning. Woods are full of snipers. They are near checkpoint 4. Col. Fooks feels he has control of it and has a request in that somebody get around that bridge and clean out those snipers because we would have to turn around if we do it. And we need that bridge crossing open for supplies.
>
> SOWUL: I'll see what I can do for you.

The division had accomplished something never done before in history: routed a defending army in the Vosges and forced that enemy to completely abandon the mountains. On 26 November, the division received orders transferring it from VI Corps to XV Corps. Jack moved back to the new battalion staging area at Moyenmoutier, just southeast of Raon L'Étape. The Germans were retreating to their next defensive position. The Centurymen of the 398th, after being trucked thirty miles north to a rest area at Troisfontaines, had a few easy days for care and cleaning of both themselves and their arms and equipment. Showers, clean clothing, and entertainment by the Division's special troops were enjoyed by all except the recon platoons which were actively gathering information on what was waiting out to the northeast. The troops were served a special Thanksgiving dinner with all of the trimmings – in pouring rain and cold, muddy surroundings.

Preparing for the Big Push

Before the move to Troisfontaines, nearly everybody assumed that the Century Division would race the 3rd Infantry Division and the 14th Armored Division to be the first to reach Strasbourg. It was not to be. The division expected to take Strasbourg as a prelude to crossing the Rhine and starting a push into southern Germany, particularly as it had just been congratulated for its Vosges performance by General Burress and his boss, Major General Edward Brooks, the VI Corps commander. Brooks had won a Distinguished Service Cross as an artilleryman in World War I and added a Silver Star at Normandy earlier in 1944 as the commander of the 2nd Armored Division.

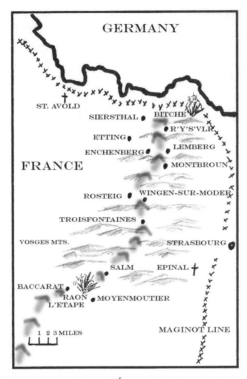

*After capturing Raon L'Étape, the Century Division
continued northeast, preparing to capture the
city of Bitche and drive German troops from the
Maginot forts back into Germany.*

At Supreme Headquarters Allied Expeditionary Forces (SHAEF), General Eisenhower decided that French forces would take Strasbourg and that the Century would be given a new assignment supporting the right flank of Gen. George Patton's Third Army as it prepared to move into Germany further north and break through the German Siegfried Line. Eisenhower saw overcoming the Siegfried Line as the cornerstone in his plan of a broad advance into Germany no matter how weak the Germans were in the upper Rhine River area beyond Strasbourg.

Jack Rhea's emphasis now swung to training instead of operations. The focus had a somewhat sinister aspect: assaulting hardened fortifications. Jack set up training exercises in special weapons with which the regiment's infantrymen had had only little experience up to that point:

Bangalore torpedoes, satchel charges, pole charges, beehive charges, and thermite grenades. The Bangalore torpedo was a long section of explosive pipe formed from shorter sections which was useful in clearing a path through barbed wire. The beehive charge, as its name implies, was a beehive-shaped, large metallic jug weighing nearly twenty-five pounds and supported by three short, squatty legs. It was intended to be placed up against a structure before detonation as was the satchel charge which could also be tossed into a structure. The pole charge was essentially a satchel charge mounted on a pole; if an opening could be found, such as one for a cannon or machine gun, the charge was shoved into the opening. Otherwise the pole could be stuck into the ground and the charge end leaned up against a bunker's outside wall prior to detonation. Thermite grenades were not strictly anti-personnel devices; rather they were designed to explode, releasing enough heat to fuse metal objects such as the moving parts of artillery pieces. Infantrymen had to be familiar with all of those explosive devices because they would be using them too, although those devices were normally intended for use primarily by the combat engineers. But what lurked ahead was not a normal target.

The explosive devices and assault training suggested that there was something monumental on the horizon. That something was truly monumental to say the least, and overpowering it would become central to the division's identity for all of its existence.

CHAPTER 8

Taking the Maginot Forts

Now as part of XV Corps, the Century Division would cross the Low
Vosges Mountains and secure that monumental obstacle, the Maginot
Line, in the vicinity of the city of Bitche. Specifically, Jack's regiment
was assigned to take out two of the Maginot's major strongholds, Fort
Freudenburg and Fort Schiesseck, both about one mile northwest of the
city, while the 399th would attack the city itself and the college that lay
before it. The 397th would attack Camp de Bitche, the military barracks to
the east of the city. To the left of the regiment, the 44th Infantry Division
would attack Maginot forts to the north. The city itself was a fortress town.
It was ideally laid out for defense, and had never been taken by an attacking
army in the 200 years since the massive hilltop citadel had been expanded
in the 1740s. The division was assigned a front nearly ten miles wide in terrain that was almost as difficult as the High Vosges.

The Maginot Line was the outcome of France's recognition of its inability to defend itself from Germany. Prior to 1940, France had been invaded
twice by the Germans in the previous seventy years: in the Franco-Prussian
War of 1870 and again in World War I. The great irony of the Maginot
Line is that, while designed to shield the French from the Germans, its
greatest use was by Germans against Americans, Britons, Canadians, and
other Allied Forces. The Maginot Line ran from the Belgian border to
Switzerland and from the southern Swiss border to the Mediterranean. The
latter section was built to defend against the Italians because the French
Army feared that the Italian dictator, Benito Mussolini, would someday
try to make good on his threats to take back the easternmost section of the
French Riviera which had been Italian territory prior to 1860. Construction
of the Maginot Line, named after French Minister of War André Maginot,
began in 1930 at great cost to the French national treasury.

In 1940, the Germans did not seriously try to break through the
Maginot Line; they made just enough noise along it to keep as many French
troops as possible in the forts occupied and unavailable for fighting elsewhere. Rather, the German *Blitzkrieg* simply avoided a costly fight over the

Maginot Line and invaded France via Belgium by storming through the Ardennes Forest.

The Maginot Line consisted of a long series of *ouvrages* (forts, small and large), moats, casemates (reinforced fortifications with at least one exposed face, firing cannons), pillboxes, *cloches* (rounded turret-like domes used for observation or firing light weapons), and retractable, armored turrets. There were massive underground complexes complete with environmental systems, subways to move troops between various sections of a fort complex, kitchens, and powered hoists to lift ammunition up to the guns. Freudenberg was a single casemate while Schiesseck was a complex consisting of eleven structures.

National Archives

Century infantrymen covering the advance into Rosteig.

On 1 December, Jack's regiment was alerted for possible movement to Metting, and on the next day the 1st and 2nd Battalion commanders were given orders to seize Wingen sur Moder and Puberg respectively while Jack's 3rd battalion was briefly held in reserve. Holding a regiment, battalion or company in reserve, typically to the rear center of the other units, was a common and prudent tactic. On 2 December the battalion moved into its forward assembly area at La Petite Pierre, and over the next two days moved to the northeast and seized Rosteig and surrounding high ground. The Germans put up a stiff resistance; two Centurymen were killed and fourteen wounded in fighting on that high ground bordering the town. At this point, the regiment had taken nearly 170 German POWs.

The Tragedy at Wingen-sur-Moder

While the battalion was taking Rosteig and surrounding high country, the 1st Battalion's Company A was approaching Wingen. Knowing what happened to that company clearly shows what a pivotal position Jack Rhea played in the 3rd Battalion and grimly reminds us of the consequences of a battalion or regimental commander not following the well-reasoned advice of his operations officer, or conversely, blindly accepting a flawed recommendation.

The dreadful scenario played out during the night of 3 December in the French village of Wingen. Accompanied by an observation team from the 375th Field Artillery and members of the 1st Battalion's heavy weapons company, Company A approached the village very late in the afternoon and was under artillery and automatic weapons fire. Having suffered some casualties already, the company commander was in contact with his superiors using the telephone line that had been laid that afternoon. The captain was bluntly told to take the village immediately. The captain pointed out the disadvantages of such an order, suggesting that the attack be launched in the morning instead. He also provided a clear assessment of the situation which included the facts that the company was already taking casualties under heavy fire, and it was very late in the day with promise of a pitch black night considering the totally overcast sky. There was a complete lack of artillery support, and the company was miles from its ammunition resupply point. The captain did not mention the fact that his troops were still relatively inexperienced.

The German unit facing the company, the 361st Volks Grenadier Division, was a relatively new unit; its predecessor organizations had basically been destroyed on the Eastern Front, although its leadership was very experienced. The newly reformed division included an experienced infantry cadre and retrained, former members of the *Luftwaffe* whose decimation left many of its members subject to transfer into the German army. The division even included a few former *Kriegsmarine* personnel. Still, it was not a completely inexperienced division; it had been battling Americans in the Vosges since early autumn.

The captain was forcefully ordered to start his attack promptly and take Wingen that night without fail. Having no other alternative, the captain led the attack in total darkness, not knowing that the Germans were preparing to surround the company after it occupied Wingen. As the company approached the town, the heavy, sustained German mortar barrage increasingly burst behind the Americans, making any retreat inadvisable. The German automatic weapons fire increased, forcing the company's platoons to seek shelter in several buildings. Those houses, in effect, became nothing more than traps into which the Germans could keep American heads down with machine gun fire while tossing grenades into those homes where most of the Centurymen had holed up in basements along with the town's inhabitants. The Germans demanded surrender in the morning, and the outnumbered, outgunned Americans really had no other option.

There were very few American survivors; some of those wounded early in the assault managed to retreat to the company aid station as the attack got under way, and several others broke free of the trap under cover of darkness. A handful of wounded soldiers avoided capture by hiding in a cellar overlooked by the Germans. Including the field artillery observers and members of the heavy weapons company attached to Company A, about 120 men were reported as missing in action. The rest of the 1st Battalion, with artillery support and tank destroyers from the 4th Armored Division, took Wingen by the afternoon of 5 December. Only then did they learn from French civilians that the better part of a company along with supporting troops had been taken prisoner and moved out for interrogation and shipment to prisoner-of-war camps.

General Burress acted decisively upon news that an entire company had been needlessly sacrificed. The 398th Regiment's commander, Colonel Nelson I. Fooks, was sacked and transferred. Being relieved of his command was career-threatening for Fooks, a West Point graduate and former instructor at the Academy. It was a sobering lesson certainly not lost upon Captain Jack Rhea.

The morning report for 10 December recorded some major changes in the battalion staff. The day before, Lt. Col. Floyd Stayton was moved up to the regimental staff as the executive officer, and his place was taken by the battalion's executive officer, Major Ernest Janes. Jack Rhea was moved from S-3 to battalion executive officer, and his place was taken by Lt. Bernard Boston who had been the intelligence officer. Taking Boston's slot was Lt. Burnus Payne, an Arkansan who had been a platoon leader in K Company which Jack had commanded in 1943. Payne was another of Jack's wartime friends, but in the process became better known by his nickname from K Company, "Payne-Less." As second in command of the battalion, Jack supervised the intelligence, operations, and supply functions. When the now Lt. Col. Janes was not at the command post, Jack was in charge of the battalion.

Several days later, Colonel Paul Daly, a World War I veteran, was sent in to become the regiment's new leader, taking the place of Col. Fooks. Daly arrived at the Century Division via Guadalcanal in the Pacific war. That he was a brave man could easily be confirmed by the ribbons on his tunic which included the Distinguished Service Cross, Silver Star, Bronze Star,

several foreign decorations, and three Purple Hearts. He had twice been nominated for the Medal of Honor. Ironically, his son, Michael, was to win the Medal of Honor several months later in Germany as a company commander with the Century's neighbor, the 3rd Infantry Division. Col. Daly had a reputation as a hard-charging commander who preferred to lead from the front of his regiment, a tendency that would soon provide him with a fourth Purple Heart and prove to be very nearly fatal.

The 10 December date would remain important to Jack for another reason. He would be decorated with the Bronze Star for gallantry in action on that date while the regiment was advancing from Rosteig through Meisenthal and St. Louis before taking Reyersviller on 13 December. With Reyersviller taken, the Centurymen had leaped the last major hurdle before attacking the Maginot Line proper. In that action, Jack's regiment took the high ground surrounding Reyersviller following a rolling barrage from the 375th Field Artillery Battalion, but still faced some opposition from snipers. The regiment's 2nd Battalion had actually reached the edge of the Maginot Line and was now the target of its heavy guns, some of which were as large as 135 mm. In the city of Bitche, the Germans had their deadly 88 mm cannons firing on the division's positions.

100th Infantry Division Archives, Marshall Foundation

A light machine gun crew from Jack's regiment moves out
toward the Maginot Line.

The advance to Reyersviller had proven to be a problem due to road-blocks, artillery, and mortar fire. Although the battalion cleared the way to the east of Lemberg, the town itself was taken by the 399th after several days of savage fighting in which well over 120 Centurymen of the 399th were killed. On 10 December, Jack had been placed in command of the battalion because the battalion commander was on a reconnaissance mission with the 100th Recon Troop. His orders were to move the battalion out of St. Louis to a position near Lemberg. As the lead company advanced toward the objective, German artillery started hitting it with great accuracy. As it became obvious that proceeding on the planned route would lead to even more carnage, Jack quickly advanced to the head of the column and was promptly knocked to the ground by an artillery shell which exploded only yards away from him. Miraculously, he was not hit by any of the resulting shrapnel. Although momentarily dazed and disoriented, Jack regained his feet and immediately selected a new route to the position near Lemberg – a route that was not in view of German artillery observers who had been directing such deadly fire. The Bronze Star citation referenced Jack's personal valor, magnificent courage, and utter disregard for personal safety while personally leading the battalion out of the trap.

Enemy resistance was strengthening, and Jack's battalion was still subjected to considerable mortar and artillery fire. The battalion had established its command post back in Lemberg prior to the assault on Reyersviller which was the last obstacle taken before reaching the Maginot Line proper. The regiment's thrust carried it several miles past Reyersviller and into range of the Maginot Line's artillery which promptly opened up on the Americans.

At that point, the Century had not yet requested much air support. Many infantrymen thought that Army Air Force aircrews got more than their share of decorations and fast promotions, especially considering how young most of them were. There was a serious downside to combat flying and Jack saw a depressing example of that while pausing near Reyersviller. It was a B-26 Marauder medium bomber flying low, but still straight and level, pouring a long plume of greasy, black smoke from one engine. The bomber bored on right over the battalion and plowed straight into one of the ridges surrounding Reyersviller and exploded in a massive fireball of flame and smoke. Jack never found out if the crew went in with their ship or if they had put the Marauder on autopilot and bailed out over enemy territory.

Assaulting the Maginot Forts

On 14 December, a cool day with fair visibility, the regiment began its assault of the Maginot Line following a heavy artillery barrage with the 1st Battalion leading. While the lighter defenses were breached, the special explosive charges were not enough to destroy Freudenberg, although the battalion poured much fire into the slits and apertures that they could reach. Murderous crossfire from the Maginot's pillboxes forced the 1st Battalion to withdraw. General Burress now had a problem that looked like only very heavy artillery and the Army Air Force could solve. Accordingly, on the next day, Freudenberg and Schiesseck were subjected to bombardment by very heavy artillery. Even direct hits by 240 mm howitzers did little more than leave blackened pock marks on the casemates.

324th Fighter Group Association via Doug Patteson

*P-47 Thunderbolts from the 324th Fighter Group provided tactical air
support for the 100th Division. Shown above is a P-47 from the group's
316th Fighter Squadron.*

The forts were worked over by P-47 Thunderbolt fighter-bombers from the
324th Fighter Group, based about twenty miles southeast of Dijon at Tavaux.
The group's three squadrons flew over fifty sorties, dropping 500-pound demolition bombs with little or no visible effect. Schiesseck was a tough nut to crack;
it was rated as one of the four strongest forts in the entire Maginot Line.

Coordinating such attacks and providing information to the division intelligence officers were the pilots and photo-interpreters from the
111th Tactical Reconnaissance Squadron, based at Azelot, near Nancy.
The squadron had trained in P-39s, flown in North Africa and Italy with
unarmed Spitfires and Lightnings, and were now flying hot, new ships with
cameras and guns: F-6s, the photo version of the P-51 Mustang. The 111th's
pilots could now defend themselves while reporting enemy troop movements, defenses at bridges and other fortifications, rail traffic, and other
essential information important to infantry operations and intelligence

officers. Unlike the 7th PRG whose mission was supporting the strategic objectives of the Eighth Army Air Force, much of the 111th's work, and that of other Ninth and Twelfth Army Air Force tactical recon groups, was in direct benefit of the infantryman on the ground. Eventually the 111th would be assigned to the 10th Photographic Reconnaissance Group which had participated in the Tennessee Maneuvers with the Century Division.

On 17 December, a very clear day, the regiment again attacked Freudenberg and Schiesseck following a rolling artillery barrage and more P-47 Thunderbolt bombing. The combined rain of steel and high explosive on the Maginot forts drove many German defenders, usually badly stunned, deeper underground. Freudenberg had been solidly hit by one 240 mm shell, after which seven Germans walked out under a white flag of surrender. That fort was out of business and quickly became the battalion command post. Unlike Schiesseck, it was not connected by passageways to other Maginot forts. There was no cover on the final dash to the Schiesseck forts; the edge of the bordering woods was several hundred yards away from the steel and concrete casemates. Men of the 3rd Battalion were heavily armed; each squad had a bazooka, satchel charges, and pole charges. Each man carried two thermite grenades and two regular grenades. The regimental commander, Colonel Paul Daly, was out in front and was very badly hit in the leg. The wound was not life-threatening, but was serious enough to require his prompt evacuation.

General Burress immediately replaced him with Major Robert M. Williams who had proven himself as commander of the 3rd Battalion, 399th Infantry. Williams, a native of Austin, Texas, was a rising star in the Regular Army and a 1938 graduate of Texas A&M University. Speaking fluent Spanish, he had done a pre-war tour in Panama prior to his return to the States after Pearl Harbor. He would very soon be a full colonel and one of the youngest regimental commanders in the United States Army.

The battalion's assault on the Schiesseck forts continued through 18 December. Regiment was anxious about the 3rd Battalion's progress as this telephone exchange clearly shows:

> MAJOR WHITUS: Where did you get the info about that
> Co. in the draw?
> RHEA: From a recon sgt. In the 44th in 755-515 just above
> Freudenburg Farm.
> WHITUS: What you got in front of you?

RHEA: Not much, they think there are some Jerries in the tunnels. In front, they are reported to have captured two of our men and one medic. We can't blast them because we don't know which tunnels they are in.

WHITUS: See if you can find out anything else, then call us back.

RHEA: L Company is reported to be in fort #3. They were getting into #2 when an MG opened up on five men, killed one, injured one, and captured two. They still have two men and a medic in #2. I Company is pretty bad off, all shot up. They are trying to reorganize now.

100th Inf. Division Collection, Marshall Foundation

Col. Robert Williams, the 398th C.O., inspects one of the Schiesseck forts after the battle.

Many Centurymen fell, but a combination of several tactics prevailed. Both tanks and tank destroyers were brought up to nearly point blank range before firing. Regiment called Jack just before the tanks arrived and ordered him to arrange for infantry guides to accompany the tanks. Heavy artillery barrages kept the Germans hunkered down long enough for infantry to race across open ground to get into position right against the forts' walls. As much as a ton and a half of explosives could not immediately breach walls of the

Schiesseck units because they could be up to twelve feet thick. However, the combat engineers, with twenty-five pound beehive-shaped charges, and infantrymen were able to locate enough apertures, ventilation shafts, and other openings to be able to toss in an adequate number of satchel and pole charges to kill or disable the defenders or at least drive them far down into the forts' depths. Very heavy 155 mm artillery had been brought up to fire at ultra-close range. Germans behind the fort's great steel doors were ordered to surrender, and some did. The combat engineers welded the steel doors shut at those fort entrances where hard-core Germans refused to give up.

By 19 December, Jack's battalion had largely secured Schiesseck, although the battalion had to rout a German counterattack that materialized from one of the underground bunkers. A "Tank-Dozer" with an attached bulldozer blade moved many tons of earth, burying as many above-ground Schiesseck units as possible beginning on 20 December. The cost of taking Freudenberg and Schiesseck could have been much worse, considering what was accomplished; of the nearly 730 officers and men in Jack's 3rd Battalion at that point, sixteen were killed and 120 were wounded. The battalion's riflemen did a good job of protecting the combat engineers who suffered only three casualties.

The regiment's other two battalions had seized the high ground north of Schiesseck, overlooking Bitche; the regiment now controlled the heights on the city's western side while the other two regiments had moved on Bitche from the south. The 399th Regiment took College de Bitche on the south side of town while the 397th Regiment attacked and held the main road to the east of Bitche.

The 3rd Battalion of the 398th Infantry Regiment would later receive notice that it had been awarded a Presidential Unit Citation for its role in taking Forts Freudenberg and Schiesseck. The citation, the first one awarded to a full battalion in the Century Division, was not just for the battalion leadership and the officers, riflemen, and scouts in the four companies; it was intended for every soldier because they had all made a contribution. That included the communications platoon linemen who risked life and limb to lay telephone wire and splice it after it had been hit by artillery; radio operators; pioneer troops who carried ammunition to those in direct contact with the Germans; the combat medics; and all others who comprised the 3rd Bn., 398th Infantry Regiment.

This German walked out of one of the Schiesseck forts and surrendered to combat engineers, was interrogated at 3rd Battalion command post.

The battalion's opponents in Freudenberg and Schiesseck were from the 25th Panzer Grenadier Division. That was a once proud division that had fought across Poland and France, but had been nearly annihilated at Minsk, in Russia. Normally such a division would have had a strength of nearly 14,000 men, but when it encountered the 100th, its numbers were closer to 7,000 – still an intimidating force.

Helping Contain the Bulge

Under normal circumstances, the regiment would have expected to immediately capitalize on its success by taking the city of Bitche and driving the Germans farther to the east. That was not going to happen because a mid-December German offensive to the north had taken the Allies by surprise, so much so that General Eisenhower had to temporarily abandon his goal of pushing the Germans eastward on a broad front. Rather, he had to blunt the German push through the Ardennes that would culminate in the Battle of the Bulge. Eisenhower's immediate need was to move forces to the vicinity of Bastogne in Belgium to stop the German advance. To do so would weaken American lines from which he had withdrawn forces for the rescue mission. The regiment was especially exposed considering how far it had advanced and the fact that many of the armor and heavy artillery assets it had come to rely upon were no longer available. Thus, the order was given to the 100th Division to abandon its newly-won territory and withdraw to defensive positions to the west. It was also feared that the sectors occupied by the 44th and 100th Divisions might be the target of another major German thrust. The war, for the time being, was headed for a stalemate in which offensive action was limited to small scale raids and intelligence gathering.

Jack had more than just a professional interest in how the Battle of the Bulge was going. The 75th Infantry Division, and with it his brother Ralph, had been moved into the northern flank of the Bulge and was now in combat with the attacking Germans.

On that clear and very cold Christmas Day 1944, the regiment was headquartered in Enchenburg to the southwest of Bitche while Jack's command post was in Sierstahl, several miles to the west of Bitche. The division initiated a policy whereby each regiment would keep two battalions on the line and the remaining battalion would be in reserve, centrally located behind the other two. Jack Rhea's living conditions during this period, and indeed during the entire period from landing in Marseille until VE Day, cannot be described as comfortable. They were however, much better than the situation faced by the average enlisted soldier assigned to a forward position. Unless the battalion headquarters was on the move, Jack could expect hot, cooked meals from the battalion headquarters field kitchen. Even a rifleman in a forward position during this relatively static period could usually rely on one hot meal a day. When the battalion was in reserve and in a small town or village, the troops could expect to bed down in a commandeered house, barn, inn, or retail shop. Jack did not have to march with a full pack, carrying a nine-pound M-1 rifle when the battalion moved, although in fluid situations he occasionally had to move on foot when a command post or observation post was in difficult terrain. Otherwise he moved by jeep.

Jack had to eat Army C-rations and K-rations when the battalion staff was in transit between locations. As a result, he probably never had a lot of patience with any Philmont rangers who complained about a steady diet of trail food. Indeed, during Jack's tour at Philmont, rangers invariably had a hot cooked breakfast and supper during their first day or two with camper groups, particularly if they were in large camps like Rayado, Cimarroncito, or Ponil. Like any army, the 100th took from the land what it might bear – local cheese, preserved fruit, the occasional pig, etc. Life expectancy for a free range chicken could be remarkably short considering the need for more calories, readily available ammunition, and very high standard of marksmanship. For the most part, men in the rifle companies ate K-rations when in combat. K-rations included dehydrated foods, the ubiquitous Spam (the meal's highlight), plenty of crackers, jelly, instant coffee, a Velveeta-like cheese, chocolate bars, and something which resembled powdered eggs. In other words, except for the coffee, K-rations bore a remarkable resemblance to Philmont trail food in the 1950s and early 1960s. C-rations were generally more popular and typically consisted of canned entrees, practically emulating the menus of Philmont dehydrated trail suppers which followed a decade later: beef stew, spaghetti, hot dogs and beans, powdered fruit drinks, and chocolate bars. Considering the cold weather and the physical challenges faced by riflemen, nobody gained weight with a steady diet of C or K-rations. Based on captured German rations, Centurymen concluded that the Allied side had, by far, the better rations.

Combatants of all sides had nicknames for their opponents. Like most Centurymen, Jack usually referred to the Germans as "Jerries" and occasionally as "Krauts." Friend and foe alike called the Americans "Yanks." Sometimes, a German soldier based in France might refer to a Yank as an "Ami" ("friend" in French) because that term was frequently used by the French when referring to an Allied soldier. There were no Brits in the 100th Division sector, but the Germans usually referred to British infantrymen as "Tommies." British soldiers typically used the term "Jerry" for a German. Members of the Royal Air Force, an organization well known for generating wartime slang, had another name for Germans: "the Huns." The French forces were located to the south of the 100th Division, so there was little contact between the two groups prior to the Occupation. There was not a lot of respect for the average French soldier of 1944, by German or American. In a disparaging mood, the average Yank would call his opposite French number a "frog." When referring to a fellow American soldier, a Centuryman occasionally used the word, "Dough." It was short for what the Centuryman's father had most likely been, a World War I "Doughboy."

On 27 December, Jack was awarded the Combat Infantryman's Badge (CIB), as was everybody else in the battalion. The award went to all infantrymen actively serving in an infantry unit while that unit was under hostile fire. The award was instituted earlier in the war to recognize those men who were at greatest risk of being killed in action. For Jack and all officers, the award had an important symbolic value, but did not include any increase in financial compensation as it did for enlisted men. For the enlisted men, the CIB brought with it an additional ten dollars in monthly pay. Added to that was another ten bucks for overseas duty. Needless to say, those twenty bucks went farther, much farther than they do today.

Over the next several weeks, Jack's command post location changed occasionally as the battalion alternated between positions in reserve and on the line. Jack's responsibility had moved from direct operations and training to supervising those functions. His replacement as S-3, Lt. Bernard Boston, was initiating new training to fit the "hit and run raid - take prisoners - ambush German patrols" mode that the battalion was now in. General Burress ordered the planting of hundreds of mines in areas from which he expected a large scale German offensive. Miles of phone wire were laid and new observation posts were established. Still, the defense was thin; the 100th was holding a front that would normally be covered by three divisions.

The battalion was complying with orders to take more prisoners; interrogation revealed that the families of any German soldier deserting would be punished. Although forbidden to talk about the progress of the war, or lack of it, the average German soldier could see the handwriting on the wall and certainly saw becoming a POW as a better outcome than being KIA (killed in action). There is an ironic story within the 100th Division that relates how one of its riflemen fell asleep while on night outpost duty. At first light, the dozing soldier woke up only to be startled by a smiling

German sitting next to him. Although the German was delighted to have been "captured," he had taken the precaution of disassembling the snoozing American's M-1 just to be sure there would be no misunderstanding.

On New Year's Day 1945, a cold, clear day with excellent visibility, the long expected German attack named Operation *Nordwind* (Northwind) came, although the brunt of it was absorbed by the 399th on the regiment's right flank. To blunt the attack, General Burress used what reinforcements he had, particularly his own 100th Reconnaissance Troop and another outside asset, the as yet unblooded 255th Infantry Regiment, which had just come up to the line. The Germans had very aggressive goals for *Nordwind*: recapturing Strasbourg and destroying the 100th Division in the process. Most companies in Jack's battalion were not in direct contact with German infantry during *Nordwind*, although K Company was briefly assigned to the 399th Regiment to cope with the German onslaught by helping to set up a defensive line around Lemberg. The battalion itself was subjected to nearly constant shelling by German heavy artillery, mortars, and rockets which wounded a number of men, although none of them required evacuation. At first, it looked as though Jack's headquarters company would very definitely be in contact because rear echelon elements of the 399th and its supporting artillery were suddenly streaming through the 3rd Battalion command post area.

Simultaneously, Regiment ordered Jack's battalion to dig in – not an easy task considering the ground was frozen solid. As it turned out, the 399th combat team and General Burress' reinforcements were able to blunt the German attack and finally stop it after giving up nearly two miles. The German advance was halted at Lemberg which had been the site of fierce fighting only several weeks before. The Century had lost some territory in falling back to Lemberg, but then its units had been opposed by two full divisions and the better part of another division. Had the Century, with the support of outside assets, failed to stop the enemy, the Germans had two *Panzer* divisions in reserve, just waiting for the opportunity to use the road through Lemberg. Had that occurred, Eisenhower would have had another "bulge" to deal with.

Early on that New Year's morning scores of Messerschmitt 109 fighter-bombers from *Jagdgeschwader* 53 (fighter wing) flew low over the Century's left flank. They were not out to strafe Jack or other American ground troops; rather, they were in the vanguard of the *Luftwaffe's* Operation *Bodenplatte* (Baseplate). The operation was actually initiated about two weeks late due to the atrocious flying weather in late December and had been originally planned to coincide with the German push through the Ardennes. Every *Luftwaffe* fighter wing in the western defense of the Reich was involved, and their targets were all of the key Allied airfields in Holland, Belgium, and France. JG53, with its three groups taking off from bases around Stuttgart, struck at the big 9th Air Force fighter base at Metz where they destroyed twenty Thunderbolts and damaged another eleven. Within a few days, more Thunderbolts were flown in from England. The *Luftwaffe*, although it could replace lost aircraft, could not replace over 200 of its pilots, including many of its remaining *Experten* (aces), who were killed by anti-aircraft fire and patrolling fighters. It was a blow from which the *Luftwaffe* never recovered. Fortunately, those Army Air Force units directly supporting the Century, being located well south of Metz, were not targets of Operation Baseplate.

By the end of the first week of the New Year, Jack Rhea was in the battalion reserve area, but still threatened by heavy artillery and mortar fire. Having been stopped at Lemberg, the Germans shifted their forces farther to the east, and within a week the 100th Division gained back the ground it had given up during the first phase of *Nordwind*. The Germans, however, continued to probe American lines, and Centurymen responded with more listening posts, ambush patrols, and warning devices such as trip flares which were useful at night. It is hard to say who was most tense when a trip flare went off: the waiting American with finger on his M-1's trigger guard, the German who expected to be cut down in the next few seconds, or, occasionally, some little wild animal which set off one of the devices.

Jack's second Bronze Star was recommended and later awarded not for a single action as at Lemberg, but for his meritorious service and devotion to duty from early November to mid-December. The citation referenced his ability to quickly visualize the situation and plan accordingly throughout two important actions: driving the Germans from Raon L'Etape and the assault on Freudenberg and Schiesseck. Lt. Colonel Janes, who initiated the award, capped it off by saying, "Any success that the 3rd Bn, 398th Infantry has had in combat has been due in part to the outstanding ability and devotion to duty of Capt. Rhea." Janes, in the award recommendation dated 6 January 1945, also noted that the award had been won during a period when Capt. Rhea had been under both small arms and artillery fire.

The battalion moved to Etting during the second week in January when the war was becoming increasingly nocturnal. The *Luftwaffe* was practically on its last legs, but a pair of Messerschmitt 109 fighters strafed the 398th's 2nd Battalion command post on 2 January. The attached 898th Anti-Aircraft Artillery Battalion confirmed the destruction of one of them. More destructive were "friendly fire" incidents in which American Thunderbolt and Mustang fighters mistakenly strafed Century Division positions several times later in January. Those tragic accidents were so damaging that the division had a number of Army Air Force fighter jocks ordered in as observers to bring pilots up to speed on how to avoid killing friendlies. Adding to the difficulty was an occasional confirmed strafing by the *Luftwaffe* using captured American fighters still in their American markings.

On 9 January 1945, there was another change in the battalion staff. During the attack on the Maginot forts in December, L Company commander Capt. Robert E. Brinkerhoff, from Knoxville, Tennessee, had been wounded in an action that also won him a Silver Star. Lt. Col. Janes was reluctant to lose Brinkerhoff's services, so he was brought in to replace Jack Rhea as the 3rd Battalion executive officer. Any German infantryman was justified in fearing Captain Brinkerhoff, a bellicose, very tall, and quite imposing man. Jack moved back to the S-3 job for the time being, and Bernard Boston left the S-3 spot and moved out to the line with L Company. Originally from North Jersey like Boston and Kleinwaks, Brinkerhoff had graduated from the University of Tennessee in 1941 with a degree in business administration.

Particular emphasis was placed on capturing prisoners and strengthening defenses. More barbed wire and concertina wire were strung. More mines were laid and cannons and mortars zeroed in on likely German approaches in case the attack was renewed. Occasionally, German and American patrols clashed, but for the most part the battalion's greatest threat was falling artillery. It was a very, very difficult time for the riflemen, forced to live out in the open with only the minimal shelter of a foxhole and winter clothing that was not really adequate. Making matters worse was the fact that the winter of 1944-45 was the coldest by far in recent memory with plenty of snow and record low temperatures. Pneumonia, hepatitis, frostbite, and trenchfoot weakened the division's strength, although replacements were steadily coming in.

Problems with feet were legion and not really helped by a controversial addition to the Army combat clothing: the shoepack, which resembled a rubber-bottomed, leather-topped lace-up L.L. Bean hunting boot of the 1940s and '50s. Standard Army footwear was a sturdy ankle-length leather shoe with durable rubber sole. The shoes were worn in the field with leggings which were identical to the Boy Scout leggings of the post-war era. The shoes and leggings were later replaced with the familiar combat boots which featured wrap-around tops and buckles. In rain and mud, the shoepack offered the tremendous advantage of keeping the water out, although it did so at the expense of very little support for the foot. Just as it kept water out, it also kept perspiration in which promptly froze if the wearer did not keep moving and/ or changing his socks frequently. Centurymen quickly learned the value of wearing clothing in layers – as many layers as possible.

Holding the Line

On 20 January, the regiment packed up and moved its headquarters to Montbroun with which it was quite familiar having passed through it on the way to attack Bitche. Jack's battalion took up defensive positions back in Lemberg, relieving the 3rd battalion of the 141st Regiment. Jack's activities during this period were dominated by sending out patrols to take prisoners and destroy German gun positions. The nocturnal patrols were aided by a novel development. The attached anti-aircraft battalion switched on their searchlights when the cloud ceiling was low, aimed them at the overcast, and the some of the light was reflected back to earth, partially illuminating suspected German positions.

The regimental weather log for the rest of January recorded a lot of cold, rain, snow, and poor visibility. The regimental bag of POWs taken topped 350 by 1 February. Interrogation showed that the Germans expected to be attacked in strength. Increasing numbers of POWs indicated that German morale was sinking fast which was not helped by threats of death to the families of deserters. Word reached Jack that his brother Ralph had been badly wounded during the Battle of the Bulge. The wound was not serious enough to assure a ticket back to the States, but it did require his evacuation to a hospital in England.

General Burress was doing what he could to maintain 100th Division morale. That included two hot, cooked meals every day for men on the line and an occasional pass to a rest area well in back of the lines. The rest areas were not resorts, but at least the food was a major improvement, there were hot showers and clean clothes, and there was no need to worry about falling artillery.

On 12 February, Jack Rhea left the division for six days of detached duty at the Army Information and Education School which was located at the Cité Universitaire in Paris. The assignment reflected the Army's growing awareness of the eventual occupation of Germany and the demands that would place on operations officers, particularly as it related to training soldiers for that assignment. The weather during this period had improved significantly, remaining mild and clear during much of Jack's absence. Jack missed a little excitement on 17 February when a raiding platoon from his battalion caught a group of Germans out in the open, exposed by light from flares, and killed or wounded fifteen of the enemy without loss. For the next several weeks, German artillery was used more sparingly with emphasis on hitting the 100th's forward positions only. By early March, the temperature was starting to moderate. The skies were clearing, but there was plenty of mud on the ground. When Jack returned from Paris, he had another opportunity to put his ranger experience to good use: continued training of raider platoons and assigning them to night operations.

Spirits were lifted by the occasional 72-hour pass to Brussels or Paris. More replacements, officially called "reinforcements," were coming from the depot in Nancy. An increasing number of non-commissioned officers were getting battlefield commissions, a trend that was greeted with great favor by the troops. That brought General Burress even closer to his Centurymen.

100th Infantry Division Archives, Marshall Foundation

During the six months it was in combat, Jack Rhea's regiment captured nearly 2,000 German soldiers.

The new training schedules issued by Captain Rhea were not greeted with any enthusiasm: instruction in assaulting hardened forts. By 14 March, Jack's battalion had moved to Enchenberg. Interrogation of prisoners revealed that the division's propaganda war was having an effect. During this period, the division's artillery battalions had been firing shells loaded with safe-conduct passes, and loudspeakers had been brought up to the forward positions to announce guaranteed good treatment for prisoners. One German POW indicated that half of his company would surrender if given the right opportunity. It was clear to all that the Century Division was about to go on the offensive, particularly since word was received that the Rhine had already been crossed to the north – at a place called Remagen. Then the plan was revealed.

Taking the Forts – Again

The 100th was to again take the Maginot forts, the city of Bitche, and its citadel along with Camp de Bitche. The 100th's old partners, the 3rd and 45th Divisions would be on the Century's left flank while the 71st Infantry Division would be on the right. The Germans in Bitche may have escaped the Century's direct attention during the recent stalemate, but they had not led carefree lives either. The 324th Fighter Group's Thunderbolts had visited Bitche several times in recent weeks on bombing and strafing missions. Once Bitche was secured, the 100th would pivot to the left, head north, and join its partners assaulting the German Siegfried Line. Burress was now approaching the city from the west with the 398th in the center. The attack was launched early in the morning of 15 March, supported by punishing artillery. During the assault, the 1st and 2nd Battalions led with Jack's battalion in reserve. In effect, the other two battalions were attacking through much of the same territory that the 3rd Battalion had covered in the first assault on the Maginot forts. The 1st Battalion succeeded in taking its objective, the high country near Schorbach while the 2nd Battalion took Freudenburg, Schiesseck, and more high ground northwest of Bitche.

Resistance from German troops was light, but German artillery, mortars, *schu* mines, and rockets created many casualties. The anti-personnel mines had been very cleverly laid out by the Germans, and it was only with great difficulty while under fire that the engineers were able to probe for and remove them. On the next day, the 1st Battalion neutralized the remaining forts in its area, finding that the Germans had not occupied the major units. The dynamiting and earth-moving carried out by the regiment in December had worked. Since they could not use the forts, the Germans simply dug in around them and became particularly vulnerable to Century artillery, mortars, and machine guns. Jack took several photos of the battle's aftermath, and although the pictures were not crisp, they do show complete devastation: trees blasted into nothing more than splinters sticking up from the earth; a landscape completely devoid of bushes, trees, and shrubbery; crater after crater of mud and dirt from the shelling and bombing; and the forts' battered, but still standing, pockmarked concrete walls.

100th Infantry Division Archives, Marshall Foundation

In one of the most iconic photos to come out of the war in Europe, Capt.
Thomas Garahan unfurls the American flag in downtown Bitche.

The 2nd Battalion occupied the city of Bitche through which Jack's
battalion passed on its way to Camp de Bitche which it seized jointly with
the 399th after a day-long battle. The Germans chose not to defend down-

town Bitche, so not a shot was fired there. At that point, nobody in the Century Division knew that in just several weeks, they would be involved in some of the worst building-to-building, street fighting of the entire war. Outside of center city Bitche, some German armor, including several heavy Tiger tanks, threatened for a while but retreated when one of their number was disabled, leaving Campe de Bitche lightly defended.

The trap was closed when the 397th also joined the fight at Campe de Bitche, thus ending the Century's conquest of a fortress city that had not been taken by any army in 200 years of conflicts. Except for some die-hard snipers, the Germans had largely abandoned the city. To try to escape the fighting, the citizens of Bitche hid in their cellars and others found shelter deep in the recesses of the citadel on the hill.

The French citizens of Bitche had been devastated when the 100th Division fell back to defensive positions in December. There was great joy when Bitche was finally liberated in March after four years of harsh, German occupation. There was great sadness too; thirty-five French civilians were killed in the taking of Bitche, 120 wounded, over 100 houses were destroyed, and almost 700 buildings were damaged.

Over the next two days, the regiment moved to its new assembly area near Schorbach. Except when in actual combat, most soldiers in rear areas had access to Armed Forces Radio which played music, variety, and news programs. Any broadcast could be interrupted locally through the battalion communications section. Jack Rhea, who had briefly been nicknamed "Texas Jack" because of his Scouting connection in Wichita Falls, interrupted an evening broadcast on 17 March. He broke in with the first news of the 3rd Battalion being awarded a Presidential Unit Citation for its December 1944 performance in taking out Forts Freudenberg and Schiesseck.

The regiment had taken over 500 prisoners to date and based on gathered intelligence it appeared that the Germans were having difficulties making it costly for Americans to pursue them. The Century's neighbors, the 3rd and 45th Divisions, had already crossed the Rhine in their sectors. Now it was the 100th's turn; crossing the Rhine and pushing into Germany at last. The Century Division had been severely tested in combat and not found wanting. The many, many months of training in the United States and General Burress' well-reasoned strategies had certainly paid off.

CHAPTER 9

Into Germany

The regiment remained in Bitche for several days. Showers were available, cooked meals were enjoyed, and Jack was again involved in setting up training schedules, particularly for new replacements. Then on 22 March, the regiment departed Bitche to catch up with the other two regiments which had already moved out to the northeast. General Burress had planned a fast, motorized thrust to cross the Rhine in the vicinity of Ludwigshaven; this goal was reached on 24 March when the 399th crossed the Rhine. The city itself had been well and truly flattened by the Eighth Army Air Force, and the only opposition in reaching the city was from snipers, a problem the Centurymen were experienced in handling.

Jack Rhea's jeep was literally speeding – covering twenty to thirty miles or more a day. Germans were surrendering in droves. The roads on which the Century moved were littered with disabled German armor which testified to the effectiveness of Allied fighter-bombers. Jack was now faced with setting up training programs designed to deal with the battalion's new circumstances: non-fraternization with former enemies, military courtesy, apprehending looters, and personal conduct among civilians in enemy territory. The battalion, though still in France, was passing through towns with decidedly non-French names: Dellfeld, Stambach, Reischweiler, Oggersheim, Maxdorf, and Reicheim.

Jack's regiment crossed the Rhine on pontoon bridges at Ludwigshaven and Mannheim, and after capturing Heilbronn swung to the east and then south to encircle Stuttgart. The dotted line traces Jack's special mission to Innsbruck in the closing days of the war.

In the evening on 31 March, the regiment crossed the Rhine unopposed and was located in an assembly area near Friedrichfeld, having used bridges at Ludwigshaven and Mannheim. The day was cool and cloudy but with good visibility. The river's fast-rushing waters occasionally threatened the pontoon bridges, but they held and all of the division's heavy trucks got across safely. On the preceding day, Centurymen were able to get showers and even enjoy a beer ration and a movie in the evening. The division encountered more and more foreign civilians who had until recently been slave laborers for the German war machine: Poles, Danes, Dutch, Ukranians, Czechs, French, Greeks, and many others. On the side of the road, Centurymen found wounded Germans, left behind by their fast-retreating comrades. Frequently, they simply found discarded German uniforms – and sullen, unkempt young men hanging around street corners in the towns through which the Century passed.

100th Infantry Division Archives, Marshall Foundation

After taking Bitche, the Century Division's advance into Germany was rapid.
Here soldiers from Jack's regiment get a lift from supporting armor as they
approach the German border.

The German army divisions were on the ropes, but not defeated. There was growing fear that with the Russians closing from the east and the other Allied forces from the west that the Germans might withdraw their available troops to the mountainous regions of Bavaria for a last ditch, titanic struggle that would prove especially costly to the Allies, i.e., the "Southern Redoubt." After all, the fighting in northern Italy had shown Allied planners how costly mountain campaigns could be. If that strategy had been followed, certainly the Germans would take many of their advanced weapons with them, including the V-1 and V-2 rockets along with their new generation jet fighters. Allied intelligence suggested that the Germans did indeed have substantial forces in reserve. Eisenhower reaffirmed his decision to push into Germany on a broad front, but included an end run that would prevent as many Germans as possible from retreating into mountainous, southern Germany. When the plans were issued, they called for General Brooks' VI Corps, consisting of the Century, the 63rd Infantry Division, and the 10th Armored Division to take two cities in southwestern Germany: Heidelberg and Heilbronn. General Burress drew Heilbronn. It was not a lucky card; as it turned out the Germans declared Heidelberg a free city and did not defend it. The intelligence professionals, quite wrongly, thought a similar circumstance might be the case with Heilbronn.

The 7th Photographic Reconnaissance Group's Spitfires and Lightnings had visited Heilbronn even before the Century Division had left the States. The Group's primary duty was mapping and providing pre- and post-strike photos for the Eighth Army Air Force whose mission was the bombing of strategic targets in Occupied Europe. In fact, the 7th had photographed not only Heilbronn, but many targets up and down the Rhine River in August and September. The Eighth's heavy bombers had only paid Heilbronn one visit in late 1944 – a 100-bomber raid in September 1944. The Royal Air Force Bomber Command had been bombing Heilbronn since 1940, although the raids up to December 1944 could really be classified as nuisance raids more than anything else. Heilbronn, with its railroad yards and industries, was an important target.

It was the Royal Air Force which pulverized Heilbronn in early December while Jack's battalion was moving into Rosteig. On that raid, Heilbronn was hit by nearly 300 bombers. This was not visible to the Centurymen because the RAF Bomber Command operated at night. When the RAF hit Heilbronn, it was with nearly 300 Avro Lancaster four-engined bombers. The "Lanc" was not especially familiar to American GIs who occasionally saw B-26 Marauders at medium altitudes and much less frequently B-17 Flying Fortresses and B-24 Liberators heading into Germany high above in daylight or on the return leg to England. The Lancaster, however, could carry a bomb load nearly three tons heavier than the Fortress and Liberator combined. In effect, the one RAF raid was the equivalent of an American force of nearly 700 bombers, depending on fuel load. Heilbronn looked as though it had been hit by just that. Unfortunately, the RAF did not hit its military objectives accurately, and thousands of German civilians were killed.

While Jack was just starting to leave in the convoy that would take him across the Rhine on that clear, last day of March of 1945, nearly sixty B-26 Marauders of the 17th and 320th Bomb Groups were taking off from their fields near Dijon to hit the rail yards, industrial district, canal, and quays on the north side of Heilbronn. The Marauders, whose groups both received Presidential Unit Citations for their precision bombing in Italy and Germany, were loaded with demolition and fragmentation bombs. Forty miles southeast of Jack, sky conditions over Heilbronn were not at all clear. One entire squadron missed Heilbronn completely, and because the bombardier in a lead ship never released his bombs, one flight of six Marauders in another squadron never toggled its bombs, turned back for Dijon, and faced landing with bombs aboard. That was never a cheering prospect in a hot ship as temperamental as the Marauder. One squadron diarist recorded the accuracy as "so-so" due to the weather while the group's official final bomb damage assessment report called the results "mediocre."

National Archives

Martin B-26 Marauders flown by the 17th and 320th Bomb Groups supported the Seventh Army's advance through France and into Germany. The Marauder was a very fast medium bomber with a heavy bomb load but its design demanded utmost skill from pilots.

Heilbronn, the Last Major Urban Battle in Europe for Americans

By 3 April the regiment was in an assembly area near Schwetzingen, and its bag of prisoners had risen to 807 to date. The assault on Heilbronn would start the next day and prove to be another major battle in the Maginot sense of the word. Although Burress had been ordered to take the city, the strategy to accomplish that was left up to him. Several of the problems he faced were similar to those encountered at Bitche. There was a metropolitan area, promising house-to-house fighting and a military base south of the city. And there were nearby heights from which the Germans could base artillery. There were two important differences. Firstly, the locals were not friendly. Indeed, there was burning hatred directed by the civilian population toward Allied soldiers because of the thousands of residents who had been killed in air raids. Secondly, the division would have to cross a river, the Neckar, whose bridges had already been blown up.

German units facing the Century were a mixed bag formed into three combat groups named after their commanding generals: Bodendorfer, Krebs, and Mockros. The latter was a regiment of the 212th Volks Grenadier Division which had fought in Russia and been reformed to participate in the December push through the Ardennes. Its troops were largely from Bavaria. Army Group Krebs had not seen as much action, having spent most of its existence as an occupation force in Holland and on coastal defense duties in northern Germany. Both of those groups were located in Heilbronn's southern section and southeastern suburbs. Army Group Bodendorfer was dug in from central Heilbronn to the north.

Jack's battalion would face Army Group Bodendorfer which was composed primarily of the 246th Volks Grenadier Regiment which itself was a reconstituted, Bavarian-sourced 337th Infantry Division. The latter unit had fought in Russia and had most recently created problems for the American Eighth Infantry Division in the Hurtgen Forest to the north. While Bodendorfer's troops included some very experienced soldiers, *Afrika Korps* veterans among them, it also included many recycled *Luftwaffe* personnel.

Commitments to protecting the Seventh Army's flank prevented General Burress from initially utilizing one of his favorite maneuvers, the pincer, to take Heilbronn. Thus he was denied the opportunity to attack Heilbronn simultaneously from the north and the south, forcing a decision to concentrate on moving from the north. His original plans for Jack's regiment were to cross the Neckar to the north at Bad Wimpfen, known for its spa resort, and proceed, supported by the 10th Armored Division, to take the high ground north and east of the city where it was assumed the Germans had located their artillery. The other two regiments would move on Heilbronn from the southeast, with the 399th on the right flank, but only after German artillery had been silenced. Unfortunately, the 10th Armored Division's infantry was having serious problems with Army Group Bodendorfer about a mile north of Heilbronn. The problems were of the magnitude that Burress was suddenly ordered to reinforce the 10th with one of his battalions.

The closest was Jack's 3rd battalion which was ordered to promptly join the 10th by crossing the Neckar as soon as possible. The battalion commander, Lt. Col. Janes, reported to the 10th's commander and was told to cross the river in darkness in the very early morning. To preserve the element of surprise, there would be no artillery in advance. Janes reported this back to Burress who took the matter up with both the 10th's commander, Maj. Gen. William Morris, and General Brooks of VI Corps. Burress was assured that a proper pontoon bridge would be put across the river right after the regiment crossed by assault boats and that armor would follow immediately. Thus, he felt that once the tanks had gotten across the river, after the battalion's infantrymen had cleaned out pockets of Germans with their mortars and *panzerfauste*, the battalion would return and he could take Heilbronn according to his original plan. There were some intelligence failures, however. Some officers doubted that the Germans would put up much of a fight for Heilbronn, yet interrogation of prisoners showed that substantial German reinforcements had been arriving in Heilbronn in recent weeks.

100th Infantry Division Archives, Marshall Foundation

Getting Centurymen across the Neckar River was the responsibility of the 325th Combat Engineer Battalion.

The crossing in darkness commenced at 3 A.M. and went easily enough with only an occasional shot from a German sniper. By daybreak, the entire battalion was across the Neckar and the CP was established on the eastern side of the river, facing a massive electrical generating plant about 400 yards away and slightly to the right of the crossing point. Jack had worked out the four companies' assignments. K Company went across first and split into two groups; the first headed to a group of factory buildings by the Heilbronn-Neckarsulm road. The other, including a radioman and mortar observer from M Company, struck out for Tower Hill in the high country northeast of Heilbronn. M Company formed the reserve, although one of its platoons had been divided and assigned to reinforce K and L Companies. L Company was to clear a lumber yard to the northeast of the crossing point. I Company was to set up a defensive perimeter between the river and the big electrical plant.

The battalion was, in fact, walking into a trap – one that would be made infinitely more desperate by General Brooks' surprisingly diverting the 10th Armored Division's tanks to another hotspot well north of Heilbronn.

Suddenly, German 88 mm cannons on the hills to the east of Heilbronn opened up on the battalion's crossing point, eliminating any possibility of getting more help across the river and preventing any chance of putting a pontoon bridge over the Neckar. That German artillery also eliminated the possibility of retreat back to the western shore of the river. Then the German infantry attacked en masse; the battalion now had to contend with a regimental size force. There was no means of retreat to the rear, except a suicidal one. Jack Rhea was now in very grave danger. The 88s were pounding the command post along with nearly every company's position. The force that had occupied Tower Hill had been isolated. Although they fought tenaciously and suffered casualties, they were so outnumbered that surrender was the only option for those remaining alive after their ammunition was depleted. On 5 April Regiment called Jack and inquired about the status of a patrol Jack had sent up Tower Hill to locate the platoons from L Company. Jack became the bearer of bad news:

> RHEA: That patrol went up last night. Couldn't get to them because the enemy was heavily entrenched on that hill and couldn't reach them. We haven't heard from them since last evening.

With Americans off the hill, the Germans had a new fire base for their artillery, and they used it effectively. The battalion's ordeal would go on for a week as it endured artillery and constant German infantry attacks. Had the battalion not been so determined, the bridgehead would have folded and the battle for Heilbronn would have been infinitely more costly.

General Burress had a massive problem because his other two regiments along with the remaining two battalions from the 398th were still on the west side of the Neckar and well to the south of Jack's position. The rapidly deteriorating situation dredged up memories of what became of Company A at Wingen Sur Moder – only this time it was an entire battalion, not just one company at risk. General Burress, the champion of squeezing an enemy from two or more sides and the "you hold him and I'll hit him" approach, was now faced with assaulting Heilbronn head on; it was the last thing he wanted to do. His immediate response was to get more troops across the river to shore up the 3rd/398th's right flank, and to do this he chose the unit closest to Jack's battalion: E Company of the 397th. That company would be followed by the rest of the 397th's second battalion as soon as possible. To make the movement as difficult as possible for the Germans to detect and hit with their 88s, the move was supported by a smoke generation company. By dark, its exact movements further hid by thick clouds of smoke, the entire battalion crossed the river by boat and was moving into position on Jack's right flank. Jack's battalion had repulsed numerous German counterattacks and was still constantly subjected to artillery, small arms, and automatic weapons fire. The Germans still had enough zeroed-in artillery to make building a pontoon bridge out of the question.

With all of the 397th across, it was assigned the task of taking the industrial district on the immediate north side of the city. That became a punishing street-to-street and building-to-building fight and was a clear indicator of how bad it would get when the Centurymen moved into the city center itself.

General Burress still had uncommitted forces and decided to use his preferred strategy now that Brooks' armor had been withdrawn from the equation: hit his opponent from a weak side while his attention was directed at another side. Accordingly, he found a place further north on the Neckar where the 2nd Battalion of the 398th could cross the Neckar near Bad Wimpfen, head east through Offenau (which was not defended), and cross the Jagdst and Kocher Rivers before turning south and closing with the enemy on the north side of Heilbronn. Unfortunately, the battalion ran into a stronger force of SS troops south of Duttenberg shortly after crossing the Jagst. The 1st Battalion had also jumped off from Bad Wimpfen and crossed the Jagst at Unter Greisheim before swinging south and being stopped cold at Odheim by artillery and mortars. By late afternoon on 7 April, several of the Century's supporting units got some light tanks and tank destroyers into position. Although their first salvos could not turn the tide at once, they would make a huge difference in a few days. The appearance of the new armor was the result of General William Morris having run into an impasse to the east where he decided that his best option was to support General Burress after all.

Air support and the division's artillery were called in, but even that could not immediately break the German artillery. Part of the problem was that American and German forces were so close together that the danger from friendly fire was about as dangerous as that from the enemy. Poor visibility also frequently limited fighter-bomber flight operations. Jack's battalion was still in great danger, but continued to repel sharp German attacks as late as 10 April. The battalion was holding a line not quite a half mile wide, and many of the German attacks were made completely across that line. These assaults were made with the support of several German tanks which were used only sparingly due to German shortages of gasoline. The accuracy of American heavy mortars, tanks, and tank destroyers still on the west side of the Neckar also kept German armor at bay. At one point, Jack and the battalion had been shoved back to the river's edge, but they rallied and eventually reclaimed the lost ground.

By 10 April, with the help of darkness and smoke generators, the combat engineers were able to put another pontoon bridge across the Neckar and get enough heavy mortar crews, tanks, and tank destroyers across to make a major difference in the outcome of the battle.

A week after Jack crossed the Neckar on 4 April, the 399th started crossing the Neckar south of Heilbronn near Sontheim. Surprisingly, its crossing by boats was not opposed, not even by artillery. Shortly, the combat engineers succeeded in putting another pontoon bridge across the Neckar which allowed many more 399th Centurymen to follow. These troops would encounter both the Krebs and Mockros Army Groups, but would eventually take their objectives: the Schlieffen army barracks and the high ground on the south side of Heilbronn. Meanwhile, savage fighting raged on in downtown Heilbronn, block to block, building to building with the 397th in the very thick of it. Except for some mopping up, German resistance had collapsed by 12 April. Among the defenders of Heilbronn were young teenagers of the Hitler Youth and grandfathers of the *Volkssturn*, the local militia. They were not real soldiers but they too had taken American lives. Over 500 Centurymen became casualties in the battle for Heilbronn. That was a high price, but it could have been much, much worse. The outcome was another testimonial to how General Burress could accomplish a goal while paying for it with only a minimal loss of Centurymen. That was one reason why he was so revered by his soldiers.

Out of the battle for Heilbronn came one Medal of Honor, to a member of the 398th Regiment for his gallantry near Odheim, a full range of other combat decorations, and many Purple Hearts. There were several Presidential Unit Citations, including those won by the 1st and 2nd Battalions of the 397th. And Jack's 3rd Battalion won a second Presidential Unit Citation for the "intrepidity and heroism" of its officers and men in holding a critical bridgehead although vastly outnumbered. It took a while for such awards to be processed and it would not be until early November that the award was actually presented.

Encircling Stuttgart

The Century did not have a lot of time to rest and refit. Jack's battalion turned north to join the attack on Neckarsulm which fell on 13 April. The battalion command post was in a different town every evening. The towns came and went as the regiment moved at a tremendous pace in trucks and riding on tanks. In many cases, the Centurymen were greeted at the outskirts of towns by the town fathers with the news that the German military had fled and that there was no need to shell the place in advance. Centurymen were still being killed, however, because some towns, such as Affaltrach, were defended by small groups of die-hard Germans. The division was covering many miles a day, stopping only when firefights erupted with last ditch defenders. The regiment's bag of prisoners had exceeded 1,700 at that point. In the week beginning on 14 April, Jack's jeep drove through Sulsbach, Willsbach, Eschenau, Rappach, Adolzfurt, Lockweiler, and Lowenstein.

100th Infantry Division Archives, Marshall Foundation

Centurymen on the move after the fall of Heilbronn in mid-April 1945.

The weather during this period was typical April: several lovely days in a row and then one or two with showers, but at least the penetrating cold of the High Vosges was a thing of the past. By 22 April, the battalion command post was in Winnendin. Elements of the other two battalions were already nearing Stuttgart's northeastern suburbs.

The race was on to cut off all German forces in southwest Germany

and prevent their escape into southern Bavaria where they might be able to prolong the war for months to come. The Seventh Army was to swing to the south, to the east of Stuttgart, and then to the southwest below the city to block all means of German escape to the southeast. The French First Army was to capture Stuttgart but only after the Americans had it completely isolated. The battalion was on the left flank of this nearly fifteen miles wide thrust across the southwest German countryside. Although the French had been ordered not to occupy Stuttgart until notified by SHAEF, the French ignored the order and went into Stuttgart anyway, giddily lording it over the German populace after decades of embarrassment over France's inability to properly defend itself. Eisenhower tolerated the French violating his orders only briefly. Very shortly the French were notified that they were welcome to occupy Stuttgart – but only at the cost of being denied a visible role in the occupation of Berlin and the rest of Germany whereupon the French swallowed their Gallic pride and turned Stuttgart over to the Century Division.

Orders from Division came to Colonel Williams to create two task forces from within his command for special missions. Both assignments went to Jack's battalion. The first was a short range mission which went to L Company to depart the battalion's command post, then at Walbingen, and establish contact with the French in Stuttgart. Under cloudy skies with intermittent rain, L Company accomplished its mission, meeting the French 3rd Infantry Division at Bad Canstatt on the Neckar River. That task force also included a platoon of tanks and engineers. Jack's communication with Regiment follows:

RHEA: Task Force made contact with 117th Recon, met no resistance. All bridges across the river blown. Also made contact with the French.

WHITUS: If you find any French soldiers in your area, take their name, rank, and organization. If they are drunk, arrest them. Upon arrival post local security and continue training. If you find any amounts of food or clothing, report the location and put guards on them. Request by 1800 condition of roads and bridges in your sector. Put a guard on electrical and water plants.

Silver Star for Captain Jack Rhea

Jack Rhea was personally in command of the other, similarly composed task force whose mission was much, much longer and infinitely more dangerous. He was to link-up with leading elements of the Fifth Army which had been fighting in Italy since the autumn of 1943 and had most recently pursued remaining German troops as they escaped from Italy into Austria over the Brenner Pass. The assignment given to Jack may well have been the defining event of his days in combat during World War II. There is no better description of it than the order awarding him the Silver Star for bravery in the face of an armed enemy. Only the Congressional Medal of Honor and Distinguished Service Cross are ranked higher than the Silver Star for valor under fire. The citation is reproduced, verbatim, below:

HEADQUARTERS 100TH INFANTRY DIVISION
Office of the Commanding General
APO 447, U.S. Army

General Orders)

23 July 1945

Number   114   )

SECTION I – AWARD OF SILVER STAR

Under the provisions of Army Regulations 600—45, as amended, the Silver Star Medal is awarded to the following individual:

AWARD OF SILVER STAR

Jack L. Rhea, 0-1296148, Captain, 398th Infantry Regiment, for gallantry in action on 23 APRIL 1945, in the vicinity of Innsbruck, Austria. In command of a small task force with the mission of contacting the Fifth Army at Brenner Pass, Captain Rhea found himself deep in enemy territory with no supporting arms and with thousands of enemy soldiers in the near vicinity. Approaching a small town, the task force was fired upon by German soldiers under cover near a building at the edge of town. Realizing that only an aggressive action would save his men, Captain Rhea climbed on a tank and ordered it to charge the enemy position. As the tank drew near, a shell from a panzerfaust hit the rear wheels of the tank temporarily demobilizing it. Leaping from the tank Captain Rhea single handedly charged the enemy posi tion. Miraculously escaping being hit by a hail of enemy fire directed at him, Captain Rhea then attacked the enemy killing three of them and forcing the remainder to surrender. His actions so inspired his men that they vigorously carried on the attack and although greatly outnumbered took the position allowing them to continue their mission. Captain Rhea's gal lant and aggressive actions prevented severe casualties to his men and insured the success ful accomplishment of their mission. Entered Military Service from Des Moines, Iowa.
****

BY COMMAND OF BRIGADIER GENERAL TYSCHEN

J.O. Kilgore
Colonel GSC
Chief of Staff

OFFICIAL:
a/ Leonard F. Oliver
t/ LEONARD F. OLIVER
Major   AGD
Adjutant General

Certified a True Copy
(signed)
Walter L. Baker
1st Lt., 398th Inf.
3rd. Bn. Adjutant

When Jack returned from that action, the battalion was still in Walbingen. The shooting was over, and the battalion was engaged in patrolling east and northeast of Stuttgart. Starting from that point his orders sounded more like those previously issued back in the States. The order of the day was training, physical conditioning, marching, and maintenance of weapons and vehicles along with rest and relaxation. While temporarily in Walbingen, companies were assigned rotating shifts of guarding installations, such as hospitals and bridges in and around Bad Canstatt. On 28 April, a cool and cloudy day, the battalion appeared in formation at 3 P.M. to take part in a special ceremony. General Burress came to present the battalion with the Presidential Unit Citation for its performance on 18 December when it took Forts Freudenberg and Schiesseck. A special streamer was attached to the battalion standard and every member of the 3rd/398th became entitled to wear the gold-bordered, blue ribbon above the right pocket. The first man to receive the ribbon was Lt. Col. Ernest Janes as it was pinned on by General Burress. Although it would not become official for another ten days, the Century's war in Europe, for all practical purposes, was over. Colonel Williams issued the last order to the regiment during the hostilities:

> Effective at once, 100th Inf. personnel will not fire upon the enemy unless fired upon or unless necessary with police duties. Peace negotiations between 7th Army HQ and German forces opposing 7th Army regarding unconditional surrender become effective 1200 6 May 45. This order affects 7th Army only.

CHAPTER 10

The Occupation

When the shooting stopped, Jack Rhea and every other Centuryman had the same thing on his mind: "When can I go home?" The answer was, "Not soon." Then there was the very real fear that the division would be sent to another shooting war on the other side of the world. In the Pacific, the war had been going well for the Allies. Iwo Jima was now an American airfield, serving as a safe haven for shot-up B-29 Superfortresses returning from Japan to bases in the Marianas. Iwo was also the home to several fighter groups whose mission was to escort the bombers and strafe Japanese targets of opportunity. Everybody realized that the invasion of Japan would be infinitely bloodier than the conquest of Germany and that the manpower needs for such an undertaking were immense.

Nonetheless, the Army had developed a point system to establish priority for return to the United States based on length of service, number of children back home, time overseas, decorations, etc. The seriously wounded had already been evacuated and just-liberated POWS had priority. Because the 100th was a latecomer to the European war, it would not occupy a favored spot as some of its neighbors such as the 3rd and 45th Infantry Divisions which had been battling the Vichy French, Italians, and Germans in North Africa, Sicily, Italy, Southern France, and Germany for more than two and one-half years. By comparison, the 100th had spent six months in combat.

Once the non-fraternization rules were relaxed, reactions to the German citizenry varied considerably. Some soldiers found the conquered Germans docile to the point of being servile, eager to perform any service for food, chocolate, or even a few cigarettes. At the other extreme were Germans who had completely swallowed Nazi master race propaganda; they were arrogant, haughty, and condescending. Many Centurymen found the average German family not unlike the folks on Main Street back home. Americans thought the typical German home was relatively up-to-date with modern conveniences – much more so than corresponding homes in France – perhaps as a result of the German obsession with technology and cleanliness.

Rhea Family Collection

Jack blinked just as the shutter snapped.
Nonetheless, this photo taken in Esslingen
shows a man relieved at no longer being a target
of the German Army.

The division's newspaper, *The Century Sentinel*, renewed its weekly publishing schedule and reflected the return to some of the soldiers' favorite leisure activities: sports. The Centurymen did not play soccer, the Germans' favorite sport. Rather, curious Germans were exposed to American baseball and football which was enthusiastically and extensively reported in the paper. The division even had swimming, bowling, boxing, and track leagues, although most of the attention was centered on baseball and football competition with other divisions also serving in the Occupation.

There was a staggering amount of work to do over a wide geographic area. Jack Rhea's job changed focus to a large extent. He was still involved in training because the need to keep the battalion's soldiering skills was ever present considering the possibility of deployment to the Pacific. Therefore, soldiers had to requalify with their weapons and there was physical training, marching, and long hikes with full packs. The other side of battalion staff work covered the waterfront of civil administration. Problems were legion: security threats, people problems, housing troubles, business difficulties, and even the most basic issues of food and sanitation in areas whose infrastructure had been obliterated by bombs, mortars, and artillery.

Third Battalion in Esslingen

The division headquarters was set up in Stuttgart. Jack's battalion was temporarily assigned occupation duties in Pluderhausen, Murrhardt, and Welzheim before finally setting up its headquarters in Esslingen am Neckar, a town about ten miles southeast of Stuttgart. The battalion command post was established in downtown Esslingen in an office building which was part of the former town hall complex just off the main square. Along with several officers from the battalion, Jack was assigned quarters in a large, private residence on the edge of Esslingen.

Esslingen came through the war largely untouched, thus it retained much of its old world charm. The division had been given an area from Heilbronn to just south of Stuttgart and west to the Neckar River and east to the city of Ulm or nearly 2,500 square miles. The battalion's first need was to guard itself and its assets including weapons, gasoline, food, ammunition, and vehicles. At the same time, similar assets of the German Army and *Luftwaffe* also had to be guarded. It was much more than just the 100th Military Police Battalion could begin to manage. The battalion was charged with policing within a triangle whose points comprised of Esslingen, Murrhardt, and Welzheim. Jack was responsible for planning and ordering all of those security activities.

Rhea Family Collection

Jack Rhea stands in front of the 3rd Battalion
Command Post just off the town square in Esslingen.

At first there was fear that the defeated Germans would expand a war-time commando force named *Wehrwolf* (Werewolf) which had functioned as a guerilla unit behind the Russian lines. The new *Wehrwolf,* largely composed of former Hitler Youth members, was to conduct sabotage and snipe at American soldiers. The threat never really materialized in Esslingen, but the battalion still had to remain vigilant and prepared. Indeed, Jack carried a sidearm, his .45 automatic, as did all officers. Others, including Lt. Sidney Kleinwaks, usually also carried an M-1 carbine in their jeeps. To make sure there were no weapons hidden among the general populace, Jack's battalion conducted a nighttime roundup shortly after arriving in Esslingen in early July which saw German citizens awakened in the middle of the night and their homes searched. Confiscated weapons were destroyed or, more typically, dumped into the deepest part of the Neckar River. It was not unusual; the same procedure had been followed in many towns through which the Century passed after it crossed the Rhine. *Wehrwolf* was assumed to have been associated with several assassinations and bombings elsewhere in Germany, including Stuttgart. General Eisenhower's orders concerning *die Werhwolfe* were harsh; by late 1947 most of them who were convicted had been imprisoned or executed. The rest gave up their aspirations, arms, explosives, and learned to live peacefully within the hated Occupation.

As with all wars, a black market quickly sprang up. There was great temptation, and a carton of American smokes which cost only two American dollars at a post exchange was worth a hundred times that in the black market. And cigarettes were only one of the more visible commodities in this illegal trade. Applying manpower to combat that corruption detracted from the massive difficulty in restoring order to a demoralized people whose physical, economic, and civil infrastructure was shattered.

Jack's duties during the Occupation were varied, including training, education, assigning guards, and relocating displaced people.

The Pentagon knew that this civil affairs mess was coming and did its best to send over as many trained public administrators and German-speakers as possible, but their numbers were so minimal that battalion leaders like Jack had to make do with existing resources. Jack Rhea did have one advantage; Captain John B. Keene, an Upstate New Yorker and fellow graduate of Jack's OCS class in 1942, was in the 3rd Battalion headquarters company, and he spoke fluent German. He had been of great service in translating during interrogation of captured Germans during the preceding six months, and his skills were still very much in demand during the Occupation. The Century Division became the "law and order" in its assigned area. There had been no legitimate judicial system since Hitler came to power in 1933, so that void was filled by the occupying force. The beginning of a German judicial system, an important aspect of the de-Nazification program, was installed by early autumn when an adequate number of judges and prosecutors free of any Nazi connections had been found and installed.

A Centuryman who had been on night outpost duty in the Vosges might find himself on guard duty at a road intersection on the edge of Esslingen, enforcing curfews or arresting thieves. A member of the communications platoon who had strung phone wire from a company CP under fire back to the battalion CP a month or two previously found himself climbing a telephone pole to re-establish telephone connections between Esslingen and Schorndorf. A soldier who had been in a heavy weapons platoon and experienced in eliminating resistance at roadblocks could find himself in charge of a German civilian labor detail dismantling bypassed roadblocks. There were no shortages of landmines for combat engineers to detect and disable. German soldiers who had abandoned their dying comrades were now supervised by Americans in the process of finding German dead and removing them from where they died, from urban rubble to hospitals, to their final resting places.

Probably the greatest problem at first was that relating to people. The division's intelligence officers were busy interrogating thousands of surrendered Germans. Many, such as young teenagers and old men were simply released and told to go home and stay out of trouble. Other soldiers were sent to labor camps where they might spend another year or two cleaning up the mess that they had started. A hard-core Nazi, whether a civilian, uniformed member of the German armed forces, or *gauleiter* (local administrator), would find himself sent up the line to higher authority for decisions on proper punishment and/or imprisonment.

With Nazi labor and death camps liberated, tens of thousands of displaced people from the Balkans to Scandinavia found themselves within the Century's jurisdiction. A squad-sized group of men from the battalion might find itself placed in charge of feeding and finding housing for groups as large as 500 of those unfortunate people until some direction could be brought back into their lives. The worst of the Nazi death camps were not within the 100th's jurisdiction; however, several small groups of Centurymen did visit Dachau, located near Munich, and came back to Stuttgart completely revolted by what they had seen.

German businesses had to be revitalized, and a few Americans emerged as something between corporate consultants and hands-on business managers. Stuttgart, although not in the battalion's occupation territory, was a target utterly destroyed by RAF and USAAF heavy bombers. In that city's businesses, large and small, soldiers with commercial experience became the bosses while former owners became employees.

A Slower Pace for the Occupying Powers

Quarters for Americans came at the expense of German citizens who were given short notice to pack up clothes and personal items and move out. In many cases, former homeowners became the new servants. An enlisted soldier could expect at least a room in a private home for his quarters and quite possibly a hotel room.

By mid-summer 1945, the division found more time for training, including marching. Part of this was for show – to impress the German populace with American prowess. Germans could not help but notice Americans during physical training and were intended to come to the conclusion that the Yanks were indeed much more powerful than Nazi "supermen." Centurymen could also enroll in classes in a variety of subjects. Many men took German, knowing that once non-fraternization rules were relaxed it would be helpful to speak to some lovely German *fräulein* in her own language. For many others, academic subjects appealed, and they wanted to have an advantage when they got back to the states and could go to college. The battalion opened a library complete with books and recent American periodicals. The Gemeindehaus Theater in Esslingen was the venue for amateur productions and a few professional productions featuring American showgirls in such shows as "Sons of Fun" and "Hells-A-Poppin." Jack enjoyed a few movies while in Esslingen. Between theaters in Stuttgart and Esslingen, there were movies every evening. Tallulah Bankhead, Spencer Tracy, Vivian Blaine, Joan Fontaine, Katherine Hepburn, and other Hollywood stars of the day were appearing in *The Southerner, Affairs of Susan, I'll Tell the World, Royal Scandal,* and *Penthouse Rhythm* among many others.

The combined Chaplain Offices of the Century Division and VI Corps offered regular Protestant and Catholic services at the existing churches in Esslingen. The synagogue in Stuttgart had survived the war to the extent that it could be used for Jewish services on Friday nights.

Jack Rhea was heavily involved in planning the battalion's activities: guard details, training, and relocating displaced persons among many other activities. He did have a few off-duty hours and that usually meant three things: getting back to some of the outdoor sports life he enjoyed at the VC Bar Ranch, renewing his bond with Scouting, and travel. Some men went hunting for deer. Hopping bunnies might have the terminal misfortune to wind up in a tasty *hasenpfeffer* (rabbit stew). Even back in the Vosges campaign, the rarely-sighted wild boar was every bit the legitimate target that a German infantryman was. There was an ulterior motive here since food, even in an officers' mess, was not quite up to Four Seasons standards. The local German populace was aghast since ordinary Germans had been prohibited from wild game hunting during the Hitler years.

Although he did participate in one deer hunt, Jack was much more interested in fishing nearby Bavarian trout streams. On several occasions he returned with a string of the wily German brown trout – nothing for the record books in terms of size, but the quantity and quality made for some fish fries of the type that Jack would someday associate with the Rayado and Agua Fria at Philmont.

Jack with a nice string of brown trout destined for a fish fry.

Jack Rhea brought the essentials of Scouting back to the German youth of Esslingen. Scouting had been very popular in Germany prior to its being banned by Hitler in 1935. Indeed, many biographies by former members of the German armed forces in World War II speak in glowing terms about their early days as a *Pfadfinder* (pathfinder or Boy Scout). It is highly unlikely that Jack ever thought about bringing uniforms back into German Scouting; even today many very elderly Germans cringe when they see a young person in uniform. Rather, it was the camping, pioneering, hiking, and personal growth aspects that Jack emphasized. Very few German boys of Scouting age in Esslingen had fathers alive in mid-1945. The few dads who were alive were elsewhere, spending a year or so in prisoner of war work camps. Scouting, with its emphasis on citizenship and character development, was exactly what Germany needed in 1945, and Jack Rhea was, therefore, really in the forefront of the Occupation although it went largely unrecognized at the time.

Rhea Family Collection

Preparing for an inspection parade on the town square in Esslingen. The tall man at center is the 3rd Battalion commander, Lt. Ernest Janes.
To Janes' right is Major Robert Brinkerhoff (looking over his left shoulder).

Postwar Travel in Europe

Captain Rhea also combined travel and Scouting. Wherever he went on leaves, he observed the local Scouting scene. It would pay dividends in later years that he could not foresee in 1945 when he was able to study Scouting close-up in France, Belgium, and England.

The frequency and length of leaves for Centurymen increased during the summer. Paris and Brussels had always been the biggest magnets, but there were other popular destinations, including the French Riviera, Switzerland, and Venice. From his foray down to Innsbruck, Jack had seen more of Germany than most Centurymen, and he added more travel in Germany with his fishing trips to Bavaria. In the company of other officers from the regiment, Jack visited Berchtesgaden and nearby Salzburg. While the latter had been bombed several times, most of its historical district was still intact. Although he could not have guessed it in 1945, Jack would someday come back to Berchtesgaden.

Jack and most of his friends acquired German cameras which were popular trading items for cigarettes, chocolate, food, etc. The most popular cameras were made by Leica, Rolleiflex or Voigtländer in both twin lens reflex and folding lens models. In many cases, the previous owner's film was still in the camera and had recorded what were obviously happier days. In Jack's Voigtländer there were photos of smiling and well fed German staff officers enjoying a picnic with several pretty *Junge Frauen*. Nearly everybody acquired another trendy item – aviator-style sunglasses. German pistols were popular and Jack, who always was interested in firearms, acquired a Walther P38 semi-automatic pistol, the sidearm that was to replace the venerable Luger in 1943.

Jack with friends in Esslingen. Back row, left to right: Sidney Kleinwaks, Jack, Harry Mignery, Carl Aschoff. Kneeling, Fred Lemr.

Based as he was in Baden-Wurttemburg, Jack and some of his fellow officers spent a few off-duty hours visiting several of the towns which had not been leveled by bombs and artillery. Baden-Wurttemburg is the third largest of the sixteen German states and is located in the southwest corner of the country; Stuttgart is its capital. Indeed, a number of attractions were located within Baden-Wurttemburg including the Black Forest, pleasant rolling countryside, and some of Germany's most important vineyards. Jack was able to visit Murrhardt, the Obberot Valley, and Gaildorf, all just east-northeast of Esslingen. Some of these towns had escaped the ravages of war while others, such as Gaildorf, had suffered some damage as the Century Division had advanced from Neckarsulm to approach Stuttgart from the east. Jack's circle of friends broadened during this period and was not limited to just the battalion leadership.

Rhea Family Collection

Jack's caption of this photo taken in Gaildorf
was short and to the point: "Jerry Arty." Church steeples
and town hall towers were favored locations for artillery
spotters and therefore quickly became targets for
opposing artillery.

Lieutenant Charles Odence and Captain William Greer from the regimental headquarters and two lieutenants from the medical detachment, Harry Mignerey and Carl Aschoff, frequently joined Jack on those excursions. His closest friends, however, were those in the 3rd Battalion leadership, such as Burnus Payne and Sideny Kleinwaks, and those men who had been company or platoon commanders, including Wilfrid Ganeau and Fred Lemr.

The British Isles were popular, particularly London, although some Centurymen traveled north to Scotland. In late June, Jack was granted enough leave to travel to London and then Paris. The United States Navy ran what amounted to a shuttle service between Le Havre and Southampton. The Navy's shuttle service was not as fast as today's "Chunnel," but it was essentially the only game in town for a soldier wanting to see London.

Although most of the shuttle fleet consisted of LSTs and LSIs (Landing Ship Tank/Infantry) that had proudly served in the invasion, Jack lucked out and went from Le Havre to Southampton on the S.S. *Marine Wolf*, a troop transport.

Rhea Family Collection

Jack on the Marine Wolf *between Le Havre and Southampton.*

Great Britain, the birthplace of Scouting, was more important to Jack Rhea than the average Centuryman on leave. Like most tourists, Jack hit all of London's high spots, including Buckingham Palace, Tower Bridge, Westminster Abbey, Big Ben, the Tower of London, St. Paul's Cathedral, Royal Albert Hall, and Parliament. Based on the photographs he took, it is possible that he visited one location that would become very important to him in just a few short years: Gilwell Park. In 1945, Gilwell and its Wood Badge heritage were essentially unknown to the mainstream of American Scouting because the only Wood Badge courses ever conducted in the United States had both taken place at Schiff in 1936 and played to very mixed reviews since they were considered too "British." It would not be until 1948 that American Scouting's awareness of Wood Badge was renewed when two Americanized courses were offered: the first at Schiff and the second at Philmont. Having taken his field executive training at Schiff in 1939, Jack would have been aware of the significance of Gilwell Park.

Exactly where Jack took this photo is unknown, but all evidence points to Brownsea Island.

There is much stronger evidence, however, that in late June Jack did visit the other important British landmark in world Scouting, and that was Brownsea Island. The majority of Americans visiting England on leave from Occupied Europe typically caught the first train they could from Southampton to London and spent most of their leaves in the big city. Yet Jack's wartime photograph album conclusively puts him in Bournemouth, about twenty-five miles west of Southampton, for a day. Bournemouth would have been very much out-of-the-way for the average American who, if he did want to see an attraction on the south coast, probably would have headed east to the resort town of Brighton. The album includes ten photos of uniformed Boy Scouts and their leaders in settings that very closely resemble the parks and campsites on Brownsea Island, the birthplace of Scouting. Once in Bournemouth, Poole Harbor is quite near and the ferry ride out to Brownsea Island takes only a few minutes.

Rhea Family Collection

Although the photo is grainy, it still captures one of the best moments of the war for Jack: meeting his brother Ralph quite by chance in Paris.

Jack visited Paris on the way back from England; his Parisian visit started just like that of any GI visiting the City of Light but ended with one of the most wonderful surprises of the entire war. With other officers from the battalion, he took in *Notre Dame*, the *Champs Elysee*, and *Place de L'Opera*. Walking along one of Paris' boulevards, Jack saw a slender soldier in a group of other soldiers seated at a sidewalk café. He could not believe his eyes, and an instant later there was a joyous reunion with his brother Ralph! With Ralph out of the hospital in England, the two brothers had been trying to see each other for months, but had trouble coordinating passes at the same time, finally gave up, and now here they were, meeting quite by chance. They finished touring Paris together and went to the grave of the French Unknown Soldier, the Eiffel Tower, and other Parisian attractions.

*Jack, as photographed by his brother Ralph, toured all
of the sights in Paris in early summer 1945.*

There is some indication, based on casual comments to his children long after the war, that Jack also visited Ireland and the American landing sites at Normandy during his Occupation duties. Omaha and Utah Beaches are little more than an hour's drive from Le Havre, a major connecting point for American soldiers arriving in or leaving France in 1944-45. Jack had an interest in seeing Normandy. Many of the enlisted men and junior officers who were transferred out of the 100th in 1943 and 1944, including friends and acquaintances, had been killed on the beaches or later in the summer as the Allies moved east across France.

Just because the war was over did not put an end to the USO tours and their famous entertainers. Bob Hope, Ingrid Bergman, Jack Benny, and Jerry Colonna were among the Hollywood stars who entertained the division at the Stuttgart Stadium. Jack was able to meet Bob Hope and shake his hand. Jack became a Bob Hope fan from that day forward, but was not at all impressed with Mr. Benny. At the time, Jack could never have envisaged the long-term consequences of shaking hands with Bob Hope. One of the division's other diversions was homegrown. That was the founding of the Society of the Sons of Bitche, which was open to any Centuryman who had a hand in the taking of Bitche and the nearby Maginot forts. The inauguration of the Society took place at what remained of the Stuttgart Opera House and was filled with appropriate ritual and humor.

Going Home

Jack's third Bronze Star came through during this period and was for his performance during the perilous days when the battalion was desperately trying to hold on to its bridgehead on the Neckar River prior to the main assault on Heilbronn. The citation referenced Jack's skill in planning and executing both the crossing under very short notice and holding the bridgehead against counterattacks and punishing artillery barrages. Again, Jack was commended for his courage while subjected to enemy small arms fire and artillery.

Any efficiency reports on Jack written by Lt. Col. Stayton do not survive. The one written by Lt. Col. Janes and endorsed by Col. Williams on 1 July 1945 still exists. It is clear that Janes considered Jack Rhea indispensable, giving him top marks for "stability under pressure, attention to duty, initiative, intelligence, leadership, ability to obtain results, judgment," and all of the other criteria.

There was a gnawing fear throughout the division relating to the future. Everybody knew that the build-up for the invasion of Japan was underway. On 10 August the division was alerted for overseas movement and notified that it was to move out on 27 August for arrival in Marseille on 10 September. Then one week later, General Burress notified the division that there would be no movement to the Pacific war because the atomic bombs had brought a close to hostilities. Two weeks after the alert notice, Jack got a personal notice himself; he was once again made executive officer of the battalion.

At that point, the battalion's strength was slipping and within several weeks would number 400 men or slightly less than half of the nearly 900 with which it went into combat ten months before. Men with the magic number of points were heading home, including Lt. Col. Janes and Major Brinkerhoff. In many cases, men with enough points were transferred out of the 100th and into other divisions scheduled for imminent return to America. With the same workload remaining, particularly guard duty, and no replacements coming in, Jack was forced to curtail some of the battalion's non-essential activities, including educational courses. By late September, Jack had become the acting battalion commander although the attending paperwork and promotion to major were still in the pipeline.

On 22 September, General Burress assumed command of VI Corps, the Century's parent organization, and Brigadier General Andrew Tyschen assumed command of the 100th. Tyschen was assistant division commander, had previously been commander of the 399th Infantry Regiment, and, like Gen. Burress, he had been with the 100th since the day of its activation. Very significantly, General Burress belonged to the inner circle of only a small handful of generals among the 91 divisions in the Army who had served the entire war with their original divisions. One of Gen. Tyschen's first acts was to approve the launch of the Century Association whose membership was open to any member of the 100th. Among the Association's first projects was the production of a history of the division, *The Story of the Century*. The little booklet was also distributed to the families of the division's dead and missing so that they would have a deeper understanding of the cause in which their loved ones gave their lives. In 1946, a 430-page, large format book of the same name was published; it included greater in-depth history, more photographs, and rosters for the entire division, including those who won the Purple Heart, Bronze Star, and the other major decorations.

On 28 October, Jack got what he was really waiting for – his own overseas movement orders – but it was not because he had just attained the right number of points. He was going home on compassionate leave because his father was seriously ill. Jack was ordered to report to Camp Herbert Tareyton near Le Havre to await transportation home. Camp Herbert Tareyton was one of the "cigarette camps" around Le Havre. That was a code name along with Lucky Strike, Pall Mall, Old Gold, Chesterfield, and others that had been temporary quarters for men arriving in France after D-Day in 1944. Now the traffic was going in the other direction. The camp was a vast collection of Nissen huts and temporary barracks that would become home to thousands of displaced persons after most GIs finally went home in 1946. Ironically, the cooks and waiters in the mess halls were German POWS, of whom some had been captured by the 100th Division.

Jack got home just in time to see his father who actually had very little time left. Charles W. Rhea died on 8 January 1946 at age seventy-one.

Jack and his older brother Charles in January 1946
just after their father died.

The Century Division was de-activated in January 1946 but shortly thereafter was reformed as an Army Reserve unit located in Louisville, Kentucky. In the following decades it went through several roles including service as an airborne unit but primarily as a training unit for replacement soldiers. Now known as the 100th OS (Operational Support) Division, its mission has also encompassed training ROTC, armor, and reconnaissance troops. In more recent years its training missions have included intelligence, civil affairs, and pre-deployment for troops fighting terrorism.

Bitche's fortress is a tourist destination nowadays. The French government briefly tried to modernize the Maginot Line, but between the Germans' hauling much of its equipment to the Western Wall, destroying some of the Line in 1940, and what the American Armies did to it late in the war, there was a lot of updating to do. Between budget crunches of the 1950s and 1960s, new military technologies, and the collapse of Communism to the east in 1989, the French government divested itself of most of the Maginot Line. Today, a few of the forts are tourist attractions, but Schiesseck and Freudenburg are not among them.

Heilbronn, along with its power plant, city hall, and cathedral, arose from the rubble of 1945 and is now the sixth largest city in Baden-Wurttemburg. It has a strong industrial base and is an important center in the German wine trade. It still conducts an annual memorial service in

December to honor those killed in the cataclysmic air raids of late 1944.

Many of Jack's acquaintances in the 100th left Germany with the main body of the 100th on 12 December and got on with their lives, but only after logistical problems with the shipping scheduled to take them home. A small contingent did get out in December, but most men had to live in tents outside of Marseille until February.

Predictably, Colonel Robert Williams, the young regimental commander, made a career of the Army and retired as a Brigadier General in 1969. During his career, he was Advisor to the Paraguayan Army in the late 1940s and later with the Military Assistance Group for Spain. Williams died in Greenville, Texas, in late 1987.

Floyd Stayton, Jack's original battalion commander, and the man with whom Jack had the most in common, started working for the Veteran's Administration in Kansas City but soon returned to education. His next move was into an area that Jack would eventually come to embrace: Native American affairs. Stayton began teaching accounting at the Haskell Institute in Lawrence, Kansas. At this institution, which is the only post-graduate school specifically for Native Americans sponsored by the government, Stayton eventually became the superintendent. He died in 1983. Jack's other battalion commander, Lt. Col. Ernest Janes, stayed in the Army and retired after service in Korea and Viet Nam. He was buried in Arlington National Cemetery in 2000.

Two more of Jack's friends from the battalion's rifle companies also made careers of the Army. Fred Lemr stayed in and served in Korea and Viet Nam; he passed away in Florida in 2005. Wilfird Ganeau also served in Korea, and retired from the Army to live in Columbia, South Carolina, where he had launched his military career at Fort Jackson in 1942. He died in 1987 at age 74.

Several other associates enjoyed careers in business or the medical profession. Robert Brinkerhoff returned to a very successful business career in Knoxville, Tennessee, a city in which he was recognized for being active in community affairs. He died in 2004 at age 87. Sidney Kleinwaks returned to North Jersey and a career in real estate and insurance, also dying in 2004. Charles Odence became a prominent stockbroker in Boston, retired to Clearwater, Florida, and also passed away in 2004. Two more of Jack's friends, both lieutenants from the 325th Medical Battalion, went to medical school after the war. Dr. Harry F. Mignerey, M.D., died in Florida in 2002.

And the last man standing was Dr. Carl Aschoff, M.D., who became a general practitioner and widely respected medical educator in Cedar Rapids, Iowa; he died in April 2011. Jack would have been delighted to know that his old friend, "Curly" Aschoff, was honored by the Boy Scout council in Cedar Rapids as a Distinguished Citizen.

The division's revered commander, Major General Withers A. Burress, became Inspector General of the European Command after leading VI Corps. He later became the European Command's Intelligence Director and concluded his career as commander of VII Corps back in the United States. He died in 1977 and is buried in Arlington National Cemetery.

The Century's war was over. Jack Rhea's division might not have had a reputation as glamorous as the six Ranger Battalions or the same level of name recognition as the 3rd Infantry Division or the 1st Marine Division. The Centurymen did not possess the same swagger as the airborne troopers from the 82nd or 101st or a fancy shoulder patch like the Indianhead Division's (2nd Infantry). Nonetheless, the Centurymen had completed a truly spectacular job. Not many other divisions put in six full months straight of hard-slogging on the line without being sent to a rest area. Few other divisions accomplished so much with such remarkably little loss of life. But the Century did. The 100th earned three Medals of Honor (two for men of Jack's regiment), a number of Distinguished Service Crosses, and its share of well-deserved Silver and Bronze Stars. Many of the division's men were awarded Purple Hearts (nearly 3,700). The division left nearly 1,000 Centurymen behind in graves in England and France and almost 200 comrades missing in action forever.

Many of the 100th Infantry Division's battle dead were brought home by a grateful nation in the late 1940s. Those who remain behind are buried in six American military cemeteries in Europe. Very small numbers of Centurymen are buried in cemeteries in England, Belgium, the Netherlands, and in Rhone American Cemetery in France. In most cases, those were men who died from disease or wounds after being evacuated from the battlefield. Most of the Centurymen who gave it all are buried near where they fell: at the Epinal American Cemetery located near Bitche and the Lorraine American Cemetery which is nearly 30 miles east of Metz in the town of St. Avold in the French Department of Moselle. Many of those men were known to Jack Rhea. In fact, of the twenty-nine original officers in the battalion's four line companies that shipped out to France in October of 1944, six were killed in action. Serving in a battalion headquarters, as Jack did, was no guarantee of safety. When the battalion H.Q. company left New York, it was composed of 117 men. Counting replacements arriving during the following six months, a total of 187 men served in the battalion headquarters. Of that number, at least twenty-seven or fifteen percent were wounded. Those statistics are based on records in the 100th Division Association, and are really a minimum figure. Actual figures, allowing for records not held by the Association, would likely place the wounded at nearly twenty percent. A further six men from the battalion H.Q. were killed in action and one was listed as missing in action.

Rhea Family Collection

*Captain Jack Rhea addresses an informal, autumn
gathering of the Headquarters Company,
3rd Battalion in Esslingen.*

Jack's last communication to the battalion as its commander is worth repeating here. Jack barely spoke of the war to family and friends over the following decades, not even late in life when many old veterans frequently become more reflective on what for many were the defining moments of their lives.

> As I look back over the last year, my emotions are mixed. Pride in the record the battalion has made for itself during combat, sorrow for the fact that the battalion is slowly dissolving, and joy for those who are now at home or are on their way to join organizations that are soon going home. The Vosges, the roadblock at La Puid, Rosteig, Bitche, Heilbronn, Affaltrach, step by step tell a glorious story. A story full of leadership and heroism, where there are no main characters, just several hundred men fighting for an ideal.

> Many of those men fell on the battlefield, many more were seriously wounded and left, never to rejoin the battalion. Let us all rededicate ourselves to the ideal for which those men were wounded and died. Never forget the sacrifices they made, never forget the hardships you endured in the fight for democracy. Your record, the record of the Third Battalion, will stand forever as a monument to the courage, unselfishness, and physical stamina of a battalion that believed in the things for which it fought, fought hard no matter the odds, and always accomplished its mission.

> Jack L. Rhea
> Capt. Inf.
> Commanding

Part III
THE UPWARD TRAIL

In a quintessentially 1950s Philmont photograph, Director of Camping Jack Rhea, at right center, greets incoming campers.

CHAPTER 11

Back Home

When the now Major Jack Rhea returned to Kansas City, heads turned when people saw the ribbons on his tunic: a Silver Star, a Bronze Star with two oak leaf clusters, a Purple Heart, the American Campaign Service Medal, the European-African-Middle East Campaign Medal (with three battle stars for Rhineland, Ardennes-Alsace, and Central Europe), the World War II Victory Medal, and the Presidential Unit Citation Award with oak leaf cluster – all appearing below what was in many ways the dearest award to those for whom likely death was constantly a very close companion: the Combat Infantryman's Badge. Although not authorized until 1947, Jack would also receive the Army of the Occupation Medal with Germany Clasp. Only four men in the regiment (including the many replacements over and above the original, pre-deployment roster of about 3,300 men) won three Bronze Stars, and Jack was one of them.

In addition to knowing that he had served his country well, Jack's World War II legacy included shrapnel wounds which would create problems many years later. Like most veterans of close combat, he rarely talked about his experiences – even to his family. The exact circumstances of Jack's being hit by shrapnel are not known; the matter is not included in any of the four citations for his major combat decorations so it is logical to assume that he was wounded on one of the occasions when the German shelling was at its most ferocious. That was most likely at Bitche or Heilbronn although Jack and everybody else in the regiment was subjected to exploding anti-personnel mines and falling artillery almost constantly during the division's six months of combat.

One of the few things Jack did mention was that his distinct aversion to roast lamb was based on its reminding him of burnt human flesh. Although he was proud to serve his country as an Army Reserve officer, he quite intentionally avoided joining the American Legion and Veterans of Foreign Wars because he wanted to put the war years well behind him. He had no reservations, however, about joining fraternal and service organizations; he became an active member of Rotary and the Lions Club, International.

If anything, the war had firmly convinced Jack Rhea of the value of

Scouting as a Peace organization. Lord Baden-Powell of Gilwell had often been accused by his critics of fostering an organization that was designed to feed pre-conditioned young men into the British military machine, yet the founder of Scouting steadfastly insisted that the World Brotherhood of Scouting was truly a peace-fostering organization.

Rhea Family Collection

Captain Jack Rhea in late 1945, just before his promotion to major.

Jack got his old job back as a field executive with the Tall Corn Council, B.S.A., in Des Moines as soon as he returned. He was released from active duty on 14 March 1946, but was actually enjoying some accumulated leave after officially starting with the Boy Scouts on 1 January 1946. He was placed in charge of Sunrise and Custer districts in Polk County along with being the director of Camp Mitigwa which is still going strong as part of today's Mid-Iowa Council, B.S.A.

It was during this period that Jack met the love of his life, Maxine Cooper, the daughter of a Des Moines grocer. Like Jack, the Coopers were originally from Missouri and were an even larger family; Maxine was the youngest of seventeen children. She was musically talented and appeared in a number of community theater productions. She also appeared as the comedic lead in two independently produced films shot locally in Des Moines near the end of the war, and she played both the piano and violin. After completing secretarial school, she got a job with Meredith Corporation, the publishers of *Better Homes and Gardens*. The late forties were the highpoint of the magazine business. In a few years, that new medium called television would substantially erode the print media advertising base, but Meredith saw it coming and diversified into television itself. *Better Homes and Gardens* was less-affected by the trend because it was a special-interest publication. Maxine's typing accuracy and speed were noticed by the magazine's publisher who promoted Maxine to become his secretary.

While the early courtship of Maxine Cooper was shaky,
the subsequent marriage was absolutely solid.

Jack's previous romances had been lighthearted and short term. The courtship of Maxine Cooper started out on a very rocky road. On a Saturday in the spring of 1946, Maxine was attending a community event at the YMCA where one aspect of the program was a speech by Major Jack L. Rhea, late of the 100th Infantry Division. Maxine's girlfriends were bowled over by Jack, but Maxine certainly was not. She thought that the Army officer with all of those combat decorations was far too full of himself. Jack asked her to dance later that day. He was refused. Persistence, however, paid off and within a few weeks, the couple went on their first date and then became engaged after a courtship lasting several months. The wedding was held in Des Moines on 20 September 1946 with Harold West, the council executive, as the best man.

Rhea Family Collection

Maxine smiles at her husband, the new assistant
council executive in Des Moines.

The Rheas remained in Des Moines for less than two years, a period in which Jack got his first promotion – to assistant council executive. On 1 November 1947, Jack became the council executive in Fort Dodge, Iowa, where the offices were downtown in the municipal building. He quickly purchased a home at 3015 Sixth Avenue, located opposite River View Park, and got off to a very fast start with the Prairie Gold Council which had been known as the Fort Dodge Area Council from its founding in 1921 to 1941 when the name changed. Within two weeks Jack was the guest of honor and main speaker at the council's annual meeting in Fort Dodge and the following week he was speaker at a district meeting at Spirit Lake in Dickinson County, near the South Dakota border.

Rhea Family Collection

The new council executive at work in Fort Dodge.

The late 1940s were critical for Prairie Gold Council. Until Jack Rhea arrived, the council never owned its own summer camp; it had leased land on Spirit Lake, near Mini Wakan State Park right on the South Dakota border for its summer camping operation. Jack led the council in the purchase of its first camp which became Prairie Gold Scout Reservation in 1950. The new camp was located about twelve miles southwest of the previous camp on an abandoned golf course by the shore of West Lake Okoboji, near Gull Point State Park. In 1972 the council retained its name in a merger with Sergeant Floyd Area Council, but the council office moved to Sioux City. By the late 1990s the Prairie Gold Council was facing substantial financial problems to the extent that a merger was necessary. In 2000 Prairie Gold merged with Mid-America Council which had been created with the merger of Covered Wagon Council and Southwestern Iowa Council in 1964. Today, Jack's old council is a district within the huge Mid-America Council which is headquartered in Omaha, Nebraska. Jack spent slightly less than three years in Fort Dodge, but they were good years – years in which he enjoyed a high profile in that small city. The council records have long since been lost, but there are indications that it was a very strong council before, during, and for years after Jack's service there.

The council got an early start with Philmont to which it sent an eighteen-person expedition in August of 1943, at a time when few councils other than those from Philmont's bordering states could do so. The contingent participated in the Service Corps Program: work for two weeks then go on the trail for two weeks. The majority of the trek was spent in the South Country where the Scouts camped at Rayado, Crater Lake, and Fish Camp. They were among the very first to see the B-24 Liberator crash site on Trail Peak – only sixteen months after the accident occurred. In 1950, just before his next promotion, Jack sent 200 Scouts to the Third National Jamboree in Valley Forge; that was a huge contingent for a not-so-large council. In fact, it was one of the largest contingents from any council.

Rhea Family Collection

*Maxine stayed at home while Jack was off
to the first of many jamborees.*

The Jamboree contingent left Fort Dodge on 25 June after a Jamboree Shakedown weekend which was held at the Lincoln Elementary School in Fort Dodge. Maxine stayed behind with their kids, and Jack was off to the first of his many Jamborees. The contingent changed trains in Chicago and later stopped in Detroit to visit the Ford Plant and Edison Museum. The next morning they woke up in Buffalo, New York, where they visited Niagara

Falls and took a ride on the *Maid of the Mist*. The next stop was New York City for tours of the Empire State Building, the United Nations, and the Statue of Liberty. While at the Jamboree they saw President Harry Truman and General Dwight D. Eisenhower who was, at that time, president of Columbia University. While at the Jamboree, Jack and the contingent visited downtown Philadelphia where they saw the Liberty Bell, Independence Hall, and the Betsy Ross House. The group left Philly very early on 7 July, but still had one more stop before heading back to Iowa. It was Washington, D.C., where they did the grand tour in one day: Arlington, the White House, Mount Vernon, the Lincoln Memorial, the Smithsonian, and the Washington Monument. The contingent entrained at 9:00 P.M. that evening and arrived back in Fort Dodge on 9 July at 4:30 A.M. It had been quite an impressive undertaking for what was essentially a small council in rural Iowa.

As the local scout executive Jack was often invited to speak to various civic and service groups. His visibility was further enhanced by his being a district governor in the Lions Club. Awareness of Jack Rhea and the Prairie Gold Council was boosted on those occasions when Jack's letters to the *Fort Dodge Messenger & Chronicle* were published. One of the letters which reveals much about Jack's philosophy on youth development was prompted by juvenile delinquency in which one of the city's beautiful parks was vandalized. Jack went right to the heart of the problem.

> The family which has no church home, the family in which school activities are unimportant, and the family in which members have little in common with each other and little interest in where the other persons go and what they do produces boys who sooner or later find themselves at odds with society.
>
> The answer is not punishment of parents for their children's behavior. The answer lies in educating the parents to take an interest in their own children. Making the church, school, and other youth programs part of the discussion in the family circle; and then not stop with just talk. Actual participation by the entire family must be part of the program. That would almost be a sure cure for our juvenile problems.

Fort Dodge is where Jack and Maxine started their family. Daughter Julie arrived in 1948 and was followed by daughter Carol in 1950 just before the family moved to Chicago when Jack was promoted.

Moving to Chicago

On 1 September 1950, Jack reported for a new job. He went to work for the National Council as an assistant director of Boy Scouting service. The new job was not located at the National Office in New York; rather his office was located in the Region Seven Headquarters in downtown Chicago. The Rheas made the first of several major moves in Jack's career; this first move was from Fort Dodge to LaGrange, a southwestern suburb of Chicago. Region Seven included Illinois, Wisconsin, Indiana, and Michigan at a time when Scouting was moving into some real growth years – the early 1950s. There were nearly 1,250,000 youth in Boy Scouts and Explorers when Jack moved to Chicago and the average growth was about six percent per year in the 1950–1952 timeframe. The job involved considerably more travel than he had ever encountered in Des Moines or Fort Dodge because he was quite literally at the beck and call of local councils. His business card might have well read, "Have Program Support – Will Travel." Council needs varied and reflected the growth in membership numbers for both youth and adult volunteers alike.

Jack was not alone in being a "National" man in a regional headquarters. He had national counterparts for Cub Scouting and Exploring in the same office as did all of the other eleven regional offices. There was some variety in the work because he was occasionally able to hone his skills as a journalist. Some of his work appeared in *Scouting Magazine* as one-page, illustrated articles with punchy headlines like "Sound-Off" and "Welcome" on subjects ranging from proper uniforming to effective use of troop committee members.

Travel was the downside of the job. While some of the work involved day trips, the journeys to Chippewa Valley Council (Eau Claire, Wisconsin), Great Lakes Council (Detroit), or Abraham Lincoln Council (Springfield, Illinois) among many others were overnighters that must have dredged up ghosts from the past – of Jack's father Charles Rhea being an absentee father most of the time. Family was becoming more important to Jack for which not the least reason was the family was growing. Son Ron arrived in 1951 and two years later son Bart was born.

Jack Rhea shortly after moving to Chicago in late 1950.

In addition to his new job, Jack stayed in the Army Reserve. On 9 October 1950 he was placed under the jurisdiction of the Chicago Detachment of the Organized Reserve Corps. This essentially turned out to be a continuation of his reserve duty in Iowa, i.e., assignment to an instructor group, a status which Jack maintained for the next two and one-half years. Jack was fortunate not to be called back onto active duty as large numbers of reservists were during the Korean War which had just broken out a mere three months before the Rheas moved to Chicago. Several of Jack's old comrades from the 3rd Battalion, 398th Infantry had remained on active duty and served in Korea – Ernest Janes, Wilfrid Ganeau, and Fred Lemr among them. Fortunately, they all got through it in one piece. In early spring of 1953, Jack was required to make a decision about resigning his commission or "re-upping" for another five-year period. With a young family and a new job that still required considerable travel, Jack left the military as a lieutenant colonel at the end of May 1953.

Earlier in 1952, Jack took on a new assignment from the National Office. Although he was still based in Chicago, he became assistant national director of volunteer training. Part of this job involved coordinating National Camping Schools and conventional training for new volunteers, i.e., scoutmasters, commissioners, etc. By far, the most important aspect of this job was rolling out Wood Badge to greater numbers of the more experienced volunteers. It is not within the scope of this book to provide an in-depth discussion of Wood Badge because that has already been authoritatively accomplished in *A History of Wood Badge* in the United States by Kenneth Davis.

Rhea Family Collection

Jack's Wood Badge woggle and beads remain with
the Rhea family. Jack started with four beads because his
training in England was for those who would be running
Wood Badge courses.

However, understanding Jack Rhea's role in Wood Badge will require just a brief recap of Wood Badge history. As the most advanced training for Scouters, Wood Badge had been offered in Britain for many years. The British version was offered twice in America during the 1930s – both times at Schiff Scout Reservation in New Jersey. It was not an immediate success because participants believed that it was too "British." The training, this time modified for American Scouters, was offered twice in 1948: once at Schiff and once at Philmont. There was still a lot of room for more "Americanization" which was part of Jack's new job. In those days, Wood Badge was offered by the National Office, never a local council. Gradually, the Regions began to offer the course. It was still very exclusive, i.e., by invitation only. It was not until the 1970s that Wood Badge would be offered by local councils, and even then it was only with input from the regional offices.

As part of this Wood Badge expansion, Jack took Wood Badge at Gilwell Park in England and became a Wood Badge Deputy Camp Chief which authorized him to conduct Wood Badge courses in the United States. Unlike most first-time Wood Badge participants who receive the thong with two beads upon completion of their tickets, Jack started off with four beads because his course in England was tailored for people who would be conducting Wood Badge courses. There were more trips to England to consult with Wood Badge authorities because the American course content was in transition which Jack noted, years later, was not always to the liking of British Wood Badge leaders. While Jack was in Chicago, Wood Badge courses for Region Seven were conducted at that region's canoe base which was located on White Sand Lake, near Boulder Junction, Wisconsin. In conducting Wood Badge courses there, Jack met the base's director, a man whom he would meet again in about ten years' time. The director's name was A.J. "Skipper" Juncker.

Jack conducted additional Wood Badge courses in a location that would prove much more important to his future career path: Philmont. In 1953 and 1954, Jack conducted Wood Badge each summer at Zastro, a South Country camp which had been built specifically for the purpose of hosting Wood Badge courses. He also was an instructor on a number of courses offered at Philmont's Training Center. Prior to 1953, he had been to Philmont at least once a year on other training assignments even as early as 1946. Jack himself was still being trained; In July of 1953, he completed Professional Scouter's Stage Three (Advanced) Training.

Jack's star was rising. He had compiled an excellent record where the rubber meets Scouting's runway – as a successful council executive. His resume included plenty of camp management experience including serving as a course director at National Camping Schools. He enjoyed high visibility at Philmont Scout Ranch at a time when the National Office was rapidly building up its training manpower and facilities, and Jack was a westerner who knew his way around horses and ranching. Jack was also involved in early 1950s Philmont staff training where he was a campcraft instructor for Philmont guides. Jack was at the right place at the right time when Director of Camping George Bullock's tour at Philmont concluded in late 1954.

Rhea Family Collection

Rhea Family Collection

In the early 1950s, Jack served as an instructor for Philmont Guides, using a National Camp School syllabus modified for use at Philmont.

Philmont Museum

*Jack Rhea arrived at Philmont in late 1954. His management philosophy was
quite simple: organize, delegate, and supervise. That, however, did not mean
that his management style was hands off.*

Getting the director of camping job was not quite as easy for Jack
Rhea as it had been for George Bullock who already had the inside track
with Philmont's general manager. In the intervening years, Philmont Scout
Ranch was receiving much more attention from the National Office where

the national personnel director screened several candidates for the job. Jack also had to have the approvals of the Chief Scout Executive, Arthur Shuck, and Philmont's new general manager, Ray Bryan. When Jack returned home to LaGrange from his office in downtown Chicago one fine evening in mid-October, 1954, he had momentous news for his family. They were going to move to New Mexico where Jack would take up duties as Philmont's new director of camping on November first.

CHAPTER 12

Taking The Reins

Jack would not make many changes in 1955, although he would start laying the foundation for major changes in 1956 and 1957. Typically, new directors of camping/program spend their first few months learning and absorbing as much as they can. Still, Jack clearly annunciated what his management philosophy was as soon as he arrived at the Ranch. That philosophy was summed up in just three words: "organize, delegate, and supervise." Anybody on the Philmont staff found that Jack was accessible and that one of his management qualities included being a good listener. People leaving the camping director's office, however, were very much aware of who was in charge. According to one old Philmont hand, "The ground shook when Jack Rhea arrived." There were certainly some tremors at first, but the real shaking would start after Jack's orientation in late 1954 and early 1955. Indeed, when many of Jack's immediate subordinates were asked to make a decision, especially by seasonal staff, a frequent response was, "See Jack."

The Rhea years were not unique in the type of talent attracted in terms of summer staff. Nearly every last young man who came to work at Philmont then wore the Eagle square knot on his uniform. OA flaps were everywhere; most were brotherhood members and here and there were some vigils. In other words, the achievement motive ran very, very high. One significant aspect of the Rhea era's uniqueness is its place early in Philmont's history, so early that an exclusive band of Rhea hirees was later able to make extraordinary contributions to Philmont – contributions that are still very much a part of Philmont itself. Looked at another way, the Rhea leadership essentially provided a ground floor opportunity for a handful of young "idea men" to make oversized, lasting contributions to Philmont.

In that regard, the statistics tell a very interesting story, or at least so as of this writing (mid-2012). Assuming that Philmont's real camping operations date from 1946, the Rhea years (1954-1962) amount to roughly twelve percent of the total years to date, but sixty percent of the Philmont Staff Association's Silver Sage Awards given to former seasonal members of the Camping Department staff were at Philmont in the Rhea years (Bates, Fossett, Gold, Hobbs, Klingler, and Replogle). Had they not died so young, several other Rhea era staffers would unquestionably have become Silver Sage honorees. We will meet Rhea's idea men in chronological order as this narrative unfolds.

Right from the beginning of their arrival in Cimarron, the Rheas hit the ground running, not only on the Ranch itself, but also in the greater "Philmont Country" communities. As might be expected, Jack was very much in demand as a speaker at men's fraternal and service organizations, especially the Lions Clubs International of which he was a very active member no matter where he lived. Those evening forays took him to Springer, Raton, and even as far as Trinidad, among other towns. Jack was also a popular speaker at school commencements, including Cimarron High School. As an experienced, polished speaker, and very frequently in venues far removed from Philmont, Jack was not one to drone on and on. He was very aware of how easy it is to lose an audience after just fifteen or twenty minutes. Jack had a notebook full of speeches which he frequently tailored for each audience. Fortunately, that little book survives to this day and reveals a man of deep religious faith, an inspirational speaker, and one who had great confidence in American youth, especially when having the good fortune of receiving some helpful guidance along the way. Philmont and Scouting were occasionally mentioned in those talks, but they by no means appear in the majority of his themes with non-Scouting-oriented audiences. Like others charged with public speaking, Jack would occasionally import a few words of wisdom or a poem from some well-known writer. One of his favorites was the Edgar A. Guest poem, "Just a Boy," for which he frequently included just the last stanza in his remarks. The poem undoubtedly rang true with audiences, but considering Jack's own nearly absentee father, the words were especially meaningful to him and probably contain the motivation which led him into education and, later, Scouting as career paths.

> Just a boy who needs a friend,
> Patient, kindly to the end;
> Needs a father who will show
> Him the things he wants to know.
> Take him with you when you walk,
> Listen when he wants to talk,
> His companionship enjoy,
> Don't forget – "he's just a boy."

Jack frequently took passages from the Bible to make certain points in his speeches. He certainly knew what he was talking about because he had been a regular reader of the Bible since childhood. His voice was a firm baritone and without any regional accent which was probably a function of growing up in Colorado, Kansas, and western Missouri whose residents tend to be free of any readily noticeable accent. Jack sounded his Rs very distinctly which may have been carried along from generation to generation in the Rhea family which was originally from Scotland.

Maxine, although she had four children at home age seven and under when she moved into the director of camping's residence, was a very high profile lady, and not just at the Ranch itself. In Raton, she was an active member and officer of the local chapter of the P.E.O. Sisterhood (Philanthropic – Educational – Organizational). Another one of her women's service groups was the Sorosis Club of Cimarron. The membership in those organizations consisted of prominent women in Colfax County, including Mrs. Linda Davis from the CS Ranch, Mrs. LaVerne Swope of the school bus fleet, Mrs. Geneva Heck of the Heck Ranch, Mrs. Howard McDaniel (UU Bar Ranch, Arizona farming, and resident of Nairn Place, now Casa Del Gavilan), and Mrs. James Dobyne. Other members were wives of men who were active or retired members of the Philmont permanent staff. The latter group included the spouses of Roy Cartwright, Buzz Clemmons, Mike Hope, Bill Tate, Joe Hawkins, and Doc Loomis among others. The Hopes and Rheas were particularly good friends; Mike Hope had become Philmont's comptroller in the late 1940s; the couples occasionally enjoyed driving over to Taos for dinner at what was then one of the best dining spots in town – Frenchy's La Doña Luz Restaurant (still there but now as a bed and breakfast). The Rheas were also friends with Gene and Lura Hayward who owned a small cattle Ranch just south of Philmont. The Hayward's place was especially popular with the Rhea children because it had a swimming pool. Gene Hayward had been Waite Phillips' first superintendent of the Philmont Ranch back in the early 1920s.

*Julie, Carol, Ron, and Bart Rhea are delighted with photographer
Dan Sheehan's dog.*

The Rheas attended the Methodist Church in Cimarron. Although Jack was not a member of the choir, he was a strong singer and considered as a very strong asset by the congregation; he was a very effective fund raiser. The Rhea family frequently attended Protestant services at the Ranch in the summer, but also made a point of occasionally attending the services of other faiths, thus providing an avenue for the Rhea children to learn about other Christian denominations and the Jewish faith. As might be expected, Jack interfaced with the chaplains only infrequently; his impression of Philmont's chaplain corps was that it was doing a superb job and therefore required little of his attention.

Jack was a very visible member of the Maverick Club and served as grand marshal at more than one Fourth of July Maverick Rodeo. The rodeos were family events for the Rheas who rode down to Cimarron on their own horses which, to save time, were taken back to the Ranch in trailers after the rodeo. Jack became a card-carrying member of the Girl Scouts of the U.S.A. because his daughters were in Brownies, for which Maxine briefly served as a leader.

Meeting the Phillips Family

Waite Phillips was an occasional visitor to Philmont during the Jack Rhea era, although he spent most of his time on those visits with General Manager Ray Bryan and Ranch Superintendent Bill Littrell. Nevertheless, Jack did become well acquainted with Phillips with whom he had much in common. Both grew up on farms, spent much of their early years on the Great Plains, were excellent horsemen, were accomplished hunters and trout fisherman, were used to hard work from an early age, and knew a lot about ranching. When speaking or writing, both drew inspiration from many of the same sources (Biblical figures, authors, statesmen, etc.). One morning not long after Jack arrived at Philmont, the two men were having breakfast when Jack asked a very incisive question. Jack later recorded the conversation in a notebook; the dialogue never made it into Phillips' well-known *Epigrams*, but is certainly worth repeating here.

> "Mr. Phillips, you gave this ranch and all of its buildings to the Boy Scouts of America at a cost to you of millions of dollars. It is now my job to help put it to good use. What one thing do you feel that boys who come here should get from their experience?"
>
> I then sat back and half-expected Phillips to tell me that the beauties of nature and love for the outdoors were uppermost in his mind. Instead Phillips rather quietly got up and motioned for me to join him.
>
> Then, pointing out the window he said, "Do you see that tall mountain? That is Black Mountain. No matter what direction you come from, the first thing you see is Black Mountain. It looks big, tall, and impressive. Much of the awe that people from the plains country get from Philmont comes from their view of Black Mountain. Yet from Clear Creek Mountain which lies behind Black Mountain and is taller and more majestic, you can look down upon all of Philmont, even Black Mountain itself. There is a trail to the top of Black Mountain, but it is little-used. Several trails go to the top of Clear Creek, and most boys want to climb it. Just point out to them that it is not the way you look or the big front you might put up, but what you are that makes you a success in life."

While Jack did not have considerable contact with Waite Phillips, he did see Chope Phillips fairly often, and with Maxine and the kids, frequently was a guest at Chope's Ranch near Las Vegas, New Mexico. The Rhea children enjoyed those afternoons spent with Chope's family, particularly because Maxine usually brought a dessert of which the kids were especially fond: a large cherry pie. Jack occasionally had the Phillips family back to Philmont as guests. The usual destination was Fish Camp where the staff in those days lived in Rayado Lodge itself. The staff surrendered their posh digs for those visits and gladly repaired temporarily to the other ranks' quarters.

Jack, Maxine, and their young family at the Ranch, spring 1955.

Welcome to the Land of Enchantment

When the Rhea family arrived in Cimarron in November 1954, Jack faced several realities. First among these was the fact that he was taking over from George Bullock, a man who was widely respected and very well-liked. Like Bullock, Jack Rhea was a warm and friendly person, but within that genial Rhea persona there was a strong "business-like" component. Al Clemmons, having just finished a tour as a Marine junior officer and eventually serving Philmont over the years as a Cito camp director, assistant chief ranger, and sector director recalls Jack very much as "the colonel." Al was hardly the only one to have that impression.

Bullock was turning over more than just the camping operation to Jack. Bullock had done a spectacular job growing the Volunteer Training Center in terms of physical plant, courses offered, family programs, and attendance in the five years since the Training Center was launched in 1949. The Training Center was part of Bullock's strategy for increasing camping attendance. He realized that having as many trained adults returning to councils across the country was a sure-fire method for boosting interest and participation on the camping side. Bullock improved more than the Training Center physical plant. Because the food quality and sanitation standards in the early days left a lot to be desired, Bullock recruited women from Oklahoma A&M to take over the kitchen, and they made a world of difference.

Philmont's place in the history of the Southwest was not lost upon Bullock; he was the one who initiated restoration of the Kit Carson homestead at Rayado. That facility's dedication was in 1951 when many artifacts that had been exhibited at a small museum in Camping Headquarters were moved down to the new museum.

In late 1954, George Bullock was leaving to become the council executive in Albuquerque, a move that puzzled many of the more senior seasonal staffers since they believed he should have been kept on at Philmont or at least been offered a larger, more prestigious council. Bullock felt that it was time to move – he had taken the Ranch from a fledgling operation to what it had become by 1954 – Scouting's premier camping operation. With Philmont's importance building rapidly, the Ranch also came under more control from the National Office, a trend with which Bullock was not always comfortable. Thus it was Bullock's decision alone to move to Albuquerque. In late 1954, he was too young to retire and was very cognizant of the fact that he could be sent Back East to the National Office or to any council across the country. Because he was anxious to stay in the Southwest, he acted quickly as soon as he became aware of the opening in Albuquerque. And as would be shown over the years, the average tour for all directors of camping is slightly under eight years, excluding A.J. "Skipper" Juncker whose death occurred just two years into his service at Philmont.

Secondly, 1955 was going to be another big season with nearly 8,000 campers expected or just about double 1953's camping total. Although the Ranch was supported by income from the Philtower Building in Tulsa, Philmont could not always count on all of the income from that property since it too required investment in maintenance and building systems updates. That fact placed a premium on making more of the Ranch pay for itself – through increased camper revenues.

Thirdly, Jack would not be able to introduce much in the way of innovations for 1955 since it would take several months just to become completely oriented. Bullock and Clarence Dunn, a Texas educator whose seasonal staff experience dated back to the close of World War II, had already made some of the key decisions for 1955, particularly those involving program and camp directors. Finally, Jack's boss, General Manager Ray Bryan, a Bostonian five years older than Jack, was relatively new in his position as well.

Jack and Ray Bryan settled into a business-like working relationship but never became especially friendly because they were cut from such different cloth. Jack was a forceful, people-oriented, outgoing program guy with plenty of camping and training experience. Bryan, a notably aloof man, was an Eagle Scout also, but that was about as much as the two had in common. Although normally rather distant, Bryan did warm up to his task of speaking to groups, particularly during staff training or when VIPs visited the Ranch. An engineer by training, he had joined the BSA as a draftsman in 1930 and by 1933 was the resident engineer in charge of developing the Schiff estate into Schiff Scout Reservation. He was very involved with designing facilities for National Jamborees from the ill-fated 1935 Jamboree to those held well after his appointment as General Manager of Phillips properties (the Ranch and the Philtower Building in Tulsa) on 1 September 1953. He had also been in charge of designing facilities for the American contingents at the World Jamborees in France and Austria in 1947 and 1951, respectively. His original connection with Philmont dated to 1938 when, as assistant national director of BSA's Engineering Service, he was part of the team from the National Office inspecting the new Philmont gift in 1938. Bryan, while located Back East, was the liaison between Philmont's general managers (B.B. Dawson, Minor Huffman, and James Fitch), until he was appointed GM immediately after the 1953 Third National Jamboree in California.

The third key player during the Rhea era was Bill Littrell, the Ranch superintendent. His job did not significantly overlap with Jack's because it was tied directly to farming, cattle breeding, timber, etc. Although Littrell's daughter Connie was a good friend of the Rhea daughters, the elder Rheas and Littrells were not members of the same social circle. Littrell's credentials were in line with the job's needs; he had grown up on a ranch, got his bachelor's degree in agriculture, and was a county agent when he accepted an offer from Philmont in 1954. He would eventually go on to become a controversial general manager at Philmont in 1974 (controversial primarily because his previous career had been spent entirely outside of the BSA). Ten years later, he left Philmont to pursue real estate interests; he eventually became secretary of agriculture in the New Mexico state government.

George Bullock's Legacy

From the roughly 1,500 youth who passed through Philmont in 1946, a handful became Philmont seasonal staff in the late 1940s. From them it is learned that George Bullock brought organization to Philmont. Among more than just one camper in 1946, there was a feeling that the Ranch was not a tightly run ship and that this was obvious in program, transportation, and logistical glitches. Today, any management consultant could easily explain the reasons for that lack of coordination. First, there was a changing cast of characters in leadership roles. In the three years before Bullock's appointment, three different men had been in the director of camping slot. There were similar changes in the Philmont general manager position, and it was a time of transition at the highest levels of the BSA. Arthur Schuck took over in 1948 and served for the next twelve years, but in the three years preceding his appointment, there had been two Chief Scout Executives (James E. West and Elbert K. Fretwell).

Philmont Museum

George Bullock, director of camping at Philmont from 1947 to late 1954.

Secondly, Philmont was new and not only was it new, it was BIG. The BSA had never been faced with developing programs, staffing, operating, and promoting an entity as large as 127,000 acres. Naturally, there were going to be some start-up bugs. In many ways, the late 1940s can really be looked upon as a new ship's shakedown cruise, i.e., a time when a great new vessel is taken to sea for its first trials. It was, thus, a time to fix that which falls short of expectations along with optimizing what looks promising.

Thirdly, it was not until 1954 that Philmont set out to create a ten-year plan, a plan which was updated in 1961, just a year before Jack moved to the National Office. To describe Philmont's immediate post-war operations as being somewhat ad hoc would be inaccurate, but by the same token, those operations were not the outcome of a disciplined process of management by objectives, strategies, tactics, and program measurement.

Bullock brought stability to Philmont camping operations but not as might be expected, i.e., with an iron hand that micro-managed. Quite the reverse was true. Bullock's strength was in developing programs and empowering subordinates, primarily the camp directors, to administer them. In that regard, he may have been Philmont's all-time leader in delegating authority. And the staff loved him for it. If a nineteen year-old camp director had to make a tough call and knew he was right, he also knew that he would have Bullock's backing on that decision.

George Bullock was a large man, well over six feet tall and approaching 240 pounds. Backpacking was not at the top of his list of leisure priorities. He was an imposing figure and an immaculate dresser who typically appeared in a dark green Explorer uniform, cowboy boots, and tan western hat. His manner with people, all people, was the same: cordial, kind, specific, and authoritative. In those days, there was a dance every Saturday night in back of Villa Philmonte. In spite of his physical stature, he was as light as a feather on the dance floor as was his lovely wife Bess. Those dances were community events for which families of local ranches such as the UU Bar and CS were in attendance. The Bullocks had two children: Bruce who worked as a wrangler and Martha, a vivacious teenager upon whom more than just several summer staffers had a crush.

Bullock was occasionally seen on a horse in the Backcountry. Fish Camp is considered "Backcountry," although it is reached by trucks and Chevy Suburbans almost daily at present. That was hardly the case in 1947 when the roads to the high South Country ended at Crater Lake and Abreu. Thus, it was usually a significant event, such as the dedication of Trappers Lodge at Beaubien in 1952, that brought Bullock to the very far Backcountry. George Bullock, however, used a horse extensively at Camping Headquarters. Instead of driving between his residence, the Training Center, or Villa Philmonte, he simply rode his big, dark sorrel horse.

Bullock had a warm personality and was a good man to have at a campfire because he was a particularly good singer. He would typically sing the first few songs and then invite others to join in either with songs, stories, or skits. That was one of the keys to his popularity. Bullock was also a commanding public speaker, one with a big booming voice. He had the capability of keeping audiences, Scouting and civic alike, engaged during his talks. One of his talks, "Our Philmont" was given to a group of Scouters gathered at Villa Philmonte. The talk also showed what a good writer Bullock was. "Our Philmont" was the precursor of much to come including the "Philmont Story" and the key themes Jack picked up for use in Philmont's annual promotional literature.

Bullock was also a very patient man; it took quite a lot to make him angry. He always had a smile on his face, and another secret to his popularity was his remembering something about each person on the staff. Dean Tooley, a guide in 1952 and years later an assistant director of program, recalls another facet of Bullock's popularity: a genuine interest in each member of the staff. Bullock was particularly fascinated with Philmont's flora and fauna, taking an active part in that aspect of guides' training. He would wind up his training session on that subject by inviting any member of the staff who had a problem identifying a certain flower or plant to bring it back to headquarters for some help with identification. Dean came across one flower that was not in the little field book he carried, so when he got back to headquarters after the trek he went to the camping office and asked to see Mr. Bullock. He was quickly ushered into the director's office where the two puzzled over George's more authoritative books. They never did positively identify the flower, but Dean was impressed with the time Bullock took with a new, seventeen year-old guide who had a question.

Rod Replogle, a young trainee in the early 50s also remembers Bullock's caring personality. Replogle had the misfortune of suffering a severe appendicitis mid-season. He was rushed to the hospital in Raton for the inevitable appendectomy. Bullock visited him there and Replogle expressed his worst fear – that he would promptly be sent home to Illinois. The young trainee asked if he could remain on the staff for the rest of the season, and Bullock did indeed find him some light duties for the remaining weeks of the summer after getting parental agreement. Rod could not have known it at the time, but he himself was destined to make a major contribution to Philmont in terms of conservation and trail building. Although his staff days were over after the 1956 season, his career in the U.S. Forest Service provided him with the expertise to become a consultant to Philmont on trail construction – a service that was much appreciated following the devastating flood in 1965. Rod can easily be considered the father of Philmont conservation and certainly was the inspiration for creating that department. His service to Philmont also includes training generations of Philmont conservation staff and channeling expertise from the Forest Service and other federal agencies to Philmont's conservation programs.

Bullock was a man of high principles; he always set the example. He never swore and would not tolerate those who did. Dan Ferguson, a guide and camp director from the late 1940s and early 1950s well recalls how

Bullock would confront the foul-mouthed, "There are three kinds of people who cuss: one that shows off his lack of language, one who does not care, and one who means it. Are you any of those?"

George Bullock was a man ahead of the times when it came to race relations. Some advisors, typically from the Deep South, arrived at Philmont and complained about the lack of "separate but equal" facilities. Bullock graciously, but firmly, replied that complaining advisors had only two choices when it came to civil rights at Philmont: accept the situation as is or go home.

Judge Richard Mills was a member of the staff during Bullock's tour at Philmont and describes Bullock as a *rara avis* (a truly unique person) and "a thoroughly honorable man who taught and lived the Scout Oath and Law, a most talented leader of men who had a tremendous impact on the hundreds of staffers who universally looked up to and idolized him." Carl Hart, who was at Cito in 1951 and Clear Creek in 1952, advises that he never knew a man who was more honest or fair in his dealings with everyone than George Bullock.

Bullock certainly brought the right credentials to the Ranch. He was a southwestern Texas farmboy who was educated at the University of Texas, and he had plenty of experience working with youth as a teacher and football coach at Oklahoma A&M where he was the Secretary of the YMCA. He had been a Scouting volunteer and a Silver Beaver recipient before turning professional in 1940 as a camping specialist in BSA Region Nine (Texas, Oklahoma, and New Mexico). By the time he arrived at Philmont, he had several years of experience in managing both Scout council and private camps. While at Oklahoma A&M, he had owned and operated Sacramento Camp for Boys, located in the Sacramento Mountains, near Cloudcroft, New Mexico. His link to Philmont came through James P. Fitch, his former boss and the Region Nine director who became manager of Phillips properties in 1946. Bullock's work on the Region Nine staff included organizing and running special events such Sea Scout regattas, Senior Scout competitive programs, and Explorer bivouacs. His management philosophy was based on working through the chain of command.

Bullock's principal assistants were two men whose careers were in education: Clarence Dunn and Doc Rouse. Dunn came from the Dallas suburb of Arlington and functioned as Philmont's personnel director among other duties. Rouse was a school teacher from Walsenburg, Colorado, who functioned as Bullock's assistant with a title of "associate director." As the years rolled on, there were many more demands on Bullock's time, including that from the rapidly escalating number of VIPs visiting from the regions and National Office. Thus Bullock increasingly relied on people like Dunn to carry out assignments and identify problem areas, particularly as the camper totals went from under 2,000 in 1947 to almost 8,000 in 1954, Bullock's last year.

In the late 1940s, there was no sustained title such as "Chief Guide," but Dunn essentially filled that role since he was involved in guide training and was the one who gave direction to guide assignments. The guides in those days were broken down into crews for training, each headed by a crew leader, and there was one senior crew leader. Dunn was the person who wrote the critiques on training and summer operations for Bullock's review and action. In the mid to late 1950s, it was to Dunn that roving rangers sent their routine reports of conditions on the trails and problems campers were having.

The quality of training improved during the post-World War II era from a fast hike over the major trails to the use of more and more specialists as the Bullock era neared its end in 1954. Representatives from the U.S. Forest Service coordinated training on how to fight forest fires and Raymond C. "Doc" Loomis instructed in cooking and woods craft skills. Specialists, such as Russ Vliet, an authority on wilderness survival, also became part of the training function. Jack Rhea was also involved in training Philmont guides as part of his duties as assistant national director of volunteer training. One of Jack's responsibilities involved National Camping School from which the Scoutcraft skills portion was adapted for Philmont guide training.

The Legendary Doc Loomis

If there was a man as closely involved with Philmont guides as Clarence Dunn, it was Raymond "Doc" Loomis who had been a key member of the staff since the late 1940s when he was brought on board as an instructor in campcraft. He became much more than an instructor. He was the Scouting skills guru, and over his roughly twelve year association with Philmont he became a legend with campers through his lively cooking and campcraft demonstrations. He was also an indispensable man in training guides and the Philmont Rangers along with serving on many JLT and Wood Badge staffs.

Philmont Museum

*The legendary Doc Loomis demonstrating the finer points
of Dutch oven cooking.*

In over more than a decade, Loomis attained iconic status in a variety of Philmont jobs: director at Ponil (through 1955), director of campcraft skills, and director of program. His teaching skills were very much in demand not only at Philmont but also by the National Office which produced literature and a film on his fire building and cooking for use by councils. It must be noted that Loomis practiced a trade that was in demand in a day when backpacking stoves were years away, hence the need for expert knowledge with an axe, the ability to start a cooking fire (perhaps right after a downpour), and the many uses of a Dutch oven. It was also an era when the Dutch oven was a very popular item at Philmont where dozens of the ovens were available at large camps and an adequate number could be had at all smaller camps.

Doc's origins might not suggest he would become an authority on western camping. He was born in Vermont in 1894 and in World War I served on the USS *Arkansas*, a dreadnought that participated in taking the surrender of the German High Fleet in 1918. Loomis had every reason to be proud of the "Arky" which was substantially updated for service in World War II when it participated in all three invasions of France, the Philippines liberation, Iwo Jima, and Okinawa.

Loomis was called "Doc" because he was a chiropractor who had practiced Back East. Unfortunately, he developed arthritis to the extent that he decided to trade the damp, dismal winters of the mid-Atlantic for the dry warmth of the Southwest. He had some involvement with Scouting and camp schools before leaving Pennsylvania and continued the association when he arrived in Texas where he became acquainted with both Minor Huffman and George Bullock. Through Bullock, Doc Loomis joined the staff in late 1947 and was a participant in the 1948 Wood Badge course held at Cimarroncito. He subsequently served on many Wood Badge and JLT courses throughout the 1950s. His last year on the Philmont staff was 1959; his health was starting to become a problem. He received the Silver Beaver from the Kit Carson Council (Albuquerque) in January of 1962, only a few months before dying at age sixty-seven. He was also especially missed in Cimarron where he was a particularly active member of the community. Seven years later, there is every reason to believe that Doc Loomis turned over in his grave in the Cimarron Cemetery – in 1969 Philmont stopped issuing three-quarter axes to rangers and in a few more years stopped issuing the bow saws which replaced the axes. Yet Doc Loomis' legend still reaches out and overshadows those little, high-tech backpacking stoves which eventually terminated the need for bow saws.

CHAPTER 13

At the Foot of the Mountain

To understand the magnitude of Jack Rhea's sweeping changes to Philmont in 1956-57 requires a thorough understanding of how the previous programs developed. During World War II, gasoline and rubber tire rationing severely arrested development of Philmont's program and facilities. Thus, 1946 was the first year when the program expanded, both in terms of activities and geography since the Ranch was able to send Scouts into what is now Philmont's Central and South Country. The program was built around the "Senior Training Program" – a month long "schedule" which started with arrival at Camping Headquarters and spending several weeks at "base camps" starting at Rayado Rancho Base Camp (today's Rayado) which was essentially a week of training in what today's Philmont Rangers impart to their crews during the first few days of a trek. From Rayado, there was a service project and an overnight burro packing trip. Then it was off to Ponil to check out nearby Indian ruins, learn some archeology, develop trail first aid skills, and try their hands at some marksmanship. That aspect of the program was a blend of what was unique to Philmont overlaid with some basic council camp activities.

The principal camps in 1946 carried names that would be confusing to those familiar with the Philmont of today. Senior Training treks spent a few days at Lookout Mountain Base Camp which was indeed none other than today's Fish Camp. That camp was also known as Agua Fria Camp which is today the small trail camp just up the Agua Fria Creek from Fish Camp. There the program emphasized fishing and sidehikes. The next to final major location was "Black Mountain Base Camp" which fortunately soon became better known as Cimarroncito where the activities again were sidehikes (Hidden Valley, Deer Lake, gold mines, and the real Black Mountain). Cito was also informally known by guides as "Horse Camp" due to the availability of horses at that location. The last base camp was Abreu with its promise of good fishing and side hikes to Fowler Mesa and the recent B-24 Liberator bomber crash on Trail Peak. The cost per Explorer was fifty U.S. dollars for four weeks of High Adventure. Almost 1,600 youth and leaders went through the program.

In 1947, three activities were offered, but the Senior Training was cut back to two weeks; it started at Rayado where training lasted for a week. Then a guide was assigned, burros were packed, and the crew was off to Fish Camp and Cimarroncito with a hike in over Tooth Ridge. One of the new programs in 1947 was one that would evolve into today's twelve-day expedition; it was the "Backpacking Schedule" a thirteen-day activity which did not include burros or horses. This was strictly a South Country activity and included three days at Abreu, time at Crater to see the B-24 crash on Trail Peak, and a stop at a place that would become Beaubien: Rincon Bonito. From the latter camp, the crew hiked over Mount Phillips, down to Cyphers Mine, and spent several days at Cimarroncito before hiking in over Tooth Ridge. In later years, expeditions, northbound or southbound, would include burros. The thirteen-day "Exploration" was the only schedule that passed through the North Country. It started at Ponil and descended to Fish Camp before winding up at Camping Headquarters which was reached via Webster Pass and Crater Lake. Roughly 1,700 participants came to Philmont in 1947.

On the Kit Carson Trail

In 1948, the first year in which George Bullock had full control of camping, the program developed even more. Attendance was up and Bullock essentially changed nearly everything and what was kept was tweaked considerably. The Exploration schedule survived but it was given a southwestern occupational slant in which participants worked with foresters, geologists, surveyors, ranchers, and farmers. The Backpacking Schedule morphed into the thirteen day "Expedition" which did include burros. The new Kit Carson Trek lasted from eight to fifteen days, was strictly backpacking and South Country-oriented, but was in no way related to the Kit Carson Men of the early 1970s or today's Rayado Programs.

Jimmy Woodyard, just then going into his high school senior year, was a Kit Carson guide in 1951. His memories of that summer are still fresh and show us how much Philmont has changed in some respects and not at all in others. Staff training for his service as one of four guides at Stockade was rather casual in comparison to contemporary Ranger training. Kay Graves was the senior of the four guides, a football player in college, and was responsible for guide training which consisted of shakedowns on the side-hikes and trails the guides would later cover with campers. The trainees did not use maps – they just followed the lead guide and tried to learn as much about the landmarks, flora, and fauna as was possible on the quick march over territory they would later cover with campers. Guides were made to clearly understand their responsibilities: get their crews from point A to B each day, see that they had good campsites, were supplied with food, and had every opportunity to see and enjoy as much of the Ranch as possible.

Stockade, the structure itself, was the starting and ending camp for the Kit Carson treks and served many purposes. There were three two-story blockhouses: two for staff quarters and one for the commissary. The remaining corner was for the water tank. Campers slept under shelters along two of Stockade's walls and all cooking, for staff and campers, was done over open fires in the courtyard. The staff collected the wood to discourage campers from wandering too far from Stockade which was known for its rattlesnake population.

Assignment of guides was simply "Who's next?" There were not a lot of campers back in those days so guides might have a few days between treks. That first afternoon the assigned guide met with his group, got acquainted, and gave them an idea of what they would be doing for the next eight days. Adult advisors were told that "running the show" was up to them. After that one or more members of the group were designated to collect food. They drew enough for the entire group plus the guide for that night's supper, the next morning's breakfast, and the next day's dinner/lunch. They were also issued enough so that the solitary member of a one-man camp, such as Black Mountain, would be able to join the group at mealtime.

Most often that first night there was a campfire with the usual singing; songs usually consisted of western ballads such as "My Darlin' Clementine" and "Red River Valley" among others. The next morning, after breakfast, the campers got together and settled on lunch preparation. They soon learned that it was easier to carry the bulk food rather than make individual sandwiches before leaving camp.

On the first day, Kit Carson groups were taken on an easy Urraca Mesa conditioning hike first, stopping frequently to catch breaths and take photos. No packs were taken on this sidehike – just canteens, food, and ponchos. Standard practice for guides was to place the fastest hikers in the rear and the slower hikers up front with the guide in the lead, setting a pace that was not threatening to the boys immediately behind him. When they reached the top of the mesa, the group had lunch and were then turned loose for exploring or taking a siesta. Total time on the mesa amounted to about two hours. On the following day, the second conditioning hike was to the Tooth of Time which was climbed directly up the gully to the right of the "solar molar," taking a couple of breathers on the way up. Lunch was taken on the Tooth itself and if the group had made good time going up, the return was via the ridge and camping headquarters; otherwise they bushwhacked down the Tooth's southwest side to return to Stockade.

The trek really started on the third day, a time when many of the campers realized that they had brought too much equipment to take on the trail. The crew was issued trail food for two days plus some food for the single staffer at Black Mountain, their immediate destination. Carrying crew equipment, including an axe, was rotated among crew members. What the crew did not see as they started was the reservoir beyond Stockade (it would be built the following year). What they did see were many trout in the small pools on the way up the canyon which occasionally became quite narrow. Infrequently, there would be a small clearing where the crew took a break and Jimmy worked with those Scouts interested in nature awards. The hike up to Black Mountain was usually uneventful, but on one occasion the crew happened upon a very fresh deer kill, suggesting that a mountain lion was very close at hand. That was a very short breather.

At Black Mountain, Jimmy would usually sleep in the little dirt-floor cabin which had several bunks inside. The cabin was even then much in need of restoration; the caulking in the walls had just about disappeared making for very cold nights. The one-man band at Black Mountain was always glad to see crews because that meant he got new food and provisions. A long dry spell between groups meant that he had to go over the hill and down to Fish Camp for supplies.

The next destination was Cimarroncito via Comanche Pass with a break for lunch (Spam sandwiches as a rule). Camping was not at today's Cito, but at an area much closer to the Cimarroncito Hunting Lodge. There was a great temptation to go rock climbing at what is now the Cito rock climbing area, but it was forbidden in 1951. The group picked up two days of food at Cito and retraced some of their tracks the next morning when they were bound for the two-man camp, Cyphers Mine. The campers' area at Cyphers was on a slight slope, but the guides usually used an open-faced shelter, the ancestor of today's Adirondacks at Cyphers. The two-man staff had an old cabin which was complete with the luxury of a wooden floor. Campers could not go near the principal mine unless accompanied by Jimmy or one of the staff. There was a huge pile of tailings in front of the mine and it was loaded with fool's gold. The other mine was partially obscured by a mudslide and was off-limits to everybody.

The next day, the sixth, was a tough one because the destination, on the designated route, was Fish Camp via Comanche Peak, Mount Phillips, and Clear Creek Camp, i.e., a long day indeed. For groups that were up for a change and wanted to bushwhack their way to Rayado Creek, Jimmy would take them off Comanche Peak and pick up the Rayado Creek at Porcupine after passing through Red Hills. Although the descent was about the same, the hiking was harder and there was more nature to observe because there was no trail in 1951. At Fish Camp, the crew picked up supplies for the next three days and contemplated the relaxing hike to Abreu, although some of the many stream crossings created a little anxiety. Upon reaching Abreu, more than just one Scout and leader were found drying out boots and socks. Jimmy's crew was now in the home stretch on the eighth day, completed the easy hike over Stone Wall Pass to Stockade and a closing campfire.

Jimmy Woodyard recalls that, other than the firm itinerary, guides were largely left on their own. He was blessed with very congenial crews and, except for one sprained ankle and one blister, enjoyed an injury-free summer. The trail food left a lasting memory: loaves of white bread, Spam, cheese, powdered milk, powdered eggs, and the Kool-Aid that became known as "bug juice." To this day, Jimmy feels that a Kit Carson Trek was truly a wilderness adventure without equal and those who have never been on one could not begin to appreciate what it was really like or what it meant to those who were fortunate to have been guides. Within just a few years, the Kit Carson Trek along with the twelve-day expedition would form the basis for what Jack Rhea established as the basic backpacking program for Philmont.

The first program designed for Scouts who could not afford Philmont was launched in 1948; it was the Pioneering Trek in which participants worked on Philmont projects, and then got a free seven-day trek with a guide. That program lasted well into the 1950s. The major innovations in 1948 involved two new programs: the Cavalcade and Wagon Train. The Cavalcade, which survives to this day, was then a six-day trek by horse that originated and ended at Camping Headquarters.

Horse Cavalcades

The late Bob Knox, who retired from Philmont as Ranch Superintendent in 1980, began his Philmont days as a wrangler on Philmont cavalcades in the late 1940s. Fortunately he recorded his adventures in his wonderful book, *Growing Up To Cowboy*, through which we can now join him on a late 1940s horse cavalcade. His job was not as easy as it might first appear. Philmont's horses, destined for duty at Philmont's horse camps (Ponil, Cimarroncito, and Rayado) had to be readied for the season. Considering the fact that they had been turned out for nearly nine months, Bob had to evaluate them and determine which were docile enough for horseback rides. He also had to break in Philmont's seasonal wranglers during a week of staff training, not a simple task considering the fact that several of those college students were really not very experienced to begin with. The results of inexperience consisted of cracked ribs, broken halters, runaway horses, horses shod improperly, and some intense, remedial training quickly administered by the head of the horse department, the legendary Boss Sanchez.

There were always two cavalcades on the trail at the same time following what was a closed loop course that started and ended at Camping Headquarters. A northbound cavalcade, led by a horseman and his wrangler, would head for Lover's Leap, Stonewall Pass, and stop to enjoy a bagged lunch at Toothache Springs before descending into Rayado. Over the following days, the group would stop at Olympia for shooting sports and spend a night at Abreu. The next day was one of the highpoints because it followed one of Waite Phillips' favorite trails: Abreu to Fish Camp using the canyon trail. For a horseman leading the cavalcade, it was spectacular but also a cause for concern at the point where the canyon narrowed. In that section, the trail moved up high on the ridge, but that trail was occasionally constricted – to the extent it was barely wide enough to get a fully loaded pack horse around a corner. Bob Knox's greatest fear at this point was that a horse might be spooked because there was nothing but sheer rock above and a long fall straight down hundreds of feet to the Rayado below.

Fish Camp was a layover waypoint and offered good fishing and jaunts up to Lost Cabin or even Philmont's boundary farther to the west. For lunch there was high trail cuisine: slices of Spam topped with peanut butter. Then Bob took the group out of Fish Camp to overnight at Crater Lake. The next day was a long one, and when the Scouts got into Cimarroncito, they were saddle sore. Fortunately, Cito was a layover camp where there was an opportunity for side hiking. The most enjoyable activity at Cito was the excursion over to Hidden Valley where Scouts could cut loose on their mounts and gallop wide open for the first time, a novel experience because most of their trip to that point had been spent in single file at a slow walk. Then the adventure ended with a return via Tooth Ridge and, for the horsemen and wranglers, maybe a day off before the next cavalcade crew arrived. Waite Phillips, wanting boys from all over America to have a western ranch experience, would probably be delighted to know that of all of the major programs of the late 1940s and early 1950s, only the horse cavalcade survived intact to this day.

Westward Wagon Trains

The Wagon Train, designed for thirty-three participants including the advisor and Philmont guide, was something of a misnomer – especially for anybody assuming that participants spent twenty-five days following a Conestoga wagon or "prairie schooner" seeing Philmont's lowlands. The wagon train, or chuckwagon, portion lasted just one day: Rayado to Abreu. The "Train" was more in the sense of BSA outdoor training which started with a Camping Headquarters check-in and the following week spent in orientation and training at Rayado. At Abreu a full week of activities was enjoyed before moving up the canyon to Fish Camp which became home for the next five days. Then the group shoved off for Urraca Cow Camp (Black Mountain) and Cimarroncito. At Cito, there were sidehikes to Webster Park, Deer Lake Mesa, and Hidden Valley; then the wagon train headed to the North Country. Dave Young was a trail guide in 1947 after having been a camper the year before. His staff experience, as recalled in the next few paragraphs nicely conveys what staff life was like in the years immediately preceding Jack Rhea's arrival and what it was like to shepherd a "wagon train" after the wagon went back to Rayado. Dave's impression of staff training was "going and doing." The intense training later to be an essential part of the Philmont ranger experience did not exist in the late 40s when training was following Dale Olsen on a quick march over the trails where the guide would be leading groups. Olsen had been a member of the seasonal staff since the World War II era and until becoming a professional Scouter was one of Jack Rhea's assistants through the 1955 season. An important part of that orientation was clearing the trails of any winter damage which provided Dave with one of his strongest memories. His training crew was taking a breather, leaning against tree trunks when, in a flash, a pack of coyotes suddenly raced through the group and disappeared down the trail.

Dave Young was assigned to be a trail guide at Fish Camp where he worked seven days a week and was provided room and board and a $50 a month paycheck in an era when the average wage was from fifteen to twenty-five cents an hour in the city. Dave got three days off a month, and usually used those days to hike to a distant location like Baldy or to catch a ride to Red River. Sometimes he put on Levis and cowboy boots and hung out in Cimarron. At Fish Camp, there was a director, full time wrangler, four trail guides, and two trainees. The trail guides were aged 16 to 22. Dave perceived himself as a trail guide, navigator, doctor, and instructor whose responsibility was getting wagon trains from Fish Camp to Cimarroncito, including an overnight at Black Mountain, the site of more wonder regarding Philmont's fauna. That included the verminous variety that lived in the little cowpuncher's cabin at Black Mountain. Dave usually stayed in that cabin along with Black Mountain's solitary staff member and the advisors; it provided some relief from the mountain lions that believed Black Mountain Camp was theirs. The big cats invariably put on a nocturnal chorus that kept campers awake and frightened. Dave accompanied the wagon train to Cimarroncito which provided the opportunity for horseback riding since it was a layover camp. When Dave deadheaded back to Fish Camp, it was leading burros packed with groceries and supplies from the Cito's commissary. Most of the food and supplies went back to Fish Camp, but some were dropped off at Black Mountain.

Returning alone with that nose-to-tail burrow string and negotiating the winding trails was always a challenge and was necessarily preceded by some "on the job learning." Dave once lost about four frustrating hours when one burro managed to get off the trail and wind up in a tug of war with the rest of the train. He had to cut the rope to keep that burro from having its face mangled by the tree in a tug of war which led to more tangled-up burros. Dave then had to cut each burro loose, tie it individually to a tree, and hobble it so it could not wander off again. Putting that string back together was a solo new experience never to forget! Actually, making the return in one day was always a challenge, but losing four hours playing "pin the tail" on the burros was an educational experience. Guides on the

Cito to Fish Camp run often got back after dark, but imagine how bushed Dave was with his one A.M. arrival after that debacle. That route did have its advantages – particularly just exploring Philmont when meeting others on the trail was not a constant occurrence. In what he describes as his "bullet-proof days," Dave was able to cover a lot of the Ranch, including exploring the depths of Cyphers Mine itself before it was staffed.

The original base camps in those days, Ponil and Rayado, were joined by others including Abreu, Cimarroncito, and Fish Camp. The landscape in those camps was very different from today. The main buildings all survived with the exception of the Old Abreu Hunting Lodge, but some structures have passed into history. There were wall tents in place at the beginning of the season, although wall tents were still available at Cimarroncito as late as the mid-1960s. The meadow that now houses the Abreu Homestead and Cantina was ringed with wall tents in the early 1950s as was the meadow across the creek from Fish Camp's Rayado Lodge. No longer does one see cooking shelters (a roof built over four poles) in those camps.

Special Programs

In 1948, there was a strictly training-oriented program called Senior Scouting Leaders Training which concentrated in traditional Scouting skills; it lasted just that one summer. No matter which schedule a group went on, there were opportunities to visit the museum at Rayado and take a tour of Villa Philmonte. Attendance in 1948 passed the 2,000 mark for the first time. Philmont could be said to be living up to Waite Phillips' vision of a western ranch for boys, but there were still vestiges of a council camp mentality because hobby/crafts, ornithology, trap shooting, archery, and rifle marksmanship among several other more traditional programs were offered.

1949 was another growth year in terms of Philmont program develop-ment. The core programs (Cavalcades, Pioneering Treks, Expeditions, and Kit Carson Treks) were joined by a number of special-interest schedules. Those two-week long, narrowly focused activities featured dedicated expe-ditions specializing in geology, forestry, and wildlife management. The regular seasonal staff was augmented with expert personnel from outside organizations such as the U.S. Geological Survey and New Mexico Game and Fish Department, thereby establishing a trend that continues to the pres-ent. Perhaps proving the old maxim that "There is nothing new under the sun," Philmont offered its first winter camping program called "Operation Ten." The ten referred to ten below zero, was conducted variously out of Cimarroncito and Beaubien, started on 27 December, and emphasized winter camping, skiing, and snow shoeing. Bullock recruited two top-flight young men to launch the program. Both had recently returned from the Antarctic where they had been involved with America's growing exploration and scientific research programs. Thus Philmont's current Kanik program is not so much an innovation as a revival.

By the early 1950s, Philmont's program was firming up and continued to be built around a core of Cavalcades, Expeditions, Kit Carson Treks, and the Pioneering Trek scholarship program. A major innovation in 1950, a year when attendance was again slightly over 2,000, was the establishment of the forty-day Junior Leader Training at Rayado. The special interest schedules were consolidated into the twelve-day Explorer Encampment which combined geology, forestry, and wildlife management. With the exception of the "Ranch Plan" (work for three weeks, get a free one-week trek with a Philmont guide) which was introduced in 1952, the program that Jack Rhea inherited in 1954 was then in place. There were only minor adjustments to the core programs, i.e., a day or two more or less at various camps. Expeditions were expanded to include northbound and southbound fixed itineraries which included burros. The twelve-day Kit Carson Trek was joined by the Lucien Maxwell Trek, a ten-day program in the South Country emphasizing frontier activities such as trapping. For Scouts who could not get enough of Philmont, there was the "Frontiersman" schedule, an eight-week, one hundred fifty dollar adventure combining Wagon Train, Cavalcade, Expedition, and Kit Carson Trek.

Due to the Third National Jamboree, 1953 was a down year for Philmont attendance: to 4,097 from the record breaking high of almost 7,500 in 1952. It was, however, still a big year for the Philmont staff which totaled near 260 including the permanent staff. By far, the largest group within the staff were Philmont guides – fifty-three of them or nearly one in five of the total staff.

Earl's 20th Century Prairie Schooners

One early Rhea innovation, or more likely an inevitable necessity, was the introduction of a modern school bus fleet to transport sharply increasing numbers of campers to starting destinations. Prior to 1955, trucks left Camping Headquarters with their human cargo; that was in an age when "loss prevention" had not crept into Scouting administration to the extent that it has now. In 1955, Jack Rhea hired Earl Swope to take charge of Philmont's rapidly escalating passenger bus needs. Jack would have been hard-pressed to find a more colorful character than Earl Swope. The CEO of the local school bus company, Earl was age fifty-seven when Jack hired him and was certainly no stranger to Philmont. Earl had been among the local workers hired to build Villa Philmonte and had also been part of the crew which completed renovation of Fish Camp after Waite Phillips bought the property. Swope was a World War I Signal Corps veteran who took a job driving school buses after droughts forced him off the family farm. Although he was truly sawed off and bow-legged, he was indeed much larger than life.

In many ways, Jack got a terrific return from his investment in Swope's bus company. Jack actually got more than the services of a modern, clean, fleet of buses with a spotless safety reputation. He got Earl Swope who turned out to be as much a fixture around Camping Headquarters as the Norton Bell in front of the dining hall. For years, Earl was listed on the staff roster as "greeter." Nominally that job was to greet buses as they arrived from councils across the country or his own buses ferrying groups down from Raton or Trinidad. There was no large-scale Welcome Center in those days, only a loading dock with a check-in desk, small roof, and a grain scale for weighing packs.

Earl was there to say "Howdy," but the other half of his job was essentially that of a court jester who specialized in boosting the spirits of downtrodden advisors – those who had been lamed on the trail and those who never even got to the trail. If he had not made it as a bus driver or greeter, he could have found success as a stand-up comic. His appearance was an essential part of the character: twinkly eyes as blue as a New Mexico sky, a big straw cowboy hat, well-faded Levis, sun-weathered face, cowboy boots, close-cropped gray hair, a well-pressed Explorer shirt, and a striking plaid neckerchief. Earl held court in a long, low building that was just west of the director of program's residence. That long-gone building served as an advisors' lounge, trip planner's office, and radio room.

Earl preferred buses built by the Georgia-based bus manufacturer, the Bluebird Company. He claimed that they held up better than any other bus, an important consideration considering the many runs to the nut and bolt-challenging Cito turnaround. From just those two buses which he started with in 1955, Earl still casts a shadow in Colfax County. The name "Swope Land and Cattle Co." was seen on the sides of many buses pulling in and out of Philmont's CHQ every summer for decades. Earl's son Jack eventually sold the company to another operator, but among the drivers are a few who got their start in Earl's day.

Philmont Training Center

In the 50s and 60s, the Philmont Training Center, or PTC, was known as "VTC" for Volunteer Training Center. When Jack arrived at the Ranch in late 1954, PTC was one of his responsibilities (primarily in terms of buildings and grounds). In those days, the director of PTC was a seasonal position and typically filled by a BSA professional from within the national volunteer training staff. The national director of volunteer training was usually in residence for a brief period at the beginning of the season. There was little contact between the camping and training operations; staff from the camping side were prohibited from attending PTC weekly dances, but each camping staffer was issued a one-time only meal card allowed to have one supper for the entire summer at the PTC dining hall. The wait was always worth it.

Because PTC history has been so expertly told by Mark Griffin in *The Other Side of the Road, The Story of the Philmont Training Center*, it will not be repeated here other than to reprise a few of the highlights. PTC experienced significant growth in attendance, course offerings, and facilities between 1954 and 1962 when the modern PTC took shape – with the addition of the assembly hall, dining hall and kitchen complex, new classroom buildings, an expanded tent city with various services, a craft lodge, trading post, VIP cottage, and new duplexes. In 1957, a $300,000 construction program doubled the Training Center capacity and resulted in an expanded kitchen/dining hall complex, more duplexes, a new health lodge, and a new recreation building. The PTC's annual growth rate then was in double digits. In 1960, which would have been a down year except for special Jamboree treks, total attendance at VTC almost reached 4,000 participants. When Jack arrived in 1954, PTC attendance had just grown through 2,500 participants. Jack was not regularly involved in the classroom any longer as he had been when he was an assistant director of volunteer training, but had a very visible role in greeting new classes, speaking to the spouses, and attending social events, such as dances. When interviewed years later in

1988 and directly asked about what was accomplished at Philmont during his tenure, Jack was quick to point out the overall growth of the VTC as one of the highpoints of his watch.

At ease, at ease! Jack Rhea strikes a familiar pose, this time speaking to a spouses group at the Volunteer Training Center as it was known in the 1950s and 1960s.

Jack Rhea was indirectly involved in one of the important Training Center programs, the VTC Trek which evolved into the PTC Mountain Men (and years later the Mountain Women) program. The VTC Trek participants, 167 of them, went out for short treks with their VTC rangers for the first time in 1956. VTC rangers reported to the Training Center directly, but Jack Rhea occasionally supported the VTC Treks with his own rangers when the VTC Treks had more campers enrolled than they could safely accommodate. The VTC Trek was a growth program, more than doubling in attendance by the time Jack left Philmont in late 1962.

Training Center participants from the fifties and early sixties do not remember Jack Rhea for the brick and mortar accomplishments, for the broadened course offering, or for the increased attendance. One of their strongest memories is the dancing on Saturday night, including seeing Jack and Maxine out on the floor for part of the evening. There was country and western music for square dancing, and the man calling "do sa do," "star promenade," "shoot the star," "wrong way thar," "walk and dodge" and "roll away with a half sashay!" was none other than Jack Rhea. For teenagers whose parents were attending PTC, there were teen dances conducted in a very 1950s fashion, girls seated on one side and boys on the other of the assembly hall.

Members of the camping department were not permitted to attend those dances, which was a great disappointment, especially to rangers. There was little opportunity for a ranger to wangle an invitation from the daughter of a Training Center attendee anyway. For members of the Horse Department, it was another matter and one vastly simplified by a clever horseman simply reminding a young lady on a PTC horseback ride to send him a dance invitation.

One young man who started his Philmont seasonal staff days at the Training Center became one of the first of Jack Rhea's idea men. It was Jerry Traut who is best remembered as the author of the campfire mainstay, the "Philmont Story," a co-founder of the Philmont Staff Association, and author of the Philmont Staff Association dedication statement. Although Jerry is usually associated with the Camping Department, he actually started at the Training Center as a Mountain Trek Ranger in 1955 and eventually headed that operation before moving to the Camping Department where he served as director of program (in an era when the top position in that department was director of camping). Over the years, Jerry became well known as the expert's expert on all matters relating to Philmont's flora and fauna. Toward the end of his Philmont days, he teamed with Larry Murphy, then the ranch historian, to become what amounted to Philmont's dynamic program duo with Jerry concentrating on nature while Larry had the last word on how accurately Philmont's programs squared with their actual historical heritage.

Jerry's story and post-Philmont career, his days as a college professor, and his devotion to teaching have been well told in *High Country* articles over the years and will not be repeated here. However, one of the most incisive looks at Jerry will be quoted below because it clearly illustrates how he was such an inspiring naturalist, teacher, and Philmont leader. The author is Steve Gregory, the wilderness survival counselor who worked with Ned Gold at Lost Cabin in 1963. At the same time, Steve's recollections of Jerry contain the essence of the Philmont experience for both camper and staffer alike.

My first impression was that he came across as a funny little guy with an odd sense of humor, strange crew cut, ears that stuck out, and screechy voice. His pants were too short and left his white socks exposed above his hiking boots. It quickly became very clear that he knew what he was talking about, had an all-abiding passion for nature, and a love of the Ranch that was infectious. He made survival training part common sense, part immersion in nature, part text book, part appreciation for the natural beauty that surrounds us that is so often overlooked, and part joking and cajoling. He was a blast to learn from and I quickly found that I couldn't best him at the come-back barb or funny story.

He issued us a textbook, *A Manual of Woodslore Survival* as developed at Philmont by Russ Vliet, published in the 1950s. I still have two copies, one of which is marked up with my underlines and notes from Jerry's expert teaching. As he wandered around the Ranch, with the program class in tow, he'd stop at a plant and begin to expound on its virtues as an edible food source. We'd whip out our little books to find the plant and he'd give a short explanation as to its merits. He gave us a set of colored pencils to use in the textbook, and we colored in between the lines to record the fact that we'd seen the plant and that this would help us identify it later on in our instruction with the Scout crews.

I think we spent nearly a week delving into shelters and beds; edible plants; fire making; animal snares; mushrooms and poisonous plants; and my favorite, fishing and fishing methods. My little book is full of hand-colored illustrations as we learned about the native plants on the Ranch. He made us build a fire without matches, a feat that turned out to be both comical and agonizing. I couldn't find a flint or hard quartz, and my wooden bow and drill set broke a couple of times. I remember he had an eagle in one of his cages that were about four-foot cubes up off the ground on wooden legs. I don't remember how he came by the bird, but it apparently had a damaged wing that he was monitoring before he let it go. He had a porcupine and a raccoon for us to study, along with a couple of snakes. He showed us how to create fishing line out of yucca and a rod out of a willow branch. I tied a rather crude, black bee-shaped fly with white wings, and Jerry showed all of us how to fish the Rayado; I think it was down at Zastro. I can't begin to tell you how thrilled I was to actually catch a fish on my hand-made rig (although the trout might have been all of six inches long). Jerry's enthusiasm was infectious and at the end of the week, I couldn't wait to begin working with the campers.

At Lost Cabin, I remember we had a group in from the Bronx, a bunch of New York smart-alecks that pretended to be bored with the trek. They reminded me of a pack of young wolves each one trying to outdo the other in an attempt to be the alpha male. However, one of the kids really took to fly tying, and we made a hand-hewn fishing pole and line from some twisted vine. I remember how excited he was to actually catch his first fish in the Agua Fria (another great excuse to go fishing and leave Ned alone in camp). We caught a lot of fish that we brought back to Lost Cabin and fried up in the kid's mess kit. The boy had never had an experience like that and I could feel his emotion bubbling up. The wise attitude slowly melted away and he seemed to become more at ease within his own group. I was so elated, proud, and ebullient at the thought of showing him a way to self-confidence and independence. THAT was one of the real virtues of being a Philmont staff member for me, and I owe it all to Jerry.

The Marketing of Philmont Scout Ranch

If the Rhea years cannot be described as the Golden Age of Philmont, the promotional effort from those days certainly can claim that title. The mid-1950s were a period of unprecedented external promotion, and it began with Jack himself. He toured the country tirelessly, promoting Philmont at every opportunity, especially at council/regional meetings and national conferences. Dick Gertler, who was on the permanent staff for nine years in the 1960s, recalls that Jack's personal salesmanship actually worked like a two-way street. Many of the High Adventure leaders from the big Philmont councils were invited out to Philmont for brief visits in the off-season for which Dick was frequently a guide. That was a period when Philmont could still absorb an increasing camper load and the National Office wanted as many Scouts to experience Philmont as possible.

Scouting was growing during the Rhea years – on an average of four percent every year during the eight years of Jack's duty at Philmont, reaching membership of 2,016,688 at the end of 1962. Attendance at Philmont increased much more dramatically. The Camping Department total for the year before Jack arrived was 3,766. In 1963, the last year for which Jack was involved with planning, the total was 12,413. Jack had prepared the way for the explosive growth that followed in the Joe Davis years when camping attendance exceeded 18,000 in 1974, Joe's last year.

In 1954, Dick Stewart, a photographer for the National Geographic Society, was at a meeting in Washington, D.C., where he heard a Mr. Frank Wiley speaking about Philmont Scout Ranch. Stewart mentioned this presentation back at his office, but nothing happened until later in the year when Wiley wrote to John Oliver La Gorce who had just become the president of the Society and editor of its esteemed magazine, *National Geographic*. La Gorce had been with the Society for decades and had a colorful past. He had been a race car driver early in life, an Antarctic explorer, and was a world-class fisherman. La Gorce saw merit in Wiley's proposal that the magazine carry an article on Philmont Scout Ranch, indicating that he thought it would appeal to younger readers and that it was very compatible with "Youth in America," which was an ongoing theme in the magazine.

National Geographic magazine was not only prestigious; it also had a long reach. Granted, it might not have had the same circulation as *Time* or *Life*, but its primary paid circulation was nearly two and one-quarter million in 1956. The pass-along readership added another four readers for every primary recipient. The total reach was almost nine million or roughly four percent of the entire American population. Mr. Andrew H. Brown, a younger member of the magazine's senior editorial staff, was assigned the project. He was an up-and-coming star at the magazine and usually took his own photographs. Over the following decades, he wrote many of the magazine's most influential articles, including those on Jane Goodall and her work with chimpanzees in Africa.

The Philmont project was a great pleasure for him considering his love of the mountains and one of his passions: trout fishing. He arrived at the Ranch in July of 1955 and spent three weeks gathering material and photographs. The timing was good because Philmont was hosting a delegation of European Scouts; they would be featured in several of the seventeen photographs the article carried. The article, "Philmont Scout Ranch Helps Boys Grow Up," was a long one by *National Geographic* standards, and the majority of its photos were in full color. Jack was frequently quoted in the article. Brown joined the European Scouts for part of their trek, rode horses into Fish Camp from Beaubien with Jack, spent a day with the Junior Leader Training contingent, camped under the Tooth at Stockade, and frequently referenced Philmont's Wild West heritage, including the Santa Fe Trail and Kit Carson's home on the Rayado. Reading between the lines in the eighteen-page article makes it clear that writer Brown was having the same wonderful experience as the youth were.

High Adventure by Norman Rockwell. © Brown & Bigelow, Inc., St. Paul, Minnesota.
Used with Permission.

While the boys of Albany Post Nine might be considered overdressed for the occasion, Norman Rockwell certainly caught their enthusiasm on the trail.

During the landmark year of 1957, Philmont benefitted from another substantial boost in awareness; the Ranch was featured on the cover of the Boy Scout Calendar for that year. Of all of the Norman Rockwell paintings that became Boy Scout Calendar covers, *High Adventure* remains as one of the most familiar. The concept dated back several years from Rockwell's returning east from the 1953 Third National Jamboree at the Irvine Ranch in California. A scene at the Jamboree inspired *The Scoutmaster*, a painting which became the calendar cover in 1956. The latter painting, also in that inner circle of the most memorable paintings, featured a Jamboree coordinator in a starlit campsite just as his Scouts were falling asleep. On the way back from the Jamboree, Rockwell stopped at Philmont and photographed the Tooth of Time. He was a meticulous artist who usually photographed models back in his studio and then introduced them into a background which had been initiated earlier. Although *High Adventure* is a bit stylized in that the boys of Albany Post Nine are on the trail wearing leggings, garrison caps, and neckties, the picture has all of the classic hallmarks that convey excitement. The focus of the boys' attention, the Tooth of Time, thrusts itself mightily into the upper third of the picture and Rockwell uses two of his most effective techniques to draw the viewer into the action: one boy pointing to the object of the group's excitement ahead and another boy shouting for the other fellows to quickly move up and see the panorama for themselves.

Jack Rhea reaped a huge benefit when the calendars for 1957 went into distribution; awareness of Philmont expanded dramatically because the calendar printer, the Brown and Bigelow Company, had by far the largest calendar sales force in the country and enjoyed a reputation for tasteful, artistic calendars. Customers were wide and varied: drug stores, banks, gas stations, hardware stores, insurance offices, and many, many more establishments. The end result was that the boys of Albany Post Nine found themselves plastered on the walls of millions of homes and business establishments across the country. The 1956 article in *National Geographic* and the 1957 appearance of *High Adventure* was about as good a publicity one-two punch as Jack could possibly have hoped for.

There is an interesting backstory regarding Rockwell's visit to the Ranch. While passing through Cimarron, he saw a scene that would become an inspiration for another painting – one that would become one of the most popular *Saturday Evening Post* covers of all time. The painting was *Breaking Home Ties* and was inspired by seeing a perky young man sitting beside his weathered cowboy father on the running board of an old pick-up truck. The young man was waiting for the bus that would take him off to college. To complete the picture, the family dog, a collie, also waits, dreading the moment his best buddy will be gone. Rockwell went through several studies for the painting before settling on the exact people he wanted to use as the final models. The tentative father was an older wrangler from Cimarron, but the man who finally appeared in the picture was a farmer who lived near Rockwell's studio which was then located in Arlington, Vermont. The bright-eyed boy heading to college was a member of the Training Center arts/crafts staff, Robert Waldrop, an Eagle Scout from Austin, Texas.

Related to the new calendar was one more 1957 project which evolved into another landmark Philmont publication. This was the U.S. Geological Survey's authoritative *Philmont Country, The Rocks and Landscape of a Famous New Mexico Ranch*. The book is actually one of a series in which the Geological Survey published in-depth but non-technical books about America's most popular national parks and monuments.

Preliminary work on this book, which is a "must have" for any serious Philmont bookshelf, was started in late 1956, but it rapidly became apparent that the geologists assigned to the job, A.A. Wanek and C.B. Read, would not have time to do justice to the project considering their other assignments. In late 1957, G.D. Robinson took on the project for which Jack Rhea provided enthusiastic logistical support. Serious work started in 1958 with the addition of two assistants, W.H. Hays and M.E. McCallum, who joined Robinson in two years of extensive fieldwork. The book also utilized the expertise of several Colfax County residents who were in a position to add some historical perspective, particularly about mining, to the project. Two other Geological Survey employees, photographer E.F. Patterson and artist/illustrator J.R. Stacy, also worked on the project in the summer of 1958. Patterson's photography rivals that of Ansel Adams while Stacy's work puts him in the same league as the noted Scouting illustrator, Remington Schuyler.

Unfortunately, the project did not have an especially high priority; the writing was not completed until 1962, the same year Jack moved Back East. Finally, the book was published in 1964. G.D. Robinson returned to the Ranch in 1964 because he was one of the principal instructors for some very special visitors: twenty Apollo Program astronauts who completed a portion of their geology training at Philmont. The book is still available through used book dealers, and is also available through the U.S. Geological Survey's website as a PDF.

That same year, 1962, Jack completed filming a promotional movie about Philmont; it was released in 1963 after Jack had moved back to the National office. The film, *Beyond the Tooth of Time*, was not the first or last movie or video about the Ranch. There had been two previous films, *The Philmont Adventure*, in 1949 and another, *The Philmont Story* produced independently of the BSA as a Hollywood short subject in 1957. Both were similar in conveying the heritage, mystery, and excitement that is Philmont. Naturally, those films produced between 1949 and 1963 have a dated quality considering the appearances of vehicles, uniforms, and programs (bronco riding for one), but they also have a timeless quality because they all vividly convey a camper's exhilaration with his Philmont adventure.

Like every director of camping or program before and since, Jack had use of the BSA's captive magazines, *Boy's Life* and *Scouting*. Whereas contemporary use of *Scouting* by Philmont is almost exclusively staff recruitment oriented, Jack's thrust was to build attendance at both the camping and training functions. The advertising programs usually featured a one-page and, less frequently, a two-page spread. The *Boy's Life* advertising was very conventional and appealed to a Scout's sense of adventure and would run along the lines of "Have a Mountaintop Experience" or "Discover Scouting's Heart." What Jack approved for *Scouting* occasionally had some interesting twists. For example in November 1958, there was the letter written home to Mom and Dad. This was a spread with action shots on the left page and the letter on the right talking about all of the activities and how trail food "actually tastes Okay" and concludes with, "Gee Mom and Dad, I wish you could come back with me next year." A similar approach was taken relative to the Training Center for which advertising was designed to dispel a spouse's fear that conditions would be too primitive (resulting in a negative vote on how the family vacation would be spent).

Jack and the Ranger Department got some good press in 1959 with the publication of a feature article about rangers in *Boys Life* magazine. The article had actually been written during Philmont's record summer of 1958 (attendance over 12,500) and mentioned three stalwarts from the banner 1957 year then in their second year as rangers: Perry Bolin, Howard Wunker, and Warren Zimmerman.

Today, the Worldwide Web serves as a cost-efficient, versatile means of promoting Philmont while simultaneously serving as a conduit for important information to council and unit treks. The Digital Age made possible the technical and cost-efficiencies of video and print production which have expanded Philmont's reach dramatically. With the exception of several movies, brochures were the principal means of non-personal promotion, and commencing in the mid-1940s, a new brochure was produced for each new camping season. Fortunately, Jack had access to the facilities of one of America's largest publishers: the Boy Scouts of America's National Office, although small run print jobs were usually sent up to Raton where they were printed by the newspaper company, *The Raton Range*.

Even in the Bullock era, Philmont's promotional literature had a contemporary look and was occasionally done in three-color, although two-color was more common in those days when four-color printing was very expensive. Until 1956 Jack essentially just updated the previous year's promotional brochure; the 1956 literature reflected the major change in Philmont's program which was consolidated into the twelve-day backpacking expedition. Similarly, Jack made no changes in Bullock's Philmont *Program Handbook* which eventually evolved into today's *Guidebook to Adventure*. Where Jack raised the bar was in brochures dedicated to Philmont history and nature. Previously, the eighty-six page *Philmont Story* combined Philmont history and nature all under one cover. When this was nearly out of print, Jack separated the subjects into two brochures with more appealing graphics and easier-reading typography. The new twenty-page, two-color *Philmont Story* came out in 1958 and the *Philmont Nature Story* in 1960. The former's text was a blend of Bullock's "Our Philmont" essay and what would become the basis of the "Philmont Story" campfire while the latter would eventually evolve into the *Philmont Fieldguide*. In 1961, Jack significantly updated the *Philmont Story* piece into a handsome four-color, twenty-eight page brochure.

From the twelve-page, two-color brochure of 1956, the pattern was set for Philmont's basic annual brochure which varied from six to twelve pages. Space was provided for a local council imprint, and the print runs were substantial: 200,000 was average. Today, Philmont's promotional literature is done in four-color and includes one large (19 x 21 inch foldout) all-inclusive brochure promoting both the camping/training operations and separate, all four-color literature for individual programs and the Philmont Training Center.

CHAPTER 14

The Wind Shifts

In the summer of 1955 the Korean War had been concluded two years previously, and although the Cold War was on everybody's mind the international Scouting movement was making great strides. One aspect of the growing internationalism was the 1955 visit of sixteen European Scouts to Philmont. There were two boys each from Turkey, Greece, Italy, France, the United Kingdom, Sweden, Germany, and Finland. Jack inquired where Gerhard Waechter and Klaus Weinert, the German boys, were from but was disappointed to learn that their homes were far from Esslingen or Stuttgart. They were accompanied by three leaders: Robert Thomas from England, Ted Holstein from the BSA National Office, and Edouard Maze from France. The original plan was to meet the international party on 25 June at the airport in Trinidad, Colorado. Early that morning, Jack Rhea was advised that the landing would be closer, at Raton's little Crews Field which had been a satellite field used by the Army Air Force in World War II for bivouac training of F-4 Lightning photo-reconnaissance squadrons based at Peterson Field in Colorado Springs. Then at the very last minute, the landing was shifted to the hilltop airport in Las Vegas, New Mexico.

Ray Bryan and Jack drove down to Las Vegas in time and parked their car at the end of the runway, assuming that the plane, a war-weary Curtiss C-46, would taxi directly up to them. Unfortunately, they parked at the wrong end of the runway and were treated to a heavy ration of exhaust and a severe dose of propwash from a pair of 2,000 horsepower engines as the plane passed just feet over their heads moments before flaring out for the landing. Once the Scouts reached Philmont, they visited JLT troops at Rayado and then received trail instruction at both Ponil and Cito. While at Philmont, they also attended the Fourth of July Rodeo in Cimarron. Their short trek got them as far into the Backcountry as Porcupine, but their main event was a horse cavalcade. While the European contingent was visiting America, sixteen Scouts from America's twelve BSA regions were on a European tour. The international Scouts would figure prominently in a *National Geographic* magazine article which was being written and pho-

tographed during their visit to Philmont. Jack was not on the trail with the
international group from start to finish, but did join it for several days when
it was in the vicinity of Fish Camp and Agua Fria where fishing was the
main attraction.

*The International Scouts of 1955 arrived courtesy of the United States Air
Force. Jack Rhea is kneeling, front left.*

Edouard Maze and Ray Bryan shale hands as Jack Rhea
and Ted Holstein look on.

The Remarkable Case of Expedition # PX-1

Although Jack had only been at the Ranch for several months, he could see a great storm cloud on the distant horizon. The looming issue took the form of a question. "How can rapidly growing numbers of campers have a mountaintop experience while management has to live within an operating budget that would not grow anywhere near as quickly?" In other words, to what extent could crews' training be compressed to the point where they would still be able to enjoy a full Philmont experience? Reducing the number of days a guide spent with a crew could dramatically extend each guide's cost-effectiveness because he would be able to serve more expeditions over the camping season. For the sake of operating efficiency, could some or all of the manpower-intensive, Bullock-era activities be streamlined into a more manageable trek without sacrificing any of those unique programs for which Philmont was attracting rapidly growing numbers of campers? Hiring enough guides to stay with each expedition for its full duration was simply not in the cards when attendance was growing in leaps and bounds. Previously, all Philmont itineraries were fixed; there was no flexibility whatsoever. Jack wondered what would happen if a crew were given some choice in the route it would follow. To answer these questions, he set up an experimental expedition which combined some of the old and a whole lot of the new.

To conduct the trial, Jack needed a typical crew, and found what he was looking for in a council expedition from the Robert E. Lee Council (now Heart of Virginia Council) in Richmond, Virginia. He had previously met the lead advisor: Ned C. Gold, Sr., the father of Philmont Staff Association founder, Ned C. Gold, Jr. Jack and Gold Senior had become acquainted at Philmont several years before when Gold was living in Santa Fe and making frequent trips to Philmont in the summer. They also had met at several conferences as a result of Gold's having moved to Richmond and become the Region Three (Pa., Del., Md., and Va.) training chairman. "Ubiquitous" might very easily have been Ned Senior's middle name. As a Navy recruiting officer, he was driving from Albuquerque to Las Cruces on 16 July 1945, when there was a brilliant flash on the eastern horizon. The first atomic bomb had just been tested. Six years previously he attended the dedication of Philturn Rockymountain Scoutcamp. In 1929 as a charter member of the Tribe of Mic-O-Say, he was photographed with that legendary professional Scouter, H. Roe "Chief" Bartle of Kansas City.

PX-1 (Philmont Experimental Expedition Number One) consisted of three adult leaders with thirty-one youth, and the expedition was aware that it was going on an experimental trek. On Tuesday 21 June 1955, Ned Cooper Gold, the younger, was the first off the bus at Philmont where he was greeted by a young Eagle Scout headquarters guide from Santa Barbara, California. The guide's name was Dave Jung and he was in his first of many years on the Philmont staff. The expedition was also greeted by Jack Rhea. Very shortly, Ned the elder and the three senior crew leaders, Lewis Flint, Friend Wilkinson, and William Hoerter, were in Jack's office confirming their itinerary. Ned Senior, who already had a working knowledge of Philmont's Backcountry, had worked up a tentative itinerary before leaving Virginia. The route selected was southbound, starting at Ponil where Doc Loomis and Terry French gave them intense Scouting skills demonstrations, with Loomis noting that the expedition was "at the beginning of something big." The expedition picked up burros before leaving Ponil (later wishing that they had left the beasts behind), and headed south as one large crew not accompanied by any guide. Over the next nine days, the trek took them down Dean Canyon, through Turkey Creek Canyon, and up to Harlan where it was discovered that Ned Junior had left the crew's home movie camera at some point back on the trail where they had taken a rest stop. Father and son left Harlan on a quick-march search mission and returned successfully hours later with Gold Senior, then forty-eight years old, much tired from a second climb into Harlan.

Gold Family Collection

Ned Gold, Sr., was the lead advisor on Philmont Experimental Expedition Number One in 1955, the model for the twelve-day expedition that was introduced the following year. This photo in which Ned Gold, Sr., is teaching rope skills dates to 1956 after the Gold family had moved from Richmond to St. Louis.

The camp directors along the way had been notified that an "experimental" group was coming their way. The crew reached Cimarroncito the next day and then started the following morning for Black Mountain. The boys in the expedition were having a fabulous time, but regretted not dropping packs on top of Comanche Pass for a quick sidehike up Mount Phillips. The crew saw Beaubien briefly in passing from the head of the Bonito Canyon on the way to Porcupine from which they also journeyed over to Crooked Creek for a conservation project. After returning to Beaubien for a two-day layover, the crew later passed through Crater Lake and hiked into Headquarters from Stockade on 3 July. While at Beaubien, the expedition encountered two legendary contingent directors. The first was Roy Swab from National Capital Area Council, the man who sent more kids to Philmont than any other Scouter, and the second was Walter Keating from Upstate New York's Finger Lakes Council. Keating had led more Philmont expeditions than any other Scouter and still had many more years of expeditions left in him.

The more significant meeting was held with Jack Rhea to whom Ned Senior relayed the highpoints and low points. Everybody had enjoyed a wonderful trek, truly their summit of Scouting experience, but Gold offered the following suggestions. The eleven by seventeen, black and white map was completely lacking. Trail signs were not always adequate in pointing the way. Most importantly, Ned Senior said it would have been beneficial to have somebody from the staff with them "on the trail for the first couple of days." The seed was planted. PX-1 departed the Ranch for home on Monday, 4 July after briefly stopping at the Cimarron Rodeo. PX-1 attended the rodeo in the company of another unique expedition which it had met earlier at Camping Headquarters – the International Expedition of European Scouts which had been brought in off the trail especially to attend the rodeo.

The Philmont Experimental Expedition was a success which led to the wide-scale implementation of the twelve-day expedition in 1956. It featured two days of intense training upfront, the crew planning its own itinerary, and backpacking for the rest of the trek without a guide. Jack Rhea almost certainly scheduled other experimental expeditions – the use of the number one in PX-1 suggests as much. He was a crafty tactician whose experiences as a battalion operations officer during the war taught him to eliminate as much of the unknown as possible. That there were more PX expeditions cannot be proven now because all registration records are long gone. Examination of crew photographs from 1955 is not possible because the Ranch did not start archiving crew photo negatives until twelve years later in 1967. Based on the supposition above, Jack probably had a number of experimental crews in 1955 – and most likely structured them so as to have small crews, large crews, geographical diversity, and to the extent possible a variety in experience levels.

From PX-1, Jack chose not to change any policy when it came to trail signs. Since the first trail signs went up, debate has raged over their value. The purists would convert all signs into campfire wood, believing that the Philmont landscape is so liberally littered with obvious landmarks that anybody with the least bit of compass savvy, a decent map, and basic cognitive skills should not get lost. Pragmatists, in the majority, would just make the signs more weather and cattle-resistant. Buster Simpson, a training ranger from the early 1960s and director of trail development in 1964 recalled a unique compromise offered by legendary staffer, Jerry Traut, who argued for signs that pointed only to major landmarks, not camps, thus forcing Scouts and leaders to use their maps for navigation. Jack, however, chose the path most frequently traveled and maintained the status quo on signage. He was painfully aware of the topographic map issue, but changing that in the very short term was beyond his control.

Rhea Family Collection

The Rhea family at home in the director of camping's residence in 1956, a very important year in Philmont's development. The Rheas always had dogs, "Lady" in this case. From left to right, the Rhea children are Julie, Carol, Bart, and Ron.

Launching the Twelve-Day Expedition

1956 was the biggest year in Philmont's history to that point; attendance climbed to 10,044, up from nearly 8,000 the year before. To serve that number of campers, Philmont hired 220 summer staffers. Of that number, there were very few guides or rangers. While attendance was up twenty percent, staffing went up by twenty-five percent. Excluding the two headquarters guides, there were nine roving rangers: two sector roving rangers, four roving rangers working out of Cito, and one roving ranger each at Ponil, Beaubien, and Abreu. Philmont's completely revised literature for 1956, a full twelve pages in two-color, announced Philmont's new program, the twelve-day expedition which could actually be extended in twelve-day increments to a forty-eight day trek. The brochure's front cover featured a dramatic photograph of a twenty-eight person expedition emerging from Stockade with the Tooth of Time dominating the center of the illustration.

Unfortunately, just as the camping season got underway, Jack received news of his mother's death. Jack had always been close to his mother and had been supporting her financially for years. She died at age seventy-nine. Although he was really needed at the Ranch, Maxine drove him to the Raton train station from which he traveled back to Kansas City for the funeral. A week later Jack returned for what was one of Philmont's most important summers.

The cavalcade was retained, but not promoted, and was dropped two years later in favor of providing everybody with an opportunity for a horseback ride. The cavalcade eventually came back but it took a long time. The wagon trains disappeared forever as did the old guide-accompanied "Expedition" which evolved from George Bullock's thirteen-day "Backpacking Schedule." The Bullock-crafted programs which had served Philmont so well when attendance was smaller were on their way out: the Kit Carson treks, Lucien Maxwell treks, and the northbound and southbound treks. Burros survived, but their use was scaled back sharply. However, many popular activities did carry over to the new program: horseback rides, gold panning, skeet shooting, mine exploration, fishing, and nature among them.

For 1956, there were two revolutionary changes in the new expedition based on what Jack had learned from the experimental expedition(s) of 1955. Crews could plan their own itineraries when they arrived at the Ranch; it was no longer dictated for them. Only if it appeared that a camp would be overwhelmed on a certain date would an itinerary variation be implemented.

Secondly, no guide would accompany them from start to finish. Training was limited to two days at one of three base camps from which crews would be launched on their own. One of the key benefits of the twelve-day expedition in comparison with many of the pre-1956 programs was its getting camper crews out on the trail and into the Backcountry much faster. Anecdotal evidence indicates that Clarence Dunn was not at all on board with completely eliminating guides from serving expeditions from beginning to end and that he vigorously expressed that reservation to Jack Rhea personally. Although Jack normally highly valued Dunn's wise counsel, this was one occasion when Jack alone charted the direction in which guides would go.

Ponil, Cimarroncito, and Rayado became the new base camps. Clarks Fork was originally planned as a starting camp that year, but its opening as a major camp was postponed. Abreu had been considered briefly as a base camp, but was dropped since it was not as logistically satisfactory as Rayado. The sequence of events for a crew arriving in 1956 was similar to that experienced by expeditions today although a crew in 1956 was not met by a ranger, but rather by one of two headquarters guides who steered the crew through headquarters on the first day much as rangers do today. Check-in, however, could also be done at Rayado instead of Camping Headquarters. The opening campfire was the highlight of the first day. The second day was devoted to intense training at one of the three base camps where a horseback ride also was available. On the third day, the group had more training with a base camp ranger and then went on a shakedown hike. That was a new context for an older word. Previously, "ranger" had referred to a one-man band at a small outpost camp where a crew might be spending the night on a trek between major camps such as Fish Camp and Cimarroncito. After reviewing and confirming the itinerary with the base camp ranger, the crew was turned loose, guideless and rangerless, on the morning of the fourth day into something short of a great unknown. In addition to rangers located at the base camps, there were the roving rangers at large on Philmont trails to aid crews who might be having difficulties. Itinerary details were sent back to Camping Headquarters and the commissary on the day the crew departed from its base camp.

The Critical Summer of '56

The summer of 1956 has been described variously as "chaotic" or "another wonderful Philmont summer." One conclusion is certain; 1956 was a critical year in terms of Philmont's core camping program with the introduction of the new twelve-day expedition. Let us now look at that state of affairs which made 1956 a failure, a success, or what is the most likely reality – something between the two extremes. "Affairs" in this context means the level of staff maturity and the extent to which Philmont could be described as a wilderness whose wildness confused crews, particularly as there was no safety net in terms of an embedded 24/7 guide. Other criteria included the availability of navigation aids (maps and trail signs), staff morale, and the incidence of such glitches as injuries, confusion on the trail, and arriving too late for program.

Staff training had improved considerably once George Bullock hit his stride; it improved even more under Jack Rhea who could have quite legitimately been called a "training expert." Examination of staff rosters from 1955 and 1956 shows that very young staff, those seventeen or younger, were rarely placed in responsible positions, and were usually hired for jobs in commissaries, dining halls, or in positions where they would not have any significant interface with camper crews. The seasonal staff of 1956, all 220 of them, included fifty-two returning from 1955 which amounts to an experienced cadre of nearly twenty-five percent or what was a fairly typical overall return rate for the 1950s (but exactly half that of today's return rate). In 1956, base camp rangers and roving rangers, as with rangers in 1957, were required to have attained their eighteenth birthday by the time they reported for employment.

There were two types of seasonal positions in the 1950s: regular and trainee. To be a regular seasonal employee, an applicant had to be sixteen years of age and have one summer of previous Philmont employment under his belt. Those aged fifteen along with sixteen year-olds with no previous Philmont experience, were hired as "trainees" who served with no regular compensation. They were, however, provided with travel expenses and if they received a satisfactory fitness report at the end of the summer they were given a red Philmont jacket. Travel expenses were not that high in those days, especially from bordering states. Indeed, in the full year before Jack arrived in 1954, approximately seventy-five percent of the staff came from Texas, Oklahoma, Kansas, Colorado, New Mexico, and Arizona.

Most of the attendance in the early 1950s was also from nearby states, but that would change dramatically during the Rhea years.

Pay would also go up during the Rhea era, but at the beginning pay scales reflected management's philosophy that seasonal employees were being extended a "privilege to serve Scouting through working as a staff member at Philmont – the largest camp of its kind in the world." The monthly pay scale for a camp director in the Bullock era ranged from 125 dollars to 175 dollars. Guides, forerunners to today's rangers received 75 to 125 dollars. As Philmont's attendance grew and the base from which he could recruit older staff expanded, Jack dropped the two-tiered employment system and was able to increase salaries. By the year he left, 1962, Jack could start a first year program counselor at 165 dollars per month – an increase of 120 percent compared to 1954.

How wild was Philmont's Backcountry in 1956? Could its remoteness have contributed to confusion in which many crews got lost on the trail and/or arrived in camps too late for program? As to describing Philmont's Backcountry as a wilderness, the term "quasi-wilderness" would be much more appropriate in 1956 as it is in the present. When Philmont's immediate post-World War II operations started, the principal Backcountry trails were already in place because they had been logging roads, horse trails to hunting/fishing lodges such as Cito and Fish Camp, cattle drive trails, and horse trails leading to mines or cow camps. Other trails dated to the 1920s and 1930s when Waite Phillips built them himself, frequently assisted by his son, Chope. There were even a few trails that had originally been blazed by hunters, trappers, and fishermen. The major trails of today were all in place in 1956 – and had resounded to hikers' footsteps for over a decade. The Philmont Staff Association's "old guard," the guides and camp directors from the late 1940s through 1951 have no recollection of trail signs, although they do recall some barbed wire fences. Guides of that era did not need trail signs; they had travelled the trails themselves before the campers arrived. Dan Ferguson, who started in '46 and later became CD at Cimarroncito, reflected upon the state of Philmont's Backcountry during the early Bullock years by observing that it was pristine country disturbed only by the conquistadores, Native Americans, trappers, hunters, miners, ranchers. And then the campers came – nearly 56,000 from 1946 through the end of the 1956 season thus further removing it from a truly pristine state.

The trail signs, minimizing Philmont as a wilderness, started appearing by 1952 and were well-sprinkled throughout the Backcountry by the 1956 season. Guides from the 1952 and 1953 seasons do recall the first trail signs – and that they did not completely prevent crews from occasionally veering off course. Rod Replogle, in 1956 a roving ranger who was responsible for the South Country, indicates that the problem was not that there were too many or too few trail signs, but that so many of them were regularly knocked over by the cattle. Rod also confirms that there was no rampant confusion on the trail in 1956 and that what problems there were hardly dampened the wonderful experiences of campers he encountered on the trail.

The principal camps of the high South Country were all in place: Crater, Fish Camp, Beaubien, Black Mountain, Porcupine, and Clear Creek. The trail camps of that sector are still with us: Agua Fria, Lost Cabin, Buck Creek, and Comanche. One trail camp grew (Crooked Creek) and one, Brownsea, went away completely. Miners Park was still in the future as was Apache Springs. The approaches to the big one, Mount Phillips, had been in place for years: via Sawmill, Clear Creek, or from Cyphers Mine.

Much the same can be said of the Central and Northern sections of Philmont once campers got out from the main base camps at Cimarroncito and Ponil. Indeed, given the fact that most trails followed canyons, it would be hard to avoid Old Camp and Indian Writings in the North Ponil Canyon, or Sioux, Bent, and Pueblano along the branches of South and Middle Ponil Creeks. In 1946, the Central Sector was just being opened up, but by 1956, there was a small camp headed for bigger things: Harlan with its clay pigeons. And, Cyphers Mine had seen two-way traffic for ten years. In 1956, the Dean Canyon had only one camp, Dean Trail Camp (but more Deans would follow).

Those crews becoming navigationally-challenged in 1956 became so based primarily on their own shortcomings, insufficient training in land navigation, and an inadequate map, not because Philmont's Backcountry was an uncharted wilderness. That is, however, not surprising considering the fact that in the mid-1950s comprehensive, pre-trek training by council High Adventure committees was the exception rather than the rule. In that era, the vast majority of the advisors were coming to Philmont for the first time which put them in a disadvantageous position compared to many of today's advisors who have had significant, previous Philmont experience. Indeed, the occasional crew today becomes momentarily perplexed on the trail even in an age of GPS, highly detailed topographic maps, and a thorough ranger session on map and compass. On the other hand, there is an element of truth in describing Philmont as "uncharted" in 1956. The old pen and ink map which had been around for years was truly simplistic and wholly inadequate as had been demonstrated in 1955. Jack Rhea had been working on that deficiency, but the comprehensive outcome was hardly an overnight solution.

The 1956 season came to a close, and although the Backcountry staff had positive feelings about the season, the advisors' reports Jack read all summer were telling a somewhat different story, forcing Jack to the conclusion that the new twelve-day expedition had not quite lived up to his expectations for it. Was the summer of '56 reminiscent of another landmark summer, 1946, which produced some bumps in the road? The answer is probably not, or at least not to the same extent, considering how key members of the Backcountry staff felt about the 1956 season. The roving rangers and the rangers at the large base camps charged with training crews had an ideal summer and were confronted with very few issues among the groups with which they worked. Indeed, Roving Ranger Boyce Farrar, whose "territory" was Cito to Ponil and back, encountered no significant problems on the trail that summer, other than blister cases. Rene de Hon, camp director at Cyphers Mine, saw a lot of traffic heading to and from Mount Phillips. He also confirms that 1956 was not an unusual year, and he was there for several years before and after 1956. George Worley, director at Fish Camp advises that '56 was like any other summer for his staff – everybody was enjoying the Backcountry life and certainly not looking forward to seeing it come to an end. One of George's staff, Dick Brammer, a young man who would be a roving ranger in a couple of years, did indicate that the only things that came to a glorious end that year were the structures associated with the old expeditions and wagon trains: tent platforms and cooking shelters. They made grand firewood for the shower's hot water heater and for makeshift saunas.

Dick did report one incident which may have helped contribute to the notion that some crews lost their bearings, only this case involved a camper who lost himself – deliberately. The lad did not get along with his fellow crewmates who were delighted when he simply decided to walk out on the crew and backpack on his own in the general Fish Camp vicinity. The felony was compounded by the advisor who apparently saw no value in counting heads as the crew left Fish Camp. The misfit was clever enough to solve his food problem by going to the Fish Camp commissary and bluffing his way into picking up trail food for his crew. That solved his food crisis for a few days, but he was eventually found out when he tried another pickup. After being at large for several days, the camper was reunited with his crew at Beaubien.

Another Backcountry camp director, Pete Silldorff at Porcupine, recalled what a wonderful summer 1956 was. Porky was on a roll with a growing staff, enjoying a good reputation based on its programs, and attracting the largest number of campers in Porcupine's history. Pete was a particularly talented artist, and his caricatures and cartoons became collectors' items. Where anonymity was required, Pete simply signed them as "The Phantom." The only problem faced by staff and campers at Porky that summer was foiling the resident bear which was attracted to the camp's new commissary. Thus, it appears that 1956 was a good year from the staff morale viewpoint. That is at least partially confirmed by the number returning for 1957; thirty percent of the 1956 staff came back in 1957 whereas the 1955-1956 carryover was at twenty-five percent.

In truth of matter, the majority of crews sailed through the Ranch on uneventful treks in 1956, and they were the ones which were older and well-prepared before they even arrived at the Ranch. The message about Backcountry problems came through to Jack Rhea in the late afternoon as he read the departing advisors' reports. Philmont's "wilderness" was not the problem; indeed, Philmont's Backcountry was and is a prized asset. It was clear, however, that something would have to be done to more fully prepare crews for the trail in 1957, a year in which Philmont attendance and total seasonal employment would decline dramatically due to the National Jamboree in Valley Forge that year. Better utilization of manpower resources within the budget, more training, and a substantially improved map clearly would go a long way in removing the critical remarks in advisors' critiques.

The Rise of Indian Writings

While the summer of 1956 may have ended with a few rough edges on the new twelve-day, guideless expedition, another program was getting off to a splendid start. That the North Ponil Canyon was archeologically significant had been known for a long time, particularly since publication of *Let The Coyotes Howl*. That remarkable book (another Philmont bookshelf essential) documented the Quinnipiac Council's archeological expedition to Philmont in 1941 under the leadership of Council Executive Samuel Bogan. Until Jack Rhea arrived at Philmont, very little had been done with Indian Writings as an important part of Philmont's programs. Even less had been done to protect and preserve the treasures that the canyon held. In 1953, Eugene Lutes, a Columbia University graduate student in archeology headed up a group of Explorers who visited Philmont and the North Ponil Canyon on the way back from the 1953 National Jamboree in California.

In that summer of 1953, Director of Camping George Bullock gave Lutes permission to take five of his Explorers up to Indian Writings. The party was driven north by John Harrison, Bullock's assistant director, to a rock shelter located above the canyon floor. The site had been badly disturbed by pot hunters, but Lutes was able to dig a small test trench and recover pottery shards, indicating the site had been a permanent dwelling. Because a mummified lizard was found at the site, it became known as Lizard Cave. Lutes took some of the shards back to Columbia and was encouraged by his professors to explore the site in depth.

Lutes later developed a specific proposal for an archeology program, including field work at Indian Writings and presented it to Ray Bryan, Philmont's general manager, at the BSA's new National Office in New Jersey. The proposal languished at the National Office until early 1956 when it was approved. That summer, Indian Writings was up and running as a three-man camp with one cooking shelter and one two-hole latrine. Lutes' two assistants were young men who had been on the 1953 trip to Indian Writings: Jim Coward and John Anderson. The new program's goals were to learn more about the ancient people of the North Ponil Canyon and to teach the basics of archeology field work. The first artifacts uncovered were estimated to date back to around the year 800. Another very significant goal was to make sure the program participants would report any significant findings to professional archeologists, or as Lutes pointed out, "better to take photographs rather than objects from the possible site." Thus, preservation was an important, early objective in the program. The early findings at Indian Writings also appeared as a fascinating article, "Secrets of the Canyon," in the June 1957 issue of *Boy's Life* magazine. Lutes later recorded the events that led to the archeology program at Indian Writings as one of the papers given at the Philmont Archeology Conference held in late 2010.

The early Indian Writings program involved much more than "digging." It also included a thorough debrief at day's end to make sure participants understood what they had accomplished. Significantly, the staff also demonstrated certain aspects of Southwestern Indian culture, including body painting and arrow making. Much was learned in the first five summers of the program, a period when a number of promising young archeologists joined the Indian Writings staff; among them were Mike Glassow, Galen Baker, and Dick Harris.

There were a number of significant finds during Indian Writings' first five summers. They included a slab house (a sunken dwelling with stone slab walls), roasting pits, human burials, and what was probably a sweat lodge. The early archeology program was not limited to human settlements. Lutes was called in to investigate a fossilized rattlesnake. It turned out not to be a snake, but rather was an ammonite fossil which was of much greater interest since it is a spiral-shaped, extinct invertebrate cephalopod of marine origin. On another occasion, he found a pre-historic mammoth's molar in gravel that was being used as a road bed. Lutes and his team tried to find more evidence of the mammoth and hoped to find any connection of mammoth hunting by finding spear points, but they were unsuccessful in the latter pursuit.

Jack Rhea was very enthusiastic about the Indian Writings program as were campers. The program became a regular part of the Training Center's tours. Within two years, Jack had a commissary cabin built at Indian Writings. Occasionally, Lutes would announce the latest find at a camp directors' meeting or less frequently by radio if it were an especially significant find. Jack invariably drove up to Indian Writings within twenty-four hours to see the new find for himself. The trips to Indian Writings added much to what was one of Jack's growing interests, Native Americans, a subject that would play an important role years later when he retired from the BSA.

One visit nearly ended in disaster, however. It was a Sunday, and Jack had taken his two boys up to the weekly Indian Writings presentation to Training Center visitors. About midway through the Lutes presentation, one of the program counselors came up and whispered something into Gene's ear. The message was cryptic, "Jack Rhea – latrine." Handing the presentation off to his assistant, Gene hastened to the latrine to find Jack sprawled on the ground trying to extract something from the latrine itself. One of the Rhea boys had tried to answer nature's call only to nearly fall into the pit as the latrine floor suddenly collapsed. The lad was hanging on for dear life, but was pulled to safety by Jack and Gene. It was discovered that some campers, who obviously could have used a little more character development, had pilfered so much of the floor's wood to use in cooking fires, that the structure collapsed, almost sending the Rhea youngster into the abyss. At 8:30 AM the next morning, Gene Pompeo, one of Philmont's carpenters, arrived at Indian Writings with an assistant to construct a camper-resistant latrine.

Although archeology was on its way to becoming one of Philmont's most popular programs, there were still a few people who did not at all comprehend exactly what it is that archeologists do. One day, a Scout riding in a pickup truck arrived at Indian Writings and wanted to see "the archeologist" because he had seen and been puzzled by something very unusual just off the Ponil road. When Gene inquired, he was told that there was a big bird with a little umbrella on its head just down the road. The Scout asked Gene to accompany him back to the fork in the road. Gene, although not a trained ornithologist, decided to see what was going on and very soon discovered a peahen complete with the little feathered crest above its head. At that time, there was a small flock of peacocks kept at Villa Philmonte and one of the hens had gotten loose and made it all the way to Six Mile Gate!

On another occasion, a wrangler arrived at Indian Writings and added to Lutes' reputation as a man of many talents. The wrangler's horse had just come off second best in an encounter with a porcupine which left four quills in the horse's nose. Although Lutes' doctorate was not in veterinary medicine, he quickly extracted the quills using a pair of pliers.

Gene Lutes is a man with a sense of humor. What is not known is if he had looked into the future and seen that it would be many years before Philmont's interpretive programs would be launched, including Apache Life. Many of Indian Writings' discoveries appeared as new features in *Staff News*, the forerunner of today's *PhilNews*. Gene always bylined those news articles from Indian Writings as Philmont's "Indian Agent." The articles ran with the headline, "Stones and Bones," and the articles were always signed-off with a unique twist, "Remember, if you have a bone to pick, see us first."

The early archeology program was a resounding success and resulted in much more than two pages of ink running in *Boy's Life*. The prestigious New Mexico-based magazine on art, history, and Indian culture of the southwest, *El Palacio*, also ran an article on the early findings at Indian Writings. Eugene Lutes was on his way to becoming a world renowned archeologist. Among the first papers he gave was one on the Philmont project – given in Chicago to an annual meeting of the American Anthropological Association. Today, Gene looks back on a very rich career and highly values the cooperation and encouragement of Philmont's management for five very productive summers.

The original shelter of the late 1950s was transformed into a cabin and eventually into a program museum building. Then a program cabin was built and finally, in 2000, a large staff cabin with a porch was built. In the very early days, Gene Lutes and his small staff commuted to work – by driving over and back every day from their quarters at Ponil. The program is much-expanded from 1956 and still includes archeological work and visits to the petroglyphs on the canyon walls. While the area around Indian Writings is acknowledged as Philmont's archeology central, other artifacts have been discovered far from the North Ponil Canyon; a good example was the discovery of a complete Indian pot found on a ledge above Miners Park in 1960. The pot was estimated to date from the 1300s. Of great interest now is the tour to the nearby Tyrannosaurus Rex footprint. Philmont hosts an annual archeological field study group from New Mexico Highlands University which continues to uncover new historical sites – adding to the existing sites that now number in excess of 1,000 in the North and Middle Ponil drainages alone.

Part IV
THE HIGH COUNTRY
AND BEYOND

*Jack Rhea credited his years at Philmont as the source of his deep interest
in Native American culture and art. The plaque above honors Chief Big Tree
of the Seneca Tribe who died at age 102 in 1967. He is associated with the
Indian image used in "buffalo" nickels which were issued between 1913 and
1938. The bronze plaque above, embedded in aspen bark, was given to Jack
by a friend on the occasion of Jack's retirement in 1974.*

CHAPTER 15

The Curtain Goes Up

With the summer of 1956 behind him, Jack deliberated on what had been learned from that year's newly introduced, twelve-day expedition *vis a vis* the realities of anticipated attendance and the operating budget. With the Fourth National Jamboree scheduled for Valley Forge in the summer of 1957, attendance would prove to be only half of the 1956 total: 5,219, down from 10,044. There would be one new income source, the Conservation Training Camp, and some real growth in another program, Junior Leader Training, but attendance at both programs was still very small. Clarence Dunn's reservations concerning guideless expeditions were very much on Jack's mind as he discussed the upcoming year with his two closest associates: Dunn and Doc Loomis.

In reality, the only solution was a compromise. Sending a guide with a crew from start to finish was certainly not in the economic picture and eliminating guides completely from the trail again would result in another summer with inadequate preparation for some crews. While Jack Rhea is best remembered for his expertise in operations, personnel, and training, he was very mindful of the financial side of running Philmont's camping department. Like the successful council executive he had been, Jack paid close attention to all bottom lines right down to the daily reports from the Philmont trading post manager and the seasonal registrar. For 1957, the one budget line item that got the most scrutiny was the seasonal staff payroll budget because it would fuel the decision on how to better prepare camper crews.

The only economic solution was to increase the time a guide stayed with the group and ram home the paramount importance of <u>thoroughly</u> training the group. Five days emerged as the logical period, which was a substantial increase over the two training days that had occurred in 1956. The new training period was comprised of a partial day in Camping Headquarters, two days at a base camp, and two full days on the trail. That would allow the new guide to evaluate the crew <u>on the trail</u> and to remediate any emerging problems before the group was truly turned loose. Crews deserved to be turned loose as a unit on their own; after all, having a guide along took some of the adventure out of High Adventure. Having an escorted tour would not be much of a growth experience; crews needed and deserved to get to the mountaintop on their own. The decision to create what eventually became the Ranger Department was made by early to mid-autumn of 1956; staff application forms going out to new applicants in late autumn included a "Ranger" job description.

However, the Philmont Rangers did not start out as a "department." Rather, the Philmont Rangers were a "program." They would remain so until their numbers swelled from the dozens into the hundreds and their management structure became stratified by several levels. In 1957, the camping operation was composed of three "departments:" Camp Operations, Camp Service, and Camp Program. Philmont Rangers were a sub-set within the latter group along with program directors, program counselors, horsemen, wranglers, and staff assigned to JLT and the Conservation Work Camp.

Naming the Rangers

Once the ranger concept was firmed up, there was the matter of what to call them. To call them guides would be a link with the past, and these new young men needed a name all of their own. The term "ranger" is traditionally defined in several ways. One is the familiar park service ranger (national, state, or local) who is associated with patrolling, visitor orientation, maintenance, and natural resource management. Another connotation is law enforcement, e.g., the Texas Rangers. Then there is the caretaker definition – one that is widely used in Scouting to describe the resident manager of a council camp whose principal function is the overall care of the camp. That term in the same context is still used at Philmont today; there is a "ranger" stationed at Ponil on a year 'round basis. His functions include opening and closing North Country camps, routine maintenance, dealing with poachers, etc.

The term "ranger" had also been in Philmont use in the late 1940s to describe the function of a solitary man operating a satellite or outpost camp where crews would overnight on the trail between major camps. For example, Clarence Baldwin, the 1949 camp director at Fish Camp was in charge of not only his own immediate staff, but also three rangers: one each at Clear Creek, Porcupine, and Black Mountain. Such rangers were phased out as those smaller locations eventually evolved into staffed operations with camp directors and counselors offering programs of their own. The term "ranger" had been used in the mid-50s as the title for a person whose job primarily involved training crews at a base camp, and the term "roving ranger" had been in use for over two years to describe the "on trail" troubleshooters who were charged with helping crews who were having problems in transit between camps.

Then there is the military context; the term "ranger" has been used all the way back to the American Revolutionary War to describe small, elite units charged with special duties. Jack Rhea had been an Army ranger himself during World War II and certainly saw many parallels between the 100th Infantry Division Rangers and this new band of high-spirited, physically fit, achievement-oriented, young, and rugged outdoorsmen who would be in the vanguard of Philmont's summer program.

Jack was also notoriously closed-mouth about his war years almost to the point of being secretive, even with his own immediate family. He would go out of his way to minimize the extent to which his family could see the shrapnel wound scars on his legs. Jack certainly was not going to divulge any details about his having been an Army ranger to any wide audience. That guarded information emerged only after scrutiny of 100th Infantry Division documents a year after Jack's death. On one of the very rare occasions when Jack ever said anything about the war to his family, it was that he "was trained in a group of men that are now known as Special Forces." Thus the term "ranger" was much more than just a casual word to Jack Rhea; it was an important part of who he was.

There are several strong similarities between the peacetime Philmont Rangers of 1957 and the wartime Century Rangers, all of which would have been very apparent to Jack. Except for the first two classes of Century Rangers, the age level of the two groups was identical – late teens and early twenties. Although Jack was not a member of the original six Ranger Battalions of World War II, he was very much aware of their motto, "Rangers Lead The Way." While the focus nowadays is to emphasize the role of the youth leader or crew leader, in the 1950s it was very much the Philmont Ranger who led the way (albeit in an unassertive manner that did not threaten the adult advisor's authority).

Philmont Ranger training has always been very intense, more so than other types of staff training because it was the most physically demanding, ran sun-up to well after dark, and was held in an essentially bivouac setting and on the trail as was Jack's ranger training experience in 1943. A Century

Ranger's uniform was easily distinguished from that of other Centurymen by its red and white shoulder tab. Philmont Rangers quickly established their own distinctive insignia which over the years has been symbolized by neckerchiefs, hats, and the prized Philmont Ranger patch. Within just a few short years, Philmont Rangers had their own song, heard nowadays as a chant and in much more public circumstances. The rangers of the 100th Division in 1943 had no single song unique to them, but did have popular marching and running songs. The Philmont Rangers do not have a motto *per se*, but the opening sentence of the Ranger Song essentially serves as one and it has been adopted by all non-ranger members of Philmont's staff alumni – "I Wanna Go back to Philmont!"

Jack's only written comment on the name was that, "The ranger title was used with the outstanding young men who were to train and serve expeditions during their first three days on the trail." Jack was not the type of man to toot his own horn and grab credit for major, very visible developments. Jack's children recall their father often saying, "Who gets credit for something is not important. What is important is getting the job done."

As to how the decision was made to name the Philmont Rangers, especially considering Jack's ranger training in the summer of 1943, his subsequent planning of ranger operations in France and Germany, and the fact that the word had already been in use at Philmont with such prefixes as "camp" or "roving," the inescapable conclusion is that Jack Rhea quickly made the naming decision himself, requiring little or no deliberation or consensus.

Rangers have always enjoyed good press – particularly in *Boys Life* and *Scouting*, commencing in 1959 when *Boys Life* carried a feature article on Philmont Rangers. Other Philmont departments have appeared in those magazines, but not at all as frequently. Adding to the perception of importance of Philmont Rangers in the early days was the special attention received from the National Office in the form of Assistant Director of Camping Bill Wadsworth who became an integral part of Ranger Training. And even before Wadsworth arrived in 1961, the National Office's director of camping, Wes Klusmann, had considered Philmont Rangers of such importance that he attended their launching in 1957 and came back again in 1958, a fact not lost upon the new rangers. And in 1970, Wadsworth wrote a glowing article about Philmont Rangers for *Scouting* magazine.

The rangers of 1957 and every ranger since got a special gift from

Mister Dunn who told his rangers to, "Know Philmont!" And know it they have. Rangers are privileged like no other Philstaff to <u>constantly</u> listen to the song of the high trail – the slosh of water in a canteen, the snarl of a pack zipper, soft footfalls and the gentle patter of falling pebbles on a High Country trail, the rip of Velcro opening a map pocket, the splash from a too shortly jumped creek, echoes across the canyon, the clickety-clank of pots, pans, and white gas bottles, a raven's raspy croak aloft, the wind's roar announcing a thunderstorm, the brush of backpack nylon fabric against scrub oak, and a camper's sigh when a break is called. Who else gets so consistently close to Waite Phillips' land as a ranger? With backpacking as Philmont's core activity, the experts in that trade are the rangers, best known as those "lean, green, hikin' machines" when staff shirts were green. On days off, rangers from day one usually do what they are paid to do, "Head for the High Country" (to quote Ranger Dave Caffey's timeless book title).

Was Jack Rhea surprised at how the Philmont Rangers almost over-night developed such a sense of identity and team spirit? Most likely, Jack would have been quite amazed and very disappointed if they had not.

The Colonel's Lieutenants

There were many details to be worked out once the die was cast. How many of these men would be needed? What qualifications were most impor-tant? Who would train them – where, using what for a syllabus, how many days for training, etc? Who would be their leader? Fortunately, Jack had time to work out the details with the two men who would play a critical role in launching the new Philmont Rangers. Clarence Dunn would become the first Chief Ranger and Doc Loomis would play a pivotal role in the training.

The iconic first Chief Ranger, Mister Clarence Dunn, is shown here speaking at his retirement dinner at Philmont in 1970.

For Jack's first two years, personnel decisions were divided between himself and Clarence Dunn, a former Arlington, Texas, school teacher and district personnel director. Jack still made many of the decisions on key appointments such as camp directors. He was not at all known as a micro-manager, but there were occasions when he very definitely was "hands-on," particularly at the end of the season. When in the Backcountry in late August, he would ask those who were planning to come back the following year to sit down with him right then and there for an employment interview.

Deals were struck and hands were shaken on the spot.

In 1957, Clarence Dunn was old enough to be Jack's father which therefore instantly also cloaked Dunn with a grandfatherly image. The effect was perfect; while a son might have sharp, angry differences with his father, a grandfather was always accorded the respect that comes with age and wisdom. Generations of Rangers referred to Dunn as "Mister Dunn" although they readily referred to directors of camping by their first names, such as Jack, Skipper, or Joe. Having been born in Belcherville, Texas, in 1891, Mister Dunn was sixty-six years of age when he became Chief Ranger – he was in fact a Philmont old-timer, having brought a crew of campers out from Texas in 1943 to work in Philmont's Service Corps Program. Time has all but obscured the fact that it was Dunn who brought a simple grace from his council in Fort Worth. The grace eventually became known as the Philmont Grace. He joined the Philmont staff in 1946, and although he had been camp director at Cimarroncito for one summer, he settled into the job of personnel director even though he was a seasonal staff member. While the Philmont Guides never really had a "chief guide," Dunn shared what amounted to leadership of the guides over the years with Russ Vliet, Doc Loomis, and Dale Olsen. He also outlasted them all and is the one person old guides usually refer to when asked to whom they reported.

During his days as Chief Ranger, Dunn came across as a gentle person although during his career as a teacher and later a school principal in Arlington, Texas, a Dallas suburb, he had been known as a tough but fair administrator. His bachelor's degree was from what is now the University of North Texas; he also held a master's degree in secondary education with a minor in elementary education. Jack, whose degree also was in education, held Dunn in very high regard, according to Jack's son Bart Rhea. Dunn was a modest man whose uniform was basically understated, although there were square knots for the Scouter's Key and Silver Beaver. Dunn had joined Scouting in 1925 as a scoutmaster before moving up to commissioner and district chairman. His good work included his community of Arlington where he received several civic honors, including having a middle school named in his honor. His retirement from Philmont in 1970 occasioned a special banquet and a bound volume of letters from many, many Rangers.

Dunn had worn many hats including functioning as Philmont's personnel manager, but that was about to change completely with the hiring of Buzz Clemmons in late 1956. In 1950, the combined permanent and seasonal staff amounted to just 113 people. By the mid-1950s, projections indicated that to serve the growing numbers of campers, a seasonal staff of 300 or more by the end of the decade would be necessary. Mr. Dunn had been Philmont's de facto personnel director up through 1955, and sharing the hiring load with Jack was only going to work for so long. Even though the 1957 Jamboree would reduce Philmont's attendance, Jack was already looking ahead to when attendance would go through 12,000 and a staff of over 400 would be required. Quite simply, the need arose for a full-time, assistant director of camping – one whose principal responsibility was the personnel management function. Jack petitioned the National Office to create a new position, assistant director of camping, with the job description concentrating on personnel administration with a secondary role in logistical support during the summer.

Several candidates were identified, but Jack only interviewed one; E.O. "Buzz" Clemmons was a BSA professional in St. Paul, Minnesota, and was about seven years older than Jack. For those generations of Philmont staffers who wondered how Buzz got his name and what the "E.O." stood for, the story can now be told. Buzz was not a 1930s barnstorming pilot;

Philmont Museum

E.O. "Buzz" Clemmons joined the permanent staff in late 1956.

the nickname dates back to his days as an infant. While most babies say "coooh," frequently accompanied with hissing bubbles, what emerged from E.O. Clemmons, the newly born baby, came out as more of a rasp or buzz. So, "Buzz" he became. The E.O. stood for Elwyn Ota, the latter being a family name.

Buzz grew up in Virden, Illinois, got a degree in education, started as a school teacher, and eventually served as a school principal in Jacksonville, Illinois. He also became a scoutmaster, something he enjoyed very much. When World War II came, Buzz tried his best to join the Navy, but was turned down: he was deaf in one ear as a result of a childhood sports injury. The BSA was desperate to hire good men into the professional service during the war because so many of their younger field execs, like Jack Rhea, had volunteered or been drafted. Buzz resigned from the school district, went through training at Schiff, and became a field executive with the Abraham Lincoln Council in Springfield, Illinois, on 1 March 1943. In June 1947 Buzz moved to St. Paul, Minnesota, for a bigger opportunity where he was hired as assistant council executive and director of camping in what is today the Northern Star Council, BSA. Buzz and his wife arrived in Cimarron in December of 1956 to start a seventeen-year career at Philmont.

There is the common misconception that in the 1950s and 1960s Philmont was flooded with seasonal employment applications – many more than were necessary to populate the summer staff with well-qualified people. That was not the case; Jack and Buzz divided the country into important sectors and each traveled extensively to recruit quality staff. Jack usually took the two coasts and Buzz mostly concentrated in the country's middle. By the time Jack left in late 1962, the seasonal staff had very definitely evolved from an overwhelmingly southwestern bias to a national composition, albeit with a rather weak showing from New England. In 1956, thirty-eight of the fifty states were represented in the seasonal staff. North Dakota and West Virginia showed up the following year, but most of New England, Alaska, and Hawaii were not represented although their day would eventually come.

Before Buzz retired from Philmont, he had bought some land over in Angel Fire in 1967. In 1971, his retirement home on that land was finished. It was a project in which he took great interest; he was a master craftsman and skilled cabinet maker in his own right. In his last two years, he commuted daily between Angel Fire and Philmont before retiring in 1973 to take up new employment as Angel Fire's first postmaster. Buzz died on 29 September 1995 at age 87 and is warmly remembered by generations of Philmont staffers because the name "E.O. Clemmons, Assistant Director of Camping" was the signature on the letter offering them employment at Philmont Scout Ranch, and he was also the first to greet them upon their arrivals at Camping Headquarters to begin employment on the seasonal staff.

In creating the Philmont Rangers, Jack went into 1957 with some more good fortune: a solid group of seasonal staff from 1956 which would form the second tier of leadership and perform a function that would later become known as "training ranger." Experienced men in this group included John Eilert, Dave Jung, Sam Kelsall, Roger Serpan, Steve Perin, Perry Bolin, and Bruce Teasley. With forty-percent of his smaller 1957 seasonal staff having been on board during the previous summer, Jack had a seasoned senior Backcountry staff in addition to the experienced ranger leadership. Jack was very well acquainted with John Eilert; the young man was his nephew. With a significant percentage of the 1956 roving ranger/guide staff coming back, Jack set about recruiting slightly more than another two dozen good men. As might be expected, most had been to Philmont before, either as campers or for Junior Leader Training. The red, white, and blue square knots of Eagle rank were abundant as were OA brotherhood pocket flaps. If a highly qualified nucleus of camping experts existed within the Philmont summer staff, itself an accomplished group to begin with, the rangers were it. And during training, the new rangers were quite definitely informed of how important that expertise would be to campers.

The new 1957 Rangers were recruited the old fashioned-way: by carefully screening applications, word-of-mouth, personal recommendations, chance encounters, and family ties. Gayle Reams, from Sweetwater, Texas, had never been to Philmont as a camper, but was very anxious to get there one way or another. His Scouting qualifications were impeccable and he got the job of his dreams: Philmont Ranger. Mister Dunn knew a couple promising Eagle Scouts (Dan Beckelman and Franklin Wilbur) from his hometown of Arlington, Texas; both were hired. Dunn had actually presented Beckelman with his Eagle award in 1955. Buzz Clemmons put his previous council staff experience to good use and recruited another Minnesot'n: Louis Chappuie. In the off-season, Jack recruited several more rangers while out on the sales circuit. While discussing upcoming arrangements with council executives, Jack requested that whatever venue, regional gathering, council banquet, or executive board lunch meeting, the council executive try to have a special youth speaker on the program – one who had attended the Ranch over the previous summer, was articulate, and anxious to talk about his experience. After Allan Rouse gave a post-luncheon talk to council leaders about his 1956 Philmont camper experience, another guest at that Cedar Rapids, Iowa, gathering came up and said what a wonderful presentation it was. The guest was Jack Rhea and the discussion with Allan quickly moved to working at Philmont. Correspondence and forms were promptly exchanged and Rouse soon had a new job at the Ranch.

These new rangers, thirty-two of them, were different from the guides and staff of previous years. Not surprisingly though, nine of them were from Texas, but only one more new ranger came from another bordering state (Arizona). Those first rangers were geographically much more diversified. Well over a quarter came from the Great Plains/Northern Plains. Twenty percent were from deep in Dixie, almost fifteen percent came from the Middle Atlantic states, and the Hoosiers and Buckeyes were represented too. The new rangers were also older than their counterparts of the early 1950s, and most had either completed their first year of college or would be heading to it in the autumn. The average age of the Philmont Rangers when they reported for work in June 1957 was nineteen years, one month. The oldest was almost twenty-two.

The First Ranger Training

Ranger training was brand new in 1957 and would set the pattern for decades to follow; it lasted longer and was much more intense than any training guides or roving rangers had received to date. Structurally, it was a patrol experience, not unlike JLT or Wood Badge, overlaid with Explorer post terminology. There were two posts, Lucien B. Maxwell Post and Kit Carson Post, with three "crews" per post. One crew had a solitary training ranger while the others had two, although the trainers' title was simply "ranger." Each of the training rangers served one day as the ranger for his post, with Dave Jung and Steve Perin taking the first day as ranger for their respective posts. The six crews were assigned four to six neophyte rangers, each of whom got to serve as crew leader for a day. The training rangers started arriving on Wednesday 12 June 1957 for their orientation and were struck by the fact that this new ranger business had attracted significant attention from the National Office. Wes Klusmann, director of camping, was there along with Don Higgins, the national director of health and safety. The other four officials were from volunteer training and both Explorer and Boy Scout Service. Klusmann's role was more symbolic, but the others would have an actual role in the training. Many of the new rangers and other staff were deposited at the train station in Raton by the Santa Fe Railroad on Thursday. The jovial Earl Swope himself was there to bus the young men down to Philmont where they were to report by late afternoon.

Two of the key instructors were Philmont permanent and seasonal staff, Doc Loomis and Bradley Davis, respectively. Loomis was already a legend in his own time and Davis was well on his way to becoming one. Davis, an Army Air Force ground instructor in World War II, was a science teacher back in Austin, Texas. His job title was naturalist and at age forty-eight, he was much older than the average summer staffer. He had a unique talent for teaching all about Philmont's flora, fauna, and earth sciences. Davis also carried a mobile zoo wherever he was assigned at the Ranch; the collection usually consisted of several snakes (including a most impressive western diamondback rattler), a skunk, raccoon, porcupine, and an albino tarantula.

Jack Rhea and Ray Bryan opened the training rangers orientation by reminding the group that the rangers' performance would be noted by crew advisors upon completion of their treks and that the secret to a good report was to always remember three concepts: democracy, volunteer spirit, and, importantly, that "the camper is king."

Mister Dunn then addressed the group by reviewing ranger job specifications, highlighting chain of command, leadership, and cooperation with other departments. His talk included personal conduct and appearance, record-keeping, responsibilities to groups and particularly its advisor, and how to set the example. After breakfast on Friday the new ranger program was outlined and job specifications were reviewed. The balance of the morning was spent much like today's arriving camper crew: medical recheck, quick tour of headquarters, picking up equipment, and the traditional shakedown.

The individual equipment consisted of a tent, ropes, stakes, basic first aid kit, a small notebook, and that enduring symbol of Rangerdom, the red-handled Plumb three-quarter axe. The tent could be purchased by the new ranger for cost at summer's end. Each crew was issued cooking gear and an Army surplus entrenching tool (shovel). Rangers had to buy the rest of their other individual equipment, and many bought two more ranger trademark items, the Bear Paw pack for ten dollars and the Philmont red jacket for six dollars. Those items could also be purchased through payroll deductions. At 1:50 P.M. the rangers left by camp bus for Ponil and six days of very intense training, beginning with axemanship, firebuilding, and Dutch oven cooking by Loomis and conservation/nature by Davis. Although legendary campfire leader Klusmann was attending, the campfire that evening was led by Frank Preston who was in a position Jack once held, assistant national director of volunteer training.

Part of ranger training was familiarization with trail food, although several meals would be taken in the Ponil dining hall. "Freeze-dried" was about ten years into the future, so Rangers went through the dehydrated menus, although when they got their real crews they could expect fresh food such as milk, mystery meat patties, and eggs when they were in a large base camp. Otherwise it was an introduction to the best dehydrated delectations Chuckwagon, Seidel, Rich-Moor, and Gumpert could offer in a plastic package: spaghetti dinner, chili beans, and that perennial love-hate favorite, vegetable-chicken-rice dinner ("vejja-vomit") among others. That was all cooked over wood fires; dishes, cooking pots, and utensils were washed and rinsed in great black buckets which began life shining in their galvanized coats. The pails overnight took on a black, sooty finish after heating water over open flames and became part of the burden borne by every crew and the occasional burro. Dishwashing was accomplished using Tetrox, a granular blue-green detergent which was also mixed with a small amount of water to create a paste with which the outsides of cooking pots were coated before they were put over a fire. The paste vastly simplified cleaning what would have otherwise been very blackened cooking pots. Rangers instructed their campers to make sure the Tetrox stayed on the outside of the pots. Any Tetrox working its way to the inside of cooking pots could also have a remarkable cleansing effect on campers' digestive systems.

During that week of ranger training, neophytes became expert with the Dutch oven with which peach cobblers and cornbread were considered child's play. Real men could make jelly rolls using Bisquick and creating the jelly from Koolaid mix. The more culinarily oriented Rangers could easily have created quiche using fresh milk, eggs, potato mix, condiment kit margarine, more ingredients from any of several trail supper menus, and a little cheese and onion begged from a camp staff. On the other hand, it may never have been tried because that was in an era when real men did not eat quiche. Pizza anybody? It was a snap with Bisquick and a quick pizza sauce derived from the spaghetti supper. Biscuits and dumplings were a stock in trade as were pancakes which were cooked by flipping a Dutch oven lid upside down to use as a frying pan. The new rangers learned old tricks – why dirty a frying pan for the sausages when they could be evenly cooked in their cans by rotating the container next to the flames of a fire?

During ranger training and the first month of operations, the fresh food and dehydrated trail food menus were always available, but by mid-July some shortages started occurring. That forced substitutions and deletions which disappointed any rangers and campers who were fond of crushed pineapple, fig bars, raisins, peanut butter, apricots, oatmeal, and fresh oranges and tomatoes which were removed from some of the menus. Worst of all, the condiment kits which were packaged in small, gray cardboard boxes, suffered the elimination of the coffee packets and one of the two sticks of margarine. They were not even to be issued by commissaries unless specifically requested.

16 June started early with a departure for New Dean where emphasis moved to tents, knots, and camping and backpacking equipment. It truly was a different era. Think canvas instead of nylon tents; sunlight-absorbing dark green official Explorer shirts instead of wicking, microfiber T-shirts; two one-quart aluminum canteens instead of Camelbaks®; shoulder straps instead of hipbelts, diamond hitches instead of nylon straps and plastic buckles; sleeping bags filled with Kapok instead of Thinsulate®; rubber ponchos for groundcloths instead of plastic film, cumbersome huff 'n' puff rubber mattresses instead of Therm-A-Rest® self-inflaters; pack frames made of wood instead of aircraft aluminum tubing; scrounging for fire-wood instead of unpacking a WhisperLite™ backpacking stove; magnetic compasses instead of GPS handhelds; leather instead of Gore-Tex®; and Tetrox detergent granules instead of liquid Campsuds, then you will get the idea. Fortunately, none of the 1957 Rangers had equilibrium issues, so hiking poles were completely unnecessary. The balance of the sixteenth was devoted to another Bradley Davis topic: geology.

The rangers, with a new man acting as crew leader each day, were on the move again the next day, bound for Pueblano with the men from National in tow. Monday, 17 June, was largely devoted to map and compass work as the Rangers were on the trail again, heading back to Ponil. There were absolutely no complaints about the map they were using. It was Jack Rhea's long-awaited, brand-new Philmont topographic map. It contained several very minor errors; a couple of short jeep trails had been marked as foot trails, for example. The few mistakes were noted on all ranger maps and recorded for correction on the next map printing. Philmont in that era never really developed home-grown experts in such subjects as first aid, health, and sanitation so those subjects were handled by Don Higgins, Frank Preston, and the other officials from the National Office using a National Camping School syllabus modified for use at Philmont.

There were some significant ups and downs attending the return to Ponil. On the morning of the eighteenth, the temperature was down to only two degrees above freezing. But ranger spirit was definitely heading skyward. Although the "Ranger Song" was still in the future, Training Ranger Perry Bolin was an especially talented guitar player and singer whose abilities could have easily made him the third of the Everly Brothers who were topping the charts in 1957 with such hits as "Bye Bye Love" and "Wake Up Little Susie." Bolin could also improvise as his transposition of lyrics from the popular old 1930s country and western song, "Tumbling Tumbleweeds" clearly attests.

> See them dragging their packs on the ground,
> Drifting along with sore and tender feet,
> I know when one group is gone,
> Another group will come drifting along.
> Drifting along with sore and tender feet.

On the eighteenth, the tables turned and the rangers-in-training now became the trainers. Doc Loomis had developed a very small flip-chart presentation that fit into a ranger's back pocket. That little flip-chart presentation recognized the importance of effective teaching and also was the direct ancestor of two critical components of the future program: the little "Campcraft" spiral-bound notebook which followed in 1958 and the comprehensive *Ranger Fieldbook* which was introduced in the late 1970s. If rangers were the world's leading authorities on map and compass, they were of no value to Jack Rhea if they could not effectively teach map and compass to teenage boys. For that reason 1957 ranger training involved a lot of "Show an' Do" followed by practice teaching on everything learned from sanitation to first aid. Loomis' flip-chart was limited to the subjects in which he excelled, but the "Campcraft" brochure covered everything from foot care to garbage disposal. The very first section of the "Campcraft" brochure was devoted to effective teaching which later became a full twenty-page section in the nearly 200-page *Ranger Fieldbook* that arrived about twenty years later.

Using Loomis' flip-chart, the new rangers gave presentations to each other on axemanship. When the presentations were over the balance of the day was spent removing the deep red, varnished finish on the axe handles and treating them with raw linseed oil. After scraping and successive sanding, oiling, and drying, the handles became so smooth that a blister-free performance was assured. Loomis taught rangers the finer points of sharpening their axes with a six-mill file. The first rangers and those during the following decade were well-versed in the proper nomenclature for all thirteen parts of the three-quarter axe and how to create a very useful fourteenth part as well. That final touch was converting the single-surfaced "doe's foot" at the end of the grip to an angled, two-surface part by sawing off the point, leaving a flat area of about one square inch called the "fawn's foot." The fawn's foot prevented the end of the handle from splitting when the grip end was tapped with a hammer or the butt of another axe to re-seat a loose axe head. A wedge would then be pounded into the eye to secure the handle, although Doc Loomis preferred using a fence staple instead of a wedge so it could easily be removed when resetting a loose axe head.

The refinished axe became the revered symbol of Rangerdom, certainly shining more brightly in a young ranger's eye than the sacred Wood Badge axe or kudu horn. The earliest axes were stamped with the Philmont brand and became prized possessions as well as Scouting collectors' items.

At dinner in the Ponil dining hall, Jack Rhea's talk was "The Ranger in Action." In that main event presentation, Jack imprinted the rangers with their mission. His talk was part comprehensive review and part pep talk. As remembered by Allan Rouse, "Jack Rhea impressed upon us repeatedly that the ranger is the key to the success of the Philmont experience for each boy who comes to the Ranch. If rangers mess up with groups, campers won't have the experience they came for."

Jack was quite frank about 1956 not being one of Philmont's big vintage years, saying of camper crews, "Philmont expected too much of them." Jack was not involved with specific instruction, but was with the rangers for at least part of every day. Except for the skills demonstrations, Mister Dunn led the daily activities, typically beginning the day by installing the day's crew leaders and closing out the campfire at the end of the day. As might be expected there were recognitions for standout crews, and the awards were presented at the campfires. Rangers were responsible for building the campfires; with the exuberance of youth and newly acquired axemanship expertise the first Ponil campfire resulted in a blaze that could be characterized by only two words, "instantaneous" and "massive." That fireball was overfueled with so much wood and so liberally doused with kerosene that the word "bonfire" seems completely inadequate. Wes Klusmann was not amused with what was nearly a barn fire and was very quick to make sure the new rangers understood that the essence of a good campfire was to allow it to build slowly as the evening program itself built intensity.

Ranger training in 1957 and 1958 was held at Ponil. Jack Rhea's talk, "The Ranger in Action," was an important part of the training.

Mister Dunn ran a tight ship during training and in the early ranger days; if a ranger wanted to head for greater Cimarron, he had to check out and check back in at the Ranger Office. Jack Rhea's insistence on proper uniforming was lovely music to Mister Dunn who could easily spot a non-regulation belt at 100 paces. Dunn's vision of the new rangers included their being exemplary in every respect, i.e., living the Scout Oath and Law to the fullest. Hanging out with "rowdies" and enjoying some Red River or Trinidad nightlife was not Ranger-like in Dunn's opinion. Within a few years, the grip was relaxed somewhat, but staying in Mister Dunn's good graces was an important aspect of the ranger mindset throughout his long tenure as chief ranger.

Mystery of the First Ranger Photo

Training was over on the nineteenth and the rangers headed back to Headquarters where the first ranger picture was taken late in the afternoon which was followed by the closing banquet. The first ranger group photo is worth scrutiny because it conveys some interesting details. Many of the first rangers are wearing a new Philmont patch – the first Philmont arrowhead which replaced the little round patch with its many segments. Jack

always shied away from taking any credit for the new patch, but years later confided in several people that it was time for the little round patch and its various segments to go because they were much too reminiscent of council camp patches. The new patch, based on Arrowhead Rock on the north side of Tooth of Time Ridge, helped popularize what has become a Philmont tradition: looking back and seeing Arrowhead Rock when leaving Philmont ensures that the viewer will someday return.

About a quarter of the new rangers had been to the Third National Jamboree in 1953 as indicated by the round patch above the right pocket flap. Official headgear for Scouts and Explorers of that era was the garrison cap (overseas cap), yet only a solitary new ranger is wearing one. Here and there, the traditionalists can be spotted – wearing the ill-fated pith helmet or a Smokey Bear field hat. Most wore a cowboy hat which was certainly not part of the uniform, but since Mister Dunn frequently wore a Stetson, the rank and file could too. Most cowboy hats were white, perhaps identifying their owners with the good guys, but there were a few individualists with black hats. The few non-conformists wore something from left-field such as a Sherlock Holmes-style autocap or no headgear at all. One thing they did have in common, whether they were conformists or not, was the preponderance of Eagle Scouts within their numbers and tremendous pride at having just become a trained Philmont Ranger.

This was Mister Dunn's version of the "official" 1957 Ranger photo.
All hats were removed to create a more uniform appearance.

There was a second 1957 Ranger picture which was the "official" picture as far as Mister Dunn was concerned. In the second picture, all headgear was removed to create a more "uniform" appearance. One person was asked to get out of the first picture; it was a publicity-hungry wrangler who inserted himself at the last minute into the third row, far right side. Unfortunately, from Dunn's viewpoint, the many-hatted version with the interloper is the photo that has gotten the most mileage over the years.

The New Era Dawns

At a mid-morning meeting on 20 June, the first expedition assignments were handed out. The lucky Dave Jung took the first expedition of the summer, 620C, a three-advisor crew from Oklahoma which arrived at the "loading dock" (the small, 1950s version of today's Welcome Center) in a large station wagon, pulling a small trailer. It would be several days before the last ranger got his first group, but it was the beginning of a new era at Philmont. How did the first crew with a Philmont Ranger work out? Many years later, Dave wrote that he knew it would be a good crew the moment he laid eyes on them. He had that ranger's intuition that can quickly size up a crew and sense whether it has plenty of outdoor experience, that the Scouts are used to working together, and that the advisor(s) have the stamina to get over Mount Phillips without difficulty. And so it turned out. The headquarters check-in went smoothly and the group confirmed an itinerary that would take it from Cito to Rayado via the best of the high South Country. The trek took Dave to Cyphers after two days of crew training at Cito, a side hike to Phillips, through Red Hills, and then to Beaubien where Dave said farewell to them before catching a ride back to Headquarters on a commissary truck.

Dave Jung had just completed his freshman year in college in June of 1956 when he reported to Philmont for his second summer – that year as a ranger based at Cito where he was responsible for itinerary planning and basic skills instruction. On the way to Philmont, he used American Automobile Association strip maps – and wondered why such maps could not be adapted for use at Philmont. Over the summer, Dave worked on the strip maps and had some comprehensive layouts to present to Jack at the end of the summer. The new strip maps, edited to remove some of Dave's wit, went into production and eventually became part of the mailings that went to all groups with reservations. The strip maps were eventually spiral-bound and seen in advisors' packs for years to come. Dave's stellar career as one of the first Rangers came to an abrupt end as July 1957 approached. The assistant director at Cito had backed out at the last moment, and Dave became the designated replacement.

The strip maps Dave devised became an integral part of a crew's itinerary planning which in the late 1950s was conducted at one of the three base camps by a member of the camp staff, usually the camp director or his assistant. Rangers typically had some influence on itinerary decisions, and in the early 1960s itinerary planning became a function of assistant chief rangers at Camping Headquarters. By 1963, when the number of days a ranger stayed with a group was reduced by one, the "base camp" concept was starting to fade as some crews were starting at such non-traditional locations as Stockade, Clarks Fork, Abreu, or Olympia. Because many of the large groups which had previously hit the trail as one group of forty or more people were breaking up, at Jack's suggestion, and hiking in several crews, ranger resources were spread very thin. Thus, the number of days of ranger orientation was reduced by one – and as it turned out, rangers were able to get the lessons across adequately in four days instead of five. And so it has been since 1963.

The Ranger Office involvement with itinerary planning proved somewhat unwieldy until 1964 when the Control Center was launched. That unit put itinerary planning, dispatching, and communications all under one roof and brought new efficiency as the result of the improved coordination. Dave Jung was in graduate school at Dartmouth during this period when he became one of the first trip planners in the new Control Center in 1964. He later served as an assistant chief ranger and was a very visible member of the Philmont Staff Association when he died, much too prematurely, of Parkinson's disease in 2004.

Ranger Life in 1957

What was it like to be a ranger in that watershed year of 1957? In some ways, it was no different than that experienced by today's rangers and what rangers will experience in another fifty years. In other ways, it was very different, beginning with what few amenities there were in a much smaller Camping Headquarters which had no Ranger City. For a laundry, rangers had access to an electric washer with a hand-cranked wringer. The great out-of-doors served as the dryer.

Philmont Museum

Philmont Ranger Shakedown, 1950s style.

Although the new rangers were empowered and feeling on top of the world, there were a few issues relating to housing. Jack Rhea had created Tent City for campers because attendance was rapidly outstripping the capacity of the Rocky Mountain shelters, Ranger City was still a couple years away. Even as late as 1955, campers were still using the big shelters. In the meantime, the new rangers took quarters in one of the Rocky Mountain shelters which contained bunks and storage bins (wire cages more than anything else). Although called "shelters," the buildings resembled low, thick-walled versions of Stockade; they contained bunks, storage space, and various camp services such as the post office. They had been used by campers in days gone by when attendance was small, but when the rangers moved in it was on a rather transient basis. Bunks were not assigned, so when a ranger was out with a group, another ranger could claim the former's bunk. John Eilert mentioned that there was some unhappiness with the arrangement to his Uncle Jack, and very shortly each ranger had his own bunk. It paid to have friends in high places.

Those first rangers of 1957 felt important if for no other reason than Jack Rhea quite firmly told them during training that they were critically important to Philmont's success. Their opinions were sought throughout that landmark summer by Messrs. Dunn and Clemmons. Ranger expertise mattered, and not just to the groups they served. Several times over the next two months, the rangers of '57 had to fill out evaluation forms that asked them to comment on the effectiveness of their training in June, quality of Philmont-issued equipment, effectiveness of Doc Loomis' flip charts, and the possibility of using a lighter-weight axe.

The feedback also involved evaluating equipment, including new types of tentpins, trail food, wax fire starter sticks, and parachute rope. They were also asked if they would like to help design a new trail tent, what they would do to improve trail menus, how blisters could be reduced, and if they would like to carry a little axe maintenance kit in their packs. Significantly, several rangers were asked to evaluate a new, aluminum Dutch oven. The new units played to rather mixed reviews since it was felt that they developed hot spots which resulted in uneven cooking. Several years later, after Philmont bought some of the units, it was demonstrated that in the absence of judicious heat control, an aluminum Dutch oven could actually be melted to the extent that it became so deformed as to be worthless.

Instant gratification, if it ever was enjoyed, might come only in the form of a stale newspaper dropped by some newly arrived advisor. Far beyond the reach of television and most radio, rangers back in the day, being essentially secluded, enjoyed more basic pursuits such as spending what precious little spare time there was writing to the folks back home, reading, bantering with peers on a wide variety of subjects, or exploring the Ranch and neighboring peaks. And frequently, a ranger's closest friends simply were not there – they were out on the trail with a group and would not be back for several days when he himself might have just caught a bus for a starting camp.

Having wheels simplified off-Ranch jaunts during what little free time there was. Steve Perin, who had previously been a guide and roving ranger, drove an old jeep which facilitated exploring. On one occasion he found a bleached steer skull which he retrieved with his friend, Ranger Bill Dailey. Unfortunately, they encountered a rattlesnake in the removal process. Actually, it was the serpent's misfortune because it was subsequently broiled in back of the Rocky Mountain shelter, much to the delight of several of the culinarily more adventurous rangers.

Doc Loomis kept a close eye on his boys that summer and knew what was going through young minds in early August when the end of the season was in sight. He also knew that some aspects of the ranger's job could result in mediocrity which he warned about in this little note, personally signed, which went out to each ranger at the end of July.

> Dear Rangers,
> We have not seen the need for a warning of this nature before, but about this time of the summer, I have always found it difficult not to slack off some in my instruction. Very often, I was not aware of doing so, but my watch told the story. It is just being human to grow tired of repetition and want to get it over with. It sure would be a shame to let a most enviable record of instruction taper off in this way. Please be aware of this tendency and double check yourselves.
> Sincerely,
> Your friend "Doc"

A chance meeting back in Camping Headquarters also always confirmed a ranger's sense of value when he heard a camper yell, "Hey, it's our ranger." That type of meeting was a rare occurrence for Philmont Guides because they took out so few crews, but for the first rangers of the late 50s who logged anywhere from eight or nine treks per summer, running into returning crews at Headquarters or even on the trail was commonplace. Nothing can replace the warm feeling of hearing campers and advisors come over and say what an exciting time they had and how grateful they were for their ranger's help up front. Collectively, hearing warm words from campers and advisors just off the trail was about as good as it got, along with the advisors' critiques, when it came to determining how successful the new Ranger Department was.

More rewarding than some praise from campers just off the trail was knowing that a ranger had made a real difference in a camper's growing up. Bill Dailey recalls a stormy day when his group was on the way from Cito to The Bench, a camp on the side of Deer Lake Mesa above today's Cimarron River Camp. The crew was heading up a steep trail with the weather deteriorating and rain on the way. Bill was at the rear of the column when one of the campers stopped and said he could go no farther. Nobody could convince the youth to take another step. Bill asked the leaders to take the others to the top and wait. As the crew moved up, Bill asked the camper to stand straight and tall, look up the trail, and then to start moving. The youngster did not budge, saying he simply just could not go. Bill gave the young man a hearty slap on the shoulder and a few strongly encouraging words. That was what it took, the boy headed up the trail, and when he and Bill reached the top, the storm broke, scattering everybody to shelter. Bill did not know what to expect when the camper walked over toward him after the storm passed. The camper's words remained with Bill over the years, "I want to thank you for getting me to the top. I didn't think I could do it but now I know I can make it all the way." If that boy had quit he would have never discovered that he had the strength and ability to succeed.

Short-Term Impact on the First Rangers

How did Jack Rhea's decision to create the modern rangers impact the lives of those who became the first rangers? Those first rangers share many common opinions on how being a Philmont Ranger influenced their lives in both the short term and long term. In the short term, it was the first time that many of them had a real title. Becoming a ranger made them somebody important, an expert at what was the core of Scouting – outing, and especially at Philmont, in a rugged, western mountain setting. To be sure, many, if not most, had been patrol leaders, senior patrol leaders, junior assistant scoutmasters, team captains, council camp counselors, or class officers, but now they were in the big leagues, a grownup's world with a real job. Granted the job did not pay a bundle, but that was unimportant because the job returned untold riches in important intangibles.

The retention rate for the 1957 rangers was quite high at sixty-five percent, placing them well above today's staff return rate of approximately fifty percent. Others wanted to come back in 1958, but education, ROTC summer camp, or family situations prevented their signing on for another season. One young 1957 ranger, Dan Beckelman, put some meaning into the lyrics of the future Ranger Song's "I wanna go back..." by coming back frequently and was on the summer staff as late as 1966.

Perry Bolin, the singing ranger, credits his 1957 experience for further developing the ability to establish lifetime personal goals and maintain the focus to reach those objectives. In Perry's case, the determination resulted in his accomplishing an early goal: becoming an architect. After having his own band in college, Bolin wrote country music in the 1980s and still sings and plays the guitar today.

For Ranger David Bell, the summer of '57 resulted in an entirely unique phenomenon – national visibility (brief though it was). Dave was selected by Jack Rhea to be "the ranger" in a film shot at the Ranch in the summer of 1957. The film was not a BSA production; rather, it was an independent Hollywood crew that filmed what became a "short subject" shown nationwide in theaters during 1958 when Dave was a cadet at the Citadel in Charleston, South Carolina. Dave had to endure some good-humored ribbing from fellow cadets about being a Hollywood "star," but like so much in Tinseltown, fame was fleeting and the film is all but forgotten today.

The first rangers felt something unique – something they shared with their Philmont Guide brothers: they had become role models. For admiring younger campers, the ranger was somebody to look up to. For the dads on the trail as advisors, the ranger was someone he hoped his son would become. If there was a better job on the pyramid of Scouting summer employment than being a Philmont Ranger, it had yet to be invented.

Rangering brought a unique sense of comradeship and mutual support on the one hand. The scramble for merit badges and rank was over. There was no competition. To be a ranger was to be in a unique peer group. On the other hand, the regimentation associated with employment by the National Council of the Boy Scouts of America hardly dampened the individualism and self-reliance of most rangers. The vast majority of 1957 Rangers interviewed for this book also noted that their leadership abilities were significantly developed as a result of their ranger training and its practical application with crews in the field.

Because the first rangers represented a more diverse geographical cross-section than their guide brothers of preceding years, there was a greater sense of the Brotherhood of Scouting. That would grow dramatically in later decades, but even the first ranger group reached from coast to coast and the Great North Woods to the Gulf of Mexico, thus enhancing what was already felt about Philmont – that it was truly a national treasure. For rangers blessed by the luck of the draw, that sense of being at the epicenter of the Scouting universe could be accentuated if they were lucky enough to get a geographically wide spread in the home councils their crews came from. For rangers with a keen interest in geography and linguistics, meeting Scouts and Scouters from all across America and around the world was a wonderful experience. Clearly, Jack's cross-country promotional tours and recruiting activities were effective in creating a geographically diversified group of rangers.

The first rangers were physically toughened to a significantly greater extent than contemporary rangers. Technology favors today's rangers who have an easier time of it with lighter packs, advanced hydration systems that weigh dramatically less than a couple of metal canteens, the lack of a nearly four-pound axe with sheath in their packs, lighter sleeping bags and tents, much lighter raingear, superior water treatment technologies resulting in fewer G.I. issues, and other technological benefits. Over the course of a two and one-half month camping season, the rangers of '57 spent more time on the trail with their groups: five days instead of four which put the rangers of yesteryear much farther up and into the Backcountry. In some cases, the trails in 1957 were more difficult, i.e., what was once a straight up climb has frequently been replaced with switchbacks or a more gentle route (Beaubien to Black Mountain and the newest trails up Trail Peak, for example).

Overall, today's rangers head back for home in late August with waistlines more closely resembling those with which they arrived in June. There are more calories and variety in today's trail food. Because trail food menus were not rotated until well into the 60s, old time Rangers started with what was supposedly one of the tastier concoctions, the chicken-vegetable-rice dinner, but its appeal waned quickly. In 1963, the five-day ranger/ group assignment was cut down to four days and trail supper number one became beef soup, cornbread, spaghetti, orange drink, and apple sauce. That resulted in rangers dining on trail supper number one very frequently; it was enough to drive some rangers away from pasta dishes and Italian restaurants for years.

There was a psychological toughening too. While rangers were used to striving for academic excellence and triumph or failure on the athletic field back home, this new rangering business very much put them on the cusp. Ranger performance was constantly evaluated by crew advisors who had a feedback pipeline direct to Jack Rhea's desk. While program counselors at staffed camps were evaluated three times over the summer, a ranger's performance was critiqued every time one of his advisors came off the trail, i.e., seven or eight critiques for each ranger in that summer of '57. Any ranger who could not attain the goals set for him by Jack Rhea faced dismal prospects about returning for another summer. For a ranger getting good marks from crew advisors and Mister Dunn, the doors were open to just about any job he wanted in 1958, although many returned as rangers.

Because the Information Age had not really dawned in 1957, the absence of that technology had a very positive impact on the first rangers' self-sufficiency. In 1957, most rangers were quite adept at what has become a disappearing social grace: writing a personal letter. For many years, there was only one public phone at Camping Headquarters. It was originally housed in a booth adjacent to one of the quads, but was later mounted on a post just outside of what is now the Tooth of Time Traders. It was rarely used if for no other reason than most rangers and H.Q. staff could not carry enough quarters, dimes, and nickels to feed the machine for a five-minute call to their girlfriends back in Fresno, Dubuque, or Glastonbury. And most were afraid to have such calls billed to their parents' home phone numbers. Thus, the technology-induced isolation made the older ranger feel even closer to the Ranch. He did not rely on technology or the outside world because they essentially were not there.

The preceding facts largely explain why some very senior, former rangers and other older staff alumni were initially rather lukewarm about helping fund Philmont's Silver Sage Staff Activity Center ("What do they need that for? Well, we certainly got by without all those cell phones, computers, DVD players, and TVs."). The insulation from the outside world drove the older ranger closer to his friends/surroundings and/or forced him to become much more self-sufficient. For those old rangers lucky enough to bridge the generations and come back on a trek in the early days of the twenty-first century, it was always a disappointing experience to see how the ranger-to-camper ratio had increased or to stand atop the Tooth and wonder about the vanishing wilderness while watching some younger advisor call his wife on a cell phone and remind her to make dinner reservations at the country club for the following Saturday night.

Long Term Impact of 1957

Although not obvious at the time, there were long term effects of having been a ranger in 1957 (or any other year for that matter). One of the most obvious and universal effects is a lasting affinity for the mountains – best described as the call of the wild. Or perhaps it is more appropriately said as, "You can take the ranger out of the High Country, but you can never take the High Country out of the ranger." Walter Thannisch serves as a good example; after Philmont and college, he worked back in Texas for five years, but the Land of Enchantment was calling. The rest of his career was spent in Santa Fe. Now retired and with a motor home, he spends summers in the Cimarron Country and is a regular visitor to the Ranch. Fellow '57 ranger Bill Dailey retired from his Illinois law practice and moved just up the road from Philmont to Raton. That the '57 Rangers were enthralled with the mountains is no surprise; nearly all came from communities where the horizon was essentially a flat line. Only Bruce Teasley and John Porter (from Tennessee and Pennsylvania respectively) could say they came from the mountains and even their round-topped Appalachians were tame in comparison with the Rockies.

Related to the enduring love of mountains, Ranger Jim "Doc" Carlson, D.D.S., made an observation that was so obvious that other 1957 rangers took it for granted and never mentioned it – and that was that Philmont confirmed their sense of adventure and whetted their appetites for even more. Doc Carlson was fortunate in being able to follow that sense of adventure over a lifetime of mountain trekking in the Rockies, Alaska, both the Austrian and Bavarian Alps, and Nepal.

Steve Perin is typical of how rangering can impact a life in several dimensions. Steve, who died in 2012, started his career in camping equipment, first with Camp Trails and then as CEO of Ocaté Corporation which also was in the camping equipment field. The mountains remained important to him, and he became an environmental activist. He also blossomed as an artist specializing in New Mexico landscapes and Native American scenes. In his art portfolio, the accompanying biographical sketch always noted his having worked at Philmont Scout Ranch. His artistic talents were much appreciated by the Rangers of '57 because Steve was the designer of the 1957 ranger neckerchief which was produced by one of the kitchen ladies using old tablecloths. The neckerchief was plaid with a white border, included the words "Philmont Ranger," and the graphic was a side and bottom view of hiking boots (the bottom view featured a deep, wide hole in the sole).

The leadership experience created by Jack Rhea was recognized by a majority of those who were interviewed for this narrative. Ed Biddulph, another ranger from Texas, became an orthopedic surgeon and always put his having been a Philmont Ranger down on application forms which led to many interesting discussions. To this day Ed feels that letting admissions officers and potential employers know about his ranger experience facilitated opening doors which helped him accomplish his life's major goals. Another '57 ranger became an M.D. It was Jack's nephew, John Eilert, who credits being a ranger with developing his ability to evaluate people, a critical asset for physicians. Howard Wunker, an Eagle Scout from Cincinnati, lumped the short and long term impact of his 1957 Ranger experience together. He credits that summer of '57 with developing his communications skills – a key attribute and quite essential to his career as a teacher.

In effect, Jack Rhea saw to it that rangers became consultants on camping and backpacking – in much the same manner as his previous training roles with Wood Badge at National Camping School. For those rangers going into the military in just a few short years (as many did back in the days when the draft and Cold War were in full swing), Philmont was a wonderful pre-conditioning experience. Hoyt Hatfield went into the Army following college and firmly believes that his 1957 ranger experience provided him with the best possible preparation for his Green Beret training.

One new ranger, Richard Galeano became motivated by seeing how much he had helped people over the summer. That led directly to a B.A. and M.A. in social work from Barry University back in his native Florida. While on active duty with the Air Force in Crete and Greece, Richard served as a scoutmaster for boys on the base and later had a career with the Veterans Administration, retiring in his last VA location, Hot Springs, South Dakota.

Regardless of what field a ranger went into, but especially for those going into a service role, the ability to work with all kinds of advisors and campers, frequently under trying circumstances, gave him a head start on developing the people-to-people skills so essential in later life. Philmont gives all rangers a real opportunity to apply the lessons they have learned about leadership, but in a much less controlled environment than in a Boy Scout troop or school setting. Thus, the Ranger Program is in many ways a "finishing school" whose lessons last a lifetime.

Bruce Teasley had a career with the Central Intelligence Agency, but was briefly a professional Scouter prior to military service. He credits his experience as one of the senior rangers in 1957 as the source of developing the interpersonal skills that were critical in his subsequent role as a training specialist in the CIA. Bruce remembers Jack as a very motivational speaker – and as a person who had that rare ability to make others feel positively about themselves.

Having been a Philmont Ranger in 1957 or any other year is a proven springboard into volunteer or professional Scouting careers. For Gayle Reams, entering the professional ranks after Philmont was an obvious choice, and a decision that Jack Rhea would uniquely benefit from in just a few short years.

Doc Loomis cast a long, very long shadow. Many '57 rangers served Scouting in a variety of roles, including Gayle Reams who taught cooking at National Camping Schools. After Doc Loomis' training and several summers at Philmont, teaching cooking was a breeze. Indeed, almost to a man, the rangers of 1957 maintained some post-Philmont link with Scouting through volunteer service as scoutmasters, assistant scoutmasters, district commissioners, or merit badge counselors. Although no studies have ever been conducted, it can safely be assumed that there is a high incidence of old rangers serving as BSA council officers, executive board members, or High Adventure chairmen considering how anxious council executives are to recruit capable volunteers. While there has never been an in-depth, career-tracking survey done among ranger alumni, it is logical to assume that there is a strong statistical relationship between having been a ranger and attainment of leadership positions in later life.

The intensity of being a ranger created strong friendships. Even fifty years later, it is not at all unusual to hear one old ranger call a ranger friend, "Brother Ranger." Indeed, the 2007 Philmont Staff Association rendezvous was a ranger reunion in celebration of the Ranger Department's fiftieth anniversary. It was by far, the largest and most successful of any PSA reunion to date. For those rangers who were in college social fraternities, the brotherhood bonds within the Ranger Department were typically stronger even than those generated in a fraternity house.

For Ranger Paul Wencko, the long term impact of 1957 is very visible every day of his life. He met the young lady who became his wife while working at Philmont. Paul, who was later to become an Air Force pilot and then have a career with Trans World Airlines, was one of a half-dozen rangers invited to a mid-summer birthday party being held at a restaurant in Ute Park for one of the daughters of Mr. and Mrs. John Harrison. In addition to the two Harrison girls, Judy and Maureen, the two daughters of Mr. and Mrs. James Dobyne, Irene and Georgeann, were among the invited guests. Jim Dobyne had retired to Cimarron after a career with Republic Steel, but had actually been employed near Philmont at the Baldy Mine in the 1930s. Lucy Harrison, who was acquainted with Maxine Rhea through the Sirosis Club, thought it would be nice to invite some young gentlemen to the party, so she contacted Jack Rhea who conveyed the invitation to several off duty rangers. For Paul Wencko and Georgeann Dobyne, the romance that began at that party blossomed and led to marriage in 1968.

Toward the end of the 1957 season Jack had a conversation with an advisor whose crew suffered rain constantly during its trek. Although Jack was apologizing for the dismal weather, knowing how rain could jeopardize an entire expedition, he was cut short by the advisor. "Please, no apology needed. This was a wonderful experience. We had a great expedition," said the advisor who went on to credit the crew's ranger with their success. Clearly, that was one crew that knew how to get a fire started in the rain, cook a warming meal, and follow it with a great cobbler. If Jack needed any reassurance on the value of the ranger program, he got it that day.

The rangers of 1957 are all now in their early seventies, and a surprising number of them have already headed up to the Great Trail Camp in the Sky, although none died in military service. A significant percentage of the group went into fairly high-stress careers (education, medicine, aviation, law, top management, etc.) which might be expected of a group of achievement-oriented Eagle Scouts. At this writing (mid-2012), eleven of the thirty-one rangers who completed the 1957 camping season have now completed their life treks, i.e., a somewhat higher mortality rate than would be expected for a group of men whose average age is now approximately seventy-four.

Jack's decision to create the Philmont Rangers in 1957 as a means of making the twelve-day expedition a complete success has certainly stood the test of time and is now a permanent part of Philmont's bedrock. Over the years, legions of campers have gotten off to a smooth start into Philmont's High Country thanks to the thousands of young men and women who have rallied to the lyrics, "I Wanna Go Back to Philmont" and taken up their duties as Philmont Rangers.

1958 Rangers

For all practical purposes, Jack Rhea took the 1957 ranger program and revised it only slightly; the 1958 playbook appeared nearly identical. Mister Dunn enjoyed a thirty-three percent ranger return rate in 1958, a year when ninety-two rangers were hired to serve 12,507 campers (by far the biggest year yet and a twenty-five percent increase over 1956). There were eight training rangers and three other returning rangers got the "to die for" job – roving ranger. Dunn did not have a monopoly on returning rangers because the long arm of Jack Rhea reached out and tapped six of the 1957 rangers for jobs as camp directors including Dave Jung who became CD at Beaubien. Several others became assistant camp directors at large camps, including Fish Camp.

Ranger training followed the 1957 Ponil example almost to the letter, including representation from the National Office. There was one important difference in 1958 – Dunn got a fulltime assistant chief ranger; his name was Don Pritchard, and he was from Lake Leelanau, Michigan. That pattern of hiring an older man who had never been a ranger to be the assistant chief ranger continued for another seven years until Giff Kessler, one of the brightest ranger stars of the early 60s, became assistant chief ranger in 1965 when he had just turned twenty-one. In that year, a young ranger reported for his first duty in a Philmont career that would see him become chief ranger in 1973; his name is Dave Caffey, author of the landmark Philmont staff adventure narrative, *Head for the High Country*.

Ranger spirit and ingenuity continued to build in 1958. Their clannishness hit a new highpoint when several off-duty rangers discovered an Army surplus field hospital tent down at the polo barns. Jack Rhea had no problem with the rangers erecting it near the old Health Lodge. It became the 1950s version of the staff activity center – except it was a ranger center. The day was coming when rangers would have their own, private tent city complete with a "clubhouse" even if its main purpose was a locker building.

Philmont Museum

Philmont and Beaubien staff attending the pilot who had just crashed in the meadow above Trappers Lodge.

One '57 ranger and his staff were witness to Philmont's second recorded aviation accident. The former ranger was Dave Jung who was camp director at Beaubien, a very aviation-minded camp in 1958. That year, small balsa wood gliders became a popular off-duty amusement. Then they graduated to rubber band-powered models and eventually had a small gasoline-powered model. The latter craft unfortunately crashed as did the next plane to swoop low over the meadow at the head of the Bonito Canyon. That plane was a sixty-five horsepower, two-place Taylorcraft which was on its way from Denver to Salt Lake City. Although the plane had a maximum service ceiling slightly in excess of 15,000 feet, the pilot did not have oxygen aboard and therefore could not climb above 10,000 feet. So he took the southern route, hoping to find his way through some mountain pass that would put him on a northwesterly heading to Salt Lake City. Unfortunately, engine failure put him on a collision course with Beaubien where he crash landed the little crimson-colored taildragger at the head of the meadow just at the base of Bonito Peak. Fortunately, Philmont's new VHF radio system resulted in the Health Lodge ambulance arriving within an hour to treat and evacuate the pilot. In the meantime, the Beaubien staff administered first aid to the unfortunate flyer who suffered two broken legs, a broken arm, broken ribs, and multiple lacerations.

Jack Rhea very nearly became a case for the ambulance himself on one of his return trips from Fish Camp and Beaubien in what was probably one of his closest calls since the war. He had started one of the steepest descents in the road on the way back when his brakes failed. He had the presence of mind to quickly radio Camping Headquarters to advise of his predicament and the location. Fortunately, he was able to guide his vehicle into a "soft landing" on the road's shoulder much as he had done years before in Colorado with a busload of Wichita Country Day School students. Unlike his previous runaway experience, his radio contact assured him that a tow was promptly on the way.

CHAPTER 16

The Rhea Way

Part of the build-up to that critical year of 1957 was some long over-due technology in the form of communication and maps. One of the most intense periods of Jack's life had been his six months of combat in France and Germany during World War II. As an operations officer at the front line, he always kept several items, call them the "tools of his trade," close at hand: steel helmet, Colt .45 automatic, his situation maps, and the field radios. At Philmont, there was no need for the helmet or Colt .45, but when he arrived at the Ranch in 1954 there was no up-to-date communications system in place and, as had certainly been confirmed in 1955 and 1956, the available maps were sadly outdated. The day had arrived when expedition crews would be on their own in the Backcountry with no ranger to bail them out when they became perplexed by a fork in the trail. Attendance, trails, camps, staff, and the need for real-time communications between camps and headquarters were growing by leaps and bounds.

The radio system Jack selected was no different than that used by avia-tion traffic control and police departments, i.e., the very high frequency radio telephone (RT) with a base set in camping headquarters and transceiv-ers at camps where there was electrical power, typically supplied by a gas-oline-powered generator. Solar panels were still in the future. Some of the generators then in use were very efficient, relatively small, and reasonably quiet. Other generators were powered by marginally muffled Army surplus engines that were large enough to power a small truck. Those contrivances had to be started by hand cranking which could be quite an adventure since the engines were very prone to backfiring. Very quickly, the transceivers were installed in various Philmont vehicles; the few with radios were easily identified because they had a very visible, long whip antenna.

Before the Ranch established repeaters at critical locations, many camps had no direct contact with Camping Headquarters due to the largely line-of-sight limitations of the VHF radio system. As a practical matter, though, even relatively remote locations, Fish Camp for example, could still get a message out by relaying it through another camp such as Abreu.

Contrast that with the situation that prevailed before the radios were introduced. In 1949, an advisor suffered a heart attack while at Fish Camp.
The response was the fastest possible: one guide took off for Camping
Headquarters over Webster Pass and past Crater Lake using the Scout pace
while another Fish Camp guide lit out for Carson-Maxwell where he could
telephone Camping Headquarters. The only medical doctor in Cimarron
was unavailable to treat the advisor, so a medical student at the Health
Lodge was called in. Fortunately, after some rest, the stricken advisor was
able to ride a horse back to headquarters.

For Jack, there was a modest amount of red tape in getting the system up and running because all users in those days had to be licensed
by the Federal Communications Commission (FCC). Therefore, Camping
Headquarters had to supply the nearest field office of the FCC (in Denver)
with the names of all people expected to use the radios. That list was dominated by camp directors whose licenses in the form of little wallet cards
were waiting for them upon check-in during staff training.

The familiar radio "Ten Code" was adapted directly from the nation's
police departments and was popularized by the beefy, gravel-voiced actor
Broderick Crawford in what was then a popular 1950s television series,
Highway Patrol. It was only a short matter of time before Philmont humor-
ists corrupted the national Ten Code with local versions. To the legitimate
tens such as 10-20 (location) or 10-4 (affirmative) came such variations as
10-33 ("Send help, our camp director is having a fit!") and 10-62 (What
is showing at the Cimarron theater?"). Yes, there was a movie theater in
Cimarron in Jack's day and it was popular if for no other reason than it
had new movies weekly whereas the staff movies shown in the dining hall
tended toward the repetitious, i.e., repeats of Disney fare, including *The
Living Desert, Treasure Island, Davy Crockett,* etc.

In setting up the modern communications system, Jack Rhea established the call signs and became the first "C-1." Bob Bashore, the seasonal
registrar in the early 1960s, was located in Camping Headquarters and
frequently observed Jack's early start to a Philmont summer day. When
Jack planned a visit to a major camp, that camp's director heard about the
impending meeting from an 8:00 A.M. call from C-1 himself.

The Modern Philmont Map

Prior to the 1956 season, expeditions embarking on a Philmont trek, cavalcade, or wagon train got by without a map because they were essentially on an escorted tour in which an experienced, trail-wise guide or horseman could be relied upon for directions. In some cases, the very familiar wall map as sketched by BSA artist Remington Schuyler actually went on the trail although it was not designed for that purpose. The "official" Philmont map was a roughly seventeen by twenty-two inch black and white representation done in pen and ink; the map was produced locally (printed at the *Raton Range* newspaper printing plant). The trails and camps were on it as was a very basic scale: one inch equaled just short of a mile and a quarter. Elevations in terms of contour lines were left to the imagination, although mountains and mesas were very roughly sketched in.

During the war, Jack worked with two types of maps at the battalion level: the operations map and the situation map. Of the two, he spent more time with the situation map because it was the one on which the battalion's various positions were overlaid along with the enemy's positions and the line of demarcation between the two forces. In one sense it was a real-time map because Jack updated it constantly based on what he was hearing on the radio or field telephone from his company commanders. Both types of maps were very similar to Philmont's first topographic map in that all three used contour lines to show elevation, colors to show vegetation and bodies of water, and similar symbols for roads, bridges, towns, etc. In effect, the only significant difference was one of scale.

Jack had to start from scratch to create Philmont's first modern map. In early 1955, after being at the Ranch for only several months, he took the matter to the Denver office of the United States Coast and Geodetic Survey which agreed to excise portions from four upcoming map projects (Cimarron, Ute Park, Tooth of Time, and Miami quadrangles) that encompassed portions of Philmont. Those relevant portions would be joined to create one new composite Philmont map which was enhanced with a legend at the bottom and a creative border featuring recycled art from promotional literature (the mountain lion, deer, buffalo head, etc.) originating as early as the late 1940s.

However, creating the new, composite map was not as simple as it might sound because land well beyond Philmont's boundaries also had to be surveyed. Then details such as roads, trails, creeks, rivers, landmarks, and buildings had to be added. The surveying alone required two years. Jack was not closely involved with the project personally, but supported it with horses, equipment, and, during the camping season, with some manpower. Several campers from the Pioneering Treks worked as surveyors' assistants in 1955 and one of them was a lad from Lees Summit, Missouri. Jack had to work hard to get the boy's mother to permit him to go to Philmont. The mom was Jack's sister, Joy Rhea Eilert, and her son, John, would work the next few years at Philmont, eventually becoming Camp Director at Ponil. Bobby Maldonado, of the Philmont Maldonado family, was then working as a cowboy on the UU Bar Ranch when his boss mentioned that the Geodetic Survey was looking for a local guide. Bobby got the job and subsequently experienced some of the best camping imaginable, ranging from near the Colorado border to Palo Flechado Pass in the west and the village of Miami in the south.

Bobby would be gone for two weeks at a time and was responsible for packing camping gear, food, and surveying equipment. The crew completed triangulations of all major peaks, basing all of the elevations from the only peak with an existing benchmark: The Tooth of Time. The job also involved locating all of the original survey points along Philmont's entire boundary and frequently pulling a survey bicycle behind his horse to measure distances. On some occasions, the surveyors would pull out an aerial photograph and request that Bobby lead them to a certain point on the map. The job was not without adversity such as getting caught in a snow storm atop Mt. Phillips.

In the early 2000s Philmont launched its own mapping information system and therefore terminated its relationship with the Geodetic Survey. Rather than update the maps every few years when the map inventory is at a low level as was past practice, changes are now made annually. Philmont currently offers a variety of well-detailed maps covering separate sections of the Ranch. The new maps' coated paper is perspiration and rain-resistant, something an old-time ranger would have appreciated because his map at the end of the season looked like an amorphous, crumbling paper maché project on its last legs.

JLT and CTC Too

The year 1957, with its new Ranger Program, new map, new Philmont arrowhead patch, and modern radio system seriously overshadowed another "new" program – the Conservation Training Camp (CTC) which was jointly promoted with Junior Leader Training (JLT). CTC was under the expert guidance of Walt Wenzel whose title was "conservationist." Wenzel would eventually move to the National Office where he would close out his professional career as director of High Adventure Conservation. In the summer of 1957, he directed CTC which was a two-week program costing fifty-four dollars. Participants were expected to learn as much as possible from their two weeks of conservation projects and take lessons learned back to their own councils where they would spread what they had learned about conservation. The projects took them around the Ranch and involved a long list of activities: pruning trees, cleaning out springs, planting trees, building trails, fishing surveys, studying trees diseases, and soil testing. Depending on which camp(s) they were near, the participants could take part in a variety of programs ranging from fly tying/fishing to campfires.

CTC as such lasted for thirteen years. In reality, it was not a new program; it was an outgrowth of several Bullock programs, including Pioneering Treks and the 1949 special interest program. CTC could also be considered a somewhat related ancestor of such contemporary programs as Roving Outdoor Conservation School and Trail Crew.

Unlike CTC which was terminated at the end of the 1970 season, Junior Leader Training (JLT) continued for years after its beginning in 1949 and later gave way to Junior Leader Instructor Training (JLIT), National Junior Leader Instructor Camp (NJLIC) and National Advanced Youth Leadership Experience (NAYLE). The only breaks in those programs have been during the Jamboree year in 1950 and a ten-year period from 1971 through 1981. During the Rhea years, JLT was something of a hybrid because it was essentially a program directed by the National Office's training function while staffing and support came from Philmont's camping side. The resident director of the program was typically a seasoned Scouter who was part of the summer staff.

One of the more popular JLT leaders was Scotty Williamson, a Florida Scouter who was also a retired Army general. His own immediate staff consisted of several teams of troop leaders, i.e., scoutmasters, assistant scoutmasters, and senior patrol leaders. Williamson, who also supervised CTC, reported to the Training Center director who supplied the course materials directly from the National Office. The national director of training spent several weeks at the Ranch at the very beginning of the season and then returned to the National Office. Jack Rhea's personal involvement with JLT was largely restricted to staff hiring and appearances at closing ceremonies. Infrequently during the off-season, he would be involved in minor issues such as maintaining some continuity with JLT as taught at Schiff, but for the most part trusted competent subordinates to manage the program. In most cases, Jack was very familiar with the JLT staff because before he hired them many had been rangers or worked elsewhere in the Camping Department. Considering the JLT, CTC, horsemen, cooks, and director and assistant, the 1962 Rayado staff was the largest camp staff on the Ranch, numbering over thirty people.

JLT and its more recent variations have been offered at several locations at Philmont, but in Jack's last few years it moved to Rayado from Cimarroncito (the Hunting Lodge location). When Jack arrived at Philmont, JLT was a four-week experience, but was eventually streamlined to twelve days. In most, but not all years, there was a "short trek" of seven days following the formal training period. The four-week version was an "on-the-trail" experience and not based at Rayado or Rocky Mountain Scout Camp. JLT, then strictly training leaders, not junior instructors as with later programs, grew during the Rhea administration. Attendance in 1955 reached 436 and peaked at 660 in Jack's last year. Indeed, attendance during Jack's last year has never been equaled since for any of the youth training/instructor programs.

Ranger City

With the dramatic increases in attendance anticipated in the 1960s, it was obvious that the Ranger Department needed much more space. Today's Advisors' Lounge, with the addition of latrines/shower, is what comprised the old Ranger Office in the 1950s and 1960s. Originally, it had been a Philmont Ranch turkey coop, but it was adequate for Mister Dunn's operations in those early days. It was clear that assigning Rangers bunks in the Rocky Mountain shelters would not be satisfactory because the department was growing so rapidly. Jack saw what was coming – from 1959 through 1962, the Ranger Program's average employment was eighty men each year, up sharply from the first group of thirty-two rangers. The solution came in the form of Ranger City in 1959; it was located on the southwest corner of Tent City (much smaller in those days) and occupied roughly a half-acre. At the center was a locker building which had two open doors, a rickety table, several chairs of dubious stability, and plenty of charm. A deck of rather worn playing cards usually graced the tabletop. The compound was built with expansion in mind because for the first few years there were many platforms without tents in position. The "compound" atmosphere was accentuated by a surrounding welded-wire fence and elevated entry steps that amounted to the human equivalent of a cattle-guard.

Photo courtesy of James R. Place

Ranger City in 1962, with Training Ranger Jim Place on his way to meet campers.

Near the entrance to Ranger City in the early days, there was a large sign identifying the compound; it did not include the word "welcome." Indeed, next to the Ranger City sign was another sign on which was boldly emblazoned, "Rangers Only." Old rangers who had moved on to become camp directors or to other staff jobs were greeted warmly upon returning to Ranger City, but anybody who lacked credentials was hardly welcomed with open arms. The entire arrangement suited the rangers perfectly and certainly bolstered their clannishness and team spirit.

1959 saw the arrival of another Rhea hiree – one who was to make a major contribution to the Philmont community little more than a decade later. This new member of the summer staff was none other than Ned Cooper Gold, Jr., today an Ohio "super lawyer," Silver Sage honoree, and active Scouter at all levels. In 1959, however, Ned was a young Philmont ranger; he later climbed the ladder to cap his Philmont years as camp director at both Fish Camp and Cimarroncito. He had a dream, conceived in 1963, about forming a Philmont staff alumni organization that would provide service to Philmont. That story and the accomplishments of the Philmont Staff Association in terms of fundraising for capital programs, reuniting former staff, service projects, and scholarships for campers and staff is well told in the magazine *High Country* and in several books, particularly *Born at the Confluence*, so it will not be repeated in depth here. It was a Jack Rhea decision to give Ned his first management job at Philmont: camp director at Lost Cabin. At that small and remote camp, Ned first conceived the idea of the staff association and discussed its possibilities frequently with Steve Gregory, Lost Cabin's program counselor. That idea took ten years to reach fruition, but what fruit it bore!

Spit & Polish Era

While it may not have had any direct relationship to Jack's Army service, the Rhea years could well be described as having a certain "spit and polish" aura, particularly in the larger, staffed camps such as Beaubien or Cimarroncito. Following a vigorous ringing of the bell on the porch at Beaubien's Trappers Lodge, breakfast was served promptly at 7 A.M. in a kitchen that could easily have passed any unannounced New Mexico or Colfax County Sanitation Department inspection. The duty roster contained the names of those who were charged with cleaning the lodge <u>daily</u>: floor swept and mopped, wood box filled for the evening fire, and porch swept (occasionally of ice late in August). Each morning, bedding, including mattresses, was aired by hanging on the porch rail. Everybody was expected to be clean-shaven, and at nearly 9,400 feet above mean sea level that was a bracing experience at the washstand in back of Trappers Lodge (except for the first in line who luxuriated in the hot, left-over kitchen dishes rinse water). Anybody in need of a haircut was expected to get one on the rare day off. For those eluding the professional barbers, amateurs cut hair on the Trappers Lodge porch. Such activity was particularly observed shortly after the radio crackled to life with advance notice that some big VIPs were expected in a day or so. There was little idle time for the staff which got one day off every two weeks. What might have otherwise been a slack hour or so was taken up with felling dead trees for the campfire using crosscut saws.

Uniforms consisted of clean Scout shorts and shirts or explorer shirts, complete with name tag. The only staff to regularly wear Levis were those associated with the Horse Department, i.e., wranglers, pack train horsemen, and western lore counselors. Jack's insistence on exemplary uniforming was in contrast to the early Bullock days where a "western" appearance was the daily dress code. Little more than a decade after Jack went to the National Office, Philmont summer staff appearance reverted to the Bullock era and far beyond with even more variations on the old theme, i.e., in some locales homesteaders, miners, loggers, and mountain men appeared in period dress (thanks to the interpretive programs ushered in by Joe Davis, director of camping from the mid-60s to the mid-70s).

Not all of Jack's uniforming innovations were popular, but he had the good sense to back off in at least one instance. It was the pith helmet, a form of headgear that never stood a chance, possibly because it was suggested by the National Office. It died a faster death than the Smokey Bear campaign hat which was issued to all Rangers a few years later.

"Groups," – the term "crews" was still years away – were personally checked out of Beaubien, Cito, or any other staffed camp with particular attention to fire rings; backpacking stoves were not part of the Philmont landscape yet and making sure a fire was really, absolutely positively dead was therefore imperative. Program then dominated the schedule during the balance of the morning and for most of the afternoon. It was an era when program counselors, the assistant camp director, and the quartermaster frequently served as merit badge counselors, initialing campers' merit badge cards, especially Conservation for which there was no shortage of projects to supervise.

Groups were checked in much as they are today, but the coffee hour following the evening campfire at Beaubien and other major camps was startlingly different. After the evening campfire in the meadow at Beaubien, coffee, bug juice, and cookies were waiting for staff and advisors inside Trappers Lodge on a table near the fireplace which always contained a roaring fire. Every member of the Beaubien staff attended the advisors' hour and enjoyed it for what it was: a good, old-fashioned crackerbarrel filled with opportunities to share stories with Scouters who were anxious to learn more about Philmont and its staff. The only excuse for missing the advisors' hour was being on the infrequent day off or being comatose. It was not at all unusual for a pair of advisors to show up with a warm cobbler for all to enjoy. The conversation which followed for about an hour was always animated and frequently accompanied by guitar music and singing – to the great enjoyment of staff and advisors alike. Coffee hour in the old days was the same no matter which camp advisors might be at. Within a couple of decades, the coffee hour was still around, but attended only by advisors who gathered out on the porch. The friendliness of the Bullock, Rhea, and Davis years had withered on the vine.

Excluding the specially hired Jambo staff, 1960 was a down year for regular seasonal staff with only about 136 being hired. The seasonal staff total in 1959 had been 205 of which fifty-five returned in 1960. Among the eighty-one new hires in 1960 was an Eagle Scout from Mount Morris, Illinois, who had previously been on a Training Center trek. His name was Dave Bates and his Training Center trek ranger had been none other than Jerry Traut. Dave started at Pueblano and later became camp director at Harlan and Beaubien with a subsequent tour in Logistics starting as a trip planner. That was in an era when Jack Rhea was using an itinerary planning system that was just adequate for camper levels of under 10,000. The system consisted of sending the trails brochure out and letting groups plan their own trek itinerary subject to approval when checking in at the Ranch. It was from Logistics that Dave later went directly into completely uncharted territory for a seasonal employee – directly to the national executive staff. It was during the Joe Davis era that Dave went far beyond his job description to introduce a genuine itinerary management/control system, including the comprehensive PEAKS books. That was followed by Dave's leadership in satisfying another burning need: a comprehensive search and rescue system. Today's PHILSAR (Philmont Search and Rescue) serves not only Philmont's summer population, but is a recognized asset within the New Mexico Department of Public Safety.

Jambo Treks

The 1960 Jamboree was held just north of Colorado Springs from 22 to 28 July at a site which was less than four hours by bus away from Philmont. In those days, Jamborees always produced a drastic reduction in Philmont attendance. The idea of a Jambo Trek or mini-expedition composed of Jamboree crews was a magnificent, one-time only opportunity to have more Scouts gain the Philmont experience while simultaneously generating some much-needed cash in what would otherwise be a very down Jamboree year. In 1960 attendance topped out at nearly 9,600. Without the Jambo Treks, attendance in 1960 would have amounted to roughly 6,200 or a thirty percent decline from 1959.

Most Jambo Rangers were hired for a three-week period although a few were hired on for the remainder of the season, and a few were hired off the trail from earlier treks. Sixty-seven Jambo Rangers were hired, and another twelve people were hired for duty as wranglers, truck drivers, commissary clerks, and health lodge staff. The Jambo Treks were scheduled before, during, and after the Jamboree. The before and after Jamboree treks were at the Ranch for only five days, but treks during the Jamboree were longer and were composed of Scouts who had been Jamboree alternates. Jack devised a separate expedition numbering system for Jambo treks; thus the second group arriving on 30 July and departing on 4 August was tagged as J-30-B-4 instead of what otherwise might have been 730-B.

There were only twenty six regular rangers, including three roving rangers, to handle the rest of the season's treks. Many camps were unstaffed, but during the Jambo treks the regular rangers "staffed" all of the camps where any Jambo groups were scheduled, i.e. Ute Gulch, Lambert's Mine, etc. In small camps, that meant one person, his tent, a tent containing food for the Jambo groups, and prayers that bears would find some other locale more inviting. All food was pre-distributed and all itineraries were pre-planned. Groups were brought directly to their starting point, Cito for example, by their Greyhound/Trailways buses which were bringing them to or from the Jamboree. The Jambo participants were actually checked in at a makeshift registration center in Cimarron because Camping Headquarters was simply not up to the task of checking so many people in during such a short timeframe. The Jambo Rangers met them at their starting point, not in Camping Headquarters. Jambo groups were large – roughly forty boys and their leaders, and many of the boys were younger than the basic required age of fourteen. Forty or less, they all got just one ranger.

Pre and post-Jambo treks got off their buses with packs ready to hit the trail. The ranger met them at their starting point in the afternoon and provided brief instruction in land navigation and axe safety. A typical pre/post short trek might involve starting at Rayado where the morning of the second day involved more instruction and a museum tour. In the afternoon, individual packs were collected and taken by truck to a point just north of the top of Stonewall Pass and were dropped there. The crew rode by horseback from Rayado to the pack drop just below Stonewall Pass, dismounted, and hiked the rest of the way to Crater. The next day involved hiking to a temporary camp called Lookout Mountain which was located much closer to Bonito Cow Camp than Lower Bonito Camp or today's Lookout Meadow Camp. After a night at Lookout Mountain, it was all downhill to Abreu. Pick-up by bus was on the following day and for those whose bus itinerary permitted the time, a brief stop at Camping Headquarters and its trading post could be arranged. That concluded what was Philmont's shortest summertime trek in history.

Many campers were from much lower elevations and/or had slept at lower locations on previous night(s). Because their first destination at Philmont might be at Cypher's or another high camp, altitude adjustment problems were legion. Not surprisingly, the Jambo ranger's top priority was to keep his group together on the trail, and make sure the destination camp was reached. All other considerations were secondary.

Groups arriving during the Jamboree were met by a ranger who took them through the check-in and confirmed the itinerary, shook them down, and stayed with them for the rest of their longer Philmont journey. A typical trek would involve starting at Cito and ending at Rayado via Cyphers, Mount Phillips, Red Hills, Beaubien, Bonito Cow, and Abreu.

With the Jambo Trek, Jack Rhea managed to turn around what would have been a very down year for attendance and revenue. What Jack did not realize at the time was the tremendous return on investment in Jambo Rangers he would reap. Out of that group came some real stars. Young men – Jim Place, Ron Baird, Ed Shea, Bob Mahn, Dave Cross, and Bill Brasher among them – went on to leadership roles as camp directors, in the Ranger Department, and the JLT staff in the years ahead.

From 1950 on, Jack Rhea attended most American jamborees, several international jamborees, and a number of international Scouting conferences too. The 1960 National Jamboree was no exception. Jack took the entire family up to Colorado Springs and spent a day at the jamboree which was held just north of the city on what was then rolling prairie. Although that site is now part of the Springs' suburban sprawl, the jamboree camp-sites offered a spectacular view of Pikes Peak and a very noticeable job site to the north where the new Air Force Academy was under construction.

Because the 1960 National Jamboree was reasonably nearby, Jack hosted more than the usual number of VIP visitors to Philmont. One of Jack's distinguished guests was a member of the British peerage. It was none other than Arthur Robert Peter Baden-Powell, Second Baron of Gilwell who also was the son of Scouting's founder, Lord Baden-Powell. In 1960, Jack and his titled guest visited Cimarroncito, then considered one of the top stops on VIP tours. As he did on many of his VIP tours, Jack parked his vehicle and talked with campers and their rangers. In 1960 at Cimarroncito, there was a hidden bonus waiting for Baden-Powell because one of the young men he spoke with was Allan Rouse who had been one of the original rangers in 1957. In the intervening years, Rouse had been educated in Germany where his professor father was on a National Science Foundation scholarship. While in Europe, Rouse took Wood Badge at Gilwell Park in 1959. The English lord and the Philmont ranger actually discovered that they had some mutual acquaintances who were senior Gilwell leaders. Rouse dearly wanted to have his picture taken with Baden-Powell, but refrained from asking, not wanting to create a potentially embarrassing moment for Jack. Sadly, little time on earth was left to Baden-Powell. In just two years at the age of 49 he was gone, dying of a heart attack complicated by leukemia and pneumonia. The pneumonia itself was a complication of bronchitis developed as a result of catching a chill at a Gilwell reunion.

Rhea Humor

Jack's sense of humor during the Baden-Powell visit was probably somewhat repressed, but for other guests Jack was a witty host. Just as he could recycle a speech and make it very interesting to new audiences, he reached back into his VC Bar Ranch days and brought out the old "bear in the woods ploy" to use on unsuspecting VIPS. Paul Dinsmore, a former camp director at Black Mountain and Beaubien, recalls that gambit as one of Jack's favorite jokes when he was taking guests into the Backcountry. Time permitting, Fish Camp was a frequent destination and as his gray station wagon headed that way, Jack would point out all of Philmont's most interesting flora and fauna. Usually, Philmont's animal kingdom was cooperative, and Jack had no problems directing attention to the mule deer, scolding Stellar's jays, strutting turkeys, gravel-voiced ravens, porcupines, grumpy badgers, and the occasional sulking, meadow-crossing coyote among others. Once in a while, the wild creatures would be on break when

Jack made his way to Beaubien and Fish Camp. That was never a problem for Jack who would suddenly, excitedly exclaim, "Hey, did you see that bear back there?" The guests usually replied in awe, "Sure, wow! How 'bout that!" Jack always saw the very same bear in exactly the same place – it was a bizarrely shaped, lightning-blackened tree stump that actually resembled the outline of a bear in the shadows of the woods' edge.

Jack Rhea's sense of humor was at its best when taking down the pompous. A case in point is the oft-told story of his handling an arrogant, condescending advisor who was a newly minted Army second lieutenant whom we shall call Lt. Myron Scatterfled. The lieutenant probably was looking forward to a career in the Inspector General's Department because all he could do was snootily complain to each and every camp director about what was wrong in his camp. The crew was on back-to-back twelve-day expeditions and Scatterfled demanded special privileges for his crew. The crisp shavetail generated so much friction that his reputation preceded him by the radio system. Dave Bates, camp director at Harlan, had just suffered a ration of grief, saw what was headed for other camps, and called Jack by radio to come up and put matters right.

Unfortunately, Scatterfled had moved on to Cito by the time Jack arrived. The ten code for "complaining advisor headed your way" has long been forgotten, but it was certainly used to warn camp directors about what was about to darken their porches. Whatever he had learned in ROTC or Officer Candidate School must have been quickly forgotten because the lieutenant obviously had not learned the basics of leadership. One must conclude that Scatterfled's tactical officers were clearly having a bad day when he was granted a commission.

The lieutenant's fury was reserved for Jack Rhea. Upon coming off the trail and completing a lengthy, vitriolic written report about everything wrong at Philmont, its camps, camp directors, and program, the lieutenant was whisked into Jack's office after demanding to see the man in charge.

Jack's greeting was typically cordial, "Well, Mister Scatterfled, come in and tell me all about your expedition."

"That's **Lieutenant** Scatterfled to you."

"Very well, Loooootenant. It's **Colonel** Rhea to you."

The lieutenant's deflation was not complete. Monday rolled around and with it the camp directors' meeting. Everybody at the meeting waited anxiously to see what was going to happen because Jack had an advisor's report in his hand; everybody knew who had written it and what it contained. Jack held the poison pen report aloft and said he was going to give it the full attention it deserved. The assembled camp directors were practically shaking in their boots because they well knew what was in the report. Camp directors nervously looked around, wondering who was going to be reprimanded or even fired. Jack waved the condemning report, tore it into shreds, and tossed the tatters into a wastepaper can. The room erupted in applause.

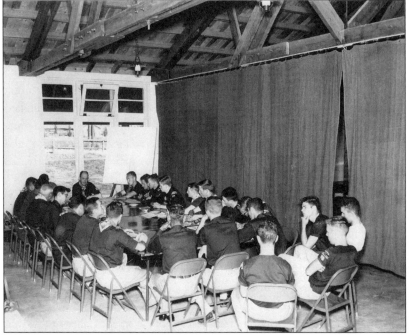

Philmont Museum

Camp director meetings were held on Mondays in the Rhea era. Those meetings were well-organized, ran to a strict agenda, and were frequently punctuated with some dry, Rhea humor.

Another balloon Jack burst belonged to none other than General Motors. Crews arriving from the Detroit area used to arrive in style – in brand-new, gleaming white GM station wagons. A ranger had to do no more than look over to the parking lot and see a row of white station wagons to know that some Michigan Scouts had arrived. The first year they arrived in such style, 1960, was marked by a very long convoy of station wagons complete with its embedded General Motors representative in addition to the contingent director. New Mexico Route 21 from Cimarron past the Ranch had not yet been paved, and was comparable to the road from Camping Headquarters to Stockade. The contingent tour director and GM rep were aghast – take these brand new, glistening white station wagons over some washboard, dirt road not far removed from its days as the Santa Fe Trail? To consider subjecting these brand new symbols of Detroit's finest technology and workmanship to dust and all that gravel scratching the shining finish off his magnificent caravans – unheard of! What to do? The director found a pay phone, contacted Jack, and demanded some sort of solution that would get his crews up to the Ranch without enduring the dents and dings his station wagons would certainly suffer on that stone-studded pig path.

Jack politely refused any assistance in the form of bus transportation or anything else. The tour director became more agitated and threatened some adverse publicity for Philmont to which Jack suggested that the same publicity would clearly demonstrate what poor primers, cheap paint, and shoddy curing techniques GM was using. The Oldsmobile convoy arrived at the loading dock within minutes.

Jack's Monday meetings with camp directors and senior staff always saw the Rhea wit in evidence. The meetings, however, were also models of efficiency. Bob Gannon, one of the '57 Rangers, attended camp director meetings in his last couple of years at Philmont, and although Gannon later attended school board meetings, city council meetings, and corporate board meetings, he recalls Jack Rhea's meetings as the most productive of all. Once operations like the Ranger Department or Junior Leader Training were up and running, Jack rarely got involved; rather he favored letting trusted lieutenants run their shows. Camp directors were another matter. The CDs were Jack's eyes and ears as to what was going on in the Backcountry, and his relationship with them was much as it had been with his intelligence officer and the battalion's company commanders during the war.

A Tornado in Camping Headquarters

Mother Nature usually has a few nasty surprises up her sleeves for Philmont's directors of camping/program, most of whom are continually plagued by drought and fire. Mark Anderson, director of program at this writing has been dealt two major adversities: the massive Ponil Complex forest fire of 2002 and the windstorm of 12/13 November 2011. The former devastated much of Philmont's northeastern quadrant and the latter, with winds clocked as high as 115 miles per hour caused substantial damage across much of Philmont's landscape, including at least $2.5 million of structural damage in Camping Headquarters alone. Joe Davis suffered the Great Flood of 1965, and Jack Rhea got off lightly with several forest fires of a magnitude smaller than that of 2002. Jack also had to deal with what he reported to the Associated Press as a "small tornado."

Miraculously, there were no fatalities associated with the 25 June 1960, tornado which devastated much of Camping Headquarters. Death very easily could have been involved, considering the wind force which drove metal devices deeply into solid wood. The tornado appeared out of nowhere on that Saturday evening around six P.M. just as many staff members were finishing their evening meal in the dining hall. The first wind gusts did not create much initial attention; the small uprooted tree blowing past the windows moments later most certainly did. Ranger City and Tent City were leveled and some automobiles were damaged, although major buildings came through with only minor damage. The same cannot be said for the brand new Protestant Chapel which was destroyed. Jack reported to the newspapers that the cost of replacing the chapel would be in the magnitude of 5,000 dollars.

Dan Sheehan, whose photography studio was in Raton, was on the scene at once and recorded the event, but did not cover the complete aftermath or just who was most impacted by the tornado. The population of Camping Headquarters that weekend had swelled beyond the normal arriving/departing groups, headquarters staff, and Rangers between groups. There were about 300 guests at Camping Headquarters: Boy Scouts from the Kit Carson Council were holding their 1960 National Jamboree Shakedown at Philmont and were cooking dinner with charcoal stoves just as the tornado hit. Instantly, there were pots, pans, spoons, and hot charcoal briquettes flying everywhere.

Jack Rhea was on the scene in a flash, the Control Center went into overdrive, and the health lodge was mobbed. The Control Center was later swamped with phone calls from all over the country wanting more information on whether callers' loved ones had been hurt. Six of the Scouts and leaders from the Jambo Shakedown were taken to the hospital in Raton with lacerations and suspected fractures. Many more of them were treated at Philmont for lesser injuries. After hitting Camping Headquarters, the tornado headed northwest along Tooth Ridge, distributing everything from sleeping bags to toothbrushes over a five square mile area. Over 300 tents were carried off in the winds. For the next several days, wranglers covered the area, brought in everything they found, and put it on display in the dining hall for owners to recover what they could identify as theirs, thus lending a lot of credibility to the age-old admonition of putting names and/ or expedition numbers on all possessions.

Old Mother Nature, in one of her more cranky moods, must have still had a soft spot in her heart for really young children. The little tent belonging to the Rhea kids, located in the Rhea's backyard, rode out the tornado in grand style and was still in place when the winds diminished.

Just two months before the tornado, Jack had a forest fire on his hands, although it was technically not on Philmont proper. It was a major fire on the Ranch's southern border, just south of the Rayado Canyon. With any misfortune, such as an adverse wind, there was every possibility that the fire would drop over LaGrulla Ridge and climb up the north side of the Rayado Canyon, thereby threatening much of Philmont's South Country. Although New Mexico and the U.S. Forest Service spearheaded the fight, Jack put out a call for volunteers – and the call was answered by hundreds of people from all walks of life who wanted to save Philmont. It took three weeks to fully contain the fire – three weeks that Jack practically never saw his family so involved was he rescuing Philmont's High Country.

Within a week after the tornado, Jack had a prominent role in a gathering at Villa Philmonte for the name change and dedication of Philmont's highest peak, what was then known as Clear Creek Mountain. At a ceremony attended by Chief Scout Executive Arthur Schuck, the mountain officially became Waite Phillips Mountain. Although the transition from "Car-Max" to Rayado and Rayado to Fish Camp took place five years later, the Clear Creek name hung on for even longer, eventually giving way to the more colloquial "Mount Phillips."

Inspired Hiring Decisions

The following year, 1961, was a rebound year – an immediate post-Jamboree year with attendance very close to 10,000. It was also a record year for seasonal staff and ranger employment which reached totals of 375 and eighty, respectively. The year was not remarkable in terms of new programs, new construction, or Mother Nature's tantrums. What is most remarkable about 1961 is the foundation it put down for major developments in the future – all made possible by some brilliant personnel hiring decisions.

Jack's experience as a classification interviewer in an Army induction center was certainly an asset at Philmont and would prove very useful in years ahead. He did not know it then, but within a few years, he would be making personnel decisions for a much larger organization than Philmont Scout Ranch. Jack was also very well-informed whether through keeping his ear to the ground or tapping into Philmont's jungle telegraph. There are several particularly good examples of his insight as an employer. One of the new first-year rangers in 1961 was a young man from Albuquerque. His name was James Talley and he had several qualifications that put him in the mainstream of Rangerdom; he was an Eagle Scout, had been a camper at Philmont, had also done JLT at the Ranch, and he had worked at his local Scout Council camp as a rifle range officer. What set him apart were his musical abilities. He was a talented singer and played both the guitar and banjo. The guitar went to ranger training at Ponil that year and was also played a lot during the first few days of the season when first year rangers usually wind up waiting for their first groups. Talley's talent was clearly far above that usually encountered among the seasonal staff

Jack heard about this singer, sought him out, and asked if he had any experience with horses. As it turned out, James was hardly a stranger to horses, having ridden from a rather early age. So, the two of them got into Jack's station wagon and drove up to Cimarroncito for which the evening campfires had always consisted of telling the Philmont story along with singing led by which ever staff member who had any musical interest and who was not afraid of getting up in front of a group to act as song leader. Jack offered James an interesting job: run the campfire and western lore program at Clarks Fork and if there were no groups in Clarks Fork, ride up to Cito and run the evening campfire there. Talley signed on and was promptly turned over to the legendary Boss Sanchez for a crash course in roping and shoeing horses. Talley was given a palomino mare, "Missy," and had a bunk in one of the Cito staff cabins as well as a tent at Clark's Fork. In 1962, he advanced to what was then Philmont's premier camp for western lore and campfire programs: Beaubien.

Although "campfire masters" were called "program counselors" on their employment contracts, Jack had another name for them: "troubadours." Talley's repertoire was varied and included popular ballads of the day, traditional folk songs, and some classics such "Ghost Riders" and "The Master's Call." In the following decade, Talley moved to Nashville, became a nationally popular recording star with Capitol Records, and sang twice at the Carter White House, including the inaugural ball. And James Talley is the first to say that it was all made possible by the opportunity that came his way through Jack Rhea's intuition.

Another interesting example of Jack's wise hiring decisions also occurred in 1961. It was the end of the season and the camp director from Porcupine stopped in to talk with Jack. The young man was Don Wilson and he had been a ranger, program counselor, and camp director. He was also disgusted with the food distribution system, a situation which was especially complicated for Porcupine because it had a relatively new commissary and also was the supply point for two satellite staffed camps, Red Hills and Comanche Creek. Don reviewed all of the problems which were primarily with how trail food and staffed camp food actually reached the camps. The problem was not so much the quality and quantity of food, but with the glitches that occurred between the warehouse and the ultimate consumer. Jack's response to the defined problem was short and sweet, "Okay, Mr. Wilson, how would you like to come back next summer as the director of distribution?" The deal was struck, and from it eventually came the development of strategically located Backcountry commissaries, introduction of new trail foods, advances in trail food packaging, and the commissary efficiencies that are still going strong today – due to Jack's seeing not a problem, but seeing an opportunity and hiring the right young man to get the job done. Years later as a BSA professional, Don also modernized food menus, packaging, and distribution systems at National Jamborees.

1961 also saw the arrival of two more young men who would both cast long shadows on the Philmont landscape. For those spending any time at all in Camping Headquarters in the mid- to late 1960s, Larry Murphy was a very familiar figure. Slender and almost frail-appearing, he was headed for an academic career and, indeed, most of his work at Philmont involved constant research. Larry, a Californian, joined the staff in 1961 near the end of Jack Rhea's tour, and spent his first summer as a commissary/trading post manager, but later really moved into his element as the museum manager at Rayado. He served on the staff through the 1969 season and in the intervening years his title evolved from ranch historian to assistant director of program, a title also carried by his program partner, Jerry Traut.

Even before his job description involved museum work, Larry would engage anybody in conversation about the history of Philmont and surrounding areas which soon resulted in a series of articles for magazines and newspapers. His interest in local history soon led to the book, *Out in God's Country: A History of Colfax County, New Mexico* which was published in 1969. That was followed in 1972 by the landmark book, *Philmont, A History of New Mexico's Cimarron Country* which, after over 25,000 copies were printed in many editions, is still the definitive book about the Philmont Country. The book did much to increase and enhance Philmont's awareness and reputation as well as serving as an inspiration and model for the next wave of Philmont researcher/writers, including Dave Caffey, Steve Zimmer, Ken Davis, Mark Griffin, and Marty Tschetter among others. Dave Caffey knew Larry as well as anybody and put it this way:

> I think Larry, along with Jerry Traut, really "unearthed" a lot of the Philmont history that we came to accept as common knowledge in later years. I know he did a good deal of oral history, maybe before it had that name, with people like Vivian and Doc Leitzel (Baldy mining and Cimarron), Narciso Abreu (Rayado, early settlement of the region), Chope Phillips (Waite Phillips, Philmont Ranch), Matt Gorman (Baldy mining), Thomas Schomburg (logging and Cimarron and Northwestern Railroad), and Victor Van Lint (Baldy mining). He made a lot of us on staff aware of books like Jim Berry Pearson's *The Maxwell Land Grant*; Agnes Morley Cleaveland and Fred Lambert's *Satan's Paradise*, and Margaret Ward's *Cousins by the Dozens*, and other items of particular local interest.
>
> As a consultant for backcountry programs, Larry was a lot of fun to have around, visiting your camp. As to the programs, he would listen and make suggestions. He did pretty good mock— or maybe it was real—exasperation at some of the liberties staff members took with historical facts in the interest of telling entertaining stories. Larry was an absolute first rate western historian. I am grateful for the Larry Murphy books we have, and sorry for the ones we missed out on that surely would have been written and published.

Larry's degrees were from the University of Arizona and Texas Christian University; indeed, his master's thesis focused on the Baldy mining district. His career path eventually led to Wayne State University in Detroit where he was Dean of the College of Lifelong Learning and a Professor of History and Social Science. He authored several books after his landmark *Philmont* and maintained his relationship with the Ranch through the PSA for which he was an early editor of *High Country* magazine. He was also the inspiration for the PSA's first book, *Tales from the High Country*, an anthology of the best articles appearing to that date, 2003, in *High Country*.

Fortunately for all historians who followed him, Larry donated all of his original Philmont research materials to the Philmont Museum. In later life, a few pounds were added to Larry's slender frame, but anybody suspecting some sort of a congenital condition when first meeting Larry in the early 60s would have been right. It was a heart problem, and he died from it on 26 September 1987 at age forty-five.

Bill Wadsworth and the Rangers

In 1961, Jack Rhea took advantage of a tremendous opportunity that was tailor made for the Ranger Department. Beginning that year, Bill Wadsworth, Assistant National Director of Camping, came out from the

Photo courtesy of Bobbie Wadsworth

Bill Wadsworth from the National Office joined Philmont Ranger training in 1961.

National Office to help train rangers. The timing was perfect; the legendary Doc Loomis had retired due to health issues and Wes Klusmann wisely decided that the rangers ought to have a younger, more ranger-like man representing the National Office. Wadsworth first got acquainted with Jack Rhea in 1960 and a year later became an integral part of ranger training, bringing the latest advances in backpacking equipment and camping techniques. It would be hard to imagine a better man for the job. Bill grew up in Fulton, New York, near the southeastern shore of Lake Ontario. An Eagle Scout (class of 1930), he went to Syracuse University where he was on the varsity swimming and skiing teams. After graduating in 1938, he spent nearly two years working in Philadelphia at a relative's company before joining the BSA professional ranks. At that point, he had a wealth of experience gained from both Scout council camps and independent private camps. After Schiff training, he went to work as a field executive in Asbury Park, New Jersey.

Then World War II came and Bill was off to Fort Benning and Officer Candidate School in January 1943, just missing Jack Rhea who had graduated from Infantry OCS only three months before. Wadsworth returned to the Boy Scouts after military service and was located in the Onondaga Council (Longhouse Council today) in Syracuse, not far from his hometown of Fulton. His first contact with Philmont was very informal; in 1948, he and his wife Bobbie, an attractive, vivacious former ski instructor, were on a Colorado skiing vacation and decided to drive south to see what Philmont was all about. They were enchanted, but it would be more than a decade before he had any official contact with the Ranch. In 1960, Bill Wadsworth moved from his job as a district executive and council camping specialist in Syracuse to the National Office as the assistant director of camping. Bill expected that job would be a short-term position and that he would be assigned back to Syracuse as the council executive in about three years. It did not turn out that way because his camping expertise was so much in demand that he remained with the National Office until retiring in 1978 after leading the camping and High Adventure departments.

Wadsworth was not a desk-bound Scout executive; he was a field-oriented innovator whose involvement with Philmont Ranger training could not have been more timely. He pioneered novel cooking methods and had created some of his own camping equipment years before, including the tab tent which became a BSA standard item. Camping equipment was changing rapidly. Contoured, exterior frame backpacks with hipbelts and nylon pack bags, lighter fabrics for tents, and backpacking stoves were beginning to emerge market-wide, and Wadsworth was on top of it along with the camping latest techniques – all of which was passed on to the rangers to keep them at the leading edge.

Every June, Wadsworth arrived to participate in ranger training, and in some ways overshadowed Mister Dunn – not surprising since Wadsworth stood six feet, four inches. Wadsworth commanded a lot of respect whether it was presenting to individual ranger training crews or leading the songs at the evening campfires during ranger training. Eventually Wadsworth became the national director of High Adventure and was a leader in the establishment of Sommers Canoe Base, Maine High Adventure, Land Between The Lakes, and Florida Sea Base.

Wadsworth is also credited with having a hand in designing the unique Philmont Ranger backpack patch. More important was his role with the training rangers of 1961, his first year as a ranger consultant. At Ponil that year, he worked with the training rangers to develop presentations that went far beyond Doc Loomis' campcraft presentations. But what is probably Wadsworth's most lasting contribution to Rangerdom was his major role in the development of the "Ranger Song." That story is well told in *I Wanna Go Back*, the 2011 book about Philmont Rangers, so it will not be repeated here except to say that the Ranger leadership of 1961 took the lyrics from Onondaga Council's "I Want To Go back To Marcy" as the model for the Ranger Song. Mt. Marcy is New York State's highest mountain, which is located close to a place very near and dear to Wadsworth, Onondaga Council's Camp Askenonta which itself is located on an island in Lake Placid.

Wadsworth clearly identified with the rangers, so much so that he made a very telling comment in his congratulatory letter to Clarence Dunn upon the latter's retirement in 1970 asking, "I hope you'll allow me to be counted as one of your rangers. It's an elite group."

More Idea Men

Yet another young idea man joined the staff in 1961, lending some validity to calling 1961 "the year the stars fell on." Gene Klingler arrived as a medical student assigned to the Health Lodge and returned two years later as a staff physician. He has been coming to Philmont every summer since then. In 1961, Gene was a medical student at the University of Kansas School of Medicine when he was called into Dean of Students' Dr. Robert Hudson's office for a discussion on how he was going to spend his summer. Gene was planning on working in the KU Medical Center emergency room, but was instead "volunteered" along with his registered nurse wife, Betsy, for a tour of duty in the Philmont Health Lodge.

In addition to strengthening Philmont's relationship with the KU Medical School over the years, Gene has served on the Ranch Committee and spearheaded the Health Lodge Task Force that raised funds to equip Philmont's new health lodge. That facility, technically, is not a health lodge – rather it is a fully licensed, equipped, and staffed New Mexico medical clinic. From that long ago summer, Gene Klingler, M.D., has spent over fifty years serving Philmont's medical needs, improving the quality of care, and training the summer medical staff. Jack Rhea's management style precluded much involvement with the health lodge; as a well-run operation, it did not require much of his attention. Once the program was up and running, Jack turned the primary responsibility for interfacing with the KU School of Medicine over to Don Higgins, the BSA's national director for health and safety.

Colorado Supreme Court Senior Associate Justice Gregory J. Hobbs, Jr. joined the staff a year later in 1962 as a ranger and was on the seasonal staff through 1966, serving as a training ranger, trip planner, and camp director. He returned as a sector director in 1968-69 after a year of service in the Peace Corps with his wife Bobbie. Based on his extensive knowledge of Philmont, he was asked by Joe Davis, director of camping from 1965 through 1974, to write in 1965 the first *Philmont Trails* guidebook which served as the foundation for the *PEAKS* book, now known as the *TREKS* book.

In the late 1960s, when the Philmont Ranch Committee was considering opening Philmont to commercial timbering operations, Hobbs organized and helped lead an ad hoc group of seasonal staff that vocally opposed the measure. His group successfully persuaded the committee and ranch management to drop the idea and renew their dedication to preserving Philmont as a wilderness for its participants. That ad hoc group facilitated the formation of the Philmont Staff Association of which Greg was a founding director. He was appointed to the Philmont Ranch Committee in the late 1980s and created Philmont's first risk management program, serving as chairman of the Risk Management Task Force for ten years. While best known as Philmont's "poet laureate" for the many poems he has written about the Ranch and its programs, Greg Hobbs is the author of a half-dozen books dealing with the law, conservation, poetry, and the American West. Several of those non-Philmont books do, however, frequently refer to Greg's Philmont days which has had the effect of broadening awareness of Philmont not only as a southwestern landmark but also as a national treasure.

Construction in the Rhea Era

Although the most readily visible aspects of construction that took place in the Rhea years are at the Training Center, Jack further developed the Backcountry in terms of new building and upgrades to existing camps. Camping attendance was growing and reached 10,457 in 1962, the second highest to date (exceeded only by the post-Jamboree attendance in 1958). Beaubien, for example, had a substantial new commissary/trading post with a walk-in freezer built in time for the 1962 season, thus making it one of four major camps offering fresh food menus.

Jack moved Cimarroncito north from its original location near the Hunting Lodge and oversaw its evolution into the major camp in the central sector. During Jack's tenure, becoming camp director at Cito was considered to be the top of the pyramid for summer staff. Cito's riding horses eventually moved to a new camp, Clarks Fork, which was scheduled to open in 1957 but did not get under way until several years later when Miners Park also made its debut.

Dean Canyon saw the opening of two camps, New Dean and Dean Cow. Three small operations, Webster Lake, Red Hills, and Old Camp came on stream, but were not destined for growth. Red Hills became a trail camp, Webster Lake is used only occasionally as a special duties camp not intended for regular camper use, and Old Camp still appears on North Country itineraries. Indian Writings grew during and after Jack's tour. Trail camps were not required on itineraries in the Rhea years. Some trail camps, such as Brownsea, disappeared forever and others like Crags and Lamberts Mine have appeared only intermittently on more recent itineraries. For those who wanted to get away from it all, the Rhea years offered many other choices, including Dan Beard, Bench, Aspen Springs, Webster Parks, Lovers Leap, Urraca, Agua Fria, Garcia, Lower Bonito, Buck Creek, Toothache Springs, Aguilla Springs, and Bear Caves.

For the Rhea family, the most obvious new construction took place at the director of camping's residence. That adobe home had been used for ranch managers during the Philmont Ranch days, but was cleaned up, painted, and modernized with the addition of a new kitchen for George Bullock in late 1947. Bullock also took out one wall and installed a new fireplace between the living room and dining room in 1950. The Rheas, with four children, significantly expanded the residence by closing in the screened front porch to gain more living space.

The Ridin' Rheas

By 1961, Jack's young family had reached ages where they could safely take advantage of living on a western ranch. In some respects, Jack's moving to Cimarron and Philmont was much like moving back to the VC Bar Ranch and Lake City, Colorado, of Jack's youth. To be sure, there were differences. He was now a manager, a married man with four young children, and his responsibilities were substantially greater than taking guests on horseback rides or catching trout for breakfast. Nonetheless, the Rhea kids were in the saddle from a very early age and each had his or her own horse. Jack always rode "Doughbelly" a large bay gelding. The horse's name did not describe any paunchy stomach, but was merely a reference to the gentle horse being like putty in Jack's hands. The girls' horses were named "Midnight" and, no surprise, "Gaucho." Ron and Bart's horses were named "Sonny" and "Geronimo" respectively.

Rhea Family Collection

A painting given to Jack upon his retirement from the Boy Scouts of America captured his interest in horses. The background consists of ghosted images of Eagle Scout rank, National Executive Staff patch, and the old, round Philmont patch.

The original Gaucho remained in Wichita with the parents of one of Jack's students after he left for Army OCS and in old age eventually had to be put down. Jack started the kids' riding lessons on burros because there was little chance of getting hurt falling off. He later graduated them to a pony named "Macaroni" before putting them on full grown horses. The Rhea kids pretty much had the run of the area around Camping Headquarters in the off season and enjoyed many rides around Coyote Mesa and out in the flats below the Tooth of Time. The kids occasionally rode with children from the Training Center during the summer. Maxine only rode horses infrequently when VIPs or relatives visited the Ranch. She easily preferred fishing over riding.

All of the Rhea children were very interested in horses, but Bart probably spent more time at the Horse Department than the others. Bart was well-acquainted with Bobby Maldonado whose father Fred was a long-time Philmont employee. Bobby also was an outstanding horseman who went on the pro rodeo tour after winning the all-around title at the Cimarron Rodeo several times. Bobby took Bart on what was an exciting day – hunting wild horses just off Philmont's southwest boundary in Wild Horse Park (where else?). That particular hunt was not a success, but it certainly made an impression on Bart – one that would be realized years later in a very big way.

Jack was always partial to horses and some of that rubbed off on the people who worked with horses. Whenever Jack's official business took him to a camp with horses, he always found time to visit the corral and talk with the horsemen. He also held the head of the Horse Department, Boss Sanchez, in the highest regard and never questioned a decision made by the Boss.

From his wartime contact with Bob Hope, Jack made the acquaintance of more Tinseltown stars which brought a curious benefit to Philmont's horse department. Some of Hollywood's aging horses, the former equine stars of their day, were not put out to pasture, put down, or sent to an old horses' home. Instead a number of them were retired to Philmont, including at least one of Roy Rogers' Triggers. Sometimes those aging horses were sent complete with their fancy saddles too.

Jack Rhea, the Sportsman

As a hunter and trout fisherman, Jack Rhea was certainly in his element when he reported to Philmont. In many ways, Philmont was very reminiscent of the VC Bar Ranch where deer, elk, turkey, and trout abounded. Before Jack arrived in 1954, Philmont's Nimrod deer hunting program was already in place. That activity was also a revenue source because guest hunters paid for the privilege of hunting. The program now has its fishing sequel in which trout fisherman pay for a weekend with guides on Philmont's Agua Fria and Rayado waters. Jack, the former fishing guide, also became a regular Nimrod guide as did Buzz Clemmons beginning with the 1957 season. Jack, however, had a couple of issues with some of the Nimrod hunters. There was one shooter who could not hit the broad side of a barn at five paces. After the deer had been stalked and just before that hunter was about to take his shot, Jack cleverly stepped out of sight. He did, however, have the same deer in his sights, and at the split-second the incompetent hunter fired, so did Jack. The poor Nimrod never knew what happened other than the fact that he had just bagged a fine Philmont deer.

There was one category of Nimrod hunter for which Jack had very little regard: the trophy hunter. Those sportsmen only wanted to shoot the biggest buck they could find and then have the mounted head with its many-pointed antlers adorn a wall in their trophy rooms back home. They were not even interested in having the carcass butchered for its venison. Jack saw to it that the venison was not wasted. It went to the less fortunate in Cimarron for whom Jack had always provided some support, especially construction materials and expertise to improve the integrity and sanitation of their modest homes.

Buzz Clemmons was a particularly good shot and had a very nice collection of hunting rifles. He once shot a huge Philmont elk with a 6 mm Remington, a rifle that is dynamite on varmints and is seen occasionally among deer hunters. To try to take down an elk with a 6 mm Remington is sporty to say the least; the hunt was written up and appeared as an article in *National Rifleman*, the National Rifle Association magazine. After the Nimrod guests had completed their hunts, Jack and Buzz went hunting separately, but it was not for deer. Elk were the preferred quarry.

There was a select group of hunters who hunted Philmont free of charge, however, thanks to Jack Rhea. Native Americans were welcome to hunt deer in the autumn. In return for that privilege, they insisted on supply-

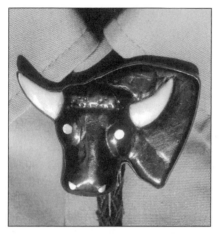

ing Jack with some of their handiwork in the form of jewelry and
bolo ties. Years later, Jack credited
his involvement with Philmont's
nearby Indians as the source of his
interest and eventual expertise in
Native American culture, art, and
jewelry. Jack held onto surplus bolo
ties and later gave them as gifts for
friends or to show appreciation to
those who had done him a favor.
Most of the ceramic bolo ties were
in the shape of a Philmont black
bull – nearly identical in appearance to the black bull patch frequently seen
on red Philmont jackets. For friends who got them, those mementos are a
treasured link with Jack Rhea.

In late November, Jack always went hunting for something to put on
the Thanksgiving Day table. Of the eight years the Rheas were at Philmont,
there were only a couple years when a Philmont wild turkey was not the
main dinner fare on Thanksgiving. Jack also hunted for quail and ducks as
a guest on other ranch properties.

When Jack hunted elk, it was with a 30:06 with a telescopic sight.
Frequently, he grilled the elk steaks in his house where the fireplace had three
sides, including the one meant for cooking. When Jack left Philmont, the rifle
gathered dust. He never went big game hunting again. Fishing was another matter. Jack caught many trout at Philmont in such prime locations as the Rayado
below Fish camp where the trail climbs up on the ridge. He also enjoyed fishing Cimarroncito Reservoir where he taught his children to fish for trout with
worms and a bobber. Otherwise, he was a dry fly fisherman who always tied
his own trout flies, a skill that he passed along to his sons. He also took his
sons to one of his favorite trout locations, a place that is seldom fished today:
the stream below the Cito Reservoir where there are a number of nice trout
pools. Jack remained a trout fisherman well into his retirement. Cathedral Rock
and the adjacent Cito Reservoir held a certain fascination for Jack; at the VC
Bar Ranch there was a very similar rock formation, albeit somewhat smaller.
Below that rocky prominence, the Lake Fork of the Gunnison River flowed and
widened, offering very good trout fishing – always a magnet for Jack Rhea.

This photograph of Jack at Cimarroncito Reservoir was taken by Philmont's 1950s photographer, Dan Sheehan, who also operated a studio in Raton. The photograph was reprinted in large format and is still seen on walls at Philmont.

Fishing frequently was a family event, although the Rhea daughters brought along a transistor radio in case the fishing got a bit slow. When the bites slackened, the radio poured out rock and roll, much to Jack's annoyance. More than once, Jack was heard saying, "Turn that down! You're scaring the fish." The Rheas also enjoyed camping, and in the off season took their tents to favorite places including Fish Camp, Porcupine, and Cito Reservoir.

Programs for Everybody

The summer of 1962 represents the peak of Jack's program development, and it is a blend of the activities unique to Philmont's heritage mixed with a significant amount of traditional council camp offerings. In that year, there were forty-two camps, of which twenty-four were staffed. There was enough western-oriented program to satisfy Waite Phillips' desire for every boy to have a western ranch experience. Horseback rides had not yet been moved to Beaubien, but were available along with western lore at Rayado, Clarks Fork, and Ponil. Burro packing was more widespread then with the animals being available at Ponil, Pueblano, all of the Deans (Old, New, and Cow), Old Camp, Dan Beard, Pueblano, and Harlan.

In those days, the geology program was concentrated at Cyphers in a pre-Baldy era, but Pueblano and Lamberts Mine also had a piece of the mining action. The shooting sports program was much more diversified in the early 1960s. Cimarroncito had the most impressive ranges (.22 caliber and shotgun), Pueblano had the biggest bang for the buck with its .30 caliber running deer range, and skeet ranges were also established at Harlan and Beaubien. The multi-part National Rifle Association's Hunter Safety Course was popular; some groups did it all at one camp on a layover, but more typically it was completed at two different camps.

Before it became a commissary location, Ute Gulch offered a field archery course. Fishing was a popular program offered at two of today's mainstays, Abreu and Fish Camp, but also at Lost Cabin, Porcupine, and Comanche (the latter was a staffed camp back then). Nature study was widely available as was conservation, and one variation on the nature study theme was wildlife photography which was located at a surprising number of camps: Ponil, Old Camp, Cimarroncito, Miners Park, Fish Camp, and Crater. Astronomy moved around from year to year and was typically offered at two of three locations: Abreu, Crater, and the now unstaffed Red Hills. And the Indian Writings program was devoted exclusively to archeology.

Dutch oven cooking was a major part of every ranger's presentation, not a separate program offered at just one camp. The ovens were everywhere and commissaries, all thirteen of them in Jack's last year as camping chief, were well stocked with Bisquick, peaches, and cornbread mix. At staffed camps, just cleaning the many Dutch ovens at the end of a season was a major part of closing camp.

While not promoted in advance of campers' arrival, merit badge work was available, and it was fairly common to see any member of a camp staff signing merit badge cards early in Jack's administration. Exactly which badges were available depended on just what special talent resided in each camp staff. Thus it was possible for a Scout to work on such unlikely badges as Radio or Woodcarving. That availability of staff as merit badge counselors was sharply cut back by 1960, not included in trip planner sessions, and what remained was tied directly to Philmont's regular programs, i.e., Soil and Water Conservation, Forestry, Nature, Geology, etc. Eventually the availability of Philmont staff as a source for merit badges or partial completions was completely dropped.

The Baldy Country

Jack missed out on developing the Baldy Country whose acquisition was announced in 1963, although he was involved in the negotiations which led up to the eventual purchase. The negotiations between the BSA and the Maxwell Land Grant Company finally came down to nineteen dollars an acre for the 10,000 acre tract, excluding mineral rights. Knowing that there was a possibility that the Baldy mines could eventually become economically viable again at some future point and wanting no restrictions, the deal was struck at twenty-one dollars an acre. Earlier, Jack had gotten permission from the Maxwell Land Grant Company to allow Baldy to be officially sidehiked from Pueblano in 1961. Those sidehikes were always led by a member of the Pueblano staff and had been one of the real highpoints of any North Country trek. Even before 1961, Baldy and neighboring Touch-Me-Not Mountain were popular hikes for off-duty Philmont staff, particularly for rangers. Jack's successor, Skipper Juncker, was the camping chief who opened the first camp in the Baldy Country, but due to his premature death in early 1965, Joe Davis was the camping director who really developed Baldy Country programs.

CHAPTER 17

Back East

In late 1962 when he was starting to prepare for the 12,413 campers coming in 1963, Jack was promoted, pretty much right out of the blue, to the position of national director of professional training. The year had been a big one with nearly 11,000 attending, and 1963 was shaping up to be even bigger with a forecast of around 12,500 campers. Jack, at age forty-seven, fought the move vigorously and made it quite clear that he did not want to leave the Ranch, but it was hopeless. The training position, a very important one, had suddenly become vacant and Jack had no choice. From a career viewpoint, it was a mixed blessing. The move placed Jack well into the upper echelon of the National Office, but if he had any hopes of becoming the Chief Scout Executive he was lacking the one key prerequisite: a successful record as the council executive in a major metro council such as Chicago or Los Angeles.

For legions of Philmont staffers, Jack Rhea is synonymous with Philmont's camping program activities, building the staff and attendance, and creating national awareness of Philmont, but the National Office also saw him as a man with many training successes, and importantly as the man who had grown the Philmont Training Center substantially during the years from 1954.

Jack's full-time Philmont days came to a close after eight years which was shaping up as a typical tour for the director of camping. He had many minor and major innovations to his credit during a period when he generated as much staff loyalty as George Bullock had enjoyed. Most importantly, Jack experimented with Philmont's core camping program in 1955, launched the new twelve-day backpacking program in 1956, refined it in 1957 with the Philmont Rangers, and cast it in metal in 1958. That four-year continuum, with its ranger and program foundation, has stood the test of time and is Jack Rhea's greatest Philmont legacy by far. Although Jack shied away from taking credit for advances, other Rhea innovations are still very much part of the Philmont landscape: the modern radio system, detailed topographic maps, creating a truly national staff, the iconic arrowhead patch (celebrating its fifty-sixth birthday when Philmont celebrates its seventy-fifth), growing the Training Center, and launching his share of new camps and substantially improving existing camps (the modern Cito, Miner's Park, Clark's Fork, Indian Writings, etc). Ranger City was built in the Rhea years as was Tent City itself. All of those developments are now taken for granted, but when they were introduced they added all new dimensions to the Philmont experience for staff and camper alike.

The move east was very difficult for the family – going from a 127,000 acre ranch to a ranch house on one acre. They could not even move into the new house immediately and had to live in a motel until their home was ready. Their residence was in Bridgewater, New Jersey, which is located midway between the National Office in North Brunswick and Schiff Scout Reservation in Mendham.

Bullock Death 1963

Less than a year after Jack moved to the National Office, the Philmont community was terribly saddened to learn of Bullock's premature death on 1 August 1963. Bullock had been out in his garden, tending flowers, when he was suddenly overcome by an intense sense of overheating combined with a crashing headache. He quickly went inside and asked his wife Bess to call an ambulance. Help arrived too late and George Bullock was gone – taken by a brain aneurysm only four days short of his fifty-eighth birthday.

Bullock's death was a great loss for what was then Kit Carson Council. His innovative programs included enrolling the support of the substantial military and scientific communities located in Albuquerque. Bullock substantially expanded Scouting's presence in the Navajo community, including developing camping operations for all of New Mexico's Native Americans. He also expanded camping opportunities for council youth when he opened a camping/aquatics operation, primarily for Explorers, on Conchas Lake. Bullock was the first council executive to hire a Hispanic district executive.

Now at the National Office, Jack's principal activity was running the course for new professional Scouters, i.e., essentially the same course that Jack had taken twenty-three years before. The move was hard on Jack's children, especially Julie and Carol; it could easily be described as culture shock. The kids, girls included, were accustomed to wearing flannel shirts, Levis, and cowboy boots. That type of apparel was not "in" where the kids went to school in well-to-do, North Jersey suburbia. When they went riding horses, even the saddles were foreign: English riding saddles instead of western saddles. The Rheas rode occasionally at the Silver Saddles Ranch in nearby Branchburg, but riding single file at a walk over several acres just did not compare with a gallop out to Stockade and back.

Rhea Family Collection

The Rhea family in the mid-1960s while at the National Office.

A few years after moving Back East, there was one light moment relating to horses. Schiff was located in a very exclusive area and is near such upscale communities as Peapack and Bernardsville. The former First Lady Jacqueline Kennedy Onassis had her New Jersey horse farm on property very close to Schiff. One of Schiff's caretakers brought a problem to Jack because it seemed that Ms. Onassis had taken to riding her horse on Schiff's trails where, as might be expected, the horse always left behind a few little, rounded calling cards. Jack decided to go walking one day and he did encounter the former First Lady. He explained to her in the most gracious manner possible that Schiff's trails were restricted to use by only those participating in the BSA's training programs. In her breathy best voice, Ms. Onassis purred, "Ooohh, Mister Rhea. I <u>am</u> <u>so</u> sorry. It will never happen again." But it did happen again (quite frequently in fact).

Jack worked himself hard and worked his students in professional training hard as well. One of his classes of staff leadership students, in late October 1964, wrote a poem chiding Jack for his thorough methods.

> To Jack Rhea
> With solutions of problems quite 'nitty;
> As problems grow rougher
> And solutions get tougher
> He cleverly forms a committee.
>
> Jack Rhea has a good deal to say,
> We hear he is handsomely paid;
> We know he'll go far
> Like a quick rising star –
> We wish he would start on his way!

Rhea Family Collection

Julie Rhea took this 1964 photo of the family at the annual BSA National Office staff picnic which was held at Schiff Scout Reservation.

Situated as he was well up in the National Office hierarchy, Jack's opinion was occasionally sought on matters other than just professional training. One case in point involved an old friend: Bob Perin who in 1964 was an assistant national director of volunteer training. Perin had been the council executive in Phoenix, was involved in Philmont ranger training in the late 1950s, and was the father of Steve Perin, who had been a training ranger in 1957. Perin coordinated a meeting between top executives of the National Office, National Executive Board, and professional and volunteer leadership of California's Monterey Bay Council. That council, under the leadership of a Hungarian immigrant, Béla Bánáthy, had developed the White Stag Program, a youth training experience which emphasized key leadership skills as opposed to what was then the norm, the patrol method and traditional Scouting skills. The purpose of the meeting was to determine if the White Stag Program had any application within the BSA's training programs. That the National Council would even listen to outside ideas was novel.

Reaction by the National Office was mixed; the traditionalists saw no value in the program, but Chief Scout Executive Joe Brunton was sufficiently impressed to order an in-depth, long-term study of the program. The evaluation saw merit in White Stag and recommended that its first implementation be in Wood Badge. Ten years after that first, critical meeting, the BSA's youth and adult training programs made the transition from traditional skills to leadership skills, crediting White Stag as the basis for the change. Just where Jack Rhea stood on the matter is unknown, but considering his reputation as an innovator and his past experience as a teacher, combat officer in WWII, and his management roles within the BSA, it is quite likely that he was one of the minority favoring a change in training direction.

It was a proud day in the Rhea family on January 19, 1966, when Ron Rhea received his Eagle Scout Award.

Jack's work at Philmont did not lend itself to much leisure time, but now that he was with the National Office, there was more time for other activities – including golf. Jack enjoyed golf very much if for no other reason than he saw himself as his major opponent. When he was in California on Scouting business, an occasional golf partner was none other than Bob Hope who introduced him to such Hollywood stars as James Garner. The golf also proved useful at various fund raising events, an activity where Jack was definitely an asset. Although son Bart was a standout basketball player, Jack never followed professional basketball; he preferred baseball and football. His reading was largely limited to religion, spirituality, and Native American life. Jack would also qualify for what many people describe as a "renaissance man." In addition to his outdoor talents, Jack was a superb carpenter, an accomplished cook, and even comfortable moving onto Maxine's turf. Jack was a maestro at the sewing machine and created curtains and bedspreads for the kids' rooms.

The Great Flood in 1965

In mid-June of 1965, right in the middle of staff training, Philmont, along with most of Colfax County, was devastated by a flood of Biblical proportions. The story of the flood has been well told in *High Country* articles and other books, so that ground will not be covered here except to say that the National Office assumed that the brand new director of camping, Joe Davis, would be more than up to his neck learning about Philmont operations. To help get Davis up to speed as quickly as possible, Jack Rhea was sent to Philmont just before staff training began. Davis had been hurriedly appointed only several weeks before as a result of the untimely death of Skipper Juncker. Jack's activities put him somewhere between that of co-director of camping and chief advisor to Joe Davis. When the flood hit, Jack was up in the Backcountry and was stranded for several days at Beaubien.

Photo courtesy of James R. Place

The Great Flood of '65 caught Jack Rhea at Beaubien. His return to Camping Headquarters was delayed – significantly.

The flood did have one positive benefit for the Rhea family; Maxine and the kids could join Jack during his temporary duty. As the Rheas drove down from Colorado Springs, it became quite obvious how bad the flood had been. Somewhere around Walsenburg, Colorado, there was a road grader turned upside down in an adjoining field. Only the wheels were visible. When Jack arrived, he stayed at one of the duplexes on the Camping Department side (the previous tenants took up temporary digs elsewhere). When Maxine and the kids arrived, the family moved to an apartment down at the Villa. The Rhea children loved every minute of their return to Philmont, but it was not a completely free ride. The girls worked at the Training Center where Carol served as a tour guide and, with Julie, also worked as a baby sitter. Ron became a helper at the polo barns while Bart worked at the trading post soda fountain.

By late July, Jack's job at Philmont was pretty well wrapped up. In the last few weeks, he had deliberately minimized his role so as not to detract from Joe's authority as the camping chief. Accordingly, Jack essentially functioned as a supernumerary sector director, a job which he enjoyed very much since it got him out into the Backcountry on a daily basis. One of his Backcountry trips was to the newly established Apache Springs which was opened by the original staff from Fish Camp which had been closed by the flood. Accompanying Jack was Joe Davis and Duke Towner, the South Country sector director. One purpose of the trip was to see how the new camp was getting along in what was still a rainy, post-flood period. The top brass visiting Apache Springs was a morale boost for Phil Yunker and his staff who had been very disappointed when they had to give up Fish Camp for the summer. The flood was still very much on everybody's mind, and the very first rumble of distant thunder prompted a sudden retreat by the visitors who were still only too aware of what sustained downpours could do to Backcountry roads.

To show appreciation for all that Jack had done in his post-flood tour, Joe Davis and available staff hosted a reception at the Staff Lounge for the entire Rhea family on Tuesday, 3 August just before the Rheas returned to New Jersey. That lounge in the 1960s was in a small building now housing the Staff Fitness Center. As master of ceremonies, Joe Davis was at his usual best, and opened the festivities by saying, "The entire permanent and summer staff pay homage to Jack Rhea, the man who first gave Philmont the idea that there are never any problems, only opportunities."

Members of the Control Center coordinated the reception and were responsible for Jack's going-away gift which was a very unique desk trophy in the form of a varnished jawbone of a horse mounted on a wood base which was inscribed with the words from the Bible, "And he took up the jawbone of an ass and slew a thousand men therewith." The "thousand" referred to the many, many problems with which Jack had to deal that summer. Several days before he returned to New Jersey, Jack sat down with Joe and Ray Bryan to look into Philmont's near-term future. Jack later summarized his thoughts in an early September letter to Joe – a letter that could easily have served as a roadmap for the innovations that would follow during Davis' tour as camping chief.

Jack could speak with some authority, of course, since he had been at the throttles during a period when the Ranch grew dramatically, and he had just completed what was quite literally an exhaustive, six-week inspection tour of Philmont. Water, in spite of the recent deluge, was a major concern, and Jack recommended that Philmont seek professional help, such as that available from the University of New Mexico or New Mexico Highlands University, to make sure that campsites of the future were well-served by water resources. As one means of water management, he suggested that every trek spend one night in a dry camp which had a program side effect: groups would come to appreciate the difficulties pioneers had as they moved west in the 1800s.

While Jack had sent out preliminary itinerary planning information to crews and councils with reservations, he recognized that it was nothing more than "planning information." He encouraged Joe to develop a means of controlling itinerary planning in the winter and spring which is exactly what came to pass several years later with Joe's approving a program devised by Dave Bates who had worked at Pueblano and Harlan during the last two years of Jack's administration. Jack also suggested that Joe develop a method of getting groups out into the Backcountry as quickly as possible in order for campers to appreciate more of Philmont's grandeur.

Jack's program suggestions could have been taken right out of Waite Phillips' wish list: much more emphasis on archeology, earth sciences, gold mines, and one activity near and dear to Jack's heart, fishing. He specifically recommended phasing out .22 rifle and archery ranges which he now considered more the bailiwick of council camps. Jack also noted that more quality time on the trail could be fostered by "roving counselors" similar to previous roving rangers and that horseback rides become optional. Thus the stage was set for the introduction of the interpretive programs which arrived later in Joe's tour.

The letter also identified problems that would become more severe as time and attendance went on. Key among those issues was the food distribution system in which the summer of 1965 saw a number of shortages, particularly with condiment kits and water purification tablets. Among other recommendations were beefing up the health lodge staff and adding another sanitarian to the staff. Finally, the summer of 1965 had certainly shown what Mother Nature could do to the road and trail system in which Jack realized that some trails had held up better than others which suggested more professionalism in Philmont's trail building. That too came to pass on the Joe Davis watch. The letter to Joe concluded with Jack's sincere thanks for Joe's open and frank rapport. It also concluded with a terrific vote of confidence since Jack called Joe, "The right man for the job."

A small and very exclusive party arrived just as Jack's temporary duty was completed. Joe Brunton, the Chief Scout Executive, and the President of the Boy Scouts of America, Tom Watson, Jr., started a two-day tour of the Ranch, and most of their visit was spent in the North Country, particularly at Baldy Town where they sampled some real Philmont trail food. Their Indian Writings sojourn included participation in the archeology program. The two leaders also were feted at a Training Center reception. Watson had reluctantly rejoined IBM after wartime service flying the VIP passenger version of the B-24 Liberator bomber. He flew high-level officials all over the world and briefly entertained the idea of staying in aviation after the war, but instead rejoined the company his father had founded. Watson swiftly steered the company into mainframes and boosted spending on R&D. He was used to dealing with high-powered people and was as shrewd a judge of character and managerial talent as there ever was. Watson never stopped flying until old age; when he came to Philmont he landed his own plane at Raton's little Crews Field where Philmont officials picked him up for the ride down to the Ranch. Watson was then into his second year as the BSA President, would continue to serve into 1968, and frequently crossed paths with Jack in the years ahead.

Major Promotions

On 1 February 1968 Jack was promoted to Director of Personnel and Training. Part of this job was supervising his successor as director of professional training, but the new part involved a range of personnel activities involving councils, regions, and the National Office. Jack was responsible for screening and recommending a short list of men who would become council executives and conducting the same activities for all regional jobs. And he was involved in all hiring decisions for positions at the National Office. Jack was also responsible for continued training of professionals as they advanced into higher levels of the BSA and for specialized, job-specific training such as finance. What he was not responsible for was volunteer training; at the time that was managed under the program group. Jack was also responsible for developing and distributing all recruiting literature.

Philmont Museum

Jack's back! Jack Rhea occasionally was at Philmont in the late 1960s for conferences and training sessions. Jack is in the back row, third from left, and Alden Barber is seated, second from left.

By this point, the number of former Philmont staff who had become professional Scouters was growing, and in Jack, those new professionals found a man who was open to new ideas. Gayle Reams, then a young professional who had been a charter Ranger in 1957, a Training Ranger in 1958, and later with Philmont's training operations, had a suggestion for Jack. In those days, college campus recruiting for BSA professionals was done by retired professionals. Gayle observed that while those men could speak proudly of rewarding careers, they could not relate as well to college seniors as a very young professional who had plenty of fire in his belly. Gayle suggested that Jack turn college recruiting over to energetic, young district executives who were still only several years out of college. Jack approved the idea and Gayle was promptly on his way to college campuses within his council's borders. And so it is today, with the exception of one person from the National Office whose principal activity is recruiting from minority groups.

During Jack's time at Philmont, the National Office was not actively engaged in recruiting professionals directly from the Philmont staff, but that would change dramatically. Recognizing what a talent pool there is among the seasonal staff, today's National Office Human Resources Department actively recruits at Philmont. Currently, Philmont's management encourages all seasonal staff to consider a career with the Boy Scouts of America, asking those interested to complete a short form for which there is a follow-up later in the summer. The follow-up is in the form of a National Office representative spending a week at Philmont conducting screening interviews and answering questions about BSA careers. There are at least two recruiting receptions at the Villa Gallery or in the Villa Gardens to which interested staff and PTC participants are invited. Those receptions are scheduled for weeks during Council Key-Three conferences, allowing prospective employees to meet key leadership from a number of councils.

Several months prior to Jack's promotion as head of personnel, Alden Barber had become Chief Scout Executive (CSE) in October 1967. That was after a year of preparation serving as the BSA's chief operating officer while Joe Brunton was preparing to retire. A Californian, Barber had served in the Army Air Force during World War II as a bombardier and, like Jack, he had been a BSA professional just before the war. When he got the nod for the top job, which included passing muster with the BSA President, Thomas Watson Jr., Barber had been the Scout Executive in Chicago. Jack's career would become closely intertwined with that of Barber over the next six years which would prove to be a tumultuous era in the history of American Boy Scouting to say the least.

BSA National leaders at Schiff during the transition from Chief Scout Executive Joseph Brunton to the incoming Alden Barber. Jack is seated at far right. To his right is Alden Barber, then Joe Brunton.

A completely independent management consultant looking at the National Office of the Boy Scouts of America would describe it as the headquarters of a large corporation marketing youth development programs, clothing, literature, camping equipment, and self-help materials. The consultant would also be quick to observe that the organization is subject to the same politics and intrigues that attend any top management succession. Barber's emerging as the Chief Scout Executive of the BSA was a good thing, a very good thing for Jack Rhea. Jack was widely admired and respected within the professional ranks, but he did have a couple detractors, and the more severe of them was in the running for the CSE position. Fortunately, the man did not get the nod because if he had Jack's career with the BSA would have turned sour. As it turned out, it was Jack's critic who wound up leaving the BSA.

If Jack had left the BSA, it would have been that organization's loss and, most likely, IBM's gain. BSA President Tom Watson had tried several times to recruit Jack Rhea into a top job at IBM with a breathtakingly high salary. The offer did not even begin to turn Jack's head. In rejecting the offers, Jack indicated that believing in what he was doing was the most important aspect of his work with the BSA and that he could never relate to IBM in the same way.

One of the first moves Barber made when becoming the chief was to shorten lines of communication by forming a cabinet made up of the key directors (field operations, personnel, training, finance, program, R&D, etc.). The cabinet met once a week at a 7:30 A.M. on Fridays. Another early initiative had been prompted by Barber's observation that the National Office staff had gotten away from traditional Scouting skills – a situation that Jack Rhea was to remediate. Thus once again Jack was in an instructor role at Schiff, but this time it was not with new men aspiring to be district executives – it was with men who had been field executives twenty or more years before.

Rhea Family Collection

With Jack being in the upper ranks of the National Office, the Rheas' travels were frequently international. Although Jack probably never dreamed of it when he was last in Berchtesgaden in 1945, he did return there with Maxine in 1969 for an international commissioners conference. The Rheas are fourth and fifth from left in a tour of local salt mines.

On 1 May 1970, Jack was promoted again – this time to national director, field operations. He replaced O.B. Evenson who had been a professional Scouter since the late 1920s and had spent many of those years in operations positions. The job had some bitter downsides. When Jack started managing the personnel and training functions, Barber's eight-year initiative, "BoyPower 76," had not been launched, but when it was introduced, Jack was increasingly involved in the council and regional personnel changes that attended the new program.

The BoyPower 76 meeting was kicked off at a national gathering of BSA professionals in 1968 at Colorado State University which Jack attended. It was, in effect, the last Top Hands Conference for the next ten years. Barber also made follow-up visits to each BSA regional headquarters to emphasize the importance of the program and to make sure all field leaders were on board with it. However, with his promotion in 1970, Jack was thrust right into the middle of BoyPower '76. The plan was to culminate in 1976, the American Bicentennial, with dramatic increases in membership, fundraising, and service to previously underserved groups. Had the objectives been attained, the positive effect on the nation and its youth would have been extraordinary. Unfortunately, the goals were set too high, many of the professionals out in the field did not buy into it, and after six years the program was cancelled. Jack became the program's "enforcer" and later described his job as one of running all over the country putting out fires.

BoyPower '76 was launched with the goal of enrolling fully one-third of Scout age boys into Scouting, i.e., a substantial increase over the one in four goals of the ten-year program of the 1930s. To accomplish this and serve the many new kids brought into the program, a fundraising goal of $65 million was established. The whole new effort did not sit well with many professionals in the field who were more oriented to traditional program activities. Membership in 1968 stood at 2,256,663, but it actually dropped by 45,000 at the end of the first year. Membership grew three percent annually from 1971 through 1973, but then started to sink. In 1974, the loss was six percent, and for the last two years of the planned program, the loss was eleven percent each year. Those council staffs which were unable to make quota were replaced, frequently by people whose backgrounds were strong in finance and marketing instead of youth service. Unfortunately, in a few councils the books were cooked to show membership figures more in line with the program goals instead of actual paid members, thus launching membership scandals which rocked Scouting over the next few decades. The focus moved to recruiting youth who were most at risk, i.e., those in the inner cities. The *Handbook for Boys* was re-written to include more of an urban slant, requirements were modified, and, in short, the BSA was moving away from its traditional base. By 1974, it was obvious that the program was not working at all, so BoyPower '76 was terminated two years before its planned completion.

Jack was on the front line of another initiative: reducing the number of regional offices from twelve down to six. The job was personally discouraging for Jack because not everybody involved in the "right-sizing" was of retirement age or could be transferred into a comparable position elsewhere in the BSA. Because of his many trips selling Philmont across the country, Jack Rhea was a well-known and respected figure in council and regional offices. That he was friends with many of those displaced by the downsizing made his job that much more difficult.

On the other hand, Jack's family was a source of comfort. Daughters Julie and Carol had decided on college "Back West," had gone out to Colorado State University, by the mid-70s were Back East, and were married and starting families. Eventually, Jack and Maxine were blessed with eight grandchildren (Julie had a son, Carol had two sons and a daughter, and Ron and Bart each had a son and daughter).

Ron started at Judson University in Illinois, but later transferred to Drew University in Morristown, New Jersey, and graduated there in 1973 with a degree in journalism. His first job was in the newspaper business in Colorado Springs.

Son Bart had started at Drew University and made the varsity basketball team in his freshman year. While in college, Bart also worked summers at Philmont as a wrangler. Unfortunately, he was injured playing basketball which put an end to his days on the court. He later transferred to Colorado College and completed his education there in 1974. Bart spent one semester abroad – at the University of Dar Es Salaam in Tanzania, which also allowed him to travel in Kenya.

In the late 1960s and early 1970s, Jack was on the road constantly. One day his son Ron came down the stairs in their home and saw his dad in the front doorway. Ron asked where his dad was headed to, but Jack told him instead that he was just getting home. As a top manager at the National Office, Jack had to travel extensively; once removed from Philmont that travel included not only National Jamborees in America but also included international travel for World Scout Jamborees and international conferences. Fortunately, Maxine was able to attend some of the distant events, but the travel was adding up. Spending the better part of several days a week cooped up in an airline seat finally came to a head in late 1973. Adding to the problem was the vascular damage to his legs resulting from his World War II shrapnel wounds. The resulting phlebitis and blood clots put Jack in the hospital and very nearly proved fatal. On top of that, Jack's weight had crept up as a result of so much travel, including out-of-town restaurants and the rubber chicken circuit at council and regional gatherings. Jack emerged from the hospital a changed man. After several months convalescence, Jack's weight was nearly back to where it had been when he was a young man, but it was obvious that he could not continue as the national director of field operations. Alden Barber gave him a new title, special assistant to the chief scout executive, during his road to recovery, but Jack officially retired from the BSA on 1 May 1974.

Rhea Family Collection

At Jack's retirement ceremony, National Director of the Program Group, John Claerhout, congratulates Jack and presents him with a retirement commendation.

Retirement Leads to Indian Arts, Inc.

In late 1974, and with his recuperation complete, Jack and Maxine began retirement by building the foundation for their second career as retailers of Native American arts in a small company called Indian Arts. To do this, they sold the house in Bridgewater and hit the road – to visit all of the major Indian reservations in the continental United States during the following two years. Jack approached this venture in a most methodical manner – by first visiting the Bureau of Indian Affairs in Washington where he learned the locations of each Indian Reservation in America. It was quite an undertaking and was preceded by buying a Buick station wagon for the journey which took them to over 150 reservations and put 50,000 miles on the car. They frequently stayed in motels, but over the years Jack had made so many good friends that they had a backlog of people to stop and visit with for a few days at a time. In that year, Jack learned as much as he could about Native American art, and he started building his initial inventory. In every case except one, Jack and Maxine were welcomed onto the reservations and in many cases to the Indians' homes. On one occasion a tall chief made it clear that Jack and Maxine were not welcome based on the contention of "what you did to us." Maxine, although she was a very petite woman, marched right up to the chief with all of her stage presence intact and bluntly said, "I never did anything to you." Confronted with such a dynamo, the chief backed down and escorted the Rheas onto the reservation.

One of the highlights of the journey was visiting Philmont for the first time in nearly six years. The Philmont interlude also provided Jack and Maxine with enough time for some fishing at Eagle Nest Lake and both the Rayado and Agua Fria.

In 1976, after more than a year of living on the road, Jack and Maxine settled in Colorado Springs where they opened a small store in a new mall called "The Depot." The structure housing the new mall was unique – it had been the original Denver and Rio Grande Railroad station but had ceased serving passengers in 1971. The opening of Indian Arts, Inc. included good coverage by the local newspaper and an appearance by Colorado Springs Mayor Lawrence D. Ochs.

Jack and Maxine's lines included art, jewelry, and clothing from over 100 Indian reservations. Any item they sold was accompanied by a card with the name of the craftsman, his tribe, and home state. Jack occasionally hated to part with some of the merchandise because he was so familiar with and appreciative of the artist's work. Indian Arts meant more to Jack and Maxine than just a source of supplemental retirement income. Jack was a man on a mission. In his dealings with reservations, he encouraged young artists to reach back and recreate the art and jewelry of generations past, and he tried to educate his suppliers in modern marketing techniques. He made sure that Indian Arts sold authentic Indian art and jewelry from tribes across the country, not just southwestern art and jewelry which dominate most Native American offerings today. Jack's marketing slogan captured his business mission perfectly, "If it's Indian, we may have it. If it isn't Indian, we won't have it."

Over the following years, the location of Indian Arts changed as Jack and Maxine settled first in Colorado Springs and later in Pennsylvania. Their prices were somewhat higher than average, but they gave considerable value with their offering because everything in their inventory was genuine. Jack had a complete story on all items because he knew exactly who had made it and what their life story was. That pair of moccasins priced at $165 was made by Eva McAdams, a Shoshone living in Wind River, Wyoming. Jack could tell the prospective purchaser just how the moccasins had been made and how Eva had stretched the deer hide on a rack, drenched it with water frequently, and used broken glass to remove hair and reach the right thickness until it became a hard leather known as parfleche.

Then Jack related how Eva had chewed on portions of the leather to make it soft for the uppers, how she had sewn them together, and how she attached the intricate bead work. The whole process took three months to produce a tough, durable moccasin that would last a lifetime. Whatever he sold, dolls or jewelry, a complete story went with it. In talking with customers, Jack also answered a fairly frequent question relating to why one sees so little Indian jewelry done in gold. The reason relates to the Spanish conquistadores who drove many of the Indians' ancestors away from the original gold sources.

Jack had a low opinion of the everyday imitation Indian jewelry – the silver plated items as opposed to the handcrafted, pounded jewelry. So much cheap stuff in the market makes it hard for real Indian craftsman to get a fair price for their work. His disdain also applied to foreign businessmen who came into reservations to buy up the valuable jewelry, making it financially attractive for Indian craftsmen to produce cheap knock-offs of such items as quality Zuni jewelry.

The directors of Hollywood and television westerns also caught some of Jack's criticism. Jack sold Indian-made war bonnets but always advised his customers that the real Indians of the nineteenth century never wore their bonnets in battle. Jack explained how the bonnets were made, including how the horsehair had to be cleaned and sized, how the feathers went through many steps before they could be attached, and how the beadwork patterns could be similar while colors were rarely the same.

Rhea Family Collection

Bart Rhea, at far right, worked at Philmont with the legendary Boss Sanchez who is seated at left in the doorway. Also seated is another long-term Philmont employee, Ben Vargas.

After Philmont, Bart Rhea worked at the UU Bar, WS, and CS Ranches.

By the late-1970s, the Rhea children's college educations had been completed and the daughters were Back East and with growing families of their own. Ron's newspaper career took him from Colorado Springs to California. Bart took a page from Jack's book and became a cowboy. For a while Bart lived at Nairn Place (now the B&B Casa Del Gavilan) when the Faudree family owned the UU Bar Ranch. Bart's work frequently took him close to Philmont's southwest border where he enjoyed some off-season fishing on the Rayado and Agua Fria. Doubtless, Bart's sojourn in the saddle made Jack think back to Gaucho and his summer at the VC Bar Ranch. After six years which also included working on the CS and WS Ranches, Bart moved Back East and went into construction equipment marketing with Caterpillar and today owns his own heavy equipment brokerage company in Flemington, New Jersey.

In the summer of 1977, Jack and Maxine went Back East for a visit with their children and the grandchildren, the eldest of whom were approaching kindergarten age. "Gramma" and "Papa" spent a lot of time with the grandchildren with Jack making sure the youngsters learned two skills at an early age: fishing and cooking. Inasmuch as Jack was well connected at Schiff Scout Reservation, he had no problem in taking the kids to Schiff's lake to catch sunfish. Then they went for bigger game in the North Branch of the nearby Raritan River.

Rhea Family Collection

One of two activities learned by Rhea grandchildren early in life was fishing. Here "Papa" Rhea instructs grandsons Haysie and Cory in one of the finer points of angling.

Rhea Family Collection

The other skill learned by Rhea grandchildren was cooking. Here Neil and Kelly get their first cooking lesson.

Jack and Maxine decided to move Back East and started looking for a place to live that would put them close to their children, but not so close as to be camped on the kids' doorsteps. Jack was still operating Indian Arts and needed a central hub from which to manage concessions with large department stores in northern New Jersey and eastern Pennsylvania. They moved in 1978 to East Stroudsburg, Pennsylvania, which is little more than fifty miles west of where they had originally been located in Bridgewater, New Jersey.

Indian Arts never provided a significant portion of the Rhea's retirement income, but the early 1980s were a time of tremendous fluctuations in silver prices. That was a factor in Jack's deciding not to continue Indian Arts, but he did find a unique way to utilize the remaining inventory. That coincided with a move west to Hershey, Pennsylvania, in 1982. At this point, Julie and her family were living in Camp Hill, a Harrisburg suburb which is not much more than a twenty-five minute drive away from Hershey. Carol, and her family lived in Branchburg, New Jersey, which is under two hours away from Hershey by interstate highway. The other major attraction in Hershey was the Hershey Museum of American Life and its substantial involvement with Native American heritage. Jack became a docent there and was also a volunteer at the nearby Milton Hershey School.

Jack's work with the Hershey Museum of American Life was recognized by the state of Pennsylvania. The state's treasurer, Catherine Baker, presents a commendation to Jack on April 23, 1993.

Jack's involvement with the museum became much more than a matter of answering questions about the many items which were on display, including much of his Indian Arts materials. Jack became, in effect, a champion of Native American causes. He also became very knowledgeable on Indian history and contemporary culture; he also dispelled the myths that many museum-goers brought with them through the front door. Jack had his facts and figures at hand: Native American population, how many reservations there were in the country (300 while Jack was at the museum), state with the most reservations (California), where the largest reservations were, traditional and contemporary religious beliefs, and much more. Jack was instrumental in establishing day-long youth programs at the museum, including programs for both Girl Scouts and Boy Scouts twice a year. Those programs were particularly helpful to boys working on their Indian Lore merit badge and covered such topics as tribal history, pottery, sand painting, origins of Indian items such as moccasins, and sketching artifacts. Jack's work with the museum was of such caliber and impact that he was commended by the state of Pennsylvania. In a special ceremony, Catherine Baker Knoll, treasurer of Pennsylvania, came to Hershey on 23 April 1993 to present Jack with a commendation from the state recognizing his valued service. Jack also was a recipient of the Rotary International's prestigious Paul Harris Award.

The Twilight Trail

The Rheas did not travel extensively in their retirement other than the nationwide tour of Indian reservations in 1975-76. There were only several exceptions and the first was out to San Francisco to visit son Ron and his family in 1985. While in California all of the Rheas drove down to Los Angeles where the big attraction for the grandkids was the thirtieth anniversary of Disneyland. Jack and Maxine did return to Philmont once after their 1976 visit; their June 1988 journey saw Jack being interviewed by the News and Information Service about his Philmont days, but most of their return was spent visiting familiar places: Villa Philmonte, the Tooth of Time, Ponil, and a sprawling Camping Headquarters that resembled a small town.

Well into his retirement, Jack was a tireless speaker at Scouting events.

Jack continued to network with his Philmont staff acquaintances and was a frequent guest at council events and banquets. Pete Silldorff, a resident of Lebanon, Pennsylvania, and the 1956 director at Porcupine, happened to be speaking with the director of the nearby Hershey Museum about the possibility of recruiting somebody to speak at a Lebanon County Council, BSA, Eagle Scout banquet. The director recommended a fellow on the museum staff who was most knowledgeable about eagles, Indian rituals, and Scouting. Then she casually mentioned his name at which Pete was absolutely thunderstruck; it was Jack Rhea. Pete promptly called Jack and started the conversation by saying, "This is Pete Silldorff, but you probably don't remember me although I was director at Porcupine in 1956." The reply came back, "Of course I know you. You're the phantom." Needless to say Lebanon County Council's Eagle Scout banquet was a major success due in no small part to the guest speaker. And that was just one of many functions at which Jack was a speaker during his retirement.

Rhea Family Collection

*Jack and Maxine
in 1993.*

Rhea Family Collection

*In 2003, Jack and Maxine welcomed their first great grandchild into the
Rhea family. Here daughter Carol holds granddaughter Ella.*

By the turn of the century, Jack was approaching eighty-five years
of age. In late 2001, Jack and Maxine moved to Hellertown, a suburb of
Allentown, Pennsylvania, to be closer to their children. Julie was living in
Allentown, and the move also put them much closer to Carol and Bart who
lived just across the Delaware River in New Jersey.

In the summer of 2008, the Philmont Staff Association honored Jack
with its Silver Sage Award. PSA founder Ned Gold and board member Bill
Cass made the presentation which was also attended by a charter Silver
Sage and Jack Rhea contemporary: Joe Davis. One of the highlights was
Jack's grandson Brandon Rhea (Bart's son) speaking at the presentation.
Anybody meeting Jack at that time could easily assume that his memory
was going, but that was not the case. It was his hearing. He refused to wear
a hearing aid; he was reading lips and not catching everything. Jack was

delighted that Joe Davis was present; the two enjoyed an animated reunion, and a moving experience it was to see those two "titans," as Ned Gold described them, reveling about the great decades of the 1950s and 1960s.

*The "Two Titans," Jack Rhea and Joe Davis, meet again
on the occasion of Jack's Silver Sage presentation.*

Both into their 90s, Jack and Joe outlived nearly all of their contemporaries. Joe was active in BSA professional retiree circles right to the very end. Jack kept up with old compatriots, but it was primarily through personal networking. Jack was also a life member of the Philmont Staff Association. Both Jack and Joe were good friends with Alden Barber who retired from the BSA in 1976 and passed away in early 2003. Ray Bryan, who had been general manager while both Jack and Joe were directors of camping retired from the BSA in 1972, moved from Princeton, New Jersey, to Easton, Maryland, and died there in February 1984. Sadly, Joe's days were numbered; he had only several more months to live, dying from complications resulting from a fall in late October 2008.

Health issues, the curse of older age, were becoming major problems for the Rheas. A cornea transplant for Maxine was unsuccessful. Increasingly after 2005 she was becoming forgetful; the situation devolved into dementia and by 2008 she was under hospice care. Maxine Rhea died in 2009.

Jack by then was a frail man, and general debility was taking its toll. He became increasingly bed-bound. It was while being treated for bedsores that Jack slipped away during lunch on 7 May 2010. He was just a few weeks short of his ninety-fifth birthday.

Jack Rhea constantly tried to earn his father's approval, but the elder Rhea never blessed Jack with a "Job well done, son." All of Jack's accomplishments prior to Charles Rhea's death – becoming an Eagle Scout, playing on a state championship basketball team, earning a bachelor's degree, becoming a teacher, completing Army OCS, and being decorated several times for heroism under fire – never earned a fatherly approval. It was one of the deepest regrets of Jack Rhea's life, and from that experience he made sure that he stuck by his kids through thick and thin. Surely, Jack must have known as he reached the end of life's twilight trail that he had the overwhelming approval of his family, the Centurymen with whom he shared great danger, hundreds of Philmont staff members, tens of thousands of Philmont advisors/campers, many volunteer and professional Scouters, and indirectly countless numbers of American youth whose lives he touched in the most wonderful ways.

Bibliography

Books

Army of the United States. *The Officer's Guide.* Harrisburg, Pennsylvania: Military Service Publishing Company. 1942.

Barber, Alden. *Recollections and Reflections: Fifty Years in the Boy Scouts of America.* Sacramento, California (privately-published). 1995.

Bass, Michael A. (editor). *The Story of the Century.* New York, New York: Century Association. 1946.

Bonn, Keith. *Friends and Enemies of the Century.* Bedford, Pennsylvania: Aegis Consulting Group, Inc. 2000.

Bogan, Samuel D. *Let the Coyotes Howl.* New York, New York: G.P. Putnam's Sons. 1946.

Boston, Bernard, editor. *History of the 398th Infantry Regiment in World War II.* Washington, D.C: Infantry Journal Press. 1947.

Davis. Kenneth P. *A History of Wood Badge in the United States.* Irving, Texas: Boy Scouts of America. 1988.

Griffin, Mark. *The Other Side of the Road,* Cimarron, New Mexico: The Philmont Staff Association. 2009.

Hillcourt, William. *Norman Rockwell's World of Scouting.* New York, New York: Harry N. Abrams, Inc. 1977

Huffman, Minor S. *High Adventure Among the Magic Mountains.* Allendale, New Jersey: TIBS Inc. 1988.

Jeal, Tim. *The Boy-Man. The Life of Baden-Powell.* New York: William Morrow and Company. 1990.

Kaufmann, J.E. et al. *The Maginot Line.* Barnsley, South Yorkshire, United Kingdom: Pen and Sword Books, Ltd. 2011.

Keen, Patricia Fussell. *Eyes and Ears of the Eighth.* Sun City, Arizona: CAVU Publishers. 1996.

Keller, Sally Altick. *The Diamond Journey, Helen and Ernie's Trail of Happiness.* Logan, Utah: (privately published). 1996.

Knox, Robert. *Growing Up to Cowboy.* Santa Fe, New Mexico: Sunstone Press. 2002.

Lewis, Paul W. *Scouting in Iowa – The Values Endure*. Des Moines, Iowa: Mid-Iowa Council, BSA. Des Moines, Iowa. 1999.

Longacre, Edward G. *War in the Ruins*. Yardley, Pennsylvania: Westholme Publishing. 2010.

Mauer, M. *Combat Squadrons of the Air Force in World War II*. Washington, D.C.: Zenger Publishing Co, Inc. 1981.

McPherson, Milton M. *The Ninety-Day Wonders*. Fort Benning, Georgia: United States Army Officer Candidate Alumni Association, Inc. 1998.

Mid-America Council, BSA. *Scouting – Our Story, A look Back at Years of Scouting in the Mid-America Council*. Omaha, Nebraska. Mid-America Council, BSA. 2010.

Murphy, Lawrence R. *Philmont, A History of New Mexico's Cimarron Country*. Albuquerque, New Mexico: 1972.

Staff of the 100th Infantry Division. *Century Division 1944* (reprint). Bedford, Pennsylvania: Aegis Consulting Group, Inc. 2000.

Vable, Neal. *The Unity Movement: Its Evolution and Spiritual Teachings*. Radnor, Pennsylvania. Templeton Foundation Press. 2002.

Wagner, Carolyn Ditte. *The Boy Scouts of America: A Model and a Mirror of American Society*. Baltimore, Maryland, Johns Hopkins University Press. 1979.

Watson, W.E., Jr., Editor. *History of the 111th Tactical Reconnaissance Squadron*. Little Rock, Arkansas. Jordan Printing. 1945.

Weber, Gerald C. *Gerald's World War II*. Louisville, Kentucky. Chicago Spectrum Press. 2007

Zimmer, Stephen and Walker, Larry. *Philmont, An Illustrated History*. Irving, Texas: Boy Scouts of America. 1988.

Newspaper and Newsletter Articles

100th Infantry Division Association Newsletter. 1973 through December 2011.

Boys Life Magazine. June 1957 and February 1960.

Century Sentinel (100th Infantry Division newspaper). February 1943 through October 1945.

Gunnison Republican. Gunnison, Colorado. 30 June - 7 July 1927.

High Country. Philmont Staff Association. Cimarron, New Mexico. October 1976, Spring 1993, Fall 1993, February 2004, April 2004, April 2005, June 2005, August 2007, June 2008, October 2008, June 2009, April 2010, June 2010, August 2010, October 2010, April 2011, December 2011, and February 2001.

Scouting Magazine. September 1972.

The Columbus Ledger. Columbus, Georgia. 14 July and 14 October 1942.

The Fayetteville Observer. Fayetteville, North Carolina. 15 January 1944.

The State. Columbia, South Carolina. 13-16 November 1942.

Documents

3rd Battalion, 398th Infantry Regiment, 100th Infantry Division. *Morning Reports.* St. Louis, Missouri: National Archives. November 15, 1942 through November 15, 1945.

"Graduation Program, Officer Candidate Course No. 79-A." Fort Benning, Georgia: 1942

Interstate Commerce Commission, Docket Number MC-93860, "Country Day School Association, Application Hearings." Reece Harrison, Examiner, Bureau of Motor Carriers. Wichita, Kansas: September 19, 1938.

Jung, David. "Ranger Training, 1957" (with notes). Cimarron, New Mexico: Philmont Scout Ranch. 1957.

"Messages, Incidents, Orders." Boxes 11733-11739. National Archives, College Park, Maryland.

Military Service Record (201 File), Jack L. Rhea, O1296148. St. Louis, Missouri: National Archives.

Philmont Scout Ranch. "Philmont Attendance Summary" (1939 to present). Cimarron, New Mexico.

Philmont Scout Ranch. "Staff Rosters 1946-1962." Cimarron, New Mexico.

Rhea, Joseph C. Jr. *Ray-Rhea Family History* (privately published genealogy), 1969.

United States Army Adjutant General's Office. *World War II Operations Reports, 100th Infantry Division, 398th Infantry Regiment Infantry Journal:*

Williams, Col. Robert M. *Operations of the 398th Infantry Regiment, 100th Infantry Division* (Regimental Monthly Operations Summary). College Park, Maryland: National Archives. November 1944 through April 1945.

Unpublished Material

Norman, Caldon R. "Whatever Happened To Company A." Portland, Oregon. 1991.

Tschetter, Marty. "Ranger Timelines." Greenville, North Carolina. 2011.

_____. Monographs on the lives of Clarence Dunn, Doc Loomis, and Bill Wadsworth. Greenville, North Carolina. 2011.

Websites

www.100thww2.org (100th Infantry Division in World War II)

www.320thbg.org (320th Bomb Group)

www.bombgroup17.com (17th Bomb Group)

www.clan-macrae.org.uk (Macrae clan)

www.convoyweb.org.uk (Convoy UGF-15b)

www.easteurotopo.org (U.S. Army Map Service, World War II)

www.marshallfoundation.org (100th Infantry Division in World War II)

www.qm.com (U.S. Army Remount Service)

www.philmontdocs.wachtu.org (1950s Philmont Maps and Literature)

Personal, Telephone, and E-Mail Interviews and Correspondence

Anderson, Mark. (Philmont Scout Ranch 1990s – 2000s)

Baker, Ted. (17th Bomb Group, WWII)

Baldwin, Clarence. (Philmont Scout Ranch, 1940s)

Barber, Mark. (BSA National Office, 1960s – 1970s)

Bashore, Bob. (Philmont Scout Ranch, 1960s)

Batchelor, Ray. (VTC Rangers)

Bates, Dave. (Philmont, 1960s)

Beckelman, Dan. (1957 Rangers)

Bell, David. (1957 Rangers)

Berry, Robin (1957 Rangers)

Biddulph, Ed. (Philmont Rangers, 1957)

Bolin, Perry. (1957 Rangers)

Bonn, Patti. (Century Division, WWII)

Brammer, Richard. (Philmont 1956)

Carlson, Don. (Philmont Rangers)

Carlson, Dr. James, D.D.S. (1957 Rangers)

Claerhout, John. (BSA National Office, 1950s – 1970s)

Clemmons, Al. (Philmont Scout Ranch, 1950s – 1960s)

Collaer, Martha Bullock (George Bullock, Philmont 1947 – 1954)

Colopy, Charlie. (VC Bar Ranch/Lake Fork Club)

Cook, Robert. (Bill Wadsworth)

Dailey, Bill. (1957 Rangers)

Davis, Ken. (Army OCS and Philmont Staff Association)

De Hon, René. (Philmont 1956)

Denman, Ray. (Century Division WW II)

Dinsmore, Paul. (Philmont 1960s)

Eilert, Dr. John B., M.D. (Philmont Scout Ranch/Rangers, 1950s)

Ferguson, Dan. (Philmont 1940s)

Galeano, Richard. (1957 Rangers)

Gannon, Robert. (1957 Rangers)

Gertler, Richard. (Philmont Scout Ranch, 1960s)

Gifford, Dave. (Philmont Rangers)

Glassow, Mike. (Indian Writings program)

Gold, Ned C., Jr. (Philmont Scout Ranch)

Gregory, Stephen. (Philmont staff training)

Griffin, Mark. (Philmont Training Center)

Groat, Myron. (Scouting in Fort Dodge)

Gulbranson, John. (BSA Professional Training)

Handy, Art. (Century Division, WWII)

Hardin, Burgin. (Norman Rockwell art)

Harris, Jack. (Philmont Rangers)

Hart, Carl. (Philmont 1950s)

Hart, Joan S. (Philmont, early 1950s)

Hatfield, Hoyt. (Philmont Rangers, 1957)

Hobbs, Gregory (Philmont Rangers)

Hopper, Robert. (Scouting in Des Moines, 1940s)

Houston, Grant. (VC Bar Ranch/Lake City, Co.)

Hunter, Cathy. (*National Geographic* Magazine)

Israel, Clark. (Scouting in Wichita, 1930s)

Johnson, Michael. (Scouting in Wichita, 1930s)

Keller, Sally Altick. (Wichita Country Day School)

Kellsall, Samuel. (1957 Rangers)

Kinsman, Brad. (Philmont 1940s)

Kirkland, Darrel. (North Texas Council, 1930s)

Kleinwaks, Michael. (398th Infantry Regiment, WWII)

Klingler, Gene. (Philmont Health Lodge)

Knox, Bettye Maldonado. (Bob Knox, Philmont Scout Ranch, 1950s)

Kozak, Jeffrey. (100th Division, WWII)

Lutes, Eugene. (Indian Writings Program)

MacArthur, Carol Rhea. (Rhea Family and Philmont)

Magendantz, Eric. (Prairie Gold Council, BSA)

Maldonado, Billy. (Philmont Scout Ranch, 1950s)

Maldonado, Bobby. (Philmont Scout Ranch, 1950s)

Marr, Ron. (Philmont 1940s)

Matthews, Bill. (Philmont Rangers)

Mills, Judge Richard. (Philmont 1950s)

Morin, Al. (BSA National Office, Personnel and Training)

Munger, Richard. (Philmont Horsemen)

Nillson, David. (Philmont JLT)

Novack, Richard. (Century Rangers, WWII)

Parsons, Edmund. (Century Rangers, WWII)

Parsons, Ellis. (Century Rangers, WWII)

Patteson, Doug. (324th Fighter Group, WWII)

Patton, Dave. (Philmont JLT, 1960s)

Perin, Shon. (Philmont Rangers)

Place, James. (Philmont Rangers)

Plamp, John. (398th Infantry Regiment, WWII)

Plummer, Bill. (Philmont 1940s)

Reams, Gayle. (1957 Rangers)

Reel, Lonnie. (VC Bar Ranch/Lake Fork Club)

Reigelman, Frank. (Philmont Scout Ranch)

Reis, Mitchell. (Lone Scout Division, BSA, 1920s)

Reisdorf, Franz. (320th Bomb Group, WWII)

Replogle, Rod. (Philmont 1952 – 1956)

Reynolds, Don. (1957 Rangers)

Rhea, Bart. (Rhea Family and Philmont)

Rhea, Julie. (Rhea Family and Philmont)

Rhea, Peter. (Rhea Family)

Rhea, Ronald. (Rhea Family and Philmont)

Rhea, Rosemarie Fillmore (Rhea Family)

Rouse, Allan. (1957 Rangers)

Saunders, Randy. (Philmont)

Scott-Davies, Daniel. (UK Scouting during WWII)

Setzer, David. (Philmont Wagon Trains)

Silldorff, Pete. (Philmont, 1956)

Stieghan, David. (Army OCS, WWII)

Talley, James. (Philmont 1961-62)

Taylor, Robin. (Philmont Museum)

Teasley, Bruce. (1957 Rangers)

Thannisch, Walter. (1957 Rangers)

Tillett, Thomas. (100th Division, WWII)

Tooley, Dean. (Philmont 1950s)

Tracey, Jamie. (Wichita Country Day School)

Trevett, Doug. (Philmont Rangers)

Tschetter, Marty. (Philmont Rangers)

Van Pelt, George. (3rd Bn., 398th Infantry Regiment, WWII)

Vickers, Larry. (VC Bar Ranch/Lake Fork Club)

Wadsworth, Bobbie. (Bill Wadsworth)

Ward, William. (Philmont JLT)

Warkoszewski, Marlene. (Col. Floyd Staton)

Weber, Gerald C. (3rd Bn., 398th Infantry Regiment, WWII)

Wencko, Paul. (1957 Rangers)

Wilson, Don. (Philmont 1950s – 60s)

Woods, Wayne (WWII Army Intelligence Tests)

Woodyard, Jimmy. (Kit Carson Guides)

Worley, George. (Philmont 1956)

Wuncker, Howard. (1957 Rangers)

Young, Dave. (Philmont Guides)

Zimmer, Stephen. (Philmont Scout Ranch)